THE
COLLEGE
WRITER'S
REFERENCE

FIFTH EDITION

TOBY FULWILER
University of Vermont

ALAN R. HAYAKAWA
The Patriot-News
Harrisburg, Pennsylvania

Prentice Hall

Upper Saddle River   London   Singapore
Toronto   Tokyo   Sydney   Hong Kong   Mexico City

Editorial Director: Leah Jewell
Editor in Chief: Craig Campanella
Executive Editor: Kevin Molloy
Project Manager: Melissa Casciano
VP / Director, Production and Manufacturing:
    Barbara Kittle
Director, Marketing: Brandy Dawson
Senior Marketing Manager: Windley Morley
Marketing Assistant: Kimberly Caldwell
Text Permissions Specialist: Lisa Black
Copyeditor: Amy Jolin
Production Liaison: Maureen Benicasa
Manufacturing Manager: Nick Sklitsis
Assistant Manufacturing Manager:
    Mary Ann Gloriande

Creative Design Director: Leslie Osher
Art Director, Interior and Cover Design:
    Laura Gardner/Running River Design
Image Resource Center Director: Melinda Patelli
Rights and Permissions Manager: Zina Arabia
Visual Research Manager: Beth Brenzel
Image Permissions Coordinator: Cynthia Vincenti
Cover Visual Research and Permissions Manager:
    Karen Sanatar
Cover Photo: Photos.com
Full-Service Project Management: Karen Berry/
    Pine Tree Composition, Inc.
Composition: Pine Tree Composition, Inc.
Printer / Binder: RR Donnelley & Sons
Cover Printer: Phoenix Color Corp.

This book includes 2009 MLA citation guidelines.

Credits and acknowledgments borrowed from other sources and reproduced, with permission, in this textbook appear on pages 505–507.

Library of Congress Cataloging-in-Publication Data
Fulwiler, Toby
    The college writer's reference / Toby Fulwiler ; Alan R. Hayakawa. — 5th ed.
        p. cm.
    Includes bibliographical references and indexes.
    ISBN 0-205-73560-6
    1. English language—Rhetoric—Handbooks, manuals, etc.   2. Report writing—Handbooks,
manuals, etc.   I. Hayakawa, Alan R.   II. Title.
    PE1408.F79 2008
    808'.042—dc22   2007002660

10 9 8 7 6 5 4 3 2

Prentice Hall
is an imprint of

PEARSON

www.pearsonhighered.com

ISBN-10:   0-205-73560-6
ISBN-13: 978-0-205-73560-0

BOX LISTS

Checklist

Critical Thinking

ESL

WRITING ACROSS THE CURRICULUM

PREFACE

This fifth edition of *The College Writer's Reference* continues to explain and illustrate the qualities of good contemporary writing as well as the logic behind the conventions of grammar, spelling, punctuation, and usage. It continues to insist that good writing is a thoughtful mix of imaginative composing, careful revising, and rigorous editing, and not the slavish following of mechanical prescriptions. In addition to updating all previous chapters, the new edition features careful attention to *critical reading, visual rhetoric, public forms of discourse, Writing Across the Curriculum,* and *practical communication beyond the classroom.*

Initially, we published this brief handbook to give undergraduates and graduates alike a highly portable yet comprehensive guide to improving their writing skills. The basic approach in all editions of *The College Writer's Reference* is to focus honestly on the needs of undergraduate writers through a process approach, examining the different but overlapping stages of planning, composing, researching, revising, and editing. The book addresses rhetorical issues of audience, purpose, situation, and voice, as well as the more technical issues of style, grammar, and mechanics, examining the range of choices rather than fixed rules writers might follow.

Varied Author Experience

A composition teacher with more than 35 years' experience teaching writing, Toby Fulwiler highlights the need for writers to gain confidence in their voices and ideas as well as to practice in a variety of formats and conventions. A practicing journalist with more than 25 years of experience writing and editing for newpapers, Alan Hayakawa understands the importance of conventional correctness and appreciates the way different writing situations and new technologies demand different approaches. For this reason, *The College Writer's Reference* devotes time to both the whys and the hows of good writing. Students who know how to analyze and address individual rhetorical situations are more likely to succeed both across the curriculum and in the world beyond college.

Pedagogical Features

As a progressive alternative to traditional handbooks, this revised, fifth edition of *The College Writer's Reference* has several important features that make this book an especially useful rhetoric and reference in writing classes, in classes across the curriculum, and in writing situations beyond the classroom.

HELP WHERE YOU EXPECT IT

The College Writer's Reference offers comphensive coverage of all the essential guidelines needed by working writers, organized according to the logic of the writing process: the opening sections focus on *planning* and *composing;* later sections examine *research, revising,* and all matters pertaining to *editing,* including *style, grammar, usage, punctuation,* and *mechanics.*

TEACHABLE TREATMENT OF THE PROCESS OF WRITING

The opening chapters of *The College Writer's Reference* examine the creative but frustrating messiness of the writing process, offering ideas and strategies to help writers shape, organize, and give voice to their work. These chapters cover many common purposes for college writing in simple and direct language—reflecting on experience, explaining ideas, arguing positions, and writing about literature, as well as composing creative nonfiction, keeping journals, and constructing essay examinations.

ATTENTION TO VISUAL RHETORIC

This edition emphasizes the importance of visual rhetoric and design in the writing even of conventional college papers. The new Chapter 5 introduces students to critical terminology for understanding and talking about visual images.

ATTENTION TO PUBLIC DISCOURSE

New to this edition of *The College Writer's Reference* is an increased emphasis on public discourse, including new chapters on "Reading and Writing with Images" and "Writing for the World." In addition, this edition includes expanded coverage of document design, writing for Web pages, and making oral presentations.

EMPHASIS ON *WRITING ACROSS THE CURRICULUM*

All editions of this handbook have been written with students and faculty across the curriculum in mind, taking great care to explain the rhetorical strategies and writing conventions of specific disciplinary areas. To the fifth edition we have added *Writing Across the Curriculum (WAC)* boxes offering suggestions for assigning and responding to writing in disciplines across the curriculum and the world of work. Supplementary material for instructors and students is also available to support teaching and learning how to write in disciplines across the curriculum and the world of work.

FULL COVERAGE OF ELECTRONIC RESEARCH METHODS

This latest edition of *The College Writer's Reference* includes up-to-date strategies for planning, organizing, and writing research papers from sources found in the library, in the field, and on the Internet. Particular attention is paid to using, documenting, and evaluating the ever-more complicated strands of electronic sources.

SPECIAL ATTENTION TO PLAGIARISM

Because of the ever-increasing ease of copying material from electronic souces, *The College Writer's Reference* has greatly expanded the discussion of plagiarism in both intentional and unintentional forms. Clear explanations and illustrations of the do's and don't's of quoting and documenting will help students avoid breaches of academic ethics.

HELP FOR THOSE WHO SPEAK ENGLISH AS A SECOND LANGUAGE

The College Writer's Reference pays careful attention to the needs of second-language students. Graphically distinct boxes throughout the text provide information on topics from grammar, idioms, and usage to the how and why of rhetorical conventions. All these boxes have been critically reexamined and revised for the fifth edition.

EDITING AS A MATTER OF CONVENTIONS, NOT RULES

The editing chapters focus on editing as a process concentrating on effectiveness, usage, grammar, punctuation, and mechanics. Hand-edited examples illustrate how writers revise and edit, showing proven strategies for focusing loose paragraphs, strengthening weak sentences, and finding precise and suitable words. *The College Writer's Reference* emphasizes grammatical and mechanical processes in everyday language and helps readers identify, analyze, and resolve confusing language problems.

UNIQUE DESIGN THAT FACILITATES QUICK REFERENCE

The carefully constructed, four-color design of the book helps students locate information quickly, as they can identify the parts of the book with their corresponding color bands. Thus, navigating the text becomes a visual as well as mental activity. The inside back cover includes a chart of proofreading symbols.

Supplements

The following supplements accompany *The College Writer's Reference* to aid teaching and learning:

FOR THE INSTRUCTOR

All of the following supplements are provided to assist instructors.

- **Instructor's Manual: Teaching Writing with the College Writer's Reference** offers guidance to new and experienced teachers in using the handbook to its best advantage.

- *MyCompLab* (*www.mycomplab.com*) offers a wealth of teaching resources, including:

    GradeTracker helps instructors track student progress.

    The *MyCompLab Faculty Teaching Guide* gives instructors strategies for using this valuable resource.

    Online course-management versions of *MyCompLab* are available in *CourseCompass, Blackboard,* and *WebCT* so instructors can manage their course in their preferred format.

    MyDropBox, a leading online plagiarism detection service, assists interested instructors in tracking plagiarism.

- *Prentice Hall Resources for Writing. A* set of supplements for the instructor designed to support a variety of popular composition topics.

    - *Teaching Writing Across the Curriculum* by Art Young is written for college teachers in all disciplines and provides useful advice on teaching writing across the curriculum.

    - *Teaching Civic Literacy* by Cheryl Duffy offers advice on how to integrate civic literacy into the composition classroom.

    - *Teaching Visual Rhetoric* by Susan Loudermilk provides an illustrated look at visual rhetoric and offers guidance on how to incorporate this topic into the classroom.

    - *Teaching Writing for ESL Students* by Ruth Spack addresses various strategies that can be employed to teach writing to non-native speakers.

FOR THE INSTRUCTOR AND STUDENT

- **Editing Activites** to accompany *The College Writer's Reference* offers exercises and activities which reinforce editing as a critical part of the writing process.

- **Open Access Companion Web Site.** The Companion Web site offers many resources to help students use their book and improve their writing. Students can use the site on their own (it is not password protected), or their instructor may direct them to portions of it as part of his or her course assignments.

The Companion Web site can be accessed at **www.prenhall.com/ fulwiler**. Click on *The College Writer's Reference* cover or title to link to the Web site and access the following:

- More than a thousand electronic exercises help students master various topics from basic grammar to research to ESL

- Our **Resources for Writing** section offers best practices related to the writing process

- The ***Research and Documentation*** tutorial provides a quick guide to writing a research paper and documenting sources

- The ***Understanding Plagiarism*** tutorial helps students understand what plagiarism is and provides strategies for avoiding plagiarism

- Links to other Web sites provide help on key topics

- Instructor support, including PowerPoint presentations, Instructor's Manual, links to helpful Web sites and more, give instructors a head start when preparing their courses

- **MyCompLab—Online Writing Support Created by Composition Instructors for Composition Instructors and Their Students.**
  MyCompLab (*www.mycomplab.com*), including an electronic and interactive version of *The College Writer's Reference,* offers comprehensive online resources in grammar, writing, and research in one dynamic, accessible place:

  - Grammar Resources include *ExerciseZone,* with more than three thousand self-grading practice questions on sentences and paragraphs; and *ESL ExerciseZone,* with more than seven hundred self-grading questions.

  - Writing Resources include a hundred writing activities involving videos, images, and Web sites; guided assistance through the writing process, with worksheets and exercises; and an extensive collection of sample papers from across the disciplines.

  - Research resources include *ResearchNavigator™,* which provides help with the research process, the *AutoCite* bibliography maker, and access to *ContentSelect™* by EBSCOhost and the subject-search archive of *The New York Times;* and *Avoiding Plagiarism,* which offers tutorials in recognizing plagiarism, paraphrasing, documenting sources in MLA or APA style, and other topics.

MyCompLab includes an intelligent system called *Grade Tracker* so students can track their work, communicate with instructors, and monitor their improvement.

Students using *MyCompLab* will also benefit from Pearson's *English Tutor Center,* offering live help from qualified writing teachers.

MyCompLab includes even more resources to help students use the book and improve their writing. They can use the site on their own, or their instructor may direct them to portions of it as part of his or her course assignments.

- Downloadable checklists and other materials from the book

- More than a thousand electronic exercises

- Video tutorials that supplement the book's explanations

- Hundreds of links to other Web sites providing help on the book's topics

- Sample research papers from various academic disciplines

- Usage flashcards on tricky words and phrases

- **Dictionary, Thesaurus, Writer's Guides, Workbooks, and Pocket Readers.** The following resources can be packaged with *The College Writer's Reference.* These valuable student resources provide additional depth on specialized topics that may only be touched upon in the text and allow you to customize the handbook to specific needs. Contact your local Prentice Hall representative for discount pricing information.

  - *The New American Webster Handy College Dictionary*

  - *The New American Roget's College Thesaurus*

  - *Writer's Guide to Research and Documentation*

  - *Writer's Guide to Oral Presentations and Writing in the Disciplines*

  - *Writer's Guide to Document and Web Design*

  - *Writer's Guide to Writing About Literature*

  - *The Prentice Hall Grammar Workbook*

  - *The Prentice Hall ESL Workbook*

  - *Applying English to Your Career (Workbook)*

  - *A Prentice Hall Pocket Reader: Argument*

  - *A Prentice Hall Pocket Reader: Literature*

  - *A Prentice Hall Pocket Reader: Patterns*

  - *A Prentice Hall Pocket Reader: Themes*

  - *A Prentice Hall Pocket Reader: Purposes*

  - *A Prentice Hall Pocket Reader: Writing Across the Curriculum*

  - *Papers Across the Curriculum*

Acknowledgments

We would like to thank these instructors who shared their insights on teaching writing and the use of handbooks, as well as for their specific suggestions on improving the fifth edition of *The College Writer's Reference:*

James M. Gentile, Manchester Community College

Virginia Skinner-Linnenberg, Nazareth College

Carolyn Harrison, Oakland Community College

Rosemary Day, Albuquerque TVI Community College

John Howe, Community College of Philadelphia

Kathy Gehr, College of Charleston

Dennis R. Perry, Brigham Young University

Eric A. Weil, Shaw University

Lou Masson, University of Portland

Mary M. Murray, Cleveland State University

John Hyman, American University

Melissa Joarder, Delaware County Community College

Judith W. Hunter, Grinnell College

Deborah Brown, University of Central Oklahoma

Joette Waddle, Roane State Community College

Gina Hochhalter, Clovis Community College

Maria Cahill, Abraham Baldwin Agricultural College

Charles Windy, Piedmont College

Thanks also to the many students at the University of Vermont who asked and answered questions about learning to write and especially to those who allowed us to reprint samples of their essays, freewrites, and journal entries.

We are grateful to the strong support staff at Prentice Hall who have made this book possible. We would like to acknowldege the strong creative and supportive counsel of our Prentice Hall editor, Paul Crockett, whose vision guided the revisions in this fifth edition. And a special thank you to assistant editor Melissa Casciano, who so dutifully helps all of us keep track of the many details both large and small of this publishing project.

We'd also like to thank Brandy Dawson, director of marketing, and Yolanda de Rooy, president of humanities and social sciences, for their enduring support of this project.

And, finally, a word of thanks to all of our friends and family members who supported us throughout this project.

chapter 1

Why Writing Matters

Whenever you share your writing with someone else, it speaks for you and tells your audience who you are, what you value, and what you want. In fact, every act of writing addresses three questions whether you actually ask them or not: (1) Why are you writing? (2) Who is your audience? and (3) What is the situation in which you are writing? How you answer these questions largely shapes your writing voice. These issues of writing—purpose, audience, situation, and voice—arise whether you are writing at home, in school, or on the job, whether you are writing letters, reports, or college papers.

1 a What is the *purpose?*

When you write a personal letter, you know why you are doing it and what you hope to accomplish. When you design a Web page to feature your accomplishments, your purpose tells you what to highlight, what to omit. However, when you write in response to a school assignment, your instructor sets the purpose for you, and it becomes your job to figure out that purpose as well as how you will try to meet it. Regardless of who instigates it, thoughtful writing is purposeful writing. To succeed, you need to know why you are writing and what you hope to accomplish. Odds are that, at one time or another, you will write for all of the following reasons.

Writing to Discover

Writing helps people think as well as record what they've already thought. Writing makes language, and therefore thought, visible and permanent, allowing writers to understand, critique, rearrange, and correct their ideas. Discovery writing is written primarily for yourself, not for some distant or judgmental audience, so style, structure, and correctness matter less than invention, exploration, and honesty. All these are forms of discovery writing.

- Freewriting
- Journal and diary writing
- Letters to trusted people

- Personal notes and lists
- Early drafts of formal papers

Instructors sometimes ask to see samples of discovery writing, but they seldom correct or evaluate it. Whether assigned or not, such informal writing will help you learn virtually any subject better. You are writing to discover when you need to figure out assignments, solve problems, find paper topics, locate research sources, or just find out what's on your mind. (See Chapters 3 and 4.)

Writing to Communicate

The general purpose of most writing in college—as well as in the world of work—is to communicate to audiences other than yourself. More specific purposes include communicating with the intention of informing, explaining, persuading, and interpreting in assignments called papers, reports, and essays of all kinds. (See Chapters 6–10.) Writing that communicates is

- clear, so that internal ideas are explained to an external audience;
- appropriate in form, style, and tone for its intended audience;
- conventional in spelling, punctuation, and grammar;
- supported by evidence and reason;
- documented to show where supporting evidence comes from.

You are writing to communicate when an assignment asks you to explain, report, analyze, describe, discuss, compare, contrast, interpret, argue, or evaluate something for an audience other than yourself. The major portion of this reference book explains and illustrates the conventions and guidelines most appropriate for academic writing.

Writing to Create

Creative writers pay special attention to form, shape, rhythm, imagery, and the symbolic qualities of language. Although the term *creative writing* is usually associated with poetry, fiction, and drama, any nonfiction text written with care, craft, and originality can be called creative. For example, researching slave conditions in 1850s Virginia, then writing a narrative from the point of view of an escaped slave, can result in a paper that is at once creative and highly factual. Such a paper is interesting to write as well as interesting to read. Although creative writing is also a type of communicative writing, its focus is less on what an audience needs than on the shape of the expression itself. The writer's goal is not so much to inform or to change the world as to portray its possibilities, both actual and imagined.

Although only a few college assignments may ask that you specifically write creative papers, many more conventional papers will profit from imaginative approaches that increase reader interest. You are invited to write creatively when an assignment asks you to suppose, speculate, design, imagine, create, or invent.

1 b Who is the *audience?*

It's difficult to define good writing in any absolute way; however, we can say that writing is "good" when it communicates clearly to its intended audience. To address readers effectively, writers need to imagine what readers know and believe as well as to anticipate their questions and concerns. Notice how differently you write to a friend compared to the way you write for a college instructor. With your friend, you assume shared experiences and a common sense of humor, so you can be playful with both content and style. With your instructor, however, you are more wary and assume very little—which means you need to explain a lot and very carefully.

Instructors are especially difficult audiences because (1) they know what they expect in their assignment, (2) they often know more about the subject of your paper than you do, and (3) each instructor has slightly different expectations. However, instructors in English as well as across the curriculum expect papers to demonstrate accurate knowledge, critical reasoning, and literate language skills.

- **Knowledge.** A successful paper demonstrates what you know and how well you know it. If you argue for or against affirmative action policies, your instructor looks to see how much you know about recent civil rights history and current political debates. A successful college paper contains accurate facts, clear definitions, careful explanations, and up-to-date information.

- **Critical reasoning.** A successful paper reveals your ability to reason logically and consistently, to support assertions, to organize information, and to argue persuasively. In arguing for or against tighter gun control laws, your paper needs to offer reasons for your position as well as refute the arguments of the opposition. Critical reasoning is witnessed in the clarity and arrangement of your ideas, the justness of your claims, and the persuasiveness of your evidence.

- **Language skills.** A successful paper is careful. Instructors cannot help but notice the clarity and correctness of your language, especially when your sentences are *not* clear or your spelling, punctuation, or grammar are *not* correct. They notice the general appearance of your writing: its neatness, legibility, and length as well as how well it conforms to standard academic conventions (see Parts 6–9).

When you write college papers, remember that you are situated within an academic community that may differ in important ways from a more familiar home, high school, or work community. This larger academic community has clear expectations for what papers should do, how they should appear, and what conventions they should follow. Although you cannot learn the particular methods and conventions of every discipline (interpretive papers written for English differ in important ways from laboratory reports, historical reviews, sociological abstracts, and so on), you can be aware of the central values that all members of the academic community subscribe to, which we might articulate as follows:

- **Knowledge.** Regardless of department or discipline, members of the university community are committed to the pursuit of knowledge that is accurate and truthful. Each academic discipline pursues such knowledge in a particular way—the sciences in one way, the social sciences in another, the humanities in still another. A successful college paper demonstrates that its writer can use the knowledge and methods of the discipline to reveal something that is true.

- **Evidence.** Scholars in all disciplines use credible evidence to support the truths they assert. Scientists make claims about the physical world and cite evidence to support those claims; art professors make claims about creative expression, and so on. As a college writer, you make claims, assertions, or arguments that you believe to be true; then you support those with the best facts, examples, and illustrations available. You must always document the sources for this evidence.

- **Balance.** Though truth is rigorously pursued in the academic world, new information and research methods constantly call old conclusions into question. Consequently, it is difficult, even impossible, to prove that something is absolutely true. Academic writers therefore make claims cautiously, with balanced, judicious language positioned somewhere between authority and doubt. Academic convention suggests that you present your inferences, assertions, and arguments in neutral, serious, nonemotional language and be fair to opposing points of view.

Writing voices range from assertive to tentative, loud to quiet, serious to sarcastic, clear to garbled, and so on. Each of us can project one or more of these voices at any given time. Some voices create belief and inspire trust, while others do not—and you must figure out which does which. An appropriate voice for a particular paper reflects both the larger academic community in which you are writing and your own unique background and personal experience. Your purpose, audience, and situation go a long way toward determining that voice—and so do who you are and where you come from. Think about the tone, style, structure, bias, and authority of the voice you present in your writing.

- **Tone.** The attitude a writer adopts toward a subject and audience is reflected in his or her tone: passionate, indifferent, puzzled, friendly, annoyed, and so on. Tone is something you control in everyday speech when you speak gently to a baby, cautiously to a teacher, sarcastically to your friends. On paper, you control tone by selecting and emphasizing words, sentence types, and punctuation to approximate the mood you want to project. To control your tone, reread out loud everything you write and ask, *Does it sound the way I intend?* If not, rewrite until it does.

- **Style.** Style includes a writer's choice of words, the construction and length of sentences, and the way grammar and mechanics present ideas on the page. Style can be described as formal (careful in respect to both convention and assertion), informal (more casual in form and mechanics), or colloquial (sounding like talk written down). Unless circumstances dictate otherwise, write college papers in a semiformal style that is clear, precise, and direct, yet sounds like a real human being speaking.

- **Structure.** Structure concerns the organization of a whole paper and the relationships among its parts. The structure of a text suggests something of the thought process that created it. For example, writing with a logical structure suggests similar habits of mind; writing with a circular or associative structure suggests more intuitive habits of mind. Some papers might call for a more logical self, others a more intuitive self; skillful writers could go either way. To control structure, ask yourself these questions: *How should the text open? Where should it go next? How should it conclude?*

- **Perspective.** When writers state or reveal their opinions directly or indirectly, they convey their social, political, and cultural beliefs as well. Unless writers deliberately mislead, their personal biases will be found somewhere in the foreground or background of everything they write. Learn where personal values are expected (personal essays) and where they are not (laboratory reports). Examine drafts for how they reveal your perspective through opinion and judgment words; then keep them, expand them, or take them out as appropriate.

- **Authority.** The conviction or authority with which you write is born of knowledge and implies self-confidence and control. Whether you write from research or personal experience, you can project real authority only over material you know well. The better you know your subject, the more self-assured your voice will be, and the more readers will believe you. To gain authority in your writing, conduct thorough research and read sources of information carefully and critically.

WRITING ACROSS THE CURRICULUM

Survey Professors Across the Curriculum

To find out how instructors across the various disciplines value writing, students in the class conduct a collaborative survey of instructors from various disciplines across campus. An easy way to do this would be for each student in class to query one instructor in another course in which he or she is currently enrolled. Each student asks his or her instructor a set of questions, such as the following:

- Why does writing matter in your discipline?
- What specific kinds of writing are most important within your discipline?
- What are the most common problems you witness in student writing?

Collate responses within the group and present your findings as a written report in a student paper or to interested college faculty, administrators, or committees.

---

chapter **2**   *The Writing Process*

The process of writing serious academic papers from beginning to end can be complicated, frustrating, and exhilarating all at the same time. Good papers begin sometimes as vague notions, other times as specific intentions. For serious writers, rewriting is an essential part of the process as they reexamine first thoughts, look for answers, fill in gaps, shore up arguments, and write new introductions. Thoughtful papers conclude with careful editing and line-by-line proofreading to guarantee clarity and correctness. Most writers wish there were simple formulas to follow to guarantee success, but such formulas do not exist.

For discussion purposes, we can describe five distinct phases of writing in the approximate order in which they might occur—planning, composing, researching, revising, and editing—though there is no necessary or fixed order for them as you write. Ideas are as likely to develop by trial and error, hunch and practice, as by preplanning and outlining. Sometimes ideas refuse to come out complete and finished on command; other times they pop up with clarity when least expected. Writers often find themselves editing when writing a first draft, revising when intending to edit, and composing new text in the midst of research. Regardless of how you mix these phases, what matters is that you learn how this process works best for you and how practicing it produces successful papers.

2 a Planning

What's your topic? What's your approach? Where should the paper start and end? When you plan to write a paper, you tackle these questions or others like them. Quite simply, planning refers to how a paper gets started. It involves asking questions, trying out answers, and developing directions. Writers plan deliberately when they make notes, turn casual lists into organized outlines, write journal entries, compose rough drafts, and consult with others. They also plan less deliberately while they walk, jog, eat, read, browse in libraries, converse with friends, or wake up in the middle of the night with an idea. Planning occurs, one way or another, every time you think about and try to solve a problem. (See Chapter 4 for strategies to help you plan and start a paper.)

2 b Composing

At some point, all writers move beyond planning and actually start writing. **Composing** happens when you try to advance your solution to a problem and see whether or not it works. The secret to productive writing is sitting down and beginning. A first draft is concerned with developing ideas, finding direction, clarifying concepts, and finding out exactly what the paper needs to say. Although writers hope their first draft will be final, a rereading often suggests otherwise. (See Chapters 6–9 for specific drafting strategies.)

2 c Researching

Authoritative papers require writers to locate new information rather than write strictly from memory or inspiration. For such papers, active researching may take place during the planning stages or while drafting and revising are going on. The library and the Internet provide new textual information, while interviews and site visits supply field data. But research also includes rereading textbooks, consulting dictionaries, conducting laboratory experiments, asking questions, and visiting museums. Writing research papers calls for detailed knowledge of disciplinary conventions. (See Chapters 11–17 for guidance through the whole process of writing research papers.)

2 d Revising

Somewhere in the middle to later stages of composing, writers begin revising the drafts they have planned, composed, and researched. Revising involves rewriting to make the purpose clearer, the argument stronger, the details sharper, the evidence more convincing, the organization more logical. Revising means re-seeing ideas and thinking again about direction, focus, arguments, and evidence. It involves cutting, adding, and modifying to make a paper say exactly what you intend—to make sure it does solve the problem you set out to solve. (See Chapter 10 for revision strategies.)

2 e Editing

Whether writers have written three drafts or five, they want the last one to be as nearly perfect as possible. Editing means sharpening, condensing, clarifying the language to make sentences express exactly what the writer intends. Editing is paying careful attention to the language, striving for the most clarity and punch possible. Editing is rearranging sentences, finding strong verbs, and eliminating wordy constructions. The final stage of editing is called proofreading—when you read line by line with a ruler, correcting errors in spelling, typos, punctuation, and grammar. (See Parts 6–9 for a full complement of editing strategies.)

2 f If English is your second language

If English is not your native language, the most important way you can improve your writing skills in English is to read, write, speak, and listen attentively to as much English as you can. Besides learning new grammar and vocabulary, be prepared to adjust to the expectations and traditions of the American classroom. For example, academic prose is often less formal in the United States than in many other countries. Students who have learned to write in more formal systems may find instructors suggesting that they make their writing more lively or personal. Also, although US schools increasingly treat writing as a multiple-draft process, instructors in many other countries may expect a piece of writing to be finished before it is handed in.

Throughout this book are boxes that provide information of particular interest to nonnative speakers. The letters *ESL* in the table of contents identify each section of the book that includes one of these specially marked boxes. An ESL index is provided at the back of the book to help you locate these topics.

WRITING ACROSS THE CURRICULUM

A Foolproof Revision Plan

The writing process described in this chapter represents an approximate way in which most published writers, both inside and outside the academy, write. Most of your professors, in other words, when they write books, articles, reports, and proposals plan, compose, revise, research, and edit to make sure their papers represent them well. At the same time, while instructors assign a paper due at a particular date, they do not actually tell you that you ought to take this paper through the rigorous multi-draft process they do in their own writing before you hand the paper in.

It's also clear that the busy-ness of your own academic schedule makes it easy to do last-minute, deadline writing. So the next time you are assigned a substantial paper in any of your college classes, take it through the stages of the writing process described in this chapter, whether asked to or not. To make this happen, write process deadlines in your academic planner so that come the night before the paper is due, the only remaining work is proofreading and printing. For example, here's a possible plan for a paper due in two weeks:

- First day, write planning notes in course notebook or journal.
- Second day, reserve one hour to begin serious first draft.
- Third night, if research is required, promise two hours at library.
- Fifth day, another hour for another serious draft sometime before evening.
- Weekend, find several hours each day to compose, research, and revise.
- Eighth day, ask for response from trusted reader (offer same back).
- Tenth day, revise and edit according to feedback received.
- Twelfth night, revise and edit.
- Night before paper is due: once over lightly—proofread and print final copy.

Following such a revision schedule will help you develop consistent, well-practiced writing habits and skills. You'll get the better grades that good writers in all subjects get. And, since there are very few good jobs out there that don't require writing skills, you'll almost guarantee yourself the more serious attention on the job market that good writers get.

chapter 3

Keeping a Journal

J ournals are notebooks in which writers can explore their personal thoughts and feelings. Instructors commonly assign journals to help students focus narrowly on the subject matter of a single discipline, but also to speculate broadly on the whole range of their academic experience.

In simplest terms, journals are daily records of people's lives (*jour* is French for "day"), similar to diaries, daybooks, or logs. When writers keep journals, they record whatever snippets of thought or life they find worth pondering. In other words, journals are whatever individual writers want them to be. Certain characteristics, however, would describe most journals.

Sequence Journals capture thoughts from one day to the next, in the order in which they occur. By dating each entry you can create an ongoing record of your constancy, change, or growth over the course of a semester or a project.

Audience Journals are written for writers rather than readers. A journal is a place to explore what's important to you, not to communicate information or ideas to someone else. By providing a place to share your thoughts and hear reactions, however, an assigned journal may initiate an informal conversation between you and your instructor.

Language Journal style is informal. Use your most comfortable voice, and concentrate on ideas rather than on grammar, spelling, or punctuation.

Freedom Journals are discovery and practice books, good for trying out new ideas. Nothing is "wrong" in a journal unless you find it so. Explore whatever you choose: Try to put new concepts into your own words, explore new lines of reasoning, or vent frustrations. Don't worry about completing every thought—journals are full of stops, starts, and fragments.

3 a Journals in the writing class

A well-kept journal will include thoughts, reactions, reflections, and questions about classes and ideas; it is the best possible record of an educational (or any other) experience.

Journals are often assigned in writing classes to help student writers discover, explore, advance, and critique their writing projects. Like private diaries, academic journals are written in the first person (*I*) about ideas important to the writer. Like class notebooks, they focus on a college subject (English, history, and so on).

Diary → Academic journal ← Class notebook

Part of the content of a writing course is the business of learning to write. Use your journal to document how your writing is going and what you need to do next to improve it. Learn to assess your writing attitudes and actions and to record the plans, strategies, and situations that promote your best writing.

Also use your journal to find paper topics, to try out introductions and arguments, to record relevant research and observations, to assess how a paper is turning out, and to make plans for what to do next. In the following journal entry, John tells himself what to do in the next draft of a paper describing his coaching of an eighth-grade girls' soccer team.

> 9/16　I'm going to try to use more dialogue in my paper. That is what I really think I was missing. The second draft is very dull. As I read it, it has no life. I should have used more detail. I'll try more dialogue, lots more, in draft 3. I'll have it take place at one of my practices, giving a vivid description of what kids were like. I have SO MUCH MATERIAL. But I have a hard time deciding what seems more interesting.

John's entry is an excellent example of a writer's critical evaluation of his own work and, on the basis of that evaluation, his plans to change something.

Use your journal to record what you've learned about writing through class discussions, through reading other students' papers, and through reviewing your own writing. Near the end of John's writing course, he reflected in his journal about what he'd learned so far.

> 11/29　I've learned to be very critical of my own work, to look at it again and again, looking for big and little problems. I've also learned from my writing group that other people's comments are extremely helpful—so now I make sure I show my early drafts to Kelly before I write the final draft. I guess I've always known this, but now I actually *do* it.

3　b　Journals across the curriculum

Journals are good tools for learning any subject. Use your journal to clarify course goals, pose and solve problems, keep track of readings, practice for exams, explore paper topics, and raise questions to ask in class. For example, Jennifer wrote the following reflection after a lecture in her education course.

3/8   Sexist language is everywhere. So much so that people don't even realize what they are saying is sexist. My teacher last year told all the "mothers-to-be" to be sure to read to their children. What about the fathers? Sexist language is dangerous because it so easily undermines women's morale and self-image. I try my hardest not to use sexist language, but even I find myself falling into old stereotypes.

In another instance, Julie, who kept a journal about all the authors she studied in her American literature course, noticed a disturbing pattern and tried to evaluate it. She used the act of journal writing to process an idea, interpret that idea, and test her hypothesis.

3/4   So far, the two authors we have read have led tragic, unhappy lives. I wonder if this is a coincidence or if it has something to do with the personality of successful writers. Actually, of all people, writers need a lot of time alone, by themselves, thinking and writing, away from other people, including, probably, close family members. The more I think about it, writers would be difficult to live with, that's it—they spend so much time alone and become hard to live with.

When your instructor poses a question, try putting it into your own language and see whether that leads you closer to an answer. If you are asked to keep journals for several classes at one time, consider using a loose-leaf notebook with dividers for each class to cut down the number of notebooks you carry. You can hand in relevant entries for each class while keeping your journals active.

 Journals for Second-language Writing

When you are writing in a language other than your native language, journals can be especially useful. Since you don't have to be concerned with correctness, you can work on developing fluency. A journal is a good opportunity for experimenting with language; you may want to try out new vocabulary or use different kinds of sentence structures.

For an academic journal, your instructor will most likely expect you to do more than summarize assigned reading. Consider a double-entry journal. Summarize what you have read in one column, and then comment on or raise questions about the reading in the column next to it.

To develop your English vocabulary, use a journal to keep an ongoing list of new words. This list can include both vocabulary you learn in your classes and words or idioms you hear outside class.

3 c Journals for personal expression

Ultimately, journals are personal—written by you, for you, and about things that matter to you. Even when they are assigned as part of a course requirement, it's important to remember that they can connect your personal and academic lives so that both are more meaningful. Journal writing helps you find a personal approach to otherwise abstract social, philosophical, and political events, not to mention the small, everyday happenings in the news. For example, in the following entry, Peter explores a personal topic for an otherwise academic assignment.

> 10/12 Well, I switched my research topic to something I'm actually interested in, a handicapped children's rehabilitation program right here on campus. My younger brother was born deaf, and our whole family has pitched in to help him—but I've never really studied what a college program could do to help. The basis of my research will be interviews with people who run the program—I have my first appointment tomorrow with Professor Stanford.

On an even more personal level, journals can help writers explore feelings about college, declaring a major, getting along with a roommate, receiving a low grade on a paper, going to a party, or meeting new friends. If you find yourself writing mostly about personal experiences in your academic journal, maybe you should start a separate personal journal that you keep strictly for yourself. After keeping a journal for the first time in a college class, Jeff wrote the entry on page 16.

Guidelines for Keeping a Journal

- **Be flexible.** Buy a loose-leaf notebook that will allow you to add, subtract, and rearrange entries so that you can edit your journal before sharing it with an instructor.

- **Be organized.** Add dividers and set aside space to write about different subjects, some personal, some academic.

- **Start each entry on a new page.** Leave plenty of white space so new thoughts can emerge without competing with previous ones. Later, use the blank space for notes or clippings.

- **Date each entry.** Record the date and other information of interest (time, place, weather, etc.). Your journal is a personal historical document, and such information may be of interest in the future.

- **Write as ritual.** Write at the same time or same place each day, whether you think you have anything to say or not. If you start writing, the ideas will come.

- **Take it with you.** Tote your journal in a book bag or backpack, in school and out. In addition to writing at your appointed time or place, stop during the day to capture snapshots of your life and to record ideas while they are fresh in your mind.

- **Write to yourself.** Write in your natural voice, your letter-writing voice. Don't worry about style, spelling, or punctuation.

- **Have fun.** Write with a favorite pen; sketch ideas; experiment with voice and style.

11/21   The journal to me has been like a one-man debate, where I could write thoughts down and then read them later. This process seemed to help clarify many of my ideas. To be honest, there is probably 50 percent of the journal that is nothing but junk, but that still leaves 50 percent that I think is important. The journal is also a time capsule. I want to put it away and not look at it for ten or twenty years and let it recall for me this period of my life.

WRITING ACROSS THE CURRICULUM

Darwin's Journal

Many scientists, philosophers, and writers have kept journals to both find ideas and create a record of those ideas to return to at a later date. The following excerpt is typed from the handwritten journal Charles Darwin kept aboard the *Beagle* in 1836 as he sailed around the Galapagos islands off the coast of Ecuador, speculating about the workings of nature and generating ideas for what would later become the theory of evolution in *The Origin of Species,* 1857. Can you see the value in such speculations written down and dated?

> In the endless cycle of revolutions, by actions of rivers currents, & sea beaches. All mineral masses must have a tendency, to mingle; The sea would separate quartzose sand from the finer matter resulting from degradation of Felspar & other minerals containing Alumen.—This matter accumulating in deep seas forms slates: How is the Lime separated; is it washed from the solid rock by the actions of Springs or more probably by some unknown Volcanic process? How does it come that all Lime is not accumulated in the Tropical oceans detained by Organic powers. We know the waters of the ocean all are mingled. These reflections might be introduced either in note in Coral Paper or hypothetical origin of some sandstones, as in Australia,— Have Limestones all been dissolved, if so sea would separate them from indissoluble rocks? Has Chalk ever been dissolved?
>
> *The Red Notebooks of Charles Darwin.* Ed. S. Herbert.
> Cornell U. Press, 1980, pp. 37–38.]

chapter 4

Strategies for Starting

For many writers, the most difficult part about writing is getting started. While you can't write if you don't have ideas, experienced writers know that you don't have to start with ideas, that ideas will come if you begin writing. In fact, one of the most productive ways of finding ideas is simply to start writing, even when you think you have nothing to say, and let the writing force ideas out. Once that happens, you're started, and you can accept, reject, or modify those ideas.

Writers are discovering when they create new ideas or relocate forgotten ideas or learn by reading or listening to others. Writers invent and discover in virtually all phases of the writing process: when limiting and focusing assignments, when finding and approaching topics, when developing answers to questions and solutions to problems, and when figuring out openings and conclusions, arranging arguments, and placing supporting examples. This chapter outlines five specific strategies to help you discover ideas when you need them: brainstorming, freewriting, clustering, outlining, and questioning.

4 a Brainstorm to find ideas

Brainstorming is nothing more than systematic list making. Ask the question you're concerned with, then list all possible answers that come to mind without evaluating or deleting any of the answers. Write these down as quickly as you can, and keep looking for more answers. Sometimes it helps to set goals: *What are seven possible topics? How many ideas can I list in five minutes?* Each item in your list becomes a possible direction for your paper.

Use free association to generate more ideas. For example, in making a shopping list, you might write *peanut butter* and it reminds you of *jelly*. To brainstorm, generate as long a list as possible, and force yourself to find and record even vague, half-formed ideas in concrete language. Then examine your list and decide which items are worth pursuing. Whenever they're stuck in any phase of their writing process, writers brainstorm by making lists, asking theoretical questions, and posing possible answers. The following exercise helps push vague subjects into shaped topics.

1. List as many topics as you can in three minutes.

2. Circle the three that interest you most, and write a paragraph about each.

3. Ask two questions about each paragraph. Find two answers to each question.

4. Select the paragraph that now interests you most, and list three different ways to start this paper.

4 b   Freewrite to advance ideas

Freewriting is writing quickly without worrying about rules. To freewrite, deliberately write as fast as possible and free associate, allowing one word to trigger the next, one idea to lead to another. Ideas happen when you write intensely, nonstop, and without censoring, drawing thoughts from wherever in your memory they may reside. If you haven't freewritten before, the following suggestions will help.

- Write quickly for a fixed period of time, say ten minutes, toward whatever problem needs solving or topic needs finding.

- Write the whole ten minutes without stopping to check spelling, ponder a word choice, stare at the ceiling, or think. So long as you continue writing, the words will generate more words, which in turn will generate ideas.

- Write to yourself. Don't worry about digressing or writing something silly. If you catch a fleeting thought that's especially interesting or think of something you've never thought of before, then the freewriting has worked.

4 c   Cluster to connect ideas

Clustering is a method of listing ideas in a nonlinear way to reveal the relationships among them. Clustering is useful both for inventing and discovering a topic and for exploring a topic after you have done preliminary

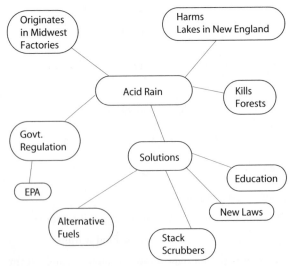

Figure 4–1   Cluster map to explore topic "acid rain."

research. Like outlining, the act of clustering helps you both invent and organize at the same time. To create a clustering diagram, follow this procedure.

- Write a word or phrase that seems to focus on what you want to write about. For example, write *acid rain* on a page and circle the words.

- Connect supporting ideas related to your circled phrase by drawing a line from the phrase to the related concepts. Circle and connect each aspect of acid rain back to the central idea.

- To expand further, draw possible clusters from each of the sub-clusters, finding ever more detailed ideas to work with. (See the figure on page 18.)

ESL *Freewriting to Develop Fluency*

Writing in a second language can be frustrating when you are trying to pay attention to ideas, sentence structures, word choices, and so on. Many ESL writers have discovered that freewriting helps tremendously with this problem. If you haven't tried freewriting before, you might find it hard at first not to stop and carefully check each sentence, but with continued practice this activity should help you to postpone editing and improve your fluency in English.

4 d Outline to organize ideas

Outlines are organized lists of ideas and information. They are a powerful way to begin and advance a writing project—so long as you understand that you can modify the outline when new and better ideas emerge. To make an outline, start with an idea, and then see how many questions you can ask about it. If you start with "acid rain," ask, *What is it? Where is it? How do you recognize it? What causes it? What problems does it cause? How can it be stopped?* Once you have such a list, arrange answers in a progression that makes sense, throwing out those that don't fit, adding others as they seem relevant.

Formal outlines establish hierarchy (major versus minor ideas) and follow logic (which ideas depend on which). Use Roman numerals for major headings, capital letters for minor ones, Arabic numbers for supporting ideas. You can extend the hierarchy to lowercase letters, Arabic numbers in parentheses, and lowercase letters in parentheses. Keep parallel ideas in parallel grammatical form (for example, use all noun clusters or all complete sentences, but be consistent). Notice, too, that each level is indented from the next higher level.

I. Definition of acid rain

II. Causes of acid rain

   A. Coal-burning power plants

      1. Power generating stations

      2. Steel mills

      3. Factories

   B. Automobile pollution

III. Effects of acid rain

   A. Deforestation in New England

   B. Dead lakes

IV. Solutions to the acid rain problem

The effort to make an outline not only helps organize the paper, but shows what the writer doesn't know and where supporting information is weak. Outlining at the beginning helps shape direction; outlining in the middle helps retain or reshape direction. Don't be afraid to modify or scrap initial outlines when your thoughts take new and better directions.

4 e   Question to test ideas

Writers who train themselves to ask questions are also training themselves to find information. Reporters train themselves to ask six basic questions about any story they are writing and do the best they can to answer these questions in their story: *Who? What? Where? When? Why?* and *How?* Using these questions will also help you discover new information. To initiate paper topics about issues, events, or personal experience, ask yourself the reporter's questions.

- Who was involved?
- What happened?
- Where did it happen?
- When did it happen?
- Why did it happen?
- How did it happen?

Asking these same questions of a first or second draft will tell you whether you have included all the relevant information or left something out. In other words, it helps to ask the reporter's questions both at the beginning and at the end of your writing.

Suggestions for Invention and Discovery

- Brainstorm a list of five possible topics to write about for your next paper assignment. (See 4a.)

- Freewrite for ten minutes about the most interesting topic on your list. (See 4b.)

- Cluster ideas about your topic until it is developed as far as possible. (See 4c.)

- Make an outline of a possible structure for your paper. (See 4d.)

- Question your topic to see that it meets all the tests for telling a complete story. (See 4e.)

WRITING ACROSS THE CURRICULUM

Writing to Discover

The term "discovery" applies to finding new ideas or recalling old ideas that you once knew but have since forgotten. The following example of writing to solve a problem was shared with us by a chemistry professor, teaching "Introduction to Chemistry."

The professor asked students to share with him their questions about the day's class. This anonymous student is puzzled by the instructor's explanation of the interaction between transfer RNA (tRNA) and messenger RNA (mRNA). In writing to the professor for clarification, however, the student an-

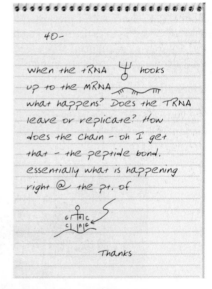

swers her own question, but hands in the note anyway, perhaps to say thanks for the opportunity to solve the problem by writing about it. Try the simple problem-solving technique of writing out where you're stuck or puzzled and see if clarification comes through writing—letting your own eyes see the dilemma from a distance and providing you with helpful objectivity. No guarantees, of course, but your chances of answering questions or solving problems greatly increase simply by writing.

5

Reading and Writing with Images

O f all five senses, the one most people trust first is their eyes. They believe what they see firsthand, and they believe the photographs, films, or videos of others. Well-known examples of the power of visual images to shape public opinion and national policy include the photographs of Depression–era poverty, Vietnam war casualties, and Iraqi prisoner-of-war abuse; films of the Nazi Holocaust victims and JFK assassination; and videos of the Rodney King beating, space shuttle disasters, and the 9/11 terrorist attacks.

5 a The elements of composition

To compose either an effective essay or a strong picture, composers use elements that turn out to be remarkably similar from verbal to visual media. Both stories and pictures present information from a composer's point of view. Pictures are arranged in two-dimensional space, while stories are ordered in sequential time, each to illustrate a certain theme, while color deepens our understanding of both.

Information

Both words and pictures convey information, but each does so in importantly different ways. In English, words are written sequentially, left to

How many words would it take?

right, and so readers' attention is directed toward meaning in a linear fashion. However, information in visual images is presented simultaneously so viewers can start or stop anywhere they like.

When we look at the accompanying photograph, "Roadside Stand," taken by Walker Evans in 1936 Alabama, where do we start? What, among all those vegetables and words, do we focus on? The informality of the roadside market in contrast with today's modern supermarkets? The careful order in what is otherwise a low-rent store? Do we focus on why the two boys are holding the watermelons? Do the verbal signs make the meaning any clearer? What do we think of a merchant who advertises "Honest Weights and Square Dealings"? Is the sign reassuring or suspicious? And if the photo supports the cliché, "a picture is worth a thousand words," with which words would you begin to explain the meaning of this photo?

To read visual *information* critically, first identify what objects, facts, processes, or symbols are portrayed in the image. Taking all the information together, ask if there is a main or unifying idea: Is the meaning open to multiple interpretations, such as the Evans photograph? Is it suggested, but not stated? Or is it clear and unambiguous?

To use images to convey additional information in your text make sure they: are thematically appropriate, are the clearest illustrations you can locate, add information difficult for text alone to impart, are inserted close to the textual discussion, and are labelled with titles or figure numbers.

Point of View

In written texts, *point of view* refers, technically, to the "person" from whose vantage point the information is delivered—commonly, first or third person. It may also refer more generally to *perspective,* which includes matters of personal value, belief, or position.

How does point of view shape this picture?

In photographs, drawings, or paintings, point of view refers, technically, to the place from which the image-maker looks at the subject—where the photographer places his camera, the artist her easel. A camera aimed east omits information north, west, and south, and so on. And as the term does in texts, it may also refer, more generally, to perspective, suggesting something of the image-maker's values, beliefs, or position. In the photograph of the Filipino lettuce pickers by Dorthea Lange (page 23), what information is conveyed? What first catches your attention—the dirt gullies, the big heads of lettuce, the open sky, or the working pickers? If you are drawn first to the people, as most of us are, what is noteworthy about the people in this picture—size? clothing? arrangement? Where has Lange placed her camera? How can you tell? In terms of personal perspective, how does her camera placement affect the photograph's meaning? Does it increase or diminish the stature of the pickers? The intensity of their labor? Your empathy or understanding of their situation?

To read point of view critically, identify the place or stance from which the image-maker viewed the subject. Ask about the effect this particular point of view has on how viewers think or feel about the subject. What would happen if the vantage point were somewhere else—above or below, left or right of what it is now? Imagine the different words you would use to describe such perspectives.

To use images to convey point of view in your written text, in first-person narratives, consider personal photos or images of yourself to allow readers to see more deeply into the world of the writer. For a third-person, more objective point of view in reports and subject-oriented texts, use images that illustrate or convey information about your subject. Also consider images that generate empathy or increased understanding for your perspective or that specifically support the position you take in an interpretative or argumentative paper.

Arrangement and Pattern

The term *arrangement* in visual texts might be compared to terms such as *order, organization,* or *structure* in written texts, though the differences are substantial. While writers arrange or put together a story, essay, or poem to take place over the time it takes a reader to follow the text, line by line, through a number of pages, photographers arrange in two-dimensional space inviting viewers to read in space rather than time. In visual texts, then, arrangement refers to the ways the various parts of a picture come together, one way or another, and how they lead the viewer's eye toward meaning.

In Dorthea Lange's photo of the plowed field, how does the curving pattern of the furrowed field lines contribute to the meaning of this photograph? How do the patterns of light and dark also contribute? And what is the role of the single human dwelling in this carefully plowed plain? Furthermore, Lange's photo is dated 1938, so historical hindsight tells us that such power plowing of millions of acres of the Great Plains was a precursor to great

How does pattern shape meaning?

dust storms that ruined crops and drove people from their homes. If the visual imagery alone suggests loneliness, poverty, and abandonment, the historical knowledge only confirms it.

To read the influence of arrangement on the meaning of visual images, identify repeated elements and ask: Where is the center of gravity or weight in a given picture? Was the center found or fabricated? Where do patterns of light, shape, weight, or number lead the eye? What does arrangement contribute to balance and order in an image, and how might those qualities contribute to meaning in a two-dimensional frame? What does the arrangement suggest about the meaning of the image?

To make images contribute to a sense of order and balance in written texts, locate them at strategic places on the page or within the paper: Images arranged flush with textual margins top and bottom, right and left, contribute to a sense of order and comfort while images that violate textual margins call extra—and perhaps distracting—attention to themselves; place according to the effect you want. Left-margin and center-page images interrupt the left-to-right flow of reading more than right-margin illustrations; place according to the effect you want. Note that text overlaying background images on the page is often difficult to read. Note that boxes around images, figures, and text separate the material from the text and call special attention to it.

Theme

Both verbal and visual texts may be said to have themes—statements that identify the larger meaning of the text being read or viewed—that operate in similar ways. In verbal texts, theme may be stated early (informational reports), late (feature stories), or accumulate by inference over the length of the whole text (personal essays). In a visual text, theme may or may not be either strongly stated or quickly apparent.

Which is more important, words or image?

Look, for example, at Marian Post Wolcott's photo of a Depression–era movie theater. What visual elements first catch your attention? The man ascending the angled staircase? The graphic and stark light and dark patterns? And what do the Dr. Pepper ad or the cowboy movie poster contribute? In this photo, you may have to look at the fine print to decide this is not a nostalgic picture of times past in small-town America, but a chilling reminder of the dark side of the American past when discrimination was once public policy.

To read theme in a visual image, notice the subject to which your eye is first drawn. Examine next all the relevant elements of the image: the placement of the subject, the information conveyed, the image-maker's point of view, the arrangement and pattern of light and shape. Find words to express what you think and feel; put the words together and you're on the track of theme.

To use images to support the theme of your written text, choose those that contribute additional information rather than those that merely decorate a page. In papers examining concrete or physical material such as people, places, or objects, illustrative images contribute to credibility and identify specific meaning. In papers using quantitative material, charts and graphs facilitate reader understanding. In papers examining abstract ideas such as arguments, interpretations, or philosophical positions, images may illustrate specific cases, characters, or examples to enhance reader comprehension.

5 b   Words

Adding words to images brings us full circle, back to the specificity of written texts. Text is often added to images to make sure the image is interpreted in a particular way. However, words may be added to images to create specific messages neither word nor image alone would convey, as in the Wolcott photo (above) where either subtracting the fine print or eliminating the photo would destroy altogether the theme of discrimination.

5 c Color

The images we've looked at so far have been in black and white since the visual elements actually stand out more clearly without the distraction of color. That said, we realize that most of the commercial and aesthetic images you'll encounter today in magazines, films, television, and the Internet will be in color, so let's look critically at what color adds or subtracts. In verbal texts, the word "color" is metaphoric and commonly refers to rich details that flesh out a description. In visual texts, color shows us the full range of colors we see with our eyes.

Look, for instance, at the photo of New York City firefighters raising an American flag at Ground Zero. The original is in color, but we added a black and white version for comparison. What is your reaction to seeing the two versions side by side? Which seems to you the more powerful? If color, why? Note how your own personal reactions to different colors may correspond to traditional symbolic values attached to different colors: Why, for instance, does red often symbolize anger or war? (Add white and blue and, in America, you get patriotism.) Why does black suggest danger or death? Why does white stand for innocence or purity? Are these meanings arbitrary or logical?

To read the impact of *color* in images, notice whether it enhances or distorts reality. Imagine the image in shades of black, white, and gray; ask:

What difference does color make?

What would be lost, what gained if color were subtracted? How do different colors suggest different emotions? Does the color add useful or believable information? Does it impact on point of view, arrangement, or theme? If so, how?

To use color, literally, in your compositions, use it to support meaning where mere black and white might lead to confusion, such as portraying seasonal landscapes, specific plants, animals, or objects. Also note that color is more useful than shades of gray in identifying different information in maps, graphs, and charts. More experimental effects can be achieved with different font and paper colors: For example, sepia tones in text, paper, or images might add a period credibility in a historical paper while mood colors might sway emotions in creative papers. And Web sites that do not use color to catch attention may not be read at all. However, be aware that academic expectations are generally conservative and that color combinations that distract from or conceal meaning will hurt rather than help credibility; black text on white paper remains the norm for hard copy papers.

As you know well, both words and pictures in the hands of skilled writers, artists, and photographers can be powerfully persuasive. Consequently, we believe that verbal language needs to be read and visual images viewed with a critical eye so that meaning and intention are revealed and understood. And we believe that, as writers and creators of images yourselves, your own critical awareness will lead to the reader and viewer understanding what you most want to achieve. The balance of attention in the chapters to come focuses on your persuasive abilities with and without images to support you.

WRITING ACROSS THE CURRICULUM

Photographs as Disciplinary Documents

Choose any single image from this chapter and write a page or two, reimagining it through the eyes of a specific academic discipline:

- Imagine it as a document from which to infer **historical** change, by comparing it to a similar photo you might take today. Where would you go to take a contemporary photo with similar subject matter?

- Imagine it as an **economic or sociological** document from which you gather clues about these people's place in society. What details would you highlight? With what specific socioeconomic group would you compare them today?

- Imagine the **poem** or **short story** you might write based on what you perceive to be the theme in the photograph. What verbal image would begin your poem? What character name would begin your story?

- Imagine the photo used in a **political** or **religious campaign:** who would use it and what purpose would the photo serve in the campaign?

- Imagine the photo as a **work of art.** What about the image is aesthetically strong and not dated? What contemporary photographer or aesthetic movement might this work have influenced?

- Imagine the photo as part of a poster for a current **advocacy group:** which group would it be, and what would the poster say?

- Imagine the photo as an **advertisement** appropriated by a contemporary product to increase sales: what would the product be and how would you write the pitch?

chapter 6

Reflecting on Experience

ood stories occur everywhere and can be told about anything. They are as likely to occur in your own neighborhood as in some exotic locale. Potential stories happen daily; what makes potential stories actual stories is putting them into language, recounting them orally or in writing. Good stories are entertaining, informative, lively, and believable; they will mean something to those who write them and to those who read them.

All stories, whether they're imagined (fiction) or true (nonfiction), are accounts of something that happened—an event or series of events—after which something or somebody is changed. Whether the story is "The Three Little Pigs" or *The Adventures of Huckleberry Finn* (both fiction), or Darwin's *The Voyage of the Beagle* or an account of your own canoe trip (nonfiction), it includes the following elements: a character *(who?)* to whom something happens *(what?)*, in some place *(where?)*, at some time *(when?)*, for some reason *(why?)*, told from a particular perspective *(how?)*. In other words, any time you render a full account of a personal experience, you answer what we called "reporter's questions" in a previous chapter (4e)—the *who, what, where, when, why,* and *how* questions reporters ask themselves to make sure their reports of news stories are complete. Whether your story is engaging depends upon the subject, your interest in telling it, and the skill with which you weave together these story elements.

The following discussion of writing papers based on personal experience is organized around the formula of "reporter's questions" so that writer's may check their drafted stories to be sure they have covered, one way or another, these basic story elements. We are not suggesting that the order of the items discussed here would be the order in which writers would begin or imagine their stories.

6 a Character (who)

In personal experience writing, your main character is yourself, so try to give your readers a sense of who you are through your voice, actions, level of awareness, and description. The characters in a good story are believable and interesting; they come alive for readers. Study the elements that give life to characters in your story: voice, actions, insight, and detail.

Voice

In your own story, your language reveals who you are—playful, serious, rigid, loose, stuffy, honest, warm, or whatever. In the following excerpt, in which Beth relates her experience playing oboe during a two-hour Saturday morning orchestra rehearsal, we learn she's serious, fun-loving, impish, and just a little lazy.

> I love that section. It sounds so cool when Sarah and I play
> together like that. Now I can put my reed back in the water and
> sit back and listen. I probably should be counting the rests.
> Counting would mean I'd have to pay attention and that's no
> fun. I'd rather look around and watch everyone else sweat.

Actions

Readers learn something about the kind of person you are from your actions. For example, when Karen recalls what she was thinking while she was playing in a basketball tournament, we learn something of her insecurity, fears, and skills all at once:

> This time, don't be so stupid Karen—if you don't take it up
> court, you'll never get the ball. Oh, god, here I go. Okay, they're
> in a twenty-one—just bring it up—Sarah's alone—fake up,
> bounce pass—yes! She hits it! I got the assist!

Insight

One of the best ways to reveal who you are is to show yourself becoming aware of something, gaining a new way of seeing the world, a new insight. While such awareness can occur for apparently unexplainable reasons, it most often happens when you encounter new ideas or have experiences that change you in some way. In writing a paper about why she goes to the library to write a paper, Judith clarifies first for herself—then for her readers—the relationship between feeling safe and being creative.

> Two weeks ago, a female student was assaulted not far
> from where I live—that's why I've taken to locking my door so
> carefully. I am beginning to understand the importance of
> feeling safe in order to be creative and productive. Here, in the
> library, I feel secure, protected from real violence and isolated
> from everyday distractions. There are just enough people for
> security's sake but not so many that I feel crowded. And
> besides, I'm surrounded by all these books, all these great
> minds who dwell in the hallowed space! I am comfortable, safe,
> and beginning to get an idea.

Telling Details

Describe yourself and other participants in your story in such a way that the details and facts help tell your story. A telling detail or fact is one that advances your characterization of someone without your having to render an obvious opinion. For example, you could characterize your little sister by pointing out the field hockey stick in the corner of her room, the photograph of the seventh-grade field hockey team on the wall, and the teddy bear next to her pillow. You could characterize her coach by pointing to the logo on the coach's sweatshirt: "Winning isn't everything. It's the only thing."

6   b   Subject (what)

People write about their personal experiences to get to know and understand themselves better, to inform and entertain others, and to leave permanent records of their lives. Sometimes people recount their experiences casually, in forms never intended for wide circulation, such as journals, diaries, or letters. Sometimes they write in forms meant to be shared with others, such as memoirs, autobiographies, or personal essays. In college, the most common narrative forms are personal experience essays.

Subjects for good stories know no limits. You already have a lifetime of experiences from which to choose, and each experience is a potential story to help explain who you are, what you believe, and how you act today. Here are some of the topics selected by a single first-year writing class:

- Playing oboe in Saturday orchestra rehearsals
- Counseling disturbed children at summer camp
- Picking strawberries on a farm
- Studying at the library
- Losing in a championship basketball game
- Touring Graceland in Memphis, Tennessee
- Working on an assembly line in a battery factory

When you write a paper based on personal experience, ask yourself: Which experience do I want to write about? Will anybody else want to read about it? Here are some suggestions.

Winning and Losing

Winning something—a race, a contest, a lottery—can be a good subject, since it features you in a unique position and allows you to explore or celebrate a special talent. At the same time, exciting, exceptional, or highly dramatic subjects, such as scoring the winning goal in a championship game or placing first in a creative writing contest, may be difficult to write because they've been used so often that readers have very high expectations.

The truth is that in most parts of life there are more losers than winners. While one team wins a championship, dozens do not. So there's a large, empathetic audience out there who will understand and identify with a narrative about losing. Although more common than winning, losing is less often explored in writing because it is more painful to recall. Therefore, there are fresher, deeper, more original stories to tell about losing.

Milestones

Perhaps the most interesting but also the most difficult experience to write about is one that you already recognize as a turning point in your life, whether it's high school graduation, winning a sports championship, being a camp counselor, or surviving a five-day solo camping trip in midwinter. People who explore such topics in writing often come to a better understanding of them. Also, their very significance challenges writers to make them equally significant for an audience that did not experience them. When you write about milestones, pay special attention to the physical details that will both advance your story and make it come alive for readers.

Daily Life

Commonplace experiences make fertile subjects for personal narratives. You might describe practicing for, rather than winning, the big game, or cleaning up after, rather than attending, the prom. If you are accurate, honest, and observant in exploring a subject from which readers expect little, you may pleasantly surprise them and draw them into your story. Work experiences are especially fruitful subjects, since you may know inside details and routines of restaurants and retail shops that the rest of us can only guess. For example, how long is it before McDonald's tosses its unsold hamburgers? How do florists know which flowers to order when?

A Caution about Love, Death, and Divorce

Several subjects that you may need to write about may not make good topics for formal papers that will be shared with classmates and instructors. For example, you are probably too involved in a love relationship to portray it in any but the rosiest terms; too close to the recent death of someone you care about to render the event faithfully; too angry, confused, or miserable to write well about your parents' divorce. Writing about these and other close or painful experiences in your journal or diary can be immensely cathartic, but there is no need to share them with others.

Experiences happen in some place at some time, and good stories describe these settings. To describe a believable physical setting, you need to recreate on paper the sights, sounds, smells, and physical sensations that allow readers to experience it for themselves. In addition to telling details that support your plot or character development, try to include evocative details, colorful memories of setting and character that will let your readers know you were really there. In the following example, Heather portrays details of the farm where she spent the summer picking strawberries:

> The sun is just barely rising over the treetops, and there is still dew covering the ground. In the strawberry patch, the deep green leaves are filled with water droplets, and the strawberries are big and red and ready to be picked. The patch is located in a field off the road near a small forest of Christmas trees. The white house, the red barn, and a checkerboard of fields can be seen in the distance. It is 5:30 a.m., and the day has begun.

The evocative details are those that appeal to your senses, such as sight, touch, and smell: *dew covering the ground, deep green leaves, strawberries . . . big and red, white house, red barn,* and *checkerboard of fields.*

The details of a setting reveal something essential about your story without you explaining them. For example, in telling a story about your sister, you might describe the physical objects in her room, which, in turn, describe important elements of her character: the hockey stick, soccer ball, gym bag, sweatpants, and baseball jersey, and the life-size posters of Tiger Woods and Jackie Joyner-Kersee. In other words, skillful description helps you "tell" the story without actually telling it outright.

In every story, events are ordered in some way. While you cannot alter the events that happened, as a writer you need to decide which events to portray and in what order to present them.

Selecting Events

You have dozens of places to start and end any story, and at each point along the way, you have many possible details and events worth relating. In selecting events, consider using one of two strategies that writers commonly use to maintain reader interest: showing cause and effect and building suspense. When writers recount an experience to show cause and effect, they pair one event (losing a basketball game) with another (a new lesson learned by losing).

In using suspense, writers raise questions or pose problems, but they delay answering or solving them. If the writer can make the question interesting enough, or the problem pressing enough, readers will keep reading to find out what happens. A typical way to use suspense in telling a championship basketball story is to tell the underdog's story, ending with a stunning upset—a good and oft-told story. An alternate and more surprising underdog story is told by Karen, a perennial basketball team bench-sitter, who wins personally, only because the team loses so badly she finally gets to play. Her basketball story starts with six minutes remaining in the game when she comes off the bench, not to shoot the winning basket, but to accomplish a personal goal:

> It's over now, and I've stopped crying, and I'm very happy. In the end I have to thank—not my coach, not my team—but Walpole for beating us so badly that I got to play. I can't get over it. I played. And my dream came true—I hit a three-pointer in the Boston Garden.

Ordering Events

The most common way to sequence events is to use chronological order, presenting events in the sequence in which they happened. Chronological order can be straightforward, following a day from morning to night, as Heather does in her narrative about picking strawberries. Chronology also orders one student's twenty-two days of Outward Bound. And chronology orders Karen's six minutes at the end of one basketball game. Sometimes, however, the order is deliberately broken up, so that readers are first introduced to an event in the present and then, later in the story, are allowed to see events that happened earlier through flashbacks. For example, the Outward Bound journal could start with the writer's first day of solo camping and then, in another entry, flash back to explain how he got there. Such a sequence has the advantage of stimulating readers' interest by opening with a point of exceptional drama or insight.

6 e   Theme (why)

We can talk about the "why" of a story on two levels. First, why did the events in the story occur? What motivated or caused them? Well-told stories will answer this question, directly or indirectly. But we can also ask the writer: "Of all the stories you could write, why did you write this one?" Or, more bluntly, every reader asks, at least tacitly: "So what? What's the meaning or significance of this story? What did I learn by reading it?" Well-told stories will allow the reader to see and understand both why you wrote it and why they read it.

However, first drafts of personal experience narratives often do not reveal clear answers to these questions, even to the writers themselves. First drafts are for getting the events down on paper for writers to look at. In subsequent drafts, the meaning of these events—the theme—should become clearer. If it doesn't, dig even deeper or drop the subject.

In experiential stories, the theme isn't usually explicitly stated in the first paragraph, as the thesis statement often is in expository or argumentative writing. Instead, storytellers may create a meaning that is not directly stated anywhere and that becomes clear only at the end of the narrative. Many themes fall into three broad categories: slices of life, insights, and turning points.

Slices of Life

Some stories simply let readers see what life is like for someone else. Such stories exist primarily to record the writer's memories and to convey information in an interesting way. Their primary theme is, "This is what my life is like." Beth's story of the Saturday orchestra rehearsal is a slice of life, as she chooses to focus on a common practice rather than a more dramatic performance. After using interior monologue for nine paragraphs, in the last paragraph she speaks to the readers directly, explaining what the meaning of music is in her everyday life.

> As hard as it is to get up every Saturday morning, and as hard as it is to put up with some people here, I always feel good as I leave rehearsal. A guest conductor once said, "Music sounds how feelings feel." It's really true. Music evokes emotions that can't be described on paper. Every human feeling can be expressed through music—sadness, love, hatred. Music is an international language. Once you learn it you can't forget it.

Insights

In contrast to the many but routine experiences that reveal slices of life is the single important experience that leads to a writer's new insight, change, or growth. Such an experience is deeply significant to the writer, and he or she makes sure that readers see its full value, usually by commenting explicitly on its meaning. In fact, many of the best personal experience stories have for themes a modest change or the beginning of growth. Although such themes may be implied throughout the story, they often become clear only in a single climactic moment or episode. In early drafts of her essay about studying at the library, it wasn't clear why Judith had selected this topic at all, as nothing of particular note seemed to happen. But in her final draft, her library study triggered an insight that tipped off the reader—and perhaps the writer—about what her story really meant:

Two weeks ago, a female student was assaulted not far from where I live—that's why I've taken to locking my door so carefully. I am beginning to understand the importance of feeling safe in order to be creative and productive. Here, in the library, I feel secure, protected from real violence and isolated from everyday distractions. There are just enough people for security's sake but not so many that I feel crowded. And besides, I'm surrounded by all these books, all these great minds who dwell in this hallowed space! I am comfortable, safe, and beginning to get an idea.

6 f   Perspective (how)

When reporters ask themselves "How?" they mean "How did the news event happen?" However, in this chapter, "How?" means "How is the story told?"—From what vantage point, position, or perspective are you telling the story? Perspective addresses the question "How close—in time, distance, or spirit—are you to the experience?" Do you write as if it happened long ago or yesterday? Do you summarize what happened or put readers at the scene? Do you explain the experience or leave it mysterious? In other words, you can control, or at least influence, the way readers respond to a story by controlling the perspective from which you tell it.

Point of View

Authorial perspective is established largely by point of view. Using the first person (*I*) puts the narrator right in the story as a participant. In personal experience writing, writers usually choose this point of view, as we saw Beth and Karen do in earlier examples.

The third person (*he* or *she*) establishes a distinction between the person narrating the events and the person experiencing them and thus tends to depersonalize the story. This perspective is more common in fiction, but it has some uses in personal essays as well. In the following example, for instance, Karen opens her personal experience essay from the imagined perspective of the play-by-play announcer who broadcasts the championship game; the point of view is first person, but from the perspective of a third person:

2:15   Well folks, it looks as if Belmont has given up, the coach is preparing to send in his subs. It has been a rough game for Belmont. They stayed in it during the first quarter, but Walpole has run away with it since then. Down by twenty with only six minutes left, Belmont's first sub is now approaching the table.

Verb Tense

Verb tense establishes the time when the story happened or is happening. The tense used to relate most of the events in a story is called the *governing tense.* Personal experience stories are usually set in either the past or the present (see 42e).

Once upon a Time: Past Tense

The most natural way to recount a personal experience is to write in the past tense; whatever you're narrating did happen sometime in the past. Lorraine uses the past tense to describe an automobile ride with her Native American grandfather to attend a tribal conference:

> I sat silently across from Grandfather and watched him slowly tear the thin white paper from the tip of the cigarette. He gathered the tobacco in one hand and drove the van with the other. I memorized his every move as he went through the motions of the prayer, which ended when he finally blew the tobacco out of the window and into the wind.

Even though the governing tense for your personal narrative may be the past tense, you may still want to use other tenses for special purposes.

Being There: Present Tense

The present tense provides the illusion that the experience is happening at the moment; it leaves no time for your reflection. This strategy invites readers to become involved with your story as it is happening and invites them to interpret it for themselves.

If you want to portray yourself thinking rather than talking—in what is called interior monologue—you may choose to use fragment sentences and made-up words since the flow of the mind doesn't obey conventional rules of language. For example, when Beth describes her thoughts during orchestra rehearsal, she writes an interior monologue; we hear her talking to herself while trying to blow her oboe. Notice the way she provides clues so that we understand what is going on around her.

> No, you don't really mean that, do you? You do. Rats. Here we go. . . . Pfff . . . Pfff . . . Why isn't this playing? Maybe if I blow harder . . . HONK!! Great. I've just made a total fool of myself in front of everyone. Wonderful.

6 g Shaping the whole paper (student essay)

The finished draft of Judith's reflective personal essay "Writing in Safety" opens and closes with a walk to and from the library. It has a loosely narrative pattern and is written in the present tense to convey a sense of the events unfolding as we read them. Her essay tells a very simple story, since it's mainly about walking and sitting down. The journey emerges as a mental, almost spiritual, quest for safety—safety in which to think and create without fear. At the same time, the physical dimensions of her journey and the attention to descriptive detail make her journey believable.

Writing in Safety

Judith Woods

It is already afternoon. I fiddle with the key to lock the apartment door after me. I am not accustomed to locking doors. Except for the six months I spent in Boston, I have never lived in a place where I did not trust my neighbors. When I was little, we couldn't lock our farmhouse door; the wood had swollen and the bolt no longer lined up properly with the hole, and nobody ever bothered to fix it. I still remember the time our babysitter, Rosie, hammered the bolt closed and we had to take the door off the hinges to get it open.

I heft the book bag onto my shoulder and walk up College Street toward the library. As I pass and am passed by other students, I scrutinize everything around me, hoping to be struck with a creative idea for a topic for my English paper. Instead, my mind fills with a jumble of disconnected images, like a bowl of alphabet soup: the letters are there, but they don't form any words. Campus sidewalks are not the best places for creativity to strike.

Approaching the library, I see skateboarders and bikers weaving through students who talk in clusters on the library steps. A friendly dog is tied to a bench, watching for its owner to return. Subjects to write about? Nothing strikes me as especially interesting, and besides, my heart is still pounding from the walk up the hill. I wipe my damp forehead and go inside.

Inside the smoke-colored doors, the loud and busy atmosphere vanishes, replaced by the soft, soothing hum of air conditioning and the hushed sound of whispering voices. The repetitive sound of the copy machine has a calming effect as I look for a comfortable place in which to begin my work.

I want just the right chair, with a soft cushion, and a low sturdy table for a leg rest. The chairs are strategically positioned with comfortable personal space around each one, so you can stretch your arms fully without touching a neighbor. I notice that if there are three chairs in a row, the middle one is always empty. If seated at a table, people sit staggered so they are not directly across from one another. People seem to respect each other's need for personal space.

Like a dog who circles her bed three times before lying down, I circle the reading room looking for the right place to sit. I need to feel safe and comfortable so I can concentrate on mental activity. Some students, however, are too comfortable. One boy has moved two chairs together and covered himself with his coat, and he is asleep in a fetal position. A girl sits at a table, head down, dozing the way we used to do in first grade.

I find my place, an empty chair near a window, and slouch down into it, propping my legs on the low table in front. If my mother could see me, she'd reprimand me for not sitting up straight. I breathe deeply, close my eyes for a moment, and become centered, forgetting both last night's pizza and tomorrow's philosophy exam. I need a few minutes to acclimate to this space, relax, and feel safe before starting my work.

Two weeks ago, a female student was assaulted not far from where I live—that's why I've taken to locking my door so carefully. I am beginning to understand the importance of feeling safe in order to be creative and productive. Here, in the library, I feel secure, protected from real violence and isolated from everyday distractions. There are just enough people for security's sake but not so many that I feel crowded. And besides, I'm surrounded by all these books, all these great minds who dwell in this hallowed space! I am comfortable, safe, and beginning to get an idea.

Hours later—my paper started, my exam studied for, my eyes tired—I retrace the path to my apartment. It is dark now, and I listen closely when I hear footsteps behind, stepping to the sidewalk's edge to let a man walk briskly past.

At my door, I again fumble for the now familiar key, insert it in the lock, open the

door, turn on the hall light, and step inside. Here, too, I am safe, ready to eat,

read a bit, and finish my reflective essay.

WRITING ACROSS THE CURRICULUM

Personal Perspective in Academic Writing

Including a personal perspective in academic writing by including either personal experiences or first-person pronouns is a matter of debate both across the curriculum and within specific disciplines.

Following are four arguments for the validity of personal perspectives in papers written in disciplines other than English:

1. A personal perspective is usually easier to read than formal academic writing because it sounds like a real person speaking: it uses first-person pronouns, contractions, and colloquial language while avoiding disciplinary jargon and complicated sentences.

2. When used in conjunction with more academic writing a personal perspective adds color, liveliness, and change of pace for the reader.

3. A personal perspective provides pertinent evidence about when the author conducted an interview, observed a situation, or recalled a relevant experience.

4. A personal perspective acknowledges the difficulty of absolute objectivity. What passes for fact today may be called into question tomorrow: for instance, only a few decades ago the extinction of dinosaurs was blamed on glaciers, whereas currently it's blamed on a meteor hitting the earth.

Following are four arguments against personal perspectives in academic writing:

1. If used without good reason: For example, if every other statement of fact is preceded by "I think that …" a personal perspective becomes tedious and irrelevant.

2. If used in place of hard evidence: For example, personal experience alone cannot attest to the validity of a political or religious idea.

3. Convention rejects it: For example, the following advice is still typical of some disciplinary style guides: "Although it is becoming increasingly common to see first person pronouns in academic texts, the use of the impersonal pronoun *one* is still generally preferred."

4. Including personal perspective may inhibit striving for objectivity. Although perfect objectivity is impossible, the sincere effort to achieve it is highly valued in meaningful, reasoned dialogue.

When in doubt, consult your instructor. For further information on the advantages of blending experiential and academic perspectives, see Candace Spigelman's *Personally Speaking: Experience as Evidence in Academic Discourse,* Southern Illinois University Press, 2004.

---

chapter **7**

Explaining Concepts

To explain something is to make it clear to someone else who wants to understand it. Explaining is fundamental to most acts of communication and to nearly every type of writing, from personal to argument to research writing. Explanatory writing is also a genre unto itself: a newspaper feature examining baseball card collecting, a magazine article explaining the extinction of dinosaurs, an Internet site clarifying the difference between socialism and communism, a textbook on the French Revolution, a recipe for chili, or a laboratory report.

7 a Writing to explain

Explanatory writing (also called *expository* or *informational* writing) answers questions such as these:

- What is it?

- What does it mean?

- How does it work?

- How is it related to other things?

- How is it put together?

▪   Why did it happen?

▪   What will its consequences be?

To write a successful explanation, find out first what your readers *want* to know, then what they *already know* and what they *don't know*. If you are able to make educated guesses about these audience conditions, your writing task becomes clear. When you begin to write, keep in mind these four general principles of explanatory writing: (1) state your purpose up front; (2) focus on the idea or object being explained, not on yourself; (3) present information in a systematic and logical manner; and (4) use everyday reader-friendly language.

7 b   Finding a topic

Topics with a limited and specific scope are easier to explain well than topics that are vague or very broad. General subjects such as mountains, automobiles, or music are so broad that it's hard to know where to begin. However, focusing on Mount Mansfield, your grandfather's 1970 Buick, or Beethoven gives you a specific place to begin. No matter how much you know starting out, consulting reference books or authorities always makes your explanations stronger. And remember to keep your audience in mind as you begin assembling information: Don't waste time researching and writing about things your audience already knows or about issues beyond the scope of your focused topic.

7 c   Developing a thesis

The thesis statement in an explanatory paper is simply the writer's declaration of what the paper is about. Stating a thesis early lets readers know what to expect and helps them predict where you're going. A thesis is the answer to the implied question your paper asks: What is it? What does it look like? How does it work? Why is it useful?

QUESTION: What's the cultural significance of fairy tales and cartoons?

THESIS: Fairy tales and cartoons are a subtle means of indoctrinating children with cultural values.

The advantage of stating a thesis in a single sentence is that it sums up the purpose of your paper quickly and lets readers know what to expect. Another way to state a single-sentence thesis is to convey an image, analogy, or metaphor that provides an ongoing reference point throughout the paper and gives unity and coherence to your explanation—a good image keeps both you and your readers focused.

QUESTION: How are the offices of the city government connected?

THESIS: City government offices are like an octopus, with eight fairly independent bureaus as arms and a central brain in the mayor's office.

Changing your thesis as you write is common and often makes good sense, since your ideas evolve while writing. Perhaps the more you learn about city government, the less like an octopus and the more like a centipede it seems. Consider your first thesis a **working thesis** to get you started and to guide further research and writing.

7   d   Using strategies to explain

Strategies that explain things include defining, describing, classifying and dividing, analyzing causes and effects, and comparing and contrasting. Which strategy is best depends on the question being asked as well as on the audience you are addressing. You could offer two very different explanations to the same question, depending on who asked it. For example, if asked by a neighbor, "Where is Westport Drive?" you would respond with local reference points ("One block north of Larson's Supermarket") while a stranger wouldn't know where Larson's was either. Here is a brief overview of possible strategies:

QUESTION	STRATEGY

■ What is it?   Define

   Example: A fairy tale is a story about imaginary characters that takes place in imaginary places.

■ What does it mean?   Define

   Example: "Three Little Pigs" is a children's story that celebrates a good work ethic.

■ What are its characteristics?   Describe

   Example: Animated cartoons are hand drawings made to move.

■ How is it related to other things?   Compare and contrast

   Example: Fairy tales and cartoons convey cultural values to children in the same way that novels and plays convey cultural values to adults.

■ How is it put together?   Classify and divide

   Example: An animated cartoon is composed of many individual images that are combined to tell a story.

■ Why did it happen?   Analyze cause and effect

   Example: The strong wind can blow down the straw house because straw is not a subtantial building material.

▪   What will its consequences be?   Analyze cause and effect

> Example: If you build a house of bricks, it will withstand strong winds and not fall down.

If your paper answers a narrow, simple question, you may need to use only one strategy. If, however, the question is more complex, you may need several strategies that can vary from paragraph to paragraph or even from sentence to sentence. For example, to explain why the government has raised income taxes, your primary strategy might be to analyze cause and effect, but you might also need to define terms such as *income tax,* to classify the various types of taxes, and to compare and contrast raising income taxes to other budgetary options. In fact, almost every explanatory effort makes use of multiple strategies: How, for example, do you describe a process without first defining it or dividing it into steps?

Defining

To define something is to identify it, to set it apart so that it can be distinguished from similar things. Writers need to define any terms central to reader understanding in order to make points clearly, forcefully, and with authority. Formal definitions are what you find in a dictionary. They usually combine a general term with specific characteristics.

> A computer is a programmable electronic device [*general term*] that can store, retrieve, and process data [*specific characteristics*].

Usually, defining something is a preliminary step accomplished before moving on to larger explanatory issues. When you need to define something complex or difficult or when your primary explanatory strategy is definition, an extended definition might be necessary, as was the case with Mark's paper explaining how computer memory works:

> Computer storage space is measured in units called
> "Kilobytes" (K). Each K equals 1,024 "bytes," or
> approximately 1,000 single typewriter characters.
> So 1 K equals about 180 English words, or a little less
> than half of a single-spaced typed page, or maybe three
> minutes of fast typing.
>   Personal computers are now measured in "gigabytes"
> (GB), each of which is a thousand "megabytes" (MB), each
> of which equal 1,048,567 bytes (or 1,000 K), which translates

into approximately 400 pages of single-spaced type. One gigabyte, then, equals approximately 400,000 pages of single-spaced type.

Describing

To describe a person, place, or thing means to create a verbal image so that readers can see, hear, taste, smell, or feel what you saw, heard, tasted, smelled, and felt. In other words, effective descriptions appeal to the five senses. Furthermore, good descriptions contain enough sensory detail for readers to understand the subject, but not so much as to distract or bore them.

However, to describe how processes work is more complicated than describing what something looks like: in addition to showing objects at rest, you need to show them in sequence and motion. It helps to divide processes into discrete steps and present the steps in a logical order—something far easier to do with making a peanut butter and jelly sandwich than manufacturing an automobile!

To help orient readers, you may number the steps, using transition words such as *first, second,* and *third*. In the following example, taken from an early draft of his paper, Keith describes the process of manufacturing compact discs. How many strategies does he use? Which are most effective?

> CDs start out as a refrigerator-sized box full of little plastic beads that you could sift your hands through. They are fed into a giant tapered corkscrew—a blown-up version of an old-fashioned meat grinder. As the beads pass down the corkscrew, they are slowly melted by the heated walls.
>
> At the bottom of their descent is a "master recording plate" onto which the molten plastic is pressed. The plastic now resembles a vinyl record, except that the disc is transparent. The master now imprints "pits," rather than grooves, around the disc, causing the surface to resemble a ball of Play-Doh after being thrown against a stucco wall— magnified five thousand times.

Comparing and Contrasting

Comparing one thing to another is to find similarities as well as differences between them. Comparing and contrasting at the same time helps people understand something two ways: first, by showing how it is related to similar things, and second, by showing how it differs. College assignments frequently ask you to compare and contrast two authors, books, or ideas.

People usually compare and contrast things when they want to make a choice or judgment about them: books, food, bicycles, presidential candidates, political philosophies. For this reason, the two things examined should be similar: You'll learn more to help you vote for president by comparing two presidential candidates than one presidential candidate and a senate candidate; you'll learn more about which orange to buy by comparing it with other oranges (navel, mandarin) than with apples, plums, or pears. Likewise, it's easiest to see similarities and differences when you compare and contrast the same elements of each thing. If you describe one political candidate's stand on gun control, describe the other's as well so voters will have a reasonable basis for choosing one over the other.

Comparison-and-contrast analysis can be organized in one of three ways: (1) a *point-to-point analysis* examines one feature at a time for both similarities and differences; (2) a *whole-to-whole analysis* first presents one object as a whole and then presents the other object as a whole; (3) a *similarity-and-difference analysis* first presents the similarities, then the differences between the two things, or vice versa.

Use a point-to-point or similarity-and-difference analysis for long explanations of complex things, such as manufacturing an automobile, in which you need to cover everything from materials and labor to assembly and inspection processes. But use a whole-to-whole analysis for simple objects that readers can more easily comprehend. In the following whole-to-whole example, a student explains the difference between Democrats and Republicans:

> Like most Americans, both Democrats and Republicans believe in the twin values of equality and freedom. However, Democrats place a greater emphasis on equality, believing equal opportunity for all people to be more important than the freedom of any single individual. Consequently, they stand for government intervention to guarantee equal treatment in matters of environmental protection, minimum wages, racial policies, and educational opportunities.
>
> In contrast, Republicans place greater emphasis on freedom, believing the specific rights of the individual to be more important than the vague collective rights of the masses. Consequently, they stand for less government control in matters of property ownership, wages and the right to work based strictly on merit and hard work, and local control of schools.

Note how the writer devotes equal space to each political party, uses neutral language to lend academic authority to his explanation, and emphasizes the differences by using parallel examples as well as parallel sentence structure. The careful use of several comparison-and-contrast strategies makes it difficult for readers to miss his point.

An *analogy* is an extended comparison showing how one unfamiliar thing is similar to a familiar thing. For example, to learn how a heart functions, compare it to a mechanical water pump; to explain a family history, construct a family *tree*. Be sure to use objects and images in analogies that will be familiar to your readers. (See the box on page 75 in Chapter 8 for a discussion of *false analogies*.)

Classifying and Dividing

People generally understand short more easily than long, simple more easily than complex. One way to help readers understand a complicated topic is to classify and divide it into simpler pieces and to put the pieces in context.

- To *classify* something, put it in a category or class with other things like it:

    Like whales and dolphins, sea lions are aquatic mammals.

- To *divide* something, break it into smaller parts or subcategories:

    An insect's body is composed of three parts: a head, a thorax, and an abdomen.

Most readers have a difficult time remembering more than six or seven items at a time, so organize a long list into fewer logical groups, as in the preceding example. Also be sure that the categories are meaningful to your readers, not simply convenient for you as a writer.

Analyzing Causes and Effects

Nothing happens without a reason. The sun shines, the air warms up; the wind blows, the waves rise; and so on. In other words, you already know about cause and effect because that's how the world seems to work. A cause is something that makes something else happen; an **effect** is the thing that happens.

Cause-and-effect analyses are most often assigned for college papers to answer *why* questions: Why are the fish dying in the river? The most direct answer is a *because* statement:

Fish are dying <u>because</u> oxygen levels in the lake are too low.

The answer, in other words, is a thesis, which the rest of the paper must defend and support.

There are three reasons for low oxygen level . . .

Cause-and-effect analyses also try to describe possible future effects.

If nitrogen fertilizers were restricted from farmland that drains into the lake, oxygen levels would rise, and fish populations would be restored.

Unless there is sound, widely accepted evidence to support the thesis, however, this sort of analysis may lead to more argumentative writing. In this example, for instance, farmers or fertilizer manufacturers might complicate the matter by pointing to other sources of lake pollution—*outboard motors, paper mill effluents, urban sewage runoff*—making comprehensive solutions harder to reach. Keep in mind that most complex situations have multiple causes. If you try to reduce a complex situation to an overly simple cause, you are making the logical mistake known as *oversimplification* (see page 75 in Chapter 8).

7 e Organizing with logic

Explain to readers where you're taking them, and they will follow more willingly. Lead carefully, step by step, using a good road map, and they will know where they are at all times and trust you. Organize your essay in a simple, straightforward, and logical manner. For example, to explain how a stereo music system works, you could (1) portray a CD inserted into a player and end with the music coming out of the speakers; (2) describe the system technically, starting with the power source to explain how sound is made in the speakers; or (3) explain it historically, starting with the earliest components developed and ending with the most recent inventions. All these options follow a clear logic that, once explained, will make sense to readers.

7 f Maintaining a neutral perspective

All writers bring with them assumptions and biases that cause them to view the world—including your explanatory project—in a particular way, so technically there is no such thing as a completely neutral perspective. Nevertheless, explanations will be clearer and more accessible to others when you present them fairly with as little bias as possible. In general, it's more effective to emphasize the thing explained than your personal beliefs and feelings about it. To do that, write from the third-person point of view, using the pronouns *he, she,* and *it,* and keep yourself in the background unless you have a good reason not to. In some instances, adopting the second-person *you*—as we do in this textbook—adds a friendly, familiar tone. If you believe personal experience will help clarify your topic, include both negative and positive examples. Remember that your goal is not to win an argument, but to convey information.

| 7 | g | **Shaping the whole paper (student essay)** |

In the following paper, Katie Moll discovered an unexpected and disturbing controversy surrounding the television cartoon show, *The Smurfs*. The essay records her step-by-step attempt to explain and understand the truth about her favorite childhood program. Here is an instance where information found on the Internet first created a problem to solve, then provided the solution. Katie's essay concludes with a personal postscript that poses interesting questions for all who rely on Web-based research. Note that this essay contains a judicious mix of primary and secondary sources: primary sources are the Smurf cartoons themselves; secondary sources are the commentators who write the Web pages about those cartoons.

The Smurfs as Political Propaganda

Katie Moll

Saturday morning cartoons were a large part of my childhood. They brought enjoyment and laughter, and they sometimes taught moral lessons. I grew up surrounded by shows like *Fraggle Rock, Rainbow Brite, The Jetsons,* and *Reading Rainbow.* My personal favorite, however, was *The Smurfs,* a cartoon focused on a village of small blue elflike creatures that lived in mushrooms and were always content with their lives. Much to my despair, they were taken off the air after the 1980s. It wasn't until about a year ago that *The Smurfs* were brought to my attention again, when I chose to attend a theme party dressed as one of the Smurf characters, such as Brainy, Handy, or Smurfette. However, after checking every party store around, I could find no costumes. When I checked the Internet for Smurf costumes, I found more than I bargained for, as Web sites popped up with titles such as "Sociopolitical Themes in *The Smurfs*" and "Papa Smurf Is a Communist." How could they make such claims about my favorite cartoon? And then I wondered, could this be true? Was *The Smurfs* television show really political propaganda?

To check this story further, I searched the Web with the keyword "Smurfs," which took me to "*The Smurfs* Official Site" at <www.smurf.com/homepage .html>. It had nothing about the communist theory, but then again, why would it? This was the home page promoting the cartoon, so I doubted it would slander the program. However, I did obtain useful background information on the origin of *The Smurfs*. The creator of the Smurf characters was Peyo, the pen name of Pierre Culliford, who lived and worked in Brussels, Belgium. *The Smurfs* first appeared as a comic strip in 1958. It was not until 1981 that the *The Smurfs* became an animated television series designed by the team of William Hanna and Joseph Barbera. Nothing on the Smurf home page suggested that either Peyo or Hanna-Barbera had subversive intentions, so I began to think the theory was a complete hoax. But I wanted to find out more.

Then, amidst a jumble of commercial topics, I found a Web site called "*The Smurfs* as a Paradigm for Communist Society" that suggested, "*The Smurfs* were actually a well-devised piece of communist propaganda to erode American society from within" (Gozer, para 2). Five points of comparison between *The Smurfs* cartoon show and a Russian communist society make the author's case: (1) Papa Smurf, the wise leader of the Smurf community, looks like Karl Marx and (2) wears red pants; (3) all Smurfs work according to their ability and receive according to their needs; (4) the villain, Gargamel, acts like a greedy capitalist; and (5) his cat, Azreal, represents "third-world despotisms that are clinging onto the coattails of first-world capitalism." He concludes, saying, "These five points provide very strong evidence pointing to the conclusion that the TV show *The Smurfs* is indeed a paradigm for communist society" (para 8).

"Strong evidence"? It is hard to take this 500-word Web site very seriously. It is short; the supporting detail in each paragraph is sketchy; some of the arguments (Papa Smurf as Karl Marx!) are far-fetched; and the author is not

accountable, providing no name and no credentials, though an e-mail address

<n9620080@cc.wwu.edu> is included. However, a second Web site, "Sociopolitical

Themes in *The Smurfs*" by J. Marc

Schmidt, outlines in much more

detail the basis for a Marxist

interpretation: "Unlike many other

cartoons, or indeed other television

programmes, *The Smurfs* is about

an entire society and its interactions

with itself and with outsiders, rather

than the adventures of a few

characters. Hence, I believe it is, in

Papa Smurf Wears Red Pants

short, a political fable, in much the same way that *The Lion, the Witch and the

Wardrobe* was a fable about Christianity. Rather than Christianity, however, *The

Smurfs* is about Marxism. (para 2)"

Note that Schmidt does not label *The Smurfs* "propaganda," but describes

the cartoon series in the same terms as other respected "political fables," such

as those by C. S. Lewis, something to be studied or learned from rather than be

brainwashed by. In Schmidt's words, "I am not accusing *The Smurfs* of being

some kind of subversive kiddie propaganda" (para 3).

Schmidt believes Peyo to be a socialist rather than a card-carrying

communist, calling the Smurf village "a Marxist utopia" rather than a police state

like the old Soviet Union (para 5). The evidence Schmidt assembles is thoughtful

and far more convincing than Gozer's hasty claims. For example, he points out

that Smurf village is "a perfect model of a socialist commune or collective" (para 5), that "the Smurfs are all completely equal" (para 6), that "everyone is equally a worker and an owner" (para 7), and that "they wear the same kind and colour of clothes" (para 9).

I found the Schmidt Web site to be quite convincing. For one thing, all that he says about the Smurfs and Smurf village matches what I remember about the show. Once he points out those similarities, I can see his point. For another thing, the Schmidt article on the Web site is carefully written, with clear explanations and concrete examples. In addition, Schmidt includes his whole name along with an e-mail address <j_marc_s@hotmail.com>—an indication that he is willing to be responsible for his ideas. Because of the way Schmidt spells certain words (*programme* and *colour*), a first reading of his site suggests that his English is British rather than American, in which case he may have more objective distance from the cartoon show than an American author would.

However, when I looked at a third Web site that addressed this propaganda issue, "Papa Smurf Is a Communist," I became confused again. At first glance, this site seemed to have been written from an angry capitalist perspective, upset that communist connections are hidden in the children's cartoon. Even the feel of this Web page was different, with a menacing black background and dark red letters as opposed to the more neutral tones on the other Web sites. At first, I was annoyed by its aggressive tone, but when I read it a second time, I found myself laughing. This Web site is not serious at all! Instead, it is making obvious fun of the communist propaganda theory as the following excerpt illustrates:

> Yes, that is correct, Papa Smurf and all of his little Smurf minions are not the happy little characters Hanna-Barbera would have us believe! The cartoon was really created by the Russian government in order to indoctrinate the youngest members of Western society with communist

beliefs and ideals, thus destroying their resistance to the imminent Russian invasion that was to occur when this generation (my generation) grew up.

When I read "imminent Russian invasion," I said, "Wait a minute." While it is true that during the Cold War many Americans feared a nuclear war with Russia, I didn't think anyone actually feared an invasion. And when he claimed that the word *Smurf* was an acronym standing for "Small Men Under Red Father," I found myself laughing again. And in yet another passage, this anonymous author argues that Papa Smurf resembles Stalin more than Marx:

> I feel that Stalin is most likely the man that Papa Smurf was modeled after. Marx believed more in the system of socialism, not communism. What is the difference, you may ask? Well, under both systems everything is supposedly shared equally among all members of the society; however, under the socialist system there are free elections for the leadership of the society, whereas under the communist system there are no elections. I sure as hell don't remember Papa Smurf being elected leader. . . . [but] Stalin's appearance also highly resembles that of Papa Smurf. His beard may not be as perfect as that of Marx, but look at that round face! (para 7)

The author does not reveal his or her identity but does provide an e-mail address <commiesmurfs@hotmail.com> to which readers can respond, along with twenty reader responses printed at the end of the site such as these two:

– "Your page was one of the funniest things I have read in a long time! Great job on it—I especially like the shot [an image on the Web page] of Papa Smurf with the hammer and sickle in his hat!"

– "The site made me open my eyes and realize that communism exists not only in society but in most of our pop culture as well. Being concerned, I am now proposing 'CASCO' (Canadians Against Smurf Communism) to rid the evils of *The Smurfs* on Sunday mornings; they are shown on a regular basis in Canada. Spread the news."

To make sense of three different Web sites, each pointing to similarities between *The Smurfs* and Marxism, I looked more carefully at the sequence in which the sites were created. Who, in other words, started this comparison? Fortunately, each site was dated. The brief Gozer site was created in September 1997. The anonymous and obvious parody "Papa Smurf" was created in March of the same year—six months *earlier* than Gozer—so the parody was first. The only serious site, Schimidt's, was not created until sometime in 1998 (exact month not available). In other words, the most obvious parody of the cartoon show, the anonymous "Papa Smurf," seemed to start a small chain reaction, with the Gozer site second and Schmidt's last.

Curious to see whether there were any connections among the three Web sites, I sent e-mail queries to each site. I never heard from the anonymous creator of the earliest site, "Papa Smurf," but I received responses from the other two authors. J. Marc Schmidt responded promptly, identifying himself as a high school teacher living in Sydney, Australia (hence the British spellings), and

explaining that he created his site after attending a museum exhibit on cartoon animation in which he found hard-to-believe interpretations of many animated shows. Schmidt writes, "I started thinking more and more about socialism, and eventually the idea just clicked. Anyway, for good or bad, that incomprehensible blurb was the seed, which led me to write an essay called 'Sociopolitical Themes in *The Smurfs*.' I turned it into a Web site and put it on the Internet."

The author of the Gozer site also responded, providing his real name, Eric Lott, but asking me not to give out his personal e-mail address. Lott writes: "In honest truth, it was/is not intended as a parody. Personally, I am an anarcho-socialist. I began thinking this up . . . and developed it into a monologue. Most people I gave [it] to found it quite amusing."

After reading the comic, the amusing, and the serious interpretations of the socialist Smurfs, I realized I had to take another look at the cartoon myself. I obtained a copy of one Smurf episode by borrowing it from a friend's younger sister (who else would collect such videotapes?) and tried to watch it with an open mind, as if I were young again.

This untitled episode portrayed Smurfette in danger of being captured by the cat, Azreal, but rescued just in time by Papa and the other Smurfs. After having read all the political ideas about *The Smurfs*, however, I found it difficult to watch an episode with an open mind. As soon as it was over, I began seeing possible socialist connections myself. For example, when Papa Smurf rounds up the rescue team, is he a communist dictator taking charge? When the villain, Gargamel, orders his cat to catch Smurfette, is he a capitalist dictator delegating his dirty jobs to the workers? Is the chase scene a reminder of the constant war between the free world and communism? Does the color red symbolize communism?

It was then I also realized that I could take virtually any children's story and make it mean something else. Do Santa Claus and Little Red Riding Hood wear red because they are communists? Do Santa's elves make toys because they are slaves? Is the Big Bad Wolf a greedy capitalist? While these interpretations are possible, I don't believe they were ever intended by the creators of these stories.

Postscript

Browsing the Internet after writing this paper, I found an interpretation of the popular children's television show *Teletubbies,* suggesting that one of the *Teletubbies* characters is a homosexual role model. According to "Parents Alert:

Tinky Winky Comes Out of the Closet," an article published in the February 1999 edition of the *National Liberty Journal*— a newsletter edited and published by the Rev. Jerry Falwell—"Tinky Winky has the voice of a boy yet carries a purse . . . is purple—the gay-pride color; and his antenna is shaped like a triangle—the gay-pride symbol" (qtd. in Reed). At this point, however, I stopped reading. Who really cares whether it's possible that Tinky Winky is gay—or a Marxist, for that matter? Not me.

Thinking about my Smurf investigation now, I think the real topic was neither the Smurfs nor the Marxists, but what I found out about the Internet itself. First, for anybody with access to a computer, the Internet is the greatest medium ever devised for the unlimited practice of free speech. Second, the Internet is also the greatest repository of both fact and fiction ever devised—but there's nobody to tell you for sure which is which, sometimes not even the author! This idea clearly needs further investigation and elaboration, but to tell the truth, I don't have the time. I'll leave that topic, along with the *Teletubbies,* for my next paper.

* * *

Works Cited

Gozer. *The Smurfs* as a Paradigm for Communist Society. 27 Sep. 1997. 7 Oct.
    2001 <http://www.ac.wwu.edu/~n9620080/smurf.html>.

Lott, Eric. Personal e-mail. 4 Dec. 2001.

Papa Smurf Is a Communist. 16 Mar. 1997. 8 Oct. 2001 <http://geocities.com/
    CapitolHill/Lobby/1709>.

Reed, David. "Falwell's Newspaper Attempts to Label *Teletubbies* Character as
    Gay." 10 Feb. 1999. 9 Nov. 2001 <http://www.sfgate.com/cgibin/
    article.cgi?file=/news/archive/1999/02/10/national0333EST0476.DTL>.

Schmidt, J. Marc. Sociopolitical Themes in *The Smurfs*. 7 Oct. 1998. 8 Oct. 2001
    <http://www.geocities.com/Hollywood/Cinema/3117/sociosmurf2.htm>.

---. Personal e-mail. 3 Dec. 2001.

The Smurfs Official Site. 2005. 7 Oct. 2001 <http://www.smurf.com/
    homepage.html>.

Teletubbies. PBS kids. 2005. 8 Nov. 2001 <http://pbskids.org/teletubbies.html>.

chapter 8

Arguing Positions

Argument is deeply rooted in the American political and social system; free and open debate is the essence of the democratic process. Argument is also at the heart of the academic process. Scholars investigate scientific, social, and cultural issues, hoping through the give-and-take of debate to find reasonable answers to complex questions.

Argument in the academic world is less about winning or losing than about changing minds or altering perceptions. Argument as rational disagreement—not quarrels, fights, or contests—most often occurs on issues of genuine uncertainty about what is right, best, or most reasonable. A position paper sets forth an arguable position on an issue about which there is some debate; if there's no debate, there's no argument. College assignments commonly ask you to argue one side of an issue and defend your argument against attacks from skeptics. This chapter explains the elements that constitute a basic position paper: an arguable issue, a claim and counterclaim, a thesis, and evidence.

8 a Selecting an issue

An issue is a controversy, something that can be argued about. For instance, mountain bikes and cultural diversity are things or concepts, not issues. However, they become the foundation for issues when questions are raised about them and controversy ensues.

ISSUE   Do American colleges adequately represent the cultural diversity of the United States?

ISSUE   Should mountain bikes be allowed on wilderness hiking trails?

These questions are issues because reasonable people could answer them in different ways; they can be argued about because more than one answer is plausible, possible, or realistic.

Take a Position

Virtually all issues can be formulated, at least initially, as yes/no questions about which you will take one position or the other: pro (if the answer is yes) or con (if the answer is no).

ISSUE	Should American college faculty represent the cultural diversity of the United States?
PRO	Yes; minority students learn better from instructors who understand their cultures.
CON	No; for learning to occur, the quality of teaching is all that matters.

A good issue around which to write a position paper will meet the following criteria.

- There is real controversy and uncertainty.

- There are at least two distinct and arguable positions.

- Resources are available to support both sides.

Consider both national and local issues. The advantages of national issues are that you are likely to see them explained and argued in national news media and that you can expect your audience to have some familiarity with them. The advantage of local issues is that you can often visit a place where the controversy occurs, interview people who are affected by it, and find generous coverage in local news media. The disadvantage is that not all of your audience may be familiar with the issue.

8 b Analyzing an issue

To analyze an issue, you need to conduct enough research to explain it and identify the arguments of each side. Treat each side fairly, framing the opposition as positively as you frame your position, and have an honest debate with yourself. Doing so may even cause you to switch sides—one of the best indications of open-minded research. Furthermore, empathy for the opposition leads to making qualified assertions and heads off overly simplistic right-versus-wrong arguments.

Establish Context

Provide full context for the issue you are writing about, as if readers know virtually nothing about it. Providing context means answering these questions: What is this issue about? Where did the controversy begin? How long has it been debated? Who are the people involved? What is at stake? It helps to use a neutral tone, as suggested in the following example about mountain bikes on wilderness trails.

With all these new riders, there is a need for places to ride, and this is where the wilderness trail controversy begins. The mountain bike is designed to be ridden on dirt trails, logging roads, and fire trails in backwoods country. However, other trail users, who have been around much longer than mountain bikers, prefer to enjoy the woods at a slow, leisurely pace. They find the rapid and sometimes noisy two-wheeled intruders unacceptable.

State Claims and Counterclaims

Claims are statements or assertions that something is true or should be done. In arguing one side of an issue, you make one or more claims in the hope of convincing an audience to believe you. Counterclaims are statements that oppose or refute claims. You need to examine an opponent's counterclaim carefully in order to refute it or, if you agree with the counterclaim, to argue that your claim is more important to making a decision.

Annotate References

Use note cards or computer files to make an alphabetical list of the references you consulted during research, briefly identifying each according to the kind of information it contains, so that each note card identifies source, relevance, and position. Some articles will be strictly informational, while others may provide both *pro* and *con* sides of the argument (see following).

Buchanan, Rob. "Birth of the Gearhead Nation." <u>Rolling Stone</u> 9 July 1992: 80–85. Marin Co., California, movement advocates more trails open for mountain bike use. Includes history. *Pro.*

Newton, Carlton. Personal interview. 13 Nov. 1995. *Con.*

Schwartz, David M. "Over Hill, Over Dale on a Bicycle Built for . . . Goo." <u>Smithsonian</u> 25.3 (June 1992): 74–84. Discusses the hiker versus biker issue and promotes peaceful coexistence. Includes history. *Pro/con.*

Take a Position

Once you have considered the two positions fairly, weigh which side is the stronger. Select the position that you find more convincing, and then write out the reasons that support this position. Order the support statements, most compelling reasons last. This will be the position to start with, not necessarily to stick with. Even though it's tentative, a working thesis focuses your initial efforts in one direction and helps you articulate claims and assemble evidence to support it. (For more information about a working thesis, see 11d, Formulating a working thesis.)

WORKING
THESIS

Hikers and mountain bikers should cooperate and support each other in using, preserving, and maintaining wilderness trails.

Your working thesis should be manageable and specific and propose a plan of action.

8 c Developing an argument

Your argument is the case you will make for your position; it is the means by which you will try to persuade your readers that your position is correct. Good arguments need solid, credible evidence and clear, logical reasoning.

Assemble Evidence

Evidence can come from a variety of sources: facts, examples, inferences, expert opinion, and personal experience all provide believable evidence.

Facts are verifiable and agreed upon by everyone involved, regardless of personal beliefs or values: *Water boils at 212 degrees Fahrenheit.* Facts are often numerical or statistical and are recorded where anybody can look them up—in a dictionary, almanac, public report, or college catalog, for example. Not all facts are of the type found in an almanac: *In Kenya, anthropologist Mary Leakey found a skull that she later concluded belonged to a 25-million-year-old common ancestor of apes and humans.* The find is a fact. If you think your audience might doubt it, you can document where you learned about it. That Leakey reached that particular conclusion is also a fact, but the conclusion itself is her expert opinion or interpretation of the fact.

Examples can be used to illustrate a claim or clarify an issue. To demonstrate that many wilderness trails have been closed to mountain biking, you might mention this example: *The New Jersey trails at South Mountain, Eagle Rock, and Mills Park have all been closed to mountain bikes.*

Inferences are generalizations based on the accumulation of a certain number of facts and examples. For example, if you check ten national wilderness trails in ten states and find they are all closed to mountain biking, you might infer that a national policy bans mountain bikes in wilderness areas; however, such an inference is not a fact, since you have not checked the other forty states or contacted the government agency that sets such policies.

Expert opinion makes powerful evidence. The testimony of a forest ranger about trail damage caused by mountain bikes or lug-soled hiking boots is more convincing than the same observation made by a casual hiker because training and experience make the ranger an expert.

Personal experience is testimony based on the writer's firsthand knowledge—he or she was there and witnessed something. When you have experienced something yourself, such as hiking or biking on wilderness trails, your knowledge cannot easily be discounted.

Demonstrate Reasoning

To build an effective argument, consider the audience you must persuade. The more you know about the audience you're trying to sway, the easier it will be to present your case. In writing about the mountain bike controversy, for example, ask yourself (1) Who will read this paper? (2) Where do I think the readers stand on the issue? and (3) What evidence would they consider convincing?

Remember that an inference based on a single piece of evidence may often be wrong. Find out more before you make simple assumptions. And sometimes audience analysis doesn't work very well when an instructor assumes a deliberately skeptical role in reading a set of papers. It's best to assume you will have a critical reader and to use the best logic and evidence available.

8   d   Organizing the paper

To organize your paper, you need to know what the main point of your argument is. It's time to consider the working thesis that's been guiding your research: confirm it, or modify it, or scrap it altogether and assert a different one. Try to articulate this thesis in a single sentence as the answer to the yes/no question.

THESIS   Wilderness trails should be open to both mountain bikers and hikers.

THESIS   Wilderness trails should be closed to mountain bikers.

Your next decision is where in this paper you should reveal your thesis to the reader. Will you state it openly up front or strategically delay it until later? Neither strategy is right or wrong, but each has a different effect on your reader.

Thesis-first Organization

When you lead with a thesis, you tell readers from the beginning of your paper where you stand on the issue. The remainder of the essay supports your claim and defends it against counterclaims. Following is one good set of steps to organize a thesis-first argument.

1. **Introduce and explain the issue.** Make sure there are at least two debatable sides. Pose the question that you see arising from this issue; if you can frame it as a yes/no, for/against construction, both you and your reader will have the advantage, throughout your answer, of knowing where you stand.

2. **Assert your thesis early.** Your thesis states the answer to the question you have posed and establishes the position from which you will argue. Think of your thesis as the major claim the paper will make.

3. **Explain the opposition's counterclaims** before elaborating on your own claims; doing so gives you something to refute. Squeezing the counterclaims between the thesis (2) and the evidence (5) reserves the strongest places—the opening and closing—for your position.

4. **Refute the counterclaims.** Point out weak spots in the opposition's argument. Use your opponent's language to show you have read closely but still find problems with the claim.

5. **Support your claims with evidence.** Spell out your own claims clearly and precisely, enumerating them or being sure to give each its own full-paragraph explanation, and citing supporting evidence. This section will constitute the longest and most carefully documented part of your essay.

6. **Restate your position in your conclusion.** Synthesize your accumulated evidence into a broad general position, and restate your original thesis in slightly different language.

Delayed-Thesis Organization

Using the delayed-thesis type of organization, you introduce the issue and discuss the arguments for and against your position but do not obviously take a side until late in the essay. Near the end of the paper, you explain that after carefully investigating both pros and cons, you have now arrived at the most reasonable position. Delaying your conclusion usually results in a paper that is more interesting for readers because you raise their curiosity about the issue but delay giving them an answer. As you reason back and forth about the issue, they must follow along, as in a mystery novel, and wait with some anticipation to find out your answer. Following is a good set of steps for writing a delayed-thesis paper.

1. **Introduce the issue and pose a question.** Both thesis-first and delayed-thesis papers begin by establishing context and posing a question.

2. **Summarize the claims for one position.** Before stating which side you support, explain how the opposition views the issue.

3. **Refute these claims.** Still not stating your own position, point out your difficulties with believing this side. (You can actually strengthen your position by admitting that some of these claims might have merit.)

4. **Summarize the counterclaims.** You are supporting these claims, so they should occupy the most emphatic position in your essay, coming last.

5. **Support your counterclaims.** Now give your best evidence; this should be the longest and most carefully documented part of the paper.

6. **State your thesis in your conclusion.** Your rhetorical stance or strategy is this: you have listened carefully to both the claims and counterclaims, and after giving each side a fair hearing, you have arrived at the most reasonable conclusion.

8   e   Shaping the whole paper (student essay)

In the following paper, Issa Sawabini, a first-year student, explores whether mountain bikers should be allowed to share wilderness trails with hikers. In the first part of the paper, he establishes the context and background of the conflict; then he introduces the question his paper will address: *Is any resolution in sight?* Note his substantial use of sources, including the Internet and interviews, cited in the MLA documentation style. (See Chapter 19 for a discussion of documentation in MLA style.) Issa selects a delayed-thesis strategy, which allows him to air both sides of the argument fully before revealing his solution, a compromise position: As long as mountain bikers follow environmentally sound guidelines, they should be allowed to use the trails. Also note the judicious use of visual images to illustrate both pro and con sides of the argument.

On the Trail: Can the Hikers Share with the Bikers?

Issa Sawabini

The narrow, hard-packed dirt trail winding up the mountain under the

spreading oaks and maples doesn't look like the source of a major environmental

conflict, but it is. On the one side are hikers, environmentalists, and horseback

riders who have traditionally

used these wilderness trails.

On the other side, looking back,

are the mountain bike riders

who want to use them too.

But the hikers don't want the

bikers, so trouble is brewing.

The debate over mountain bike use has gained momentum recently because of the increased popularity of this form of bicycling. Technology has made it easier for everyone to ride these go-anywhere bikes. These high-tech wonders incorporate exotic components including quick gear-shifting derailleurs, good brakes, and a more comfortable upright seating position—and they can cost up to $2000 each (Kelly 104). Mountain bikes have turned what were once grueling hill climbs into casual trips, and more people are taking notice.

Mountain bikes have taken over the bicycle industry, and with more bikes come more people wanting to ride in the mountains. The first mass-produced mountain bikes date to 1981, when five hundred Japanese "Stumpjumpers" were sold; by 1983 annual sales reached 200,000; today the figure is in the millions. In fact, mountain biking is second only to in-line skating as the fastest growing sport in the nation: "For a sport to go from zero to warp speed so quickly is unprecedented," says Brian Stickel, director of competition for the National Off Road Bicycle Association (Schwartz 75).

With all these new riders, there is a need for places to ride, and this is where the wilderness trail controversy begins. The mountain bike is designed to be ridden on dirt trails, logging roads, and fire trails in backwoods country. However, other trail users, who have been around much longer than mountain bikers, prefer to enjoy the woods at a slow, leisurely pace.

They find the rapid and sometimes noisy two-wheeled intruders unacceptable: "To traditional trail users, the new breed of bicycle [is] alien and dangerous, esthetically offensive and physically menacing" (Schwartz 74).

"The problem arises when people want to use an area of public land for their own personal purpose," says Carl Newton, forestry professor at the University of Vermont. "Eventually, after everyone has taken their small bit of the area, the results can be devastating. People believe that because they pay taxes for the land, they can use it as they please. This makes sense to the individual, but not to the whole community." Newton is both a hiker and a mountain biker.

When mountain bikes first came on the scene, hikers and environmentalists convinced state and local officials to ban the bikes from wilderness trails (Buchanan 81; Kelly 104). The result was the closing of many trails to mountain bike use: "Many state park systems have banned bicycles from narrow trails. National Parks prohibit them, in most cases, from leaving the pavement" (Schwartz 81). These trail closings have separated the outdoor community into the hikers and the bikers. Each group is well organized, and each group believes it is right. Is any resolution in sight?

The hikers and other passive trail users have a number of organizations, from conservation groups to public park planning committees, who argue against allowing mountain bikes into narrow trails traditionally traveled only by foot and horse in the past. They believe that the wide, deeply treaded tires of the mountain bikes cause erosion and that the high speeds of the bikers startle and upset both hikers and horses (Hanley; Schwartz 76).

The arrival of mountain bikes during the 1980s was resisted by established hiker groups, such as the Sierra Club, which won debate after debate in favor of closing wilderness trails to mountain bike activities. The younger and less well organized biking groups proposed a compromise, offering to help repair and maintain trails in return for riding rights, but their offers were ignored. "Peace was not given a chance. Foes of the bicycle onslaught, older and better connected, won most of the battles, and signs picturing a bicycle crossed with a red slash began to appear on trail heads all over the country" (Schwartz 74).

In Millburn, New Jersey, trails at South Mountain, Eagle Rock, and Mills Park have all been closed. Anyone caught riding a bike on the trails can be arrested and fined up to $100. Local riders offered an amendment calling for trails to be open Thursday through Sunday, with the riders helping maintain the trails on the other days. The amendment was rejected. According to hiker Donald Meserlain, the bikes "ruin the tranquillity of the woodlands and drive out hikers, bird watchers, and strollers. It's like weeds taking over the grass. Pretty soon we'll have all weeds" (Hanley).

Many areas in western New York, such as Hunter's Creek, have also been closed to mountain bike use. Anti-biking signs posted on trails frequently used by bicyclists caused a loud public debate as bike riding was again blamed for trail erosion. Until more public lands are opened to trail riding, mountain bikers must pay fees to ride on private land, a situation beneficial to ski resorts in the off season: "Ski areas are happy to open trails to cyclists for a little summer and fall income" (Sneyd). For example, in Vermont, bike trails can be found at the Catamount Family Center in Williston, as well as at Mount Snow, Killington, Stratton, and Bolton Valley. At major resorts, such as Mount Snow and Killington, ski lifts have actually been modified to go to the top of the mountains, and each offers a full-service bike shop at its base.

However, the real solution to the conflict between hikers and bikers is education, not separation. In response to the bad publicity and many trail closings, mountain bikers have banded together at local and national levels to educate both their own member bike riders and the nonriding public about the potential alliance between these two groups (Buchanan 81).

The largest group, the International Mountain Bike Association (IMBA), sponsors supervised rides and trail conservation classes and stresses that mountain bikers are friends, not enemies, of the natural environment. "The IMBA wants to change the attitude of both the young gonzo rider bombing downhill on knobby tires and the mature outdoorsman bristling at the thought of tire tracks where boot soles alone did tread" (Schwartz 76). IMBA published guidelines it hopes all mountain bikers will learn to follow:

Ride on open trails only.

Leave no trace.

Control your bicycle.

Always yield the trail.

Never spook animals.

The New England Mountain Bike Association (NEMBA), one of the largest East Coast organizations, publishes a home page on the Internet outlining goals: "NEMBA is a not-for-profit organization dedicated to promoting land access, maintaining trails that are open to mountain bicyclists, and educating riders to use those trails sensitively and responsibly. We are also devoted to having fun" (Koellner).

At the local level, the Western New York Mountain Bike Association (WNYMBA) educates members on proper trail maintenance and urges its members to cooperate with local environmentalists whenever possible. For instance, when angry cyclists continued to use the closed trail at Hunter's Creek, WNYMBA used the Internet to warn cyclists against continued trail use: "As WNYMBA wishes

to cooperate with Erie County Parks Department to the greatest extent possible on the use of trails in open parks, WNYMBA cannot recommend ignoring posted signs. The first IMBA rule of trail is 'ride on open trails only' " (JTYL).

Educated mountain biking, like hiking and horseback riding, respects the environment and promotes peace and conservation, not noise and destruction. Making this case has begun to pay off, and the battle over who walks and who rides the trails should now shift in favor of peaceful coexistence. "Buoyed by studies showing that bicycle tires cause no more erosion or trail damage than the boots of hikers, and far less than horses' hooves, mountain bike advocates are starting to find receptive ears among environmental organizations" (Schwartz 78).

Even in the Millburn, New Jersey, area, bikers have begun to win some battles, as new trails have recently been funded specifically for mountain bike use: "After all," according to an unnamed legislator, "the bikers or their parents are taxpayers" (Hanley).

The Wilderness Club now officially supports limited use of mountain bikes, while the Sierra Club also supports careful use of trails by riders as long as no damage to the land results and riders ride responsibly on the path. "In pursuit of happy trails, bicycling organizations around the country are bending backward

over their chain stays to dispel the hell-on-wheels view of them" (Schwartz 83).

Education and compromise are the sensible solutions to the hiker/biker

standoff. Increased public awareness as well as increasingly responsible riding

will open still more wilderness trails to bikers in the future. It's clear that

mountain bikers don't want to destroy trails any more than hikers do. The surest

way to preserve America's wilderness areas is to establish strong cooperative

bonds among the hikers and bikers, as well as those who fish, hunt, camp, canoe,

and bird-watch, and to encourage all to maintain the trails and respect the

environment.

Works Cited

Buchanan, Rob. "Birth of the Gearhead Nation." *Rolling Stone* 9 July 1992: 80-85.

Hanley, Robert. "Essex County Mountain Bike Troubles." *New York Times* 30 May

1995: B4.

JTYL, ed. *Western New York Mountain Bike Association Home Page.* Western

New York Mountain Bike Association. 4 Oct. 1995

<http://128.205.166.43/public/wnymba/wnymba.html>.

Kelly, Charles. "Evolution of an Issue." *Bicycling* 31 (May 1990): 104-105.

Koellner, Ken, ed. *New England Mountain Bike Association Home Page.* 19 Aug.

1995. New England Mountain Bike Association. 30 Sep. 1995

<http://www.ultranet.com/~kvk/nemba.html>.

Newton, Carlton. Personal interview. 13 Nov. 1995.

Schwartz, David M. "Over Hill, Over Dale on a Bicycle Built for . . . Goo."

Smithsonian 25.3 (June 1992): 74-84.

Sneyd, Ross. "Mount Snow Teaching Mountain Biking." *Burlington Free Press*

4 Oct. 1992: E1.

WRITING ACROSS THE CURRICULUM

False Arguments

The following false arguments are often made when a writer does not have enough evidence to support his or her claims. Learn to recognize and avoid them.

- **Bandwagon.** Encourages people to accept a position simply because others already have: *More than three-fourths of Americans have already begun to recycle paper and plastics—shouldn't you recycle too?* (Those other people could have made bad decisions.)

- **Begging the question.** Treats a questionable statement as if it had already been accepted: *If the United States is to maintain its position as the foremost military power on the planet, defense spending must be increased.* (Many people question whether the United States should try to maintain its military supremacy.)

- **Does not follow (non sequitur).** Presents a conclusion that does not logically follow from its premises: *Catharine MacKinnon has been an ardent supporter of women's rights, so she would be a good senator.* (The fact that MacKinnon supports women's rights does not mean that she has, or does not have, the skills to be a good senator.)

- **False cause (post hoc).** Assumes that if one event happened after another, the earlier event must have caused the later one: *Federal spending on schools should be decreased because the last time the government decreased education spending, SAT scores went up.* (There is no clear connection between spending on education and SAT scores.)

- **False analogy.** Uses analogy to show that two things are alike for the purpose of the argument when, actually, they are different: *Just as the lioness is the one to protect her cubs, so do women bear the responsibility of caring for their children.* (Lions and humans are not alike.)

- **Oversimplification.** Reduces a complex system of causes and effects to an inaccurate generalization: *Bill Clinton's first election led to a stable economy in the 1990s.* (Clinton's election may have been one factor in the economy of the 1990s, but there were no doubt many other forces at work.)

chapter 9

I
n the humanities and social sciences, instructors commonly assign critical and analytical essays about course readings that ask for interpretation. If you are given a choice, the best texts to select for an interpretive assignment are the most questionable and problematic ones—texts whose meaning seems to you somewhat slippery and elusive—because these give you, the interpreter, the most room to argue one meaning against another. Whether given a choice or not, you have the same job: to make the best possible case that your interpretation is reasonable and deserves attention.

A fully developed interpretation incorporates several rhetorical strategies to make its case. It explains what the text says, in and of itself. It also argues for a particular version of the text's meaning—what the text implies or suggests about something beyond itself—and, like any argument, an interpretive essay should be as persuasive as possible, though it can never be an absolute proof. And it may also evaluate the importance or quality of the text being interpreted.

A typical assignment may ask for an interpretation of a poem, story, essay, or historical document—a complex task that draws on all of your reasoning and writing skills. You may have to describe people and situations, retell events, and define key terms. You may need to analyze passages and explain how they function in the text, perhaps by comparing or contrasting one part of the text to another—or this text to other texts. Finally, you will argue for one meaning rather than another, usually by stating a thesis and defending it with sound reasoning and convincing evidence. (See Chapter 7 for more on explanatory strategies; see Chapter 8 for more on argument strategies.)

9 a Presenting a text

This chapter demonstrates a methodical approach to developing an interpretive essay on one specific text, the poem "We Real Cool" by Gwendolyn Brooks, a short text, rich with interpretive possibilities. We believe our approach to examining this single poem also applies to interpreting many other kinds of texts. Please read "We Real Cool" and follow along as we look at what the poem might mean.

We Real Cool

THE POOL PLAYERS.
SEVEN AT THE GOLDEN SHOVEL.

We real cool. We
Left school. We
Lurk late. We
Strike straight. We
Sing sin. We
Thin gin. We
Jazz June. We
Die soon.

9 b   Exploring a text

Interpreting requires understanding. Plan to read the text more than
once. The first time, read the text to understand it on a literal level: Who
are the characters involved? Where are they? What happens? How does the
situation end? As you read, mark passages that interest you, that seem important or are difficult to understand. Now read the text a second time,
more slowly, making notes about passages that are interesting, questionable, or problematic. As you do this, look for answers to your previous concerns, rereading as many times as necessary to further your understanding.
Using "We Real Cool" as an example, we will explore ways of interpreting
a short poetic text as well as general guidelines applicable to interpreting
most prose texts.

9 c   Finding a topic

A good topic for an interpretive essay must involve an interesting question with more than one possible answer. Without the possibility of more
than one answer, there is no need to argue for one interpretation over another. If your question isn't interesting, you and your readers will be bored.
Here are suggestions for finding and exploring topics.

■   **Identify.** Ask, What genre is this text—poem, play, story, or essay? What
is its title? Who is the author? When was it published? Tell your reader: *"We
Real Cool" is a poem by Gwendolyn Brooks, published in 1963.*

■   **Annotate.** Locate ideas, problems, or puzzles, both small and large, that interest or intrigue you. Good topics for analyzing any genre of text arise
from material in which the meaning is not obviously stated. In "We Real
Cool," what is the setting? Who is speaking? How many characters are
there? What does "Jazz June" mean? Why do the characters "die soon"? If
you are analyzing a poem, it helps greatly to read it out loud to get the feel
of the language, the rhythm of the ideas.

- **Notice patterns.** Look for repeated words, ideas, or images that serve as clues to the author's main ideas. In both poetry and prose, writers use repetition to call attention to their central ideas and indicate their importance to the meaning of the text: *In "We Real Cool," why does each line except the last one end with "We"?*

- **Examine structure.** Analyze how the text is put together or organized. Authors arrange ideas and information to help readers understand the point they want to make. Whether in a chapter of a book or in a short story, organization is a major clue to meaning. Ask why the author made the choices he or she did: *Brooks creates rhythm in "We Real Cool" through a series of four rhymed pairs: "Cool / school," "late / straight," "sin / gin," and "June / soon." What effect does this use of rhythm have?*

- **Consider context.** Compare or contrast the text with other things you know about culture, history, or similar texts. Bring to bear all of your knowledge to situate the work in a context that sheds light on possible meaning. If you are comparing one text to other texts, use other works by the same author or a similar work by a different author: *"We Real Cool," written more than forty years ago, has characteristics similar to the lyrics and rhythm of a rap tune. Is Brooks's message similar to that of rap artists? If not, how does her message differ?*

9 d   Developing an interpretation

An interpretation starts by asking questions but concludes by presenting answers. Your essay will argue that a text means one thing rather than another, and it will explain why. These suggestions may help.

Choose a Perspective

Many college assignments ask you to interpret a text objectively—to focus on the object (text) under study instead of the subject (yourself) doing the study. When adopting an objective stance, write from the third-person point of view. Keep yourself and references to yourself to a minimum, and use language that is emotionally neutral and unbiased. Possible themes to explore in "We Real Cool" could be companionship, mischief, rebellion, or death.

Some college assignments, however, call for a more personal, subjective stance, encouraging you to acknowledge your own history as a reader. Instead of keeping your opinions or emotions out of the paper, you incorporate them as they suit your purpose. In the subjective stance, write from the first-person point of view and refer to personal experience to support the theme you are developing. *"We Real Cool" . . . reminds me of the gang in high school who used to skip classes and come back smelling of cigarette smoke and cheap liquor—not that I knew it was cheap back then.*

Take a Position

To write an interpretation from any point of view, you need to locate, identify, and understand what you consider to be the text's central meaning. It is customary to state your version of this central meaning as a claim or thesis directly in the first paragraph. Your thesis is a clear, concise statement of your interpretation, explaining to readers your argument for what the text means. They expect your thesis to be advanced and supported with sound reason and good evidence: *"We Real Cool" explores the meaning of the word "cool" in the actions and attitudes of a group of young, urban black males, known in the poem as "the pool players."*

If you write from a more personal perspective, instead of stating a thesis outright, you commonly develop your essay around a theme that holds your interpretation together—though sometimes the theme is implied rather than stated. Your first paragraph often signals such an interpretation by using the first-person point of view and featuring your ideas, memories, or values. Personal writing is commonly more speculative and less argumentative, often supported by memories, experiences, or associations that dovetail with textual evidence: *Brooks's pool players "Die soon," so we never know where else their adventurous spirits might have taken them. In the end, this poem just makes me sad.*

Provide Support

An interpretive thesis should be tightly focused so that you can support your argument with evidence from the text itself. Refer to your underlinings, highlightings, margin notes, and journal entries to bring specific textual references into your paper to serve as evidence, or proof, that your own reading of the text is a valid one.

When you draw on the text itself or bring in additional sources to support your view, you will have to decide when to summarize, when to paraphrase, and when to quote directly. In general, summarize larger ideas in your own language to conserve space; paraphrase more specific ideas also in your own words; and quote directly to feature especially colorful or precise language: *The companionship seen in the urgent repetition of the word "We" becomes the coercive force of a street gang, until the poem ends with what seems to be their mass suicide, as suggested by the ending—"We / die soon."* (For more information about using quotations, see Chapter 16, Using Research Sources.)

If you write from a subjective perspective, it's a good idea to identify or quote specific textual passages that trigger memories, associations, or personal ideas. The more specific your examples, the better. For example, one reader explains her reason for not hanging around pool halls: *I was always afraid . . . of the consequences, so I practiced piano, did my algebra, and stayed put.*

Guidelines for Writing About Literature

- **Identify text.** No matter which kind of interpretation you choose to write, personal or analytical, identify title and author of the text.

- **Position yourself.** Early in the essay, let your reader know what approach you are taking. If analytical, make that clear by writing your first paragraph in carefully neutral prose; if personal, make that clear by writing in the first person and advancing your own experience as part of your authority.

- **State your thesis.** You may state the main point your essay makes on the first page (common in analytical essays), or you may delay it, inviting readers to witness how you arrived at it. In either case, state your thesis clearly, so that after they have finished reading your paper, they know where you stand.

- **Support your thesis.** If you take an analytical approach, provide evidence for your assertions from lines in the text as well as other relevant cultural information. If you take a personal approach, provide evidence from the text itself, but also include your own experience as a form of evidence to support your position.

- **Document assertions.** Give credit for ideas that are not your own or passages of text that you quote or paraphrase.

- **Apply the writing process.** Interpretive essays need to be careful and tight. One idea needs to lead clearly to the next until a final position is stated. In writing this kind of essay, make time to reread your first draft critically, organize it logically, provide more evidence as needed, and edit for clarity.

9   e   Shaping the whole paper (student essays)

This chapter concludes with two short interpretive papers on Brooks's poem. One is a critical essay written to keep the focus on the argument of the poem, not on the writer's own opinion. The writer has a personal opinion, of course, but by writing from the third-person point of view, he doesn't draw attention to it. The other interpretation is written in a genre we might call a personal essay or reader-response paper—the essay is triggered by the poem, but it is admittedly as much about the writer as the poem, as evidenced by frequent first-person pronouns and allusions to personal experience. In the more subjective essay, the writer's experience and values become as important as the text under discussion.

Limited Textual Response to the Poem "We Real Cool"

Kelly Sachs writes a brief interpretation of "We Real Cool," keeping himself in the background by writing from the third-person point of view and limiting his focus to the language of the poem. He presents his thesis early and supports it with frequent quotations from the text. This close reading of a single short primary document does not call for MLA documentation apparatus; however, in the study of a longer poem (fifteen lines or more), including line numbers following quoted material would help readers locate the language under discussion.

High Stakes, Short Life

Kelly Sachs

The three interrelated themes in "We Real Cool" are companionship, mischief, and revelry. The speakers in the poem, referred to as "We," are teenagers who have dropped out of school, and these three qualities are inseparable elements of adolescent hedonism. For teenagers, fitting in or conforming to a group identity is more important than developing an individual identity. This need for companionship is suggested in the poem's subtitle, "Seven at the Golden Shovel"; the Golden Shovel proves to be their regular hangout. It is also supported by the plural point of view, "We," repeated at the end of each line.

Mischief is what these dropouts do instead of attending school. They "Lurk late," "Strike straight," "Sing sin," drink "Thin gin," and move to their own music, "Jazz June"—actions frowned upon by society and deliberately harmful to other people. This is a bunch of kids to watch out for. If you see them coming, cross the street.

However, this gang is also out to celebrate the high moments that life gives them—references to feeling cool, singing, and drinking gin all support this. To themselves, they are not so bad, not dangerous, maybe even happy and full of life. But, as their language tells us, they are young and not well educated and see little hope in the adult future—the simple one-syllable words reinforce this single-minded, simplistic view of a short life.

The poem's last line calls their bluff and suggests that their pleasures—companionship, mischief, and revelry—are brief and doomed. Brooks declares the fate of misfits who violate social norms in the last and shortest line of the

poem: they "Die soon."

Personal Response to the Poem "We Real Cool"

In the following essay, Mitzi Fowler writes about her personal reaction to Brooks's poem, describing how it reminds her of her own high school experience. Mitzi does not state a thesis, but the theme of sadness opens and closes the essay, providing the necessary coherence. Although she quotes the text several times, her primary supportive example from this subjective response come from her own memories.

Staying Put

Mitzi Fowler

"We Real Cool" is a sad poem. It reminds me of the gang in high school who

used to skip classes and come back smelling of cigarette smoke and cheap

liquor—not that I knew it was cheap back then. I think everybody who ever went

to a public high school knows these guys—at least, most of them were boys—

who eventually "left school" altogether and failed to graduate. They dressed a

little differently from the rest of us—baggier pants, heavier boots, dirtier shirts,

and too-long hair, never washed. And if there were girls—too much makeup or

none at all.

They had their fun, however, because they stayed in their group. They came

late to assemblies, slouched in their seats, made wisecracks, and often ended up

in detention after school or on Saturday morning. And no matter how strait-laced

and clean-cut the rest of us were, we always felt just a twinge of envy toward

these careless, jaunty rebels who refused to follow rules, who didn't care if they

got detentions, who didn't do homework, and whose parents didn't care if they

stayed out all night. I didn't admit it very often—at least not to my friends—

but some part of me wanted to have their pool hall and adventures, the adult freedoms they claimed for themselves. However, I was always afraid—chicken, they would have said—of the consequences, so I practiced piano, did my algebra, and stayed put.

Then I think of the poem's last line and know why I obeyed my parents (well, most of the time), listened to my teachers (at least some of them), and stayed put (if you don't count senior cut day). These "cool" ones paid for their rebellion in drug overdoses, jail terms, police shootouts, and short lives. Brooks's pool players "Die soon," so we never know where else their adventurous spirits might have taken them. In the end, this poem just makes me sad.

9 f Using secondary sources

The two interpretive essays that conclude this chapter use the work of literature itself as a primary source for writing the essay; that is, the poem "We Real Cool" is our single source of information, and both Kelly's and Mitzi's essays draw solely upon their own experience and insights gained by reading the poem. In contrast, they could have written the essay using secondary sources to support, expand, or challenge their initial readings of the poem, which would have changed the writing into an interpretive research essay. In other words, adding information from other interpretations of the poem is adding *second (and third and fourth, etc.) opinions* about the poem's meaning. (For an example of a research essay about literature that uses secondary sources, see end of Chapter 19 "MLA: Writing in Languages and Literature.")

WRITING ACROSS THE CURRICULUM

Literature Across the Curriculum

In disciplines other than English, there are occasions to introduce themes, characters, and insights derived from reading fiction, drama, and poetry in assigned papers. As with personal experience anecdotes, literary perspectives supplement rather than replace more discipline-specific or objective information in science, social science, humanities, and fine arts courses. Below are some examples.

History, Political Science, or American Studies. In writing a paper about social, cultural, or political conditions during the Civil War, adding insights from well-known fiction about the same period, such as Mark Twain's *The Adventures of Huckleberry Finn* or Harriet Beecher Stowe's *Uncle Tom's Cabin,* would show both your breadth of knowledge and illustrate your larger understanding of the issues being discussed in your paper.

Psychology or Sociology. In writing a paper on adolescent psychology or social norms, using fictional examples such as sixteen-year-old Holden Caufield from J. D. Salinger's *The Catcher in the Rye* or a character from the Harry Potter series (book or film) would provide an apt example to demonstrate an interdisciplinary understanding of your topic—you are not just writing from textbook or lecture material.

Religion or Art History. A paper examining medieval or Renaissance ideas about Christianity might introduce ideas from Dan Brown's *The Da Vinci Code* or Nikos Kazantzakis's *The Last Temptation of Christ,* to support or refute the argument of another critic. Such a strategy could illustrate your literary knowledge as well as your ability to extract parallels from personal reading.

Biology or History of Science. By referencing or including an example from Michael Crichton's *Jurassic Park* (book or film), in a paper on evolution, you might provide a lively and apt illustration of the contemporary view that dinosaurs were warm-blooded and therefore fast-moving creatures rather than cold-blooded and sluggish ones. Again, the fictional reference reinforces textbook understanding and adds a lively, interesting dimension to an otherwise fact-based paper.

chapter **10** | *The Revising Process*

L earning to write means learning to rewrite. While inexperienced writers may see revising as an alien activity and waste of time, experienced writers know that revising is the primary way of developing thoughts and preparing them to be shared with others.

It helps to separate revising from editing. Revision is conceptual work, in which you reread, rethink, and reconstruct your thoughts until they match those in your mind. Revising means re-seeing your topic, thesis, argument, evidence, organization, and conclusion, and making major changes that affect the content, direction, and meaning of your paper. Editing, however, is primarily sentence-level work, in which, once you know what you want to say, you make sure to say it as clearly, emphatically, and correctly as possible. For more on editing, see Parts 6–9.

10   a   General revising strategies

Although there is no one best way to revise, many of the following strategies have proved helpful to experienced writers and so may be useful to you as well.

- **Plan to revise.** You cannot revise a paper you haven't yet written. Finish drafting your paper before the night before it is due.

- **Make false due dates.** Write personal deadlines in your academic planner that remind you to draft, revise, edit, etc., on dates *before* the final instructor deadline.

- **Establish distance.** Let your draft sit at least overnight. When you return to it the next day, you'll see more clearly what works well, what doesn't, and where your writing can be improved.

- **Ask, "So what?"** Writing should teach readers something. Reread your paper and ask what can be learned from it. If you're not sure, it's time to revise.

- **State the theme or thesis.** Most papers make assertions early on that say, in effect, "Here's what this paper is about." If yours does not, revise.

- **Evaluate evidence.** To convince readers that your claims or assertions are good ones, double-check your facts and examples. Ask yourself: What evidence supports my thesis or advances my theme? What objections can be raised about this evidence? What additional evidence will answer these objections?

- **Reconsider everything.** When you return to your draft, reconsider the whole text. If you change the information on one page, it may change ideas on another. If a classmate or instructor suggests improvements on certain pages, don't assume the others are perfect.

- **Make a paragraph outline.** A paragraph outline creates a map to check for logical organization. Number each paragraph. Describe briefly the topic of each paragraph. Keep all related paragraphs together. Reorganize so that your paper has a beginning, middle, and end.

- **Play with titles.** Titles tell readers whether they want to read your essay. Changing a title can also give you, the writer, a new sense of direction. So, use titles as prompts to revision. Try some of these:

Use one good sentence from your paper.

Ask a question that your paper answers.

Use a strong sensory word or image from your paper.

Locate a famous quotation that relates to your paper.

Write a one-word title (a two-word title, a three-word title).

- **Listen for your voice.** Read your paper out loud. Does it sound like you—your ideas, your commitments, your style? If not, revise so that it does.

- **Seek response.** Share your early drafts with an audience you trust, and ask for a response about the strength of your claim, the credibility of your evidence, the clarity of your conclusion, and so on. The fresh eyes of other readers can usually spot things in your writing that you can no longer see for yourself.

- **Let go.** No matter how well an idea is expressed, if it no longer matches your paper's purpose, get rid of it or revise it until it does. When writers let go of early drafts, they trust that the power, creativity, and authority they found for their first draft will return for the second draft (and the third).

- **Start over.** Instead of always returning to the language of your original text, start over and let fresh language point you in new directions. Starting over may generate better writing as you delete dead ends and false starts.

10 b   Focused revising strategies

Sometimes you can bring new life to a paper by challenging yourself to see it in an entirely new way. Four specific suggestions for creatively refocusing your work are (1) limit your focus or scope, (2) add new material, (3) switch perspective, and (4) transform into another genre. These moves can be done as experiments at one sitting or as a sequence of drafts over several days or weeks.

Limit

Early drafts of papers are often too broad and cover too much ground in too few pages. Rather than continue writing many more pages, consider limiting your topic. How much of it should you cover? Ask these limiting questions: What are the parts of my paper? How many different parts are there? What are the subsections of each part? What is a specific example of each part? Could I write a complete paper about any of these smaller units?

Instead of writing a personal essay covering the two months last summer when you worked at McDonald's, for example, limit your draft to one specific day, afternoon, or hour, and tell that story with specific details so your readers can hear the hamburgers sizzle. Instead of writing a research paper about gun control as a national problem, limit your study to gun control in your own neighborhood, using local people and newspapers as resources.

When you limit your topic from something general to something specific, from something national to something local, you can find a lot of interesting and detailed information. When you select a specific and local issue, you have the opportunity to visit a place and talk to real people.

The following suggestions will help you limit a second draft:

▪ **Limit ideas.** Focus on one idea covered in a single paragraph or sentence of your first draft. Develop that single idea into your whole paper.

▪ **Limit time.** Focus on "real time" so that what you describe could really happen in the amount of time it takes to read your paper.

▪ **Limit place.** Focus on a single setting in which something happens or somebody speaks. Write as if you were a video camera, recording everything you witness.

Add

Drafts get stale when writers keep revising over the same ground. Make a resolution to add new information each time you revise. For example, when you limit your topic to something local, it's easy to add material you discover through field research. A paper is more fun to write when the research process includes living as well as textual sources.

In a personal experience paper, for example, add dialogue between yourself and a customer or a coworker, and let readers hear other voices in your paper. In a research paper on gun control, add interviews with local police officers, members of Handgun Control and the National Rifle Association, politicians, and members of the clergy to better explain your case for or against gun control. Take notes or use a tape recorder to ensure accuracy.

Whatever your new sources of information, take careful notes. Include details that appeal to the senses of sight, sound, touch, smell, and taste. When using quotations from an interview, be faithful to the spirit of the occasion and the character of the person talking.

The following suggestions will help you add new material to later drafts:

▪ **Add local people.** Find a local person who knows something about your topic and include his or her testimony in your paper.

▪ **Add recreated dialogue or interior monologue.** Close your eyes to help you visualize the experience from your memory, and make your recreated words faithful to the spirit of the occasion.

▪ **Add text research.** Use books, periodicals, or Internet sources to teach readers more than you knew when you started researching your topic.

Switch

Writers sometimes lock themselves into one way of seeing a topic. They write draft after draft from the same perspective and the same point of view, in the same tense, tone, and style. A good way to revitalize a later draft is to change one of these mechanical elements and see the effect on the conceptual elements. For example, in retelling a personal experience, instead of always writing in the past tense—which is normal—switch to present tense: instead of *I walked,* write *I walk.* In writing about your experience as a volunteer at the local hospital, switch from first-person point of view and past tense to third-person point of view and present tense.

Signal tense changes within the same piece of writing by giving clear typographical signals (subheadings, indentations, type changes, or white space) or by including careful transitional phrases. Notice how you re-see the experience as well as how readers respond to it. The present tense places you and your readers at the scene, so that you both witness it. Instead of summary and generality, readers experience drama and life.

Consider switching other elements of your composing to force yourself to see your topic in a new light. If you have been writing in the first person, switch to third person. If you've been writing in an academic voice, switch to a personal voice. If you've been writing in term-paper style, switch to letter or journal style, and vice versa. If you have been writing an argument paper in support of legalizing marijuana or euthanasia, write a draft in which you argue convincingly against legalizing it.

You don't need to stay "switched" in any of these cases for your final draft, but the change will be mentally challenging and lead to new insights. The following suggestions may help you switch effectively.

- **Switch point of view, verb tense, style, or voice.** Look at your ideas from a different perspective.

- **Switch audience.** Write a draft to your younger brother, your mother, or the local newspaper, and notice how change in audience results in change in style, tone, or voice.

- **Switch from exposition to narrative.** Instead of reporting the results of research, write a research draft detailing how you went about your search for information, telling whom you talked to and when, where you went next, and with what results.

Transform

College writers often write in the same academic forms over and over: a critical essay for literature class, a personal narrative for writing class, a position paper for political science, a term paper for history, and so on. For your next draft, experiment with a new form or genre for reporting information or telling a story.

For example, instead of writing a traditional comparison-and-contrast paper about Edgar Allan Poe and Stephen King, transform a draft into a dialogue between King and Poe sitting in a coffee house. Instead of writing a position paper on alcohol abuse or gun control, transform your research into a script for *60 Minutes,* complete with interviewer, interviewee, settings, and camera angles.

No matter what your new form or genre, be consistent with its conventions. Note that although you may use the techniques of fiction and drama, your facts, events, dialogue, and feelings should remain true to the experience. If you write a paper on personal organizers as if it were an article for *Consumer Reports,* follow the magazine's style and conventions all the way through.

Remember that you will not know the full effect of a new form until you actually create one. Even if you don't like the results of these experimental drafts, the new ideas generated by experimenting will usually find their way into your final paper. The more you experiment, the more you will grow as a writer. The following suggestions provide ideas for when to transform and what to transform to:

- **Transform for a good reason.** Use a form that complements and enhances the content of the paper.

- **When you have time to experiment, transform from one genre to another.** If the new form doesn't work, you still have the time to write conventionally.

- **Just do it.** Don't imagine what the new form will do to your ideas—write in it long enough to see what the possibilities are.

When you try a switching or transforming experiment, make sure you treat the content of the paper just as seriously as if you wrote in a more conventional mode. To be safe, check with your instructor before turning in your final draft.

WRITING ACROSS THE CURRICULUM

Focused Revising

Review the examples below and invent your own imaginatively focused version of a paper you need to write somewhere across the curriculum. Compare the result with a more traditional draft. What are the strengths and weaknesses of each?

Art history. Review a local art exhibit as a reporter for a local or campus newspaper, making sure your review is intelligible to a lay audience.

Biology. Write a science fiction story that includes carefully researched biological facts and principles but includes one fiction that creates havoc for our species after the fashion of *War of the Worlds* or *The Andromeda Strain*.

Business. Invent a product case study including perspectives from several corporate points of view (marketing manager, CEO, technical support) as well as several consumers with realistic, but colorful complaints.

Communications. Recreate a fictional television show dialogue as hosted by a Jon Stewart, Don Imus, or Rush Limbaugh, interviewing an expert about a critical issue in contemporary communications.

Education. Write an editorial supporting a local school board decision with a major impact on local schools; then write half a dozen letters to the editor in response to the editorial.

Geology. Interview the survivor of a natural disaster such as a forest fire, flood, tornado, or drought; then research the same event on the Internet and in the library. Write an account of this event as it might appear in *Time* or *Newsweek* magazine.

History. Adopt the role of an historical figure and compose a fictional letter exchange between this figure and his or her historical nemesis.

Literature. Invent the missing chapter or compose an alternate ending for a literary work you are studying in your English class; be sure to replicate the style and form of the work and make your new content consistent with the content and theme of the original.

Political science. Write a public opinion column on a troublesome political issue in the style of a syndicated columnist representing a particular point of view such as conservative George Wills or liberal Ellen Goodman; conclude with letters to the editor sparked by the column.

Psychology. Contrast two major psychological theorists by sitting them down in a coffee shop (or bar or mall or talk show debate) for a conversation about a current issue of some psychological importance.

Sociology. Write an advice column in response to a question of some social concern after the fashion of "Dear Abby."

chapter 11

Beginning the Research Process

Although doing a research paper is demanding, it also can be rewarding if the subject interests you and if you have the time and resources necessary for the job. The real secret is to start early, work steadily, and locate a personal interest. Following are some suggestions for how to do that.

11 a Keeping a research log

The best way to manage a complex research project is to log in a notebook every aspect of it from start to finish. That way, you'll always know where you are, what your questions are, how they've changed, what you've done, how much information you have, what it's worth, and where you need to go next. A research log is essentially a journal dedicated to thinking methodically about a research project. Your log helps you keep track of the whole research project from beginning to end—to write about your curiosity, to pose questions, to brainstorm where answers might be found, to keep track of sources found (and not found), and to explore modifications of research questions as new information leads your thinking in new directions. Use the log to answer questions such as these.

- What subject would really interest me?

- Why am I interested?

- How many specific questions could I ask about it?

- Where am I likely to find answers?

Writing out answers to these questions in your research log clarifies your tasks as you go along. It forces you to articulate ideas and examine supporting evidence critically. This, in turn, helps you focus your research activities. When you keep notes in a research log, record each as a separate notecard. Or, if using a computer, clearly identify the file containing your notes. Here is a sample from a research log for an investigation of ozone holes in the atmosphere.

> 11/12 Checked the subject headings—found no books on ozone depletion. Ref. librarian suggests looking at magazines because books take much longer to get published. Found twenty articles in the General Science Index—got printouts on about half. Start obtaining the sources and reading them tomorrow.

11/17   Conference today with professor about the ozone-hole thesis—said I didn't really have much of a thesis yet, just a lot of notes on the same subject. I should look at what I've got, then step back and decide what question it answers—that will probably point to my thesis.

11 b   Finding a topic

Many instructors let students choose their own research topics as long as they are consistent with course goals. Begin by asking these questions: What do I care about and why? What are the course goals? How would my research project fit in? What sources are available? How much time do I have? Why would anyone else care about the results?

Limiting a Topic

Whether your topic is assigned or created, it's better to do more with less than less with more: Limit your topic to a manageable scope and size. Instead of trying to analyze all the fiction of Alice Walker, limit the topic first to a book you want to investigate, say *The Color Purple;* then decide what specific aspect of the novel to investigate—the development of a specific character? a particular theme? the historical setting? and so on.

Owning the Topic

Conducting research means entering an ongoing conversation with a select community of people who are knowledgeable about a subject. As you collect information, you too become an author, an authority who can teach your classmates—and your instructor—something they didn't know before.

The best way to take control of your topic is to put the facts and ideas you collect into your own words at every chance—in your research log, on your notecards, in your computer file drafts. Finding your own language to express an idea guarantees that you understand the idea and increases your chances of saying something useful, interesting, or provocative.

11 c   Developing a research question

As we've suggested, research projects are designed to answer questions the answers to which you do not already know, so spend some time formulating a good research question. By isolating a particular aspect of the subject, the research question helps you tighten and maintain focus.

What Makes a Good Research Question?

- You find it interesting.

- You have a question to pursue.

- You don't already know the answer.

- You have the resources to track down the answer.

If source materials are not available, adapt your question to fit the materials at hand. If you are unsure about resources, consult a reference librarian. Ask your instructor to check your research question before you invest a lot of time in it. He or she can help you hone the question and save you time on a project too large to manage.

11 d   Formulating a working thesis

To research in a specific direction, it helps to formulate a working thesis, which is simply a tentative or possible answer to the question you plan to pursue. Essentially, it's a hunch or an educated guess to guide your investigation. If more research leads in a different direction—and you're interested in this new direction—redirect your investigation and revise your thesis.

For an informational report, try to begin with an open mind (*What would be the effects of legalizing marijuana?*) and be sure to find out as much background information about your topic as you can by searching the

Research Strategies

- **Ask questions.** Begin by asking questions about a subject, both of yourself and of others. Preliminary questions lead to more specific inquiries.

- **Read extensively.** Texts of all kinds—books, journal and magazine articles, and studies—are the raw material from which you will build your research paper.

- **Question knowledgeable people.** Start with people you know. If they can't help, find out who can and interview them.

- **Seek first-hand information and experience.** No matter how many answers other people offer you, seek out information yourself.

- **Evaluate your sources.** Sources vary in their accuracy and objectivity. Try to confirm the information you gather by checking more than one reliable source.

- **Write at every stage.** Remember that reading and taking field notes as well as log entries all help you gain control of your subject.

Internet or a library catalog before you commit to a single answer (*Legalizing marijuana would be a disaster—or maybe not.*). In other words, when you don't have a thesis in mind, informational research can help you find one, at which point your paper can either present the information you found in a neutral manner (*There are both pros and cons to legalizing marijuana*) or make an argument favoring one idea over another.

In contrast, if you begin a research project with a working thesis already in mind (*Legalizing marijuana for medical purposes is a good idea.*), you'll spend most of your time locating evidence to support and strengthen your position. However, be open to the possibility that your writing could change your thesis, and it's difficult to write a convincing paper when you, the writer, no longer believe in your position. In other words, even in *thesis-driven research,* you'll work best with an open mind!

11 e   Using the writing process

Take your research through all the stages of the writing process: plan, investigate, compose, revise, and edit. At the same time, note that research writing presents a few special problems.

Planning

The technical requirements of research writing—length, format, the nature and number of the sources you need, and the special documentation system required—take extra time, so plan schedules for trips to the library, online research, and interviews. Most important, allow enough time for writing, revising, and editing your paper. Whenever you fall behind in your schedule, revise your plan.

Researching

To evaluate sources, you first need to understand how different kinds of sources work as evidence. Primary sources contain original material and/or raw information. Secondary sources report on, describe, interpret, or analyze someone else's work. If you explore the development of a novelist's style, for example, the novels themselves are primary sources. Other people's reviews and interpretations of the novels are secondary sources.

Many research essays use both primary and secondary sources. Primary sources ground a paper in first-hand observations and facts; secondary sources supply context and support for your own analysis and argument.

Composing

Write your first draft early so you will have time for further research in case you find yourself creating a new working thesis or discover gaps in your coverage. The tentative answer to your research question has been your working thesis. As you gather material and begin drafting, however, this answer crystallizes into a more definite thesis statement, usually required in an academic research paper.

Remember that in an informational paper, your thesis states what you found but does not advance one position over another. For example, if you are asked to report on holes in the ozone layer, your paper will define, describe, or explain ozone holes but will not argue any point about them. Your research question (*What are ozone holes?*) leads to the neutral thesis statement answer (*Huge gaps in the earth's stratospheric ozone layer are caused by chlorofluorocarbons and other chemicals that react with and destroy ozone.*). In contrast, in a paper that interprets, argues, or assesses, you state your position on an issue and support it with evidence. Your research question (*Should Congress regulate handgun ownership?*) leads to a yes/no answer supported with evidence (*The ownership of handguns in the United States should/should not be strictly regulated by the federal government.*).

Many research essays present the thesis statement at the beginning, in the first or second paragraph, where it establishes what will follow. Some research papers delay the thesis statement until the end, where it acts as a conclusion or a summary. If you take the delayed-thesis approach, be sure that the topic and scope of your paper are clear to your readers in the beginning paragraphs.

Revising

Revising may entail modifying both the writing and the research that underlies it. Once research begins, your questions and answers multiply and change. Be prepared to find new questions more interesting to you than your original question. Keep the research process flexible, keep an open mind, and keep your eye focused on your topic. Remember, the act of writing—both informal and formal—focuses the brain: the more you write, the better you focus.

Editing

Editing and proofreading a research paper require extra time as you need to check the writing, the information, and the documentation. The editing stage is a good time to assess your use of quotation, paraphrase, and summary to make sure you have not misquoted or used a source without crediting it.

WRITING ACROSS THE CURRICULUM

Collaborative Research

Of all writing assignments, those involving research profit most from collaboration, no matter the subject area. In the corporate, business, and scientific worlds, nearly all work is collaborative, including posing, processing, and solving problems; reaching decisions; evaluating production; and writing reports. For most complex problems, two heads are better than one, and three are better than two. If your assignment lends itself to collaboration, and if your instructor approves, find out with which classmates you could work. The following suggestions will aid collaboration:

- **Start with either a group or topic.** Either form a group you want to work with and then choose a topic you all want to research, or choose a topic that interests you and see whether you can interest others in joining you.

- **Control size.** Small groups (two to three people) work better than large groups, because they make it easier to find time to meet outside of class and to synthesize the information found.

- **Organize.** Divide tasks early, specifying who will do what when. Divide tasks equitably. And divide tasks so that members make best use of their different skills, abilities, and interests.

- **Share.** Agree to duplicate the reading, interview, and observation notes so that each member has full sources of information.

- **Compose.** A group writing a single paper can write together by (1) blending voices—passing the drafts back and forth so that each writer overwrites the others each time; (2) sequencing voices—each writer writing a different section (as in chapters in a book); or (3) weaving voices, so that the final product has different writers' voices emerging at different times throughout the paper.

- **Synthesize.** Ask each group member to write his or her own version of what the paper might be. Share early drafts and look for consensus in topic and thesis. If no consensus emerges, share research but write separate papers.

- **Revise and edit.** Near the end, balance the workload, with different members volunteering to type, prepare references, edit, proofread, and reproduce the final paper. To encourage group ownership of the project, conduct a round-robin reading, whereby each member takes a turn editing the final draft.

- **Assess responsibility.** Ask group members to privately rank individual contributions to assess equity. When all group members meet their responsibilities and deadlines, all should receive the same reward; when they don't, they shouldn't.

---

chapter **12** | *Conducting Library Research*

The college library is the heart of the academic community and the most reliable source of credible information in all academic subjects. Many informative resources are also available on the Internet and in the field, though their reliability varies immensely. In contrast, resources screened by professional librarians for authenticity and credibility are likely to be reliable. Librarians can save you precious time by showing you the most helpful resources. If you are not sure how to begin, follow this research plan.

12 a Planning library research

To learn about the library, go there, walk slowly through it, read the signs, poke your nose into nooks and crannies, and browse through a few books or magazines. If there is an introductory video, pause to see it. If there is a self-paced or guided tour, take it. Read informational handouts and pamphlets. By the time you leave, know how to find the following:

The online catalog, a computerized database that tells you which books and other sources your library owns and where they are located.

The stacks, where books and periodicals are stored.

The circulation desk, where you check out and reserve books and get information on procedures and resources.

The periodical room, which houses current issues of magazines, journals, and newspapers.

The reference room, which contains general reference works, such as dictionaries and encyclopedias, along with guides and indexes to more specific sources of information.

To take full advantage of library resources, keep the following suggestions in mind:

Visit early and often. As soon as you receive a research assignment, visit the library to find out what resources are available for your project. Even if your initial research indicates a wealth of material, you may not be able to find everything the first time as a book may be checked out or your library may not subscribe to a certain periodical, or there are still resources you haven't learned about.

Take notes. Even in this computerized world it helps to bring index cards to the library—3″ × 5″ cards for bibliographical information and 4″ × 6″ cards for notes—from your first visit on. Good substitutes, of course, include your laptop computer or research log notebook.

Check general sources first. Look at dictionaries, encyclopedias, atlases, and yearbooks for background information about your topic. An hour spent with these general sources will give you a quick overview of the scope and range of your topic and will lead you to more specific information.

Ask for help. Talk to librarians. At first you might show them your assignment and describe your topic and your research plans; later you might ask them for help in finding a particular source or ask whether they know of any sources that you have not checked yet. Librarians are professional information experts, so use them.

12 b   Finding sources of information

Most of the information you need to find will be contained in reference books, in other books, and in periodicals (journals, magazines, and newspapers). To locate these sources, you'll need a variety of tools including the *online catalog* and *databases* as well as *periodical indexes*. To use these resources efficiently, use the following process.

Consult General Reference Works

Use databases (also called indexes) at your college or university library to locate general reference sources. Databases are guides to the material published within works, sometimes within books but more often within periodicals (magazines, journals, newspapers), which are published at set periods throughout the year. They focus on particular areas of interest, and their information is more current than that found in books. Because so many periodical issues are published each year and because every issue can contain dozens of articles on various topics, using a periodical index or database is essential to finding the article you need. Each index or database covers a particular group of periodicals. Make sure that the index you select

What You Need to Know About Keyword Searching

When you are looking for materials on a particular topic, a keyword search is often your best bet. A keyword search is a comprehensive way to search, and it tells the computer to look for your word or words anywhere in a record—in the title, the author name, the subject headings, the journal title, or the abstract. Keyword searching allows you to combine terms in different ways using Boolean connectors to either broaden or narrow your search results. Truncation is another powerful keyword searching tool that allows you to add greater flexibility to your searches by telling the computer to search for variant word endings. Both techniques are described below.

BOOLEAN CONNECTORS

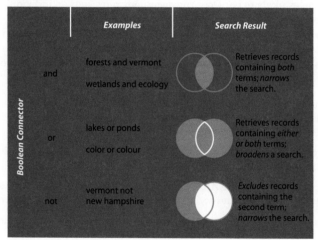

▶ **BOOLEAN CONNECTORS**

Boolean Connector		Examples	Search Result
	and	forests and vermont wetlands and ecology	Retrieves records containing *both* terms; *narrows* the search.
	or	lakes or ponds color or colour	Retrieves records containing *either* or both terms; *broadens* a search.
	not	vermont not new hampshire	*Excludes* records containing the second term; *narrows* the search.

TRUNCATION

Truncation	*Example*	*Search Result*
Use a truncation symbol at the end of a word or a root word, and the computer will search for all its different word endings. Different databases use different symbols (?, *, |, or #), so check the online help to learn what symbol to use.	environment*	*The use of "*" retrieves …* environment environmental environmentalist environmentalists environmentalism environmentally environments

contains the journals, magazines, and newspapers that you want to use as sources.

Many indexes, called full-text databases, allow you to print out the full text of an article you find, thus simplifying your search process. But beware: some texts are abbreviated when they are stored on the computer, and others omit accompanying information such as sidebars or graphics. In some cases, you may have to pay to retrieve the full text of an article. If an article looks important but is not retrievable in full-text form, be sure seek out the periodical (paper or electronic version) and read the article.

Whichever search tool you use, there is nothing magic about information transferred over a computer. You will need the same critical skills you use to evaluate printed materials, although the clues may be harder to understand when you find documents online. Is the author identified? Is that person a professional in the field or an interested amateur? What are his or her biases likely to be? Does the document represent an individual's opinion or peer-reviewed research?

The best way to locate and search for general reference works is to use the databases available online at most university libraries. Access is usually restricted, so check to see which of the following databases your university subscribes to.

> ***Academic Search Premier.*** Indexes over 3,400 scholarly publications including humanities, sciences, social sciences, education, engineering, languages, and literature in full-text access.
>
> ***ArticleFirst.*** Indexes over 15,000 journals in business, humanities, medicine, sciences, and social sciences.
>
> ***Expanded Academic ASAP.*** Indexes over 2,000 periodicals in the arts, humanities, sciences, and social sciences, as well as many newspapers.
>
> ***Factiva.*** Full-text access to major newspapers, business journals, and stock market reports.
>
> ***LexusNexus Academic.*** Indexes a wide range of magazines, newspapers, and government documents, all available full-text.

Consult Specialized Reference Works

Plan to use university online databases to search for s*pecialized reference works* that contain articles by well-known authorities and sometimes have bibliographies and cross-references that can lead to other sources. Access is usually restricted, so check to see which databases your university subscribes to.

A major online system commonly found in college libraries is *Dialog,* which offers more than 400 specialized databases. Some of the most commonly used databases (content identified by title) within *Dialog* include Arts and Humanities Search (1980–present), ERIC (Educational Resources

Information Center, 1966–present), MLA International Bibliography (1963–present), PsycINFO (1967–present), Scisearch (1974–present), and Social Scisearch (1972–present).

To use *Dialog,* you usually need the assistance of a reference librarian. The library is charged a fee for each search, calculated according to the time spent and the number of entries retrieved. Some libraries have the person requesting the search pay the fee; others limit the time allotted for each search. Be sure to ask what your library's policy is.

Consult the Online Catalog

All catalogs provide the same basic information. They list items by author, title, and subject; describe their physical format and content; and tell where in the library to find them. Consult the online catalog to find all books, journals, newspapers, and audiovisual material the library owns. Most online catalogs can be accessed from locations outside the library.

Plan to use the library catalog in several ways. If you already know the title of a work, the catalog confirms your library owns it and tells where it's located. You can also browse the catalog for works relevant to your topic. And you can also search the online catalogs of other libraries via the World Wide Web. Many libraries can obtain a work owned by another library through an interlibrary loan, a process that may take anywhere from a few days to a few weeks.

Note: You will not find individual journal articles listed in the catalog; to find those you will need to consult the periodical indexes.

Most online catalogs also allow you to perform keyword searches, allowing the computer to search different parts of the record at once. To perform a keyword search, use the words you've identified as describing your topic, linked by *and* or *or* as appropriate. For example, if you're trying to research fictional accounts of Dakota Indians, you can search for *"Dakota Indians" AND "fiction."* The computer will present you with a list of works that fit that description.

Two meta-library search tools that allow you to search multiple card catalogs simultaneously are LibWebCats <http://www.librarytechnology .org/libwebcats/> and Libdex <www.libdex.com>.

Other Sources of Information

Government documents. The U.S. government publishes numerous reports, pamphlets, catalogs, and newsletters on most issues of national concern. Consult the *Monthly Catalogue of United States Government Publications* and the *United States Government Publications Index,* both available electronically.

Nonprint media. Records, CDs, audiocassettes, videotapes, slides, photographs, and other media may also be located through the library catalog.

Pamphlets. Pamphlets and brochures published by government agencies and private organizations are generally stored in a library's vertical file. The *Vertical File Index: A Subject and Title Index to Selected Pamphlet Material* (1932/35–present) lists many of the available titles. Many are also available via the World Wide Web.

Special collections. Rare books, manuscripts, and items of local interest are commonly found in a special room or section of the library.

Maps and geographic information systems (GIS). Maps and atlases depict much more than roads and state boundaries, including information on population density, language patterns, soil types, and much more.

12 c   Taking notes

Taking good notes will make the whole research process easier, enabling you to locate and remember sources and helping you use them effectively in your writing. Use either a card-based system or laptop computer to record and sort sources and information.

Make Bibliographic Notes

A bibliographic note identifies the source, not what's in it. When you locate a useful source, write all the information necessary to find that source again on a 3″ × 5″ index card or computer equivalent, using a separate card for each work. Do this as you find each source, even before taking notes from the source. If you create *bibliographic notes* as you go along you can easily arrange them in alphabetical order to prepare the reference list required at the end of formal academic papers. (For complete information on bibliographic information appropriate for each discipline, see MLA, APA, or other documentation conventions in Chapters 19–22.)

Make Information Notes

Make paper or electronic notes to record the relevant information from every source you intend to use. Focus them on your research question, so that their relevance is clear when you read them later. If using paper cards, use 4″ × 6″ index cards for information and 3″ × 5″ for bibliographic sources. A typical notecard should contain only one piece of information or one idea to allow you to arrange and rearrange the information in different ways as you write. At the top of each notecard, identify the source through brief bibliographic identification (author and title), and note the page numbers on which the information appears. Personal notes, including ideas for possible use of the information or cross-references to other information, should be clearly distinguished from source.

Quote, Paraphrase, or Summarize as Needed

When recording information, take steps to avoid plagiarism (see Chapter 17) by making distinctions among *quoting directly, paraphrasing,* and *summarizing.* A direct quotation is an exact duplication of the author's words in the original source surrounded by quotation marks. A paraphrase is a restatement of the author's words in your own words to simplify or clarify the original author's point, restating the original facts or ideas fully and correctly. A summary is a brief condensation or distillation of the main point of the original source in your own words, with all facts and ideas accurately represented.

WRITING ACROSS THE CURRICULUM

Suggestions for Talking with Librarians

The following suggestions apply to any research situation in any discipline where the writer wants to advance the research project and learn more about the way libraries work.

- Bring with you a copy of the research assignment and be prepared to describe the course/discipline for which you are conducting the research. Also bring along a copy of the course syllabus.

- Be ready to explain the assignment in your own words: purpose, format, length, number of sources, and due date.

- Identify any special requirements about sources: Should information come from government documents? Rare books? Films?

- Describe the particular topic you are researching and the tentative question you have framed to address the topic.

- Describe any work you have done so far: Web sites, books, or periodicals looked at, log entries written, people interviewed, and so on.

- Think about it this way: Reference librarians don't like to sit around with nothing to do. The more difficult the questions, the more interesting their work.

Although many students turn first to the World Wide Web to look up information of any kind, using the Internet effectively for academic research requires
good search skills and the ability to evaluate sources for relevance and reliability. This chapter focuses on how to search for information. Evaluating Internet
sources for their value to your research is covered further in Chapter 15.

13 a Search engines

Search Engine Design

One kind of search engine uses a *directory,* an index organized in the
manner of a library subject catalog and usually evaluated by human editors. One familiar example is the Yahoo directory http://dir.yahoo.com/.
Another main approach uses *crawlers,* automated programs that evaluate
sites in part by counting the key terms that appear in them and the other
sites that link to them. One crawler you'll recognize is Google, http://www
.google.com/. (Just to make it confusing, Yahoo, which started as a directory, also now offers a crawler, and Google, which started as a crawler, now
offers a directory.)

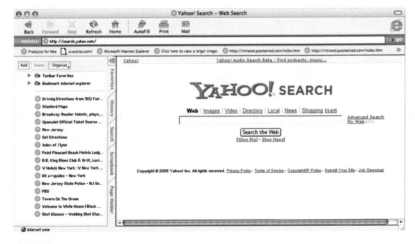

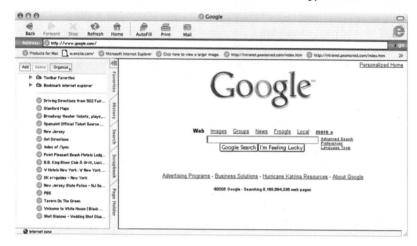

Directories are good at providing an overview of a subject. For example, if you enter the term *molecular biology* in a Yahoo! directory search, you'll find links to subcategories such as *molecular biology: imaging* or *molecular biology: proteins*. The list returned will include many gateway (specialized index) and overview sites.

A crawler search on a similarly general term yields an assortment of individual sites, including reference sites, gateways, course outlines, and journal archives. Some of these resources might be of great value, but it can be hard to know where to start. On the other hand, when your search terms are more specific, such as *molecular biology proteins myosin,* a crawler search is often more useful. To see the differences, try those two searches in Google and the Yahoo! directory http://dir.yahoo.com.

To learn more about search engines and how they work, visit Search Engine Watch www.searchenginewatch.com. For a tutorial on Internet searching, visit the University of California at Berkeley site at http://www .lib.berkeley.edu/Teaching Lib/Guides/Internet/.

13 b   Limiting your search

Searching for *music* on Google locates 2.5 billion pages; limiting the search to *classical music* yields a mere 320 million. Even searching for *composer Edvard Grieg* retrieves 454,000 pages. Narrowing further to *composer Grieg biography* yields a slightly more manageable list of 97,300 pages.

To get the most out of each search engine, visit its "advanced search" or help page, which will tell how it works and describe any special tools. For example, if you enter more than one word in Google, by default it returns only pages that contain *all* your search terms. That's why *classical music* yields fewer pages than *music* or *classical*. To search within those results, simply add another term: *American classical music.*

Most search engines ignore prepositions (*in, on, around*) and other small, common words. To guarantee that a word is included, some engines let you put a plus sign in front of it: *breakfast +in bed* yields more specific results than *breakfast bed* but doesn't eliminate all the *bed and breakfast* results.

The words *and, or* and *not* have special meaning, and some search engines require capitalization to distinguish these terms. They are terms of Boolean logic, used in search phrases such as *rights AND human OR civil,* which is equivalent to searching for *human rights* and then for *civil rights.* (See "What You Need to Know About Keyword Searching," 12b.) Using quotation marks or a "search for the exact phrase" field, you can find a specific phrase such as "Give me liberty or give me death." (Compare the results of that kind of search with a search for *liberty OR death.*)

Many search engines use *stemming* to search for related words at the same time. For example, searching for *parent* would also find *parents, parenting,* and *parental.* Some routines let you use an asterisk to include multiple forms: *parent**. On engines that do not use stemming, you must search separately: *rights AND parent OR parenting OR parents.*

Try some of these searches on the Google advanced search page and note the different results each one yields. (Some sites code these functions differently; check the help files.) The point of this exercise is that when you're having trouble finding what you need, be ready to try lots of different approaches.

13 c   Search strategies

When you find a Web site devoted to your topic, check for links to other sites. Chances are its author has listed sources of related information. For example, the National Museum of the United States Air Force has an extensive site http://www.nationalmuseum.af.mil/museum/history/vietnam/index.htm describing the role of aircraft in the Vietnam War. If you find a dead link, try shortening the Web address. For example, if you can't bring up the specific Air Force Museum site, shorten the URL to http://www.nationalmuseum.af.mil/ and look for useful links.

Examine different sites on the same subject, which may provide information from a different perspective or have different degrees of reliability. In addition to focused searching, leave time for open-ended "surfing."

Here are some specialized, academic, and library resources.

- Bartleby.com http://www.bartleby.com: Offers complete, searchable text of works of literature, poetry, and criticism.

- Biographical dictionary http://www.s9.com/biography/.

- CIA World Factbook http://www.cia.gov/cia/publications/factbook/index.html: Comprehensive information on every country.

- Information Please http://www.infoplease.com: Online almanac with topics from architecture to biography to historical statistics to weather.

- The Internet Public Library http://www.ipl.org/.

- Learn the Net Inc. http://www.learnthenet.com/english/index.html/: A primer on searching.

- Librarians' Index to the Internet http://lii.org/: A professionally compiled gateway to research sites.

- LibrarySpot http://www.libraryspot.com/: Another reference-oriented gateway.

- LibWeb http://lists.webjunction.org/libweb/: A list of library servers in more than 125 countries.

- Reference.com http://www.reference.com/: Dictionaries, thesauri, encyclopedias, and more.

- Shakespeare Web http://www.shakespeare.com/: Resources related to Shakespeare.

- Social Science Research Network http://www.ssrn.com: Abstracts and full text of many current papers in business, economics, and legal scholarship.

- U.S. Census Bureau http://www.census.gov: A primary source for government demographic and economic data. Also see Statistical Abstract of the United States http://www.census.gov/compendia/statab/.

In a research notebook (which can itself be a computer file), record search terms and the addresses of sites you visit. When you locate a useful site, print a copy of the page and, if your printer doesn't automatically print the URL, record the address and the date and time in your notebook. If you're using your own computer, enter useful locations in your browser's bookmark or favorites file.

13   d   E-mail, lists, and newsgroups

Once you have an e-mail address, you can correspond with people around the world—if you know their addresses. People often post their e-mail addresses on their own Web sites, and institutions such as universities often have faculty e-mail directories on their Web pages. If you know someone works at an institution but can't find his or her e-mail address, try writing to a contact address provided on the Web site. To search for an e-mail address, try Search.com at http://www.search.com/search?channel=10 or an e-mail address metasearch at http://my.email.address.is/. You can also use newsgroups or e-mail lists to communicate with groups of people.

Newsgroups

Information submitted (or *posted*) to a newsgroup is collected on a computer "bulletin board." Readers interested in a group's topic must download messages to read them. The oldest newsgroups began on a network called Usenet. Many search sites now offer tools that search Usenet groups and enable users to create groups outside Usenet. (At Google, www.google .com, click the Groups link, then follow the Usenet link.)

Many of the tens of thousands of Usenet groups are open to the public. Some require membership, which is usually easy for researchers to obtain. (Note that unmoderated groups often contain irrelevant or objectionable material or heated debate.) Google, Yahoo, and other gateways host groups that are not part of Usenet.

The archives of a scholarly newsgroup can be a gold mine for a patient researcher. They can also help you find people knowledgeable about your topic whom you can contact directly, usually by e-mail.

Before you post a query to a newsgroup or contact a member, do your homework. Most major groups list frequently asked questions (FAQs) and answers. The FAQs (pronounced fax) often will tell you whether you're in an appropriate group, list the key contacts, and answer many preliminary questions. The sources you contact will appreciate not having to repeat information they have already set out for you.

E-mail Lists

If you write to an e-mail list, your message is delivered to all members of the list. Both newsgroups and e-mail lists allow one writer to reach many readers with similar interests. The difference is that while a newsgroup posting must wait for interested readers to find it, anything you post to a list will quickly be delivered to list members' inboxes.

Many lists have Web pages with FAQs that include the name and address of the moderator and instructions for joining or leaving the list. Many also have searchable archives available to members of the list. A request for membership for research purposes will usually be accepted. And most members will welcome questions from newcomers, especially those who have familiarized themselves with the list's FAQs or archives before posting.

WRITING ACROSS THE CURRICULUM

How to Read an Internet Address

Every site on the Internet has a unique electronic address called the *universal resource locator,* or URL. In addition to identifying a specific computer file, a URL also includes information about the owner of the site. Here are the parts of a URL:

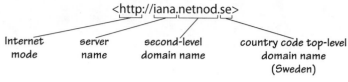

The two or three letters at the end of a URL are called the *top-level domain name*. Two letters are a *country code* (.se for Sweden, .jp for Japan). A *generic top-level domain name* has three letters (.org, .net, .biz) indicating the type of organization that owns the site. Here are the generic top-level domain names:

- **.aero** aviation groups or companies
- **.biz** businesses
- **.com** commercial/business
- **.coop** cooperative association
- **.edu** educational institution
- **.gov** government agency
- **.info** informational site, including commercial
- **.int** intergovernmental organization
- **.museum** accredited museums worldwide
- **.mil** military
- **.name** reserved for individuals
- **.net** news and other networks, including broadband service providers
- **.org** nonprofit agency
- **.pro** professionals and professional organizations

Looking at the top-level domain name can give you a clue about the purpose and viewpoint of a Web site: **.com** and **.biz** sites are commercial, oriented toward sales; **.coop, .pro,** and **.org** may have commercial or political purposes but also may promote general public welfare; **.int, .mil** and **.gov** are official sites; **.edu** and **.museum** are primarily educational and cultural; **.info** and **.name** can be almost anything. A tilde (~) in a file name denotes a personal site, often representing one person's point of view.

Depending on your research question, you may need to conduct research outside the library and away from computers. Field research simply means visiting places (a lakeshore, a downtown, a factory, a museum) or people (a biologist, a police officer, a farm worker, a professor) and taking careful notes. Field research gets you fresh, local information about people, places, events, or objects that you cannot find in books or cyberspace. Your observation and interview notes provide you with original data to incorporate into research papers.

14 a Observing places

Unlike a library, which bundles millions of bits of every kind of information in a single location, fields are everywhere. A college campus is an ideal place in which to conduct field research since there are many potential sites for investigation: academic departments, administrative offices, labs, libraries, dining and sports facilities, and dormitories. In the neighborhood beyond the campus, sites for field research include theaters, malls, parks, playgrounds, business offices, homes, and so on. Furthermore, accessing the Internet opens up the possibility of field research in cyberspace, from e-mail on your own campus to contact with a site halfway around the world. Field information is not cataloged, organized, indexed, or shelved for your convenience. Obtaining it requires diligence, energy, and careful planning.

The following suggestions will increase your chances of successful site visits.

- **Select relevant sites.** When doing research at local sites, visit places that will be the primary focus of your paper or offer supplementary details to support your major points.

- **Do homework.** To observe with understanding and use onsite time efficiently, consult reference room or online sources such as encyclopedias, dictionaries, and atlases to inform yourself about the places you will visit.

- **Call ahead.** Find out directions and convenient times to visit and let people at the site know you are coming; also let them know if you need to cancel.

- **Bring a notebook with a stiff cover.** It will help you write while walking or standing. Record both general impressions and specific details. Double-entry notebooks record facts in one column and your reactions in the other.

- **Use a handheld audio recorder** for onsite dictation to supplement or replace written notes.

- **Review, transcribe, and rewrite** both written and dictated notes within twenty-four hours after your visit. Both your memory and the completeness of your records will benefit.

- **Sketch, photograph, map, or videotape** useful visual information. Supplement visual records with measurements or notes as appropriate.

Electronic Research Tools

Use electronic media to capture interview data when conversations in person are difficult or impossible to arrange.

- **Telephone.** Use your telephone to interview people you cannot talk to in person. Even a ten-minute phone conversation can give you insights and quotable nuggets to enliven your paper. Keep a pen handy and take good notes.

- **Telephone answering machine.** Pose simple questions to interview subjects and ask them to call back to record their answers on your answering machine (when you know you won't be home). You can transcribe the recording later.

- **E-mail.** Send queries by e-mail to interview subjects with a limited number of questions, and allow them to e-mail their responses. This technique is convenient for subjects as it allows them to answer you when they have time; it also provides you with a written record for quotations.

- **Home page.** Ask interview subjects to visit your Web home page on which you've described situations or posed questions as well as provided a means to record responses (e-mail or listserv, chat box). You will spend time setting up the page to serve research purposes, but you will save time later if many people access your questions and respond in writing.

- **Camera.** Use your digital or film camera to capture color and details from both interview subjects and site visits.

14 b   Interviewing people

A good interview provides the researcher with timely, original, and useful information that often cannot be obtained by other means. Getting such information is part instinct, part skill, and part luck. In many respects, a good interview is simply a good conversation. If you find talking to strangers easy, then you have a head start on being a good interviewer. If you do not, you can still learn how to ask good interview questions that will elicit the answers you need. Your chances of obtaining good interview material increase when you've carefully selected your interview subject and thought about what questions you want to pose ahead of time.

Keep in mind that people differ in both the amount and the kind of knowledge they have. Not everyone who knows something about your research topic will be available to be interviewed. In other words, before you make an appointment with a local expert, consider whether this is the best person to talk to. The following guidelines should help you conduct good interviews.

■ **Select relevant people.** Determine what information you need, who is likely to have it, and how to approach them. To find such people, start by asking people you know. Use the Yellow Pages and the Internet to locate experts.

■ **Call ahead for an appointment.** Let your subject know when you are coming or when an appointment needs to be changed or canceled.

■ **Do homework.** Consult library or Internet sources for background information on your interview subject. Experts will say more and provide greater depth if you know more; they will say less if you seem ignorant and settle for superficial answers.

■ **Prepare questions in advance.** Plan to ask general questions early to establish context; plan to ask more specific questions as you become more informed. Write these out in a small notebook so that you remember to ask them.

■ **Ask open questions.** Open questions elicit general information and set the context for further questions: *How did that situation develop? What are your plans for the future?* Open questions allow your interviewee to add new information, insights, and direction that you may not have thought of but that might prove crucial for your paper.

■ **Ask closed questions.** Closed questions elicit facts or concrete details to support a point or to focus the direction an interview is taking: *On what date did that policy take effect? What is the name of the district manager?*

■ **Ask follow-up questions.** If answers are incomplete or confusing, the follow-up question allows your interviewee to provide you with more depth and detail: *How many gallons does it hold? How long ago was that?* Get all the information possible at one sitting.

■ **Use silence.** Often when people don't answer immediately, it's because they are thinking or formulating an answer. If your subject does not respond right away, allow time for him or her to think, recall, or reflect before you fill the silence with another question.

■ **Read body language.** Notice how your subject acts: Does the person look you in the eyes? Fidget? Look bored? Smile? Pace around the room? Each of these actions suggests whether someone is speaking honestly, avoiding your question, or tiring fast. In your notes, describe body language along with conversation to add color, context, or extra meaning to recorded words.

- **Use a tape recorder.** Ask permission in advance and make sure your equipment works. Continue to make written notes of conversation highlights to help you remember questions that occur while your subject is talking and to describe the subject's appearance and manner.

- **Confirm important assertions.** Read back important or controversial statements to check for accuracy and allow for further explanation.

14 c Conducting surveys

A type of field research commonly used in the social sciences is the survey, a structured interview in which respondents, representative of a larger group, are all asked the same questions. Their answers are then tabulated and interpreted. Researchers usually conduct surveys to discover attitudes, beliefs, or habits of the general public or segments of the population. They may try to predict how soccer moms will vote in an election, determine the popularity of a new movie with teenage audiences, compare the eating habits of students who live off campus to those of students who eat in college dining halls—the possible topics are infinite.

Respondents to surveys can be treated like experts for research purposes because they are being asked for their own opinions or information about their own behavior. However, you must ask your questions skillfully to get useful answers. Instead of collecting candid responses, wording that suggests a right or wrong answer reveals the researcher's biases and preconceived ideas. Furthermore, questions should be easy to understand and answer, and they should be reviewed to make sure they are relevant to the research topic or hypothesis. The format for questioning and the way the research is conducted also have an influence on the responses. For example, to get complete and honest answers about a sensitive or highly personal issue, the researcher would probably use anonymous written surveys to ensure confidentiality. Other survey techniques involve oral interviews, in person or by phone, in which the researcher records each subject's responses on a written form.

Surveys are usually brief to gain the cooperation of a sufficiently large number of respondents. And to enable the researcher to compare answers, the questions are usually closed, although open-ended questions may be used to gain additional information or insights.

Survey research is a complex and much studied field so that we are unable in this handbook to provide in-depth coverage needed to conduct a meaningful survey. However, useful information on conducting different kinds of surveys and designing questionnaires can be found on the Internet as well as in basic handbooks, including the following sources we found especially useful to students conducting a survey research project.

- Colorado State University has a highly informative Web site that provides an overview of survey types (oral, electronic, written), including the advantages and disadvantages of each plus an outline of various methodologies and procedures for collecting and analyzing the result. See http://writing.colostate.edu/guides/research/survey/index.cfm.

- StatPac is an online public service designed to tutor first-time researchers in the art and science of *Designing Surveys and Questionnaires,* including pointed information on composing, editing, and ordering survey questions, as well as time and cost considerations for written questionnaires. See http://www.statpac.com/surveys.

A textual source worth investigating is *Designing and Conducting Survey Research: A Comprehensive Guide,* by Louis M. Rea and Richard A. Parker. This text is a practical guide to conducting survey research, including chapters on designing questionnaires as well as processing, anaylzing, and reporting the results.

chapter 15 | *Evaluating Research Sources*

Good sources inform your papers and make them credible. To evaluate a source, ask these questions: Is the source itself credible? Is it useful in my paper? This chapter provides guidelines for evaluating the credibility and usefulness of sources found in the library, on the Internet, and in the field.

15 a Evaluating library sources

The research sources—periodicals, documents, special collections, and electronic resources—in a college library carry some credibility because they have been chosen by scholars and librarians with expertise in the subjects that the library catalogs. However, just because *some* authorities judged a source to be credible *at one time* does not necessarily mean that it still is, or that it's the best available, or that its findings are not contested, or that it's relevant to the paper you're writing. Two of the main reasons for challenging any source have to do with *time* (When was it written? Is it still valid?) and *perspective* (Who said it, and for what reason?).

Identifying Dated Sources

Most library documents include a date of publication inside the cover, and in most cases this will be a fact that you can rely on. In some cases, such as articles first published in one place and then reprinted in an anthology, you may have to dig harder for the original date, but it's usually there (check the permissions or credits page).

One of the main reasons any source may become unreliable—and less credible—is the passage of time. For example, any geographical, political, or statistical information true for 1950 or even 1999 may have changed by the time you examine it—in many cases, radically so. (See atlas or encyclopedia entries for Africa or Asia from 1950!) Yet at publication, this information was held to be accurate.

Check the critical reception of books when they were published by reading reviews in *The Book Review Digest* (also online); often you can tell whether the critical argument over the book twenty years ago is still relevant or has been superseded by other events and publications.

At the same time, dated information has all sorts of uses. In spite of being "dated," works such as the Bible, the I Ching, the novels of Virginia Woolf, and the beliefs of Malcolm X are invaluable for many reasons. In studying change over time, old statistical information is crucial. Knowing the source date lets you decide whether to use it and how.

Identifying Perspective

Who created the source? With what purpose or agenda has someone or some organization written, constructed, compiled, recorded, or otherwise created this source in the first place? This second critical question is difficult to answer by reviewing the source itself. While most library texts include the dates they were published, few accurately advertise their purpose or the author's point of view—and when they do, this information cannot always be believed.

To evaluate the usefulness of a text, ask questions about the assumptions it makes, the evidence it presents, and the reasoning that holds it together. Finding answers to these critical questions reveals an author's bias.

- What is the writer's purpose—scholarly analysis, political advocacy, entertainment, or something else?

- Can you classify the author's point of view (liberal, conservative, radical) and differentiate it from other points of view?

- What is the author's reputation in the field? How is he or she regarded by contemporaries or successors?

- What does the writer assume about the subject or about the audience? (What does unexplained jargon tell you?)

- How persuasive is the evidence? Which statements are facts, which inferences are drawn from facts, which are matters of opinion? (See Chapter 8.)

- Are you aware of relevant points that the writer *doesn't* mention? What does this tell you?

- How compelling is the logic? Are there places where it doesn't make sense? How many?

Your answers to these questions should influence the degree to which you accept the author's conclusions.

Cross-Referencing Sources

At first it may seem daunting to answer all these questions, but have patience and give the research process the time it needs. On a relatively new subject, you won't know many answers; however, the more you learn, the more you learn! As you read further, you begin to compare one source to another and to notice differences, especially if you read carefully and take notes to keep track of each source's timeliness and perspective. The more differences you note, the more answers to the above questions you find, and the more you know whether a source might be useful.

15 b   Evaluating Internet sources

Although the Internet provides marvelous information sources, it can also be a trap for unwary researchers. Material published on the Internet does not have to meet the same standards of fairness, accuracy, or statistical validity as, say, a peer-reviewed journal or a daily newspaper. Anyone with a computer and an Internet connection can publish personal opinion, commercial pitches, satire, bogus claims, even bomb-making instructions, on the World Wide Web. So how do you distinguish the credible from the questionable? And what do the differences mean for your research writing?

To identify an Internet source, look first at the electronic address or Uniform Resource Locator (URL). The extension at the end, such as .com or .gov, is called the *top-level domain name*. It indicates the type of organization sponsoring the site.

The domain extensions are your first clue to the nature of the source. Those with .gov and .mil can be expected to present official information. Nonprofit organization sites—.org—usually reflect the viewpoint of the sponsoring organization. For examples of how a point of view can saturate a site, visit the Sierra Club (www.sierraclub.org), the New England Mountain Bike Association (www.nemba.org), or any other special-interest site you are interested in. Pages designated .com and .biz can be promotional, sales-oriented, or informational. The top-level domain .info—for information—is not yet common, but it will be available to all Internet users

Identifying the Ownership of Internet Resources

Every Internet domain name, such as *randomnumbers.com* or *google.com,* must be registered, and you can look up the name of each registered owner. Registries also usually contain e-mail addresses or postal addresses. The tool for finding this information is called *WHOIS.* Click on the WHOIS button at Network Solutions (www.netsol.com). Enter only the second-level and top-level domain name (google.com, not www.google.com), and WHOIS returns the owner's name and contact information. However, a site that makes you search for this information, rather than providing it, should not inspire confidence.

wanting to publish information of almost any kind. Personal sites with a tilde (~) or .name in the URL usually represent one person's point of view, and in that case you have to make a judgment about that individual's credibility and relevance to your project.

An address extension isn't a certain indicator of a site's value. If you're writing about history, for example, you may find a .edu site covering your topic published by a history class at another school. For your purposes, that site is a secondary source that you may not want to use directly, but it might contain useful links to primary sources that are highly relevant. Similarly, a commercial site isn't usually a primary source for information about history, but it can be a primary source for what the sponsor says about itself or perhaps for trends in marketing.

Question every Internet source as thoroughly as you would a print source. If the source has a print counterpart, such as a peer-reviewed journal or a respected periodical, you may assign it roughly the same credibility as its print cousin. But most Internet sources are not so easy to classify. Try asking a reporter's questions—*who, what, when, where, why,* and *how.*

WHO IS THE AUTHOR?

- Look for an individual's name. Check the top and bottom of the page and in the URL.

- Look for a link that says "about us" or "about this site."

- Does the author have credentials as a scholar, scientist, physician? College degrees? Experience?

- Does the author have connections to a university? A publication? A government agency? An advocacy group?

- If no individual is named, is there a sponsoring organization? What can you tell about that organization's purpose, credibility, or politics?

- Look for links to the author's or agency's home page.

- Look for a way to contact the author or sponsoring organization by e-mail, phone, or letter to ask further questions.

- If you cannot tell who created the site or contact its sponsor, assign the site a low credibility, and don't rely on its information.

WHAT IDEAS OR INFORMATION DOES THE SITE PRESENT?

- Look for familiar concepts and terminology. Are they used in the ways you would expect?

- Summarize the site's claims or central ideas in your own words. How does the site fit your research needs?

- Examine how clearly the author distinguishes facts from opinions or speculation. Be wary of speculation. Be especially wary of any author who presents opinion or speculation as fact.

- When opinions are expressed, are they part of a balanced presentation or one that is biased toward one point of view? What tips you off? Which is more trustworthy? Why?

- Is any key information missing? Why do you think it's not there?

- If advertising is present, is it clearly labeled and separate from the factual material? Does the information in the site tend to support the aims of the advertisers?

HOW IS THE INFORMATION PRESENTED?

- Examine how carefully the site is constructed, an indication of the educational level and sophistication of its creators. If the site contains spelling or grammatical errors or unexplained jargon, do you trust it? Will your readers?

- Do the graphics and multimedia features contribute to the content or detract from it?

- Are there links that help you put the information in context?

WHERE DOES THE INFORMATION COME FROM?

- How carefully does the author identify the source of material that is not his or her own? Are links provided so you can check for yourself? Documenting sources increases a site's credibility, as it shows respect for standards of accuracy and verifiability.

- Are there related print sources for the information? How credible are they?

- Has the information been refereed or peer-reviewed?

WHEN WAS THE SITE CREATED?

- A site more than a year old suggests information could be outdated. If there is no date, check the links to see whether the sites they point to are current. How important is the datedness or currency of the information to your purpose?

- If the site is not dated, how does that affect your assessment of its credibility?

Critically Evaluating Two Web Sites

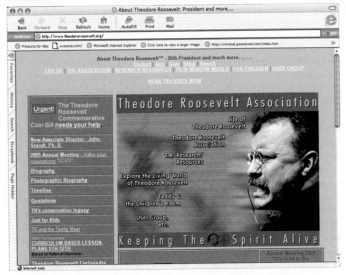

The Theodore Roosevelt Association site, http://www.theodoreroosevelt.org. Reprinted by permission of Theodore Roosevelt Association.

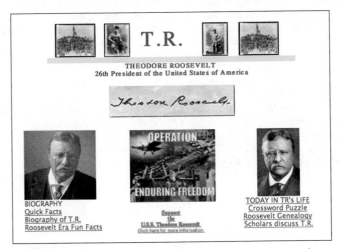

The Almanac of Theodore Roosevelt site, http://www.theodore-roosevelt.com.

Here's the situation. You are looking for primary source material about Theodore Roosevelt, the 26th president of the United States, especially contemporary photographs and facsimiles of manuscripts. After ruling out several sites by actors who impersonate

Roosevelt for special occasions and after reading a good biographical sketch at www .AmericanPresident.org, a University of Virginia site, you have narrowed your search to two very similar sites, the Theodore Roosevelt Association (www.theodoreroosevelt.org) and The Almanac of Theodore Roosevelt (www.theodore-roosevelt.com). Both appear to have primary documents, including many contemporary photographs. The two sites share a very positive view of Roosevelt—neither contains any material critical of him, but the sites' origins differ. Which would make the more reliable source? Here's how the "reporter's questions" help differentiate the two.

The Theodore Roosevelt Association site (http://www.theodoreroosevelt .org):

- **Who?** The site says it's the official publication of an association chartered by Congress in 1920. Officers of the association are named. The appointment of a new director is announced.
- **What?** A wealth of facts, a timeline, images of pages from Roosevelt's diaries, and photos. The diary pages and photos are representations of primary sources, and they are identified and dated.

- **Where?** A mailing address, e-mail link, and phone numbers are provided.
- **When?** Home page isn't dated, but the site includes information on an upcoming meeting and one that occurred very recently.
- **Why?** A mission statement says the organization exists "to instill in all who may be interested an appreciation …" of Roosevelt.
- **How?** Site mixes some primary materials with secondary accounts to present a positive view of Roosevelt.

The Almanac of Theodore Roosevelt site (http://www.theodore-roosevelt .com):

- **Who?** No author is identified on the home page. The site appears to be the work of one person with a great enthusiasm for all things related to "TR."

- **What?** The site has extensive texts of writings and speeches by Roosevelt. There are many photos, most of which do not have captions or dates. There are a number of facsimiles of documents, but many lack identification. Some photos appear on both the association and almanac sites.
- **Where?** There is no mailing address or phone number.
- **When?** The site says it was modified within the past week.

- **Why?** A mission statement says the site was created to "preserve and expand upon the memory and ideals of Theodore Roosevelt."
- **How?** The site mixes historical documents with advocacy, such as offering readers a chance to vote (for Roosevelt) in a History Channel poll on "Who is the greatest American?"

Some Conclusions

Both sites show a heavy pro-Roosevelt bias, so their stories of Roosevelt's actions and triumphs (which for this purpose are secondary sources) need to be checked against other, more balanced accounts. The almanac site, the work of one person who presents no scholarly credentials, is an example of an excellent "fan site," a collection of materials gathered to express and spread the author's enthusiasm for the subject. The absence of key information about photographs and some other materials limit its usefulness for scholarly research. Many items here that appear to be primary documents would need to be supported by other sources.

While the association site apparently began with similar enthusiasms, the group's longevity and official recognition and the fact that it appears to have hired professional staff enhance its credibility. The association shows greater respect for research standards by providing more information about the primary documents it presents.

To judge for yourself, visit the sites online. Be aware that they may have changed substantially since this writing.

15 c   Evaluating field sources

People and places are, by their nature, not as carefully documented, reviewed, cataloged, and permanent as library sources or as widely available as Internet sources. The reliability and credibility of field sources is problematic because it is often more difficult for readers of your paper to track down field sources than textual sources. An interview is usually a single event, so a subject available one day may not be there the next for follow-up questions or confirmation of responses. A location providing information one day  may change or become off-limits the next. To examine field sources critically, you need to "freeze" them and make them hold still. Here's what to do.

Interviews

To freeze an interview, use a tape recorder and transcribe the whole session. (See 14b.) Once an interview is taped, apply to it the critical questions you would a written source. (See 15a and b.) If you cannot tape-record, be sure to take careful notes, review main points with your subject before the interview ends, and apply these same critical questions.

Site Observations

To freeze a site, make photographic or video records of what it looks like and what you find. Take copious notes about time and details of location, size, shape, color, number, and so forth. If you cannot make photo records, then sketch, draw, or diagram what you find. Pictures and careful verbal descriptions add credibility by providing specific details that would be difficult to invent had the writer not been present. Even if you don't use them directly in your paper, visual notes will jog your memory of other important site events. (See 14a.)

Personal Bias

Evaluating personal observations is complicated since you are both the creator and the evaluator of the material at the same time. The world is out there, and in and of itself, it has no meaning or value until you, the recorder, assign it. This material has not been filtered through the lens of another writer. You are the interpreter of what you witness, and when you introduce field evidence, it's your own bias that will show up in the way you use language; you will lead your reader one way or another depending on the words you select to convey what you saw: Was the lake water *cloudy, murky,* or *filthy?* Was the electric car *slow, relaxed, hesitant,* or *a dog?* You also shape interview material by the questions you ask, the manner in which you conduct the interview, and the language of your notes. In other words, in field research, the manner in which you collect, record, and present information is most likely to introduce the bias that is the most difficult to control—your own.

WRITING ACROSS THE CURRICULUM

Questions to Ask Any Source, Any Discipline

- **Who?** What author or agency is speaking? If you are working with a printed or electronic document, run a name check on the World Wide Web or in the library catalog to find the author's credentials, or look in one of the library's invaluable *Who's Who* reference books. If you are checking an interview subject, examine any evidence of expertise available, from job title to neighborhood opinion. When a document has no verifiable authorship, it is not a strong source. In your main text, if you have important information about author credibility, include it in a signal phrase introducing quoted material.

- **What?** Whatever information in a source interests you, check at least two other sources claiming to have the same information and look for similarities and/or differences. In your main text, include some acknowledgment that you've checked more than one source.

- **Where?** Notice the location of the source: an article in an academic journal will count more than one in a popular magazine, which will count more than an anonymous Web site. In your main text, mention strong academic sources in a signal phrase or parentheses.

- **When?** How recent is the information? This year's is better than last, which is better than last decade, etc. In your main text, if your source is recent, include that information in a signal phrase or parentheses.

- **Why?** Sometimes it's apparent that a source exists with a particular bias—a media commercial promoting a new product, a newspaper editorial supporting government policy, electoral campaign literature, etc. Information from such sources is best balanced by information from more neutral sources as well. In your main text, acknowledge your awareness of biased sources.

chapter **16** *Using Research Sources*

Locating potential sources for a research project is difficult enough; deciding which ones to include, where to use them, and how to incorporate them is even more so. No matter how you begin writing with sources, there comes a time when you will need to incorporate them finally, smoothly, effectively, and correctly into your paper.

Serious research is vital and dynamic, which means it's always changing. Just as you can't expect your first working thesis to be your final thesis, your first outline to be your final, so you can't expect to know in advance which sources will be useful, and which won't. At each step in the process you see your research question more clearly and know better what sources you need to answer it. Similarly, and perhaps especially when engaging in field research, writers of research essays often gain an increased sense of audience as their research progresses, which pays off in increasingly reader-oriented writing.

16 a   Organizing sources

Control your sources rather than letting them control you, so outline your ideas independent of any research notes taken so far. This will be a working outline to remind you of where you intend to go. Outline first and you won't be tempted to find a place for every note and to gloss over areas where you haven't done enough research. Then arrange the bibliographic cards in alphabetical order, last name first, integrating field notes as best you can. Now, go back to your outline and annotate it according to which source goes where, noting especially areas where you have, as yet, no sources, so you can identify any ideas that need more research.

Next, decide on some balance among your sources so you remain the director of the research production, your ideas on center stage, and your sources as the supporting cast backing you up. Keep in mind that referring too often to a single source suggests overreliance on a single point of view. If you find yourself referring largely to one source, go get more to add other points of view to your paper.

16 b   Integrating information

The notes you made during your research may be in many forms: direct quotations, paraphrases, summaries, as well as interview and observation notes. As you write, make decisions about how to use sources based on your goals, not on the format of your research notes. Different disciplines have different conventions for documentation so be aware that the examples in this chapter use those of the Modern Language Association (MLA), the style preferred in English and foreign language departments. (For documentation styles of specific disciplines, see Chapters 19–22.)

Integrating Quotations into Your Paper

Direct quotations will be most effective when you integrate them smoothly into the flow of your paper. You can do this by introducing the source and reason for the quotation in a phrase or sentence. Readers should be able to follow your meaning easily and see the relevance of the quotation immediately.

Introduce Quotations

Readers need to know who is speaking, so introduce quoted material with a signal phrase (sometimes called an attributory phrase) so the reader knows the source and purpose of the quotation.

If the source is well known, name alone will be enough.

> Henry David Thoreau asserts in *Walden,* "The mass of men lead lives of quiet desperation" (5).

If your paper focuses on the published work itself, introduce a quotation with the work's title rather than the author's name, as long as the reference is clear.

Walden sets forth one individual's antidote against the "lives of quiet desperation" led by the working class in mid-nineteenth-century America (Thoreau 5).

If neither the author or source is well known, introduce the quotation with a brief explanation to give your readers enough context to understand the quotaton.

> Mary Catherine Bateson, daughter of anthropologist Margaret Mead, has become, in her own right, a student of modern civilization. In *Composing a Life,* she writes, "The twentieth century has been called the century of the refugee because of the vast numbers of people uprooted by war and politics from their homes" (8).

Quote Smoothly and Correctly

To use a *direct quotation* you must use an author's or speaker's exact words, though slight changes in wording are permitted so long as they are clearly marked. Although you can't change what a source says, you do have control over how much of it you use. Too much quotation can imply that you have little to say for yourself. Use only as long a quotation as you need to make your point.

To *shorten* a quotation, so that only the most important information is included, integrate it smoothly and correctly in the body of your paragraph to provide minimal disruption for your reader. Unless the source quoted is itself the topic of the paper (as in a literary interpretation), limit brief quotations to no more than two per page and long quotations to no more than one every three pages. The following examples illustrate both correct and incorrect use of quoted material.

ORIGINAL PASSAGE	The dialogue throughout the movie is once again its weakest point: The characters talk in what sounds like Basic English, without color, wit or verbal delight, as if they were channeling Berlitz. The exceptions are Palpatine and of course Yoda, whose speech (voiced by Frank Oz) reminds me of Wolcott Gibbs' famous line about the early style of *Time* magazine: "Backward ran sentences until reeled the mind." (Roger Ebert review of *Star Wars Episode III: Revenge of the Sith,* Roger Ebert.com)
DISTORTED QUOTATION	According to film critic Roger Ebert, all the characters in *Star Wars Episode III: Revenge of the Sith* "talk in what sounds like Basic English, without color, wit or verbal delight, as if they were channeling Berlitz."

The exceptions noted by Ebert in the original passage are missing.

ACCURATE QUOTATION	According to film critic Roger Ebert, all the characters, with the exceptions of Yoda and Palpatine, "talk in what sounds like Basic English, without color, wit or verbal delight, as if they were channeling Berlitz."

Omit or Substitute Words Judiciously

Cutting out words for the sake of brevity is often useful, but do not distort meaning. Indicate omitted words by using ellipsis points (three dots within a sentence, four to indicate a second sentence). Indicate any changes or additions with brackets. (See 54b and 55b for more on brackets and ellipses.)

<table>
<tr>
<td>DISTORTED
QUOTATION</td>
<td>In reviewing the last episode of the Star Wars saga, film critic Roger Ebert claims that, "The dialogue throughout the [Revenge of the Sith] . . . sounds like Basic English, without color, wit or verbal delight, as if they were channeling Berlitz."</td>
</tr>
</table>

While use of the ellipsis and brackets are technically correct, the missing words indicated by the ellipsis leave out Ebert's exceptions and again distort the meaning of the original passage.

Use Block Format for Long Quotations

Brief quotations should be embedded in the main body of your paper and enclosed in quotation marks. All of the previous examples are brief and would be embedded within paragraphs as normal sentences. According to MLA style guidelines, a brief quotation consists of four or fewer typed lines.

However, longer quotations (five or more lines) should be set off in block format, indented, but spaced the same as the normal text.

- Introduce the quotation in the last line of normal text with a sentence that ends with a colon.

- Indent ten spaces, then begin the quote. Do not use quotation marks because the indentation signals a direct quotation.

- Include the page number after end punctuation in parentheses.

> In *The Magical Classroom,* Michael Strauss says:
>
> > If they were candid, most magicians would say they are trying to entertain us by hiding the truth. They challenge us to discover what they have hidden. And we respond by trying to figure out the underlying causes of the magical effects and illusions we see. Like scientists, we search for the truth, for what might be hidden from our senses. (2)

Explain and Clarify Quotations

Sometimes you will need to explain a quotation in order to clarify why it's relevant and what it means in the context of your discussion.

> In *A Sand County Almanac,* Aldo Leopold invites modern urban readers to confront what they lose by living in the city: "There are two spiritual dangers in not owning a farm. One is the danger of supposing that

breakfast comes from the grocery, and the other that heat comes from the furnace" (6). Leopold sees city-dwellers as self-centered children, blissfully but dangerously unaware of how their basic needs are met.

You may also need to clarify what a word or reference means. Do this by using square brackets.

Adjust Grammar for Clarity

A passage containing a quotation must follow all the rules of grammatical sentence structure: tenses should be consistent, verbs and subjects should agree, and so on. If the form of the quotation doesn't quite fit the grammar of your own sentences, you can either quote less of the original source, change your sentences, or make a slight alteration in the quotation. Use this last option sparingly, and always indicate any changes with brackets.

UNCLEAR   In *A Sand County Almanac,* Aldo Leopold follows various animals, including a skunk and a rabbit, through fresh snow. He wonders, "What got him out of bed?" (5).

It is not clear whether "him" refers to the skunk or the rabbit.

CLEAR   In *A Sand County Almanac,* Aldo Leopold follows various animals, including a skunk and a rabbit, through fresh snow. He wonders, "What got [the skunk] out of bed?" (5).

GRAMMATICALLY   In *A Sand County Almanac,* Aldo Leopold said that living in
INCOMPATIBLE   the city is a "spiritual danger" if people "supposing that breakfast comes from the grocery."

To be grammatically correct, the writer needs to change supposing *from a gerund (-ing word) to the verb form* suppose. *One way is to make the change inside the quotation marks with brackets.*

GRAMMATICALLY   In *A Sand County Almanac,* Aldo Leopold said that living in
COMPATIBLE   the city is a "spiritual danger" if people "[suppose] that breakfast comes from the grocery."

Another option is to start the quotation one word later.

GRAMMATICALLY   In *A Sand County Almanac,* Aldo Leopold said that living in
COMPATIBLE   the city is a "spiritual danger" if people assume "that breakfast comes from the grocery."

Still another option is to recast the sentence completely.

GRAMMATICALLY   According to Aldo Leopold, city-dwellers who assume "that
COMPATIBLE   breakfast comes from the grocery" are out of tune with the world of nature (*A Sand County Almanac* 6).

16 c Paraphrasing

When you paraphrase, you restate a source's ideas in your own words. The point of paraphrasing is to make the ideas clearer by simplifying and explaining the author's original language to both your readers and to yourself, and to express the ideas in the way that best suits your purpose. In paraphrasing, attempt to preserve the intent of the original statement and to fit the paraphrased statement smoothly into the immediate context of your essay.

The best way to make an accurate paraphrase is to stay close to the order and structure of the original passage, to reproduce its emphasis and details. However, don't use the same sentence patterns or vocabulary or you risk inadvertently plagiarizing the source.

ESL Strategies for Paraphrasing

Writers who are inexperienced at paraphrasing in English sometimes just substitute synonyms for some of the author's words, keeping the sentence structure and many of the words the same. This kind of paraphrasing is unacceptable in academic writing; it can be considered a form of plagiarism. (See 17a.) Here are some suggestions that may help you write effective paraphrases:

- Before you begin writing a paraphrase of a sentence or passage, make sure that you understand the author's meaning. Look up in a dictionary any words you don't know, and ask a native speaker of English about any idioms or slang with which you are unfamiliar.

- Look away from the original source and put the ideas into your own words.

- If you are paraphrasing a passage, don't paraphrase the information one sentence at a time. Instead, try to express the meaning of the entire passage.

- Consider the context of the sentence or passage you are paraphrasing. Are there any references that are clear only from the surrounding sentences? Make sure you have given your readers enough information to understand your paraphrase.

- Use a thesaurus to find synonyms if you need to, but use only words you are familiar with. Not every synonym for a word listed in a thesaurus will be appropriate in your sentences.

If the original source has used a well-established or technical term for a concept, you do not need to find a synonym for it. If you believe that the original source's exact words are the best possible expressions of some points, you may use brief direct quotations within your paraphrase, as long as you indicate these with quotation marks.

ORIGINAL
PASSAGE

The affluent, educated, liberated women of the First world, who can enjoy freedom unavailable to any woman ever before, do not feel as free as they want to. And they can no longer restrict to the subconscious their sense that this lack of freedom has something to do with—with apparently frivolous issues, things that really should not matter. Many are ashamed to admit that such trivial concerns—to do with physical appearance, bodies, faces, hair, clothes—matter so much.

—NAOMI WOLF, *THE BEAUTY MYTH* (9)

INACCURATE
PARAPHRASE

In *The Beauty Myth,* Naomi Wolf argues that first world women, who still have less freedom than they would like to have, restrict to their subconscious those matters having to do with physical appearance—things that are not really important to them (9).

ACCURATE
PARAPHRASE

In *The Beauty Myth,* Naomi Wolf asserts that first world women, despite their affluence, education, and liberation, still do not feel very free. Moreover, many of these women are aware that this lack of freedom is influenced by superficial things having primarily to do with their physical appearance—things that should not matter so much (9).

16 d Summarizing

To distill a source's words down to the main ideas and state these in your own words is to summarize. A summary includes only the essentials of the original source, not the supporting details, and it is consequently shorter than the original. You should occasionally supplement summaries with brief direct quotations or evocative details collected through observation to keep readers in touch with the original source and avoid too much generalizing.

Summaries vary in length, and the length of the original source is not necessarily related to the length of the summary you write. Depending on the focus of your paper, you may need to summarize an entire novel in a sentence or two, or you may need to summarize a brief journal article in two or three paragraphs. Remember that the more material you attempt to summarize in a short space, the more you will necessarily generalize and abstract it. Reduce a text as far as you can while still providing all the information your readers need to know. Be careful, though, not to distort the original's meaning.

ORIGINAL
PASSAGE

For a long time I never liked to look a chimpanzee straight in the eye—I assumed that, as is the case with most primates, this would be interpreted as a threat or at least as a breach of good manners. Not so. As long as one looks with gentleness, without arrogance, a chimpanzee will understand and may even return the look.

—JANE GOODALL, *THROUGH A WINDOW* (12)

INACCURATE
SUMMARY   Goodall learned from her experiences with chimpanzees that they react positively to direct looks from humans (12).

ACCURATE
SUMMARY   Goodall reports that when humans look directly but gently into chimpanzees' eyes, the chimps are not threatened and may even return the look (12).

16 e Identifying Internet sources in signal phrases

When you quote, paraphrase, or summarize *authoritative* sources from the World Wide Web—and there are many such sources on the Web—you need to be sure to emphasize the nature of that authority when you introduce the source. Although library and field sources also need to be introduced carefully, readers don't regard them with quite the skepticism and distrust they've learned while surfing the Net.

For example, in looking for information about the zebra mussell infestation in Lake Champlain, a team of students located the following sources on the Internet, noting the first two, a university site (.edu) and a nonprofit site (.org), were more likely to be impartial than the third commercial site (.com).

Zebra Mussels and Other Nonindigenous Species
. . . **Zebra mussels** also had colonized New York's Finger **Lakes, Lake Champlain,** Wisconsin's **Lake** Winnebago, Kentucky **Lake,** and nearly 100 smaller inland **lakes . . .**
www.seagrant.wisc.edu/communications/great**lake**s/GLnetwork/exotics.html - 23k - Cached - Similar pages

Invasive Species Lake Champlain
. . . **Zebra Mussel** Monitoring Program - Excellent explanation of the **Lake Champlain** Basin Program's **Zebra Mussel** Monitoring program. . . .
www.lclt.org/invasive.htm - 47k - Cached - Similar pages]

Zebra Mussel filters by ZeeStop Filter designed to stop **Zebra Mussels**
. . . your **lake** water line from sand, silt and the ever present **Zebra Mussel** . . . **Lake Champlain,** Mississippi River, Erie Canal, Hudson River and most **lakes . . .**
www.zeestop.com/

However, the researchers used both educational and the commercial information in the two following examples by specifying in careful signal phrases what was to be learned from each source:

1. Information supplied by the University of Wisconsin Sea Grant Institute details the destructive nature of the zebra mussel in freshwater lakes:

> The prolific mollusk tends to biofoul and restrict the flow of water through intake pipes, disrupting supplies of drinking, cooling, processing and irrigating water to the nation's domestic infrastructure. The mussel also attaches to boat hulls, docks, locks, breakwaters and navigation aids, increasing maintenance costs and impeding waterborne transport.

2. The pesky zebra mussel had given rise to new commercial enterprises to help lakefront homeowners cope with the destructive mollusks. For example, Zeestop.com promises:

> The use of a Zeestop Filter should prolong the life of your entire plumbing system. Valve seats and washers should last longer without the grit that shortens their life expectance. Hot water tanks should not accumulate sediment brought in with the water, leading to longer element life. Other water filters such as carbon filters should not need to be replaced as often.

16 f   Incorporating visual images

It is easy to incorporate visual images into papers, portfolios, and Web pages to inform, entertain, and engage readers in ways text alone does not. Images are often included in verbal texts to break up dense textual space or signal a shift in content. While readers appreciate such images, they seldom pay close attention to them.

Whenever possible, use images to expand understanding rather than merely decorate the paper you're writing. Here are some possibilities:

- Use images that save you a thousand words. For example, many of the images that illustrate Chapter 5 in this handbook are especially rich in visual information.

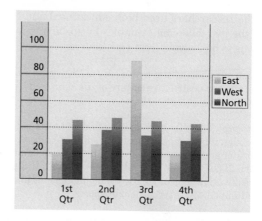

- Use images that convey useful information quickly in the shorthand way of charts and graphs, as does this *Regional Sales Distribution* chart above.

- Use images that make abstract ideas concrete. It would take a lot of words and a long time to describe a cartoon character such as a Smurf to somebody who had never seen the television show.

- Control the size and layout of images using a computer program such as *MS Paint* or *Adobe Photoshop* or by judicious cutting and pasting with scissors and tape.

- Position images where they belong—or as near as possible—in your text.

- Refer to an image in text to explain reason for its presence.

- Label each image appropriately, following conventions such as MLA style in formal papers (*Figure 1: Roadside Stand Near Birmingham, AL, by Walker Evans*) or more casually as we did with captions in Chapter 5.

- If publishing on a Web site, make sure image is in public domain (as is the Walker Evans photograph above) or secure permission from copyright holder.

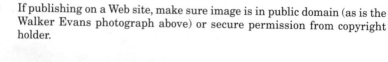

WRITING ACROSS THE CURRICULUM

Embedding Sources in Popular Literature

Whether you are writing for readers in college or out, you always need to credit your sources. The simplest way of giving credit is embedding source information directly in the sentence where the source is used and not attaching a separate reference page at the end. Embedded references are used in all the popular—as opposed to academic—periodicals, including *Time, Newsweek, Harpers', The New Yorker, The Atlantic Monthly, GQ, Sports Illustrated, Esquire, Elle,* etc., as well as in the *New York Times,* the *Los Angeles Times,* the *Washington Post,* and all the other local papers in the country.

Embedded references in more popular publications are not as detailed or precise as academic systems such as MLA or APA require (see Part Four of this handbook); however, they always include enough information for a curious reader to track down the source if necessary. For example, in Chapter 5 of this textbook, we identified photographs by photographer, title, and date without referring to more specific source location:

> When we look at the accompanying photograph, "Roadside Stand," taken by Walker Evans in 1936 Alabama, where do we start?

In choosing this embedded reference style, we knew that a curious reader could find more about a particular photo or photographer simply by conducting a search with that most wonderful research tool, Google!

In like manner, *The New Yorker* uses an embedded style, as illustrated in Jonathan Weiner's article, "The Tangle" (April 11, 2005):

> In August 2003, Cox and Banack reported in *Neurology* their discovery of high concentrations of BMAA in the bat tissues and in the cycad seeds.

While Weiner doesn't give us the volume number or page, interested readers can locate the Cox and Banack article should they wish to.

Another kind of embedded documentation is used in book reviews, where reviewers cite precise identifying information at the beginning of the review (title, author, total pages, publisher, price) but do not include specific page references when they include a quotation. For example, in reviewing *A Land of Ghosts,* by David Campbell, *New York Times* book reviewer Elizabeth Royte writes:

> Darwin gushed upon entering the Brazillian rain forest; Campbell writes more coolly, though with precision. At a rubber estate, "six hammocks are pregnant with indolent men."

So our advice is this: when writing college papers, always use the appropriate academic documentation for the discipline in which you are writing. However, when you are writing to an audience outside the academy, try embedded documentation. The bottom line is, one way or another, always credit your sources.

17

Avoiding Plagiarism

The rule is simple: When you use other people's ideas or language in writing a paper, you need to give credit to those people whose ideas and words you have used. If you don't, you have stolen their ideas or words and are guilty of plagiarism. In Western culture, plagiarism is a serious offense, one that has cost writers, reporters, artists, musicians, and scientists their reputations, jobs, and enormous amounts of money. Recent charges of plagiarism against historian Doris Kearns Goodwin, *New York Times* journalist Jayson Blair, and even the late civil-rights leader Dr. Martin Luther King, Jr., have cast shadows on their otherwise excellent reputations. Plagiarism is especially serious within academic communities where the generation of original research, ideas, and words is the central mission of the institution.

In fact, students who knowingly plagiarize cheat both themselves and their sources. Perhaps the primary value of writing in the first place is the author's right—nay, duty—to shape knowledge according to his or her own unique point of view and voice. In essense, to plagiarize is to forfeit one's independence of thought and settle for intellectual conformity, laziness, and dishonesty. Whew! You lose a lot when you copy rather than create.

Unfortunately, the Internet, which puts a world of research at the writer's fingertips, has also made the copying of research sources especially easy—which is a blessing to serious writers but a potential problem for casual or dishonest writers who do not treat their copied sources with the respect they deserve. In other words, the ease of blocking-copying-pasting almost any Internet source has also made both intentional and unintentional plagiarism especially easy. To avoid plagiarizing, you need to know exactly *what it is* and *how to avoid committing it*.

17 a What plagiarism *is*

Plagiarism is putting one's name on a paper written by a friend and passing it in. Plagiarism is buying a term paper from an Internet term-paper factory and pretending to have written it. Plagiarism is downloading a report from the Internet and pretending to have written it. And plagiarism is pasting in a phrase, sentence, paragraph, passage, or portion of anybody else's work in any paper and not giving that author credit. In any of these flagrant examples, the intent to plagiarize is deliberate and obvious, something that serious and honorable students would never do.

However, plagiarism also occurs when well-meaning students get careless in taking notes from library or Internet sources or in copying those notes into paper drafts. Following are four examples of *unintentional* plagiarism:

(1) A student copies a passage word-for-word from an Internet site and pastes it word-for-word into a paper but forgets to include quotation marks or author attribution. (2) A student summarizes, but does not directly quote, a published author's idea and omits both author name and source title. (3) A student credits an author's idea in a signal phrase (According to John Smith . . .) but omits quotation marks around the author's exact phrases. (4) A conscientious student includes borrowed sources on a Bibliography page but neglects to acknowledge it in the text itself. None of these may be intentional, but each is an act of plagiarism, and each could be easily avoided by clearer knowledge and more careful research and writing practice.

17 b   What plagiarism is *not*

Writers don't need to attribute everything they write or say to specific sources. For example, what we call *common knowledge* does not need documentation. You do not need to credit common historical, cultural, or geographical information that an educated adult American person can be expected to know. Nor do you need to attribute to specific authorities the factual information that appears in multiple sources such as the dates of historical events (the sack of Rome in 410 AD, the Declaration of Independence in 1776), the names and locations of states and cities, the general laws of science (gravity, motion), or statements of well-known theories (feminism, liberalism, evolution).

You don't need to document phrases in widespread use in your own culture (global warming, cloning, urban sprawl). Nor do you need to document what is well known in the field in which you are writing that can be found in textbooks and lectures. For example, in a paper written about Sigmund Freud for a psychology professor, don't document the terms *libido* or *superego*. In a paper written for English, history, art, or philosophy, don't document *Victorian, the Roaring Twenties, modern,* or *postmodern*. In other words, within a given interpretive community, basic ideas and knowledge can be assumed to be the common property of all members of that community. However, specific positions or interpretations within a community do need to be specifically identified: how fellow psychotherapists Jung and Adler viewed Freud; how one specific critic viewed Victorian manners compared to another critic; and so on.

Nor do you need to document useful suggestions from friends, classmates, parents, instructors, tutors, or writing groups about possible changes to a paper you are writing. In such cases, if their suggestions proved especially useful, you might write a short endnote thanking them for their help. Such notes do not show up on Reference or Works Cited pages.

However, if you have borrowed ideas in any of the common knowledge situations illustrated above and you quote an author's formulation exactly, you need to put the author's words in quotation marks and acknowledge it on a reference page.

Finally, most colleges and universities have codes of academic integrity or honor published on their Web sites and in their catalogs. At some institutions, for instance, it is a violation of institutional rules to submit the same paper to more than one instructor. At another institution a student taking two deliberately linked courses, say English and History, may actually be required to submit the same paper to two instructors. Be sure to check the particular policies that govern your institution.

17 c Recognizing and avoiding plagiarism

Intentional plagiarism is simply cheating, which honest students avoid. *Unintentional plagiarism,* a far more common problem, occurs when a writer paraphrases or summarizes another author but stays too close to the wording or sentence structure of the original. The following examples will help you avoid unintentional plagiarism. This first example shows the student writing a paper on Machiavelli's *The Prince,* where he is citing a scholarly text:

Original

Notwithstanding the widely different opinions about Machiavelli's work and his personality, there is at least one point in which we find a complete unanimity. All authors emphasize that Machiavelli is a child of his age, that he is a typical witness to the Renaissance.

—ERNST CASSIRER, *THE MYTH OF THE STATE*

Plagiarized Paraphrase

Despite the widely different opinions about Machiavelli's work and his personality, everyone agrees that he is a representative witness to the Renaissance (Cassirer 43).

Even though Cassirer is credited with the idea, the writer does not credit him with the specific wording that the writer has copied almost word for word.

Acceptable Paraphrase

Although views on the work and personality of Machiavelli vary, everyone agrees that he was "a typical witness to the Renaissance" (Cassirer 43).

In this second example, from a popular culture source, the student is writing a paper for a film professor about comic book heroes portrayed in the movies. She decides to use this passage in Roger Ebert's review of *Spider-Man* for *Chicago Sun-Times,* May 3, 2002:

Remember the first time you saw the characters defy gravity in *Crouching Tiger, Hidden Dragon?* They transcended gravity, but they didn't dismiss it: They seemed to possess weight, dimension and presence. Spider-Man as he leaps across the rooftops is landing too lightly, rebounding too much like a bouncing ball. He looks like a video game figure, not like a person having an amazing experience.

Ebert's whole review is readily available on the Internet, easily accessed via the Internet Movie Database (http://www.imdb.com/), so that it's especially easy to block and copy parts to paste directly into the paper you are writing instead of onto a notecard for further study. *(In an*

Guidelines for Avoiding Plagiarism

Plagiarism is a serious offense in every field and department across the curriculum. In simplest terms, it's the act of copying somebody else's work and passing it off as your own. In addition to the many obvious cases described in this chapter, it's also plagiarism to copy the results of a neighbor's biology experiment in your lab report; it's plagiarism to copy a chart or graph from an economics textbook and not attribute it; and it's a form of plagiarism to hand in somebody else's field notes and claim them as yours. Below are simple guidelines for avoiding plagiarism:

- For all copied sources, note *who said what, where,* and *when.*

- When using quoted material, do not distort or intentionally modify an author's meaning.

- Print out and save at least the first page of all online material, making sure it contains the Internet address and date.

- Hand copy identifying information (name, title, date, place of publication) on all photocopied or printed source pages.

- In using direct quotations, place all exactly copied language in quotation marks.

- In writing a paraphrase or summary, credit the author *and* recast the original material into your own language.

- Identify all borrowed ideas and language with appropriate references using the appropriate documentation system (MLA, APA, CMS, etc.).

academic paper, the citation would appear on a "Works Cited" (MLA) or "Reference" (APA, CMS) page; if academic style is not required, including author and title in a signal phrase would give proper credit.) If the research writer does not follow proper citation guidelines, he or she might inadvertently plagiarize, as the following examples illustrate.

- It is plagiarism if the student cut and pasted the *Spider-Man* passage above directly into the paper without acknowledging that it was written by Roger Ebert.

  - To fix, credit in a signal phrase (*According to Roger Ebert . . .*), put the passage in quotation marks, and in an academic paper, identify where the passage came from and when it was published on a "Works Cited" page (MLA), "References" page (APA), or footnote (CMS) page as appropriate (see Chapters 19–22).

- It is plagiarism if the student wrote:

  > *The problem with* Spider-Man *is the video-game quality of the characters who bound from roof to roof and don't seem to be affected by gravity—unlike the more realistic figures in the movie* Crouching Tiger, Hidden Dragon.

  - In this case the student lifts Ebert's idea in clearly identifiable ways but does not quote Ebert directly. To fix, credit in a signal phrase (***Roger Ebert claims** the problem with* Spider-Man *is the video-game quality . . .*) and, if an academic paper, identify where the passage came from and when it was published in the appropriate academic convention.

- It is plagiarism if the student lifted key portions of Ebert's exact language from the passage without using quotation marks:

  > *Roger Ebert claims that the characters in* Crouching Tiger, Hidden Dragon *transcended gravity, but they didn't dismiss it.*

 Plagiarism in American English

In many countries, it is customary to use another writer's words in your writing. This is done to demonstrate knowledge; to honor intellectuals, writers or philosophers; or to rely on the words of an authority to add credibility to your writing. In this country, however, if you are not extremely careful about diligently acknowledging each time you use the words, thoughts, or teachings of someone else, you will be accused of plagiarism. It is not enough to rearrange the words or to replace them with synonyms; even if you completely rewrite the words of the original, you are still borrowing the ideas of another person. U.S. schools treat the idea of plagiarism very seriously, and you could find yourself in serious trouble if ever accused of plagiarizing. Talk to your instructors to make sure you really understand what they mean by quoting, paraphrasing, and summarizing another writer's words.

■ Though Ebert is credited with the idea, he is not credited with the specific language. To fix, put quotation marks around the words borrowed: *Roger Ebert claims that the characters in* Crouching Tiger, Hidden Dragon *"transcended gravity, but they didn't dismiss it."* Again, if this is an academic paper, identify where the passage came from and when it was published on the appropriate reference page.

WRITING ACROSS THE CURRICULUM

The Pros and Cons of Anti-Plagiarism Software

The Internet offers powerful software for identifying suspicious sources of information in any text, including Internet search engines and subscription programs that claim to locate even more sources. For a brief summary of each method—along with an opposing view to both—see below.

Search it Yourself
The American University of Beirut suggests using Internet search engines that allow searching exact phrases or even whole sentences (through "advanced search"). To search, choose unusual phrases in the text and copy them in a search engine within "inverted commas." The following search engines will bring to you all Internet documents in which the phrase appears AND which were indexed in its huge database:

AlltheWeb www.alltheweb.com/

AltaVista: www.altavista.com

Google: www.google.com

Dogpile: www.dogpile.com

HotBot: www.hotbot.com/

MetaCrawler: www.metacrawler.com

If the suspicious phrase is not found, remember that (1) no search engine covers all Internet pages and (2) Portable Document Format (PDF) files are not accessed by many search engines. For more information see wwwlb.aub.edu.lb/~eplagio/Ident_plag.htm and www.robcol.k12.tr/library/teachers/detectplagiarism.

Anti-Plagiarism Sofware
Claremont McKenna College surveyed faculty, students, and relevant support staff that assessed the relative effectiveness of anti-plagiarism programs including Prentice Hall, Turn It In, and the universities of Michigan and Purdue. writing.claremontmckenna.edu/Examining.

The top-rated program for teaching students about plagiarism was the Prentice Hall Companion Website:

- **The Prentice Hall Companion Website "Understanding Plagiarism."** This program identifies two goals: 1) to help you understand what plagiarism is, and how to avoid it, and 2) how to atribute, quote, summarize, paraphrase, and cite a reference source. wps.prenhall.com/ hss_understand_plagiarism.

The most effective program for detecting student plagiarism proved to be the most popular, Turn It In:

- ***Turn It In*** One of the most popular anti-plagiarism programs will check a student's paper for more than eight consecutive words in common with another source; if a matching source is located, the copied words are highlighted, alerting the instructor to possible plagiarism. www.turnitin.com/.

Anti-Anti-Plagiarism Software
Student leaders at Mount Saint Vincent University in Bedford (Nova Scotia, CA) have won faculty support to ban the use of anti-plagiarism software on campus: "Students go to university for a higher education. They don't go to be involved in a culture of mistrust, a culture of guilt," said Chantal Brushett, president of the students' union. www.cbc.ca/ns/story/ ns-msvu-plagiarism.

ood writing satisfies the expectations of an audience in form, style, and content. But different audiences come to a piece of writing with different expectations, so writing that is judged "good" by one audience may be judged "less good" by another. Although all college instructors value good writing, each area of study has its own set of criteria by which writing is judged. For instance, humanities and literature instructors may be especially pleased with the loose form, informal style, and speculative content of a reflective essay, while social science instructors may be more comfortable with the predictable format and more neutral voice of a position paper. At the same time, exceptions to such general expectations are many. This chapter provides a broad outline of common differences and expectations among different disciplines as well as important similarities for writing across the curriculum.

18 a Differences among disciplines

As a rule, knowledge in the humanities focuses on texts and on individual ideas, speculations, insights, and imaginative connections. Interpretation in the humanities is thus relatively subjective. Accordingly, good writing in the humanities is characterized by personal involvement, lively language, and speculative or open-ended conclusions.

In contrast, knowledge in the social and physical sciences is likely to focus on data and on ideas that can be verified through observing, measuring, and testing. Interpretation in these disciplines needs to be objective.

Accordingly, good writing in the social and physical sciences emphasizes inferences based on the careful study of data and downplays the personal opinion and speculation of the writer.

But boundaries between the disciplines are not absolute. For example, at some colleges history is considered one of the humanities, while at others it is classified as a social science. Geography is a social science when it looks at regions and how people live, but it is a physical science when it investigates the properties of rocks and glaciers. Colleges of business, engineering, health, education, and natural resources all draw on numerous disciplines as their sources of knowledge.

The field of English alone includes not only the study of literature but also literary theory and history, not only composition but also creative and technical writing. In addition, English departments often include linguistics, journalism, folklore, women's studies, African American studies, and sometimes speech, film, and communications. In other words, within even one discipline, you might be asked to write several distinct types of papers: personal experience essays for a composition course, interpretations for a literature course, abstracts for a linguistics course, short stories for a creative writing course. Consequently, any observations about the different kinds of knowledge and the differing conventions for writing about them are only generalizations. The more carefully you study any one discipline, the more complex it becomes, and the harder it is, make a generalization that doesn't have numerous exceptions.

Formal differences exist among the styles of writing for different disciplines, especially in the conventions for documenting sources. Each discipline has its own authority or authorities that provide rules about such issues as spelling technical terms, preferred punctuation, editing mechanics, as well as documentation style. To cite one specific example, the method of documenting sources within the text of an English paper, is to lead with the author and follow with title of the work, then the page number (Machiavelli, *The Prince* 18), following proper Modern Language Association (MLA) style. In contrast, the same citation in a social science, such as political science, would follow the conventions of the American Psychological Association (APA), and include the author's name followed by date of publication, then the page number (Machiavelli, 1517, p. 18).

The reason for the difference? The study of literature places primary importance on the uniqueness of an individual's work, less on how recently it was published, as one novel, play, or poem seldom builds directly on another. In contrast, the social sciences place primary importance on the timeliness of a study, as one work is expected to build directly on preceding work in the field. These differences are carried through on the Works Cited page in MLA which includes each author's full name (Machiavelli, Niccolo), while authors on an APA Reference page are identified only by initials (Machiavelli, N.). For more information on why MLA differs from APA, see Chapters 19a and 20a.

In addition, if you write for publication in a magazine, professional journal, or book, the publisher will have a *house style,* which may vary in some details from the conventions listed in the authoritative guidelines for the discipline in which you are writing. The following table lists the sources of style manuals for various disciplines.

DISCIPLINE	STYLE
Languages and literature	Modern Language Association (MLA) (See Chapter 19.)
Social sciences	American Psychological Association (APA) (See Chapter 20.)
Humanities	*Chicago Manual of Style* (CMS) (See Chapter 21.)
Sciences	
Life sciences	Council of Science Editors (CSE) (See Chapter 22.)
Chemistry	American Chemical Society
Physics	American Institute of Physics (AIP) (See Chapter 22.)
Business	Varies (See Chapter 23.)
Journalism	Associated Press (AP)
Medicine	American Medical Association (AMA)

18 b Similarities among disciplines

Regardless of disciplinary differences, certain principles of good writing hold true across the curriculum.

Good Writing Is Grounded in a Field of Disciplinary Knowledge.

Each field of study attempts to develop knowledge about a particular aspect of the physical, social, or cultural world in which we live. For example, the physical sciences observe nature to learn how it works, while

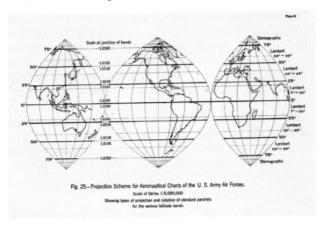

Fig. 25—Projection Scheme for Aeronautical Charts of the U. S. Army Air Forces.
Scale of Series 1:5,000,000
Showing types of projection and notation of standard parallels
for the various latitude bands.

history and anthropology examine civilizations over time, sociology looks at human beings in groups, and psychology attempts to explain the operation and development of the individual human mind. In writing for a particular course, keep in mind the larger purpose of the field of study, especially when selecting, introducing, and concluding your investigation.

Good Writing Follows Disciplinary Methods of Inquiry.

Each field has accepted methods of investigation. Perhaps the best known is the scientific method, used in most of the physical and social sciences. One who uses the scientific method first asks a question, then poses a possible answer (a hypothesis), then carries out experiments in the field or in a laboratory to test this answer, and finally, if it cannot be disproved, concludes that the hypothesis is correct. However, while research in the

social sciences follows this scientific pattern, some disciplines, such as anthropology, rely instead on the more personal approach of ethnographic study. Literary research may be formal, historical, deconstructive, and so on. It is important to recognize that every discipline has its accepted—and its controversial—methods of study. Any conclusions you discuss in your writing should reflect that awareness.

Good Writing Argues Its Claims Through Relevant Evidence.

In every field, any claim you make about the subject of your study needs to be supported by evidence. If, in order to identify an unknown rock, you scrape it with a known rock in the geology laboratory, the scratch marks of the harder rock on the softer rock will be part of your evidence to support your claims about the unknown rock. If you analyze Holden Caulfield on the basis of his opening monologue in *The Catcher in the Rye,* his words will be evidence to support your interpretation. If you conduct a survey of students to examine college study habits, counting and collating your findings will be evidence to support your conclusions. In other words, although the *nature* of evidence varies greatly from one discipline to another, the *need* for evidence is constant. In some cases, when you need to support an assertion, you will consult certain sources for evidence and will need to have clear documentation for these sources. (Chapters 19–23 provide detailed guidelines for documenting sources in various disciplines.)

Good Writing Is Clear, Honest, and Accurate.

Each field values clarity, honesty, and accuracy, and each has its own specialized vocabulary for talking about these qualities. Writers are expected to explain terms carefully and use them precisely, according to disciplinary conventions. They are expected to acknowledge—not avoid—problems about the ideas they present. In addition, when you write within a discipline, you should know the correct form in which to communicate a literary analysis in English, a research report in sociology, or a laboratory report in biology. Each discipline also values conventional correctness in language. Your writing will be most respected when it reflects standard use of grammar, punctuation, and mechanics.

chapter 19 | *MLA: Writing in Languages and Literature*

This chapter describes the aims, style, and forms required for most kinds of writing in English, comparative literature, and foreign languages, where the primary focus is on the study of texts. Many specialized areas, such as film and cultural studies, also follow the conventions described here. Papers in language and literature use the documentation system of the Modern Language Association (MLA).

19 a   Aims

Language and literature courses are concerned with reading and writing about texts such as poems, novels, plays, and essays written by published authors as well as by students. (The term *text* is defined here broadly to include films, visual arts, advertisements—anything that can be read and interpreted.) What sets literary studies apart from most other disciplines, including others in the humanities, is the attention devoted to all elements of written language. In these courses, writing is not only the means of study but often the object of study as well: Works are examined for their *form* and *style* as well as their *content*. Texts are read, listened to, discussed, and written about so students can discover what these texts are, how they work, what they mean, and what makes them exceptional or flawed. Moreover, literary studies often draw on ideas from other disciplines. For instance, reading a single novel such as Charles Dickens's *David Copperfield* can teach readers a little about sociology, psychology, history, geography, architecture, political science, and economics, as well as the esthetics of novel writing.

When you write in language and literature, you can focus on a text's ideas, authors, formal qualities, or themes. For such essays, you usually refer mainly to primary sources, the text itself and perhaps other works to which you may compare it. You can also consider the culture that produced the text, the text's relationship to other texts, its place in history, and its politics. You may refer to secondary sources, writing by others about the text or about the context in which the primary text was written. Modern literary study may engage in any of five basic activities with texts:

- **Appreciating** texts. You write about the text's most moving or interesting features, the beauty or strangeness of the setting, the character with whom you most identify, the plot as it winds from beginning to end, or the turns and rhythms of the language.

- **Analyzing** texts. You ask questions such as *How is it put together?* or *How does it work?* Analysis involves looking at a text's component parts (chapters, for example) and the system that makes it work as a whole (such as the plot), defining what they are, describing what they are like, and explaining how they function.

- **Interpreting** texts. You ask, *What does it mean? How do I know what it means?* and *Why was it made?* Interpretations often vary widely from reader to reader and may provoke quite a bit of disagreement.

- **Evaluating** texts. *How good is it? What makes it worth reading?* and *How does it compare with other texts?* These are questions of judgment, based on criteria that might differ considerably from person to person. One reader might judge a poem good because its rhythm and imagery are pleasing (esthetic criteria), while another reader may praise the same poem because it subverts common assumptions about power relationships (political criteria), and a third may do so because it evokes fond childhood memories (personal criteria). However, a fourth reader might look for underlying assumptions or values (philosophical criteria), and a fifth might contrast it to another poet's work (comparative criteria).

- **Inferring cultural values.** You can also use literature to study culture by asking, *What are the values of the people depicted in the text?* and *How do the scenes, settings, and characters reveal the character of the broader culture?* To find answers to these and other questions, it is common to compare the text with other texts produced at the same time or different times.

MLA MLA MLA

19 b Style

Writing in languages and literature demands clarity, variety, and vitality to create a strong connection between the writer and reader. Direct, unpretentious language and an engaging tone are valued over obscure terminology and an artificially formal style. Observing the standard conventions of grammar, punctuation, and mechanics is expected, as are creative deviations.

Because literary studies center so closely on the multitude of ways readers approach texts, writing can range from the highly personal to the highly theoretical, from deeply impressionistic to sharply rational, from journalistic to experimental to political. Indeed, a single essay may knit together all these styles.

As a student, you may do much of your writing in language and literature in a relatively conventional academic style—asserting a thesis and supporting it with textual evidence and reasoned insight. But do not be surprised if you find yourself responding in different styles and voices for different kinds of assignments.

The MLA system is explained in more detail in the *MLA Handbook for Writers of Research Papers,* seventh edition (New York: MLA, 2009) aimed specifically at undergraduate writers, as well as *The MLA Style Manual and Guide to Scholarly Publishing,* third edition (2008) aimed at graduate students and faculty.

19 c Guidelines for formatting manuscripts

The MLA guidelines for submitting college papers are fairly conservative and do not reflect the wealth of visually interesting fonts, type sizes, graphics, and other options available with most modern word processing programs. If your instructor requests MLA format, follow the guidelines below. If your instructor encourages more open journalistic formats, use good judgment in displaying the information in your text.

Paper and Printing

Print all academic assignments on 8½″ ×11″ white paper, in a standard font (for example, Times New Roman or Courier) and type size (11 or 12 point), using a good-quality printer.

Margins and Spacing

Allow margins of one inch all around. Justify the left margin only. Double space everything, including headings, quoted material, and the Works Cited page. Indent five spaces for paragraphs.

Indent ten spaces for prose quotations of five or more lines or poetry of more than three lines. (Do not use quotation marks around these long quotations. See 53a.)

Identification

On page 1, include your name, your instructor's name, the course title, and the date on separate lines, double spaced, flush with the upper left margin.

Title

Center the title on the first page, capitalizing key words only. If your instructor asks for strict MLA style, avoid using italics, underlining, quotation marks, boldface type, unusual fonts, or large type for the title. (MLA does not require a title page or an outline.) Double space to the first paragraph.

Page Numbers

Print page numbers in the upper right margin, one-half inch below the top of the paper. If you are following strict MLA format, include your last name before each page number to guarantee correct identification of stray pages (*Turner 1, Turner 2*).

Punctuation

One space is required after commas, semicolons, colons, periods, question marks, and exclamation points and between the periods in an ellipsis. Dashes are formed by two hyphens, with no extra spacing on either side.

Visual Information

Label each table or chart as *Table 1, Table 2,* and so on. Label each drawing or photograph as *Figure 1* or *Fig. 2,* and so on. Include a clear caption for each figure, and place the figure in the text as near as possible to the passage that refers to it.

19 d   Guidelines for in-text citations

The MLA system provides a simple, concise, and thorough way for writers to acknowledge their research sources. In the MLA system, authors use footnotes and/or endnotes to provide additional, explanatory information, but not to cite information provided by external sources. Whenever possible, the MLA system includes explanatory information in the text itself and limits the use of footnotes or endnotes. Pay careful attention to the practical mechanics of documentation so that readers can readily identify, understand, and locate your sources.

- All sources are briefly documented in the text by an identifying name and page number (generally in parentheses).

- A Works Cited section at the end of the paper lists full publication data for each source cited.

- Additional explanatory information provided by the writer of the paper (not by external sources) goes either in footnotes at the foot of the page or in a Notes section after the close of the paper.

The following examples illustrate the most common types of in-text citations.

1. Author identified in a signal phrase

When you include the author's name in the sentence introducing the source, add only the specific page on which the material appeared, in parentheses following the information.

> Carol Lea Clark explains the basic necessities for the
> creation of a page on the World Wide Web (77).

Do not include the word *page* or the abbreviation *p.* before the number. The parenthetical reference comes before the period.

For a work by two or three authors, include all authors' names.

> Clark and Jones explain. . . .

For works with more than three authors, list all authors or use the first author's name and add *et al.* (Latin abbreviation for "and others") without a comma.

> Britton et al. suggest . . .

2. Author not identified in a signal phrase

When you do not include the author's name in your text, add it in parentheses along with the source page number. Do not punctuate between the author's name and the page number(s).

> Provided one has certain "basic ingredients," the Web
> offers potential worldwide publication (Clark 77).

For a work by two or three authors, include all authors' last names.

> (Smith, Web, and Beck 210)

For works with more than three authors, list all authors' last names or list the first author only, adding *et al.*

> (White et al. 95)

3. Two or more works by the same author

If your paper refers to two or more works by the same author, each citation needs to identify the specific work. Either mention the title of the work in the text or include a shortened version of the title (usually the first one or two important words) in the parenthetical citation. There are three correct ways to do this.

> According to Lewis Thomas in *Lives of a Cell*, many bacteria become dangerous only if they manufacture exotoxins (76).

> According to Lewis Thomas, many bacteria become dangerous only if they manufacture exotoxins (*Lives* 76).

> Many bacteria become dangerous only if they manufacture exotoxins (Thomas, *Lives* 76).

Identify the shortened title by italicizing (for books and other long works) or quotation marks (for short works, such as articles in periodicals) as appropriate. Put a comma between the author's last name and the title.

4. Unknown author

When the author of a work is unknown, give either the complete title in the text or a shortened version in the parenthetical citation, along with the page number.

> According to *Statistical Abstracts*, in 1990 the literacy rate for Mexico stood at 75 percent (374).

> In 1990 the literacy rate for Mexico stood at 75 percent (*Statistical* 374).

5. Corporate or organizational author

When no author is listed for a work published by a corporation, foundation, organization, or association, indicate the group's full name either in the text or in parentheses.

> (Florida League of Women Voters 3)

If the name is long, cite it in the sentence and put only the page number in parentheses.

6. Authors with the same last name

When you cite works by two or more authors with the same last name, include the first initial of each author's name in the parenthetical citation.

> (C. Miller 63; S. Miller 101-04)

7. Works in more than one volume

Indicate the pertinent volume number for each citation before the page number, and follow it with a colon and one space.

> (Hill 2: 70)

If your source is one volume of a multivolume work, do not specify the volume number in your text, but specify it in the Works Cited list.

8. One-page works

When you refer to a work that is one page long, do not include the page number, since that will appear in the Works Cited list.

9. Quotation from a secondary source

When a quotation or any information in your source is originally from another source, use the abbreviation *qtd. in.*

> Lester Brown of Worldwatch feels that international
>
> agricultural production has reached its limit (qtd. in
>
> Mann 51).

10. Poem or play

In citing poems, name the part (if divided into parts) and line numbers; include the word *line* or *lines* in the first such reference. This information will help your audience find the passages in any source where those works are reprinted, which page references alone cannot provide.

> In "The Mother," Gwendolyn Brooks remembers
>
> "the children you got that you did not get" (line 1).

When you cite up to three lines from a poem in your text, separate the lines with slash marks. (See 55c.)

> Emily Dickinson describes being alive in a New England
>
> summer: "Inebriate of air am I / And debauchee of dew /
>
> Reeling through endless summer days" (lines 6–8).

When you cite more than three lines, use a block quotation and indent ten spaces.

Cite verse plays using act, scene, and line numbers, separated by periods. For major works, such as *Hamlet,* use identifiable abbreviations.

> (*Ham.* 4.4.31-39)

11. More than one work in a citation

To cite two or more works, separate them with semicolons.

> (Aronson, *Golden Shore* 177; Didion 49-50)

Note that more than one work by Aronson is cited in this paper, so the title is given as well.

12. Long quotation set off from text

To set off quoted prose passages of five or more lines, indent one inch or ten spaces from the left-hand margin of the text, double space, and omit quotation marks. The parenthetical citation *follows* end punctuation (unlike citations for shorter, integrated quotations) and is not followed by a period.

> Fellow author W. Somerset Maugham had this to say
>
> about Austen's dialogue:
>
>> No one has ever looked upon Jane Austen as a great
>>
>> stylist. Her spelling was peculiar and her grammar often
>>
>> shaky, but she had a good ear. Her dialogue is probably as
>>
>> natural as dialogue can ever be. To set down on paper
>>
>> speech as it is spoken would be very tedious, and some
>>
>> arrangement of it is necessary. (434)

13. Electronic texts

The MLA guidelines for documenting online sources are explained in detail online at http://www.mla.org.

Electronic sources are cited in the body of the text in the same style as print sources: by author, title of text or Web site, and page numbers. If no page numbers appear in the source, include section (*sec.*) number or title and/or paragraph (*par.*) numbers.

> *The Wizard of Oz* "was nominated for six Academy
>
> Awards, including Best Picture" (Wizard par. 3).

However, Web pages commonly omit page and section numbers and are not organized by paragraphs. In such cases, omit numbers from your parenthetical references. (For a document downloaded from the Web, the page numbers of a printout should normally not be cited, since pagination may vary in different printouts.)

> In the United States, the birthrate per 1,000 people has
>
> fallen steadily from 16.7 in 1995 to 14.6 in 1998 (*Statistical*).

14. Endnotes and footnotes

MLA style uses notes primarily to offer comments, explanations, or additional information (especially source-related information) that cannot be smoothly or easily accommodated in the text of the paper. In general, however, you should omit additional information that is outside the main body of your paper, unless it is necessary for clarification or justification. If a note is necessary, insert a raised (superscript) numeral at the reference point in the text. Introduce the note itself with a corresponding raised numeral, and indent it.

TEXT WITH SUPERSCRIPT

The standard ingredients for guacamole include avocados, lemon juice, onion, tomatoes, coriander, salt, and pepper.[1] Hurtado's poem, however, gives this traditional dish a whole new twist (lines 10-17).

NOTE

[1] For variations see Beard 314, Egerton 197, and Eckhardt 92. Beard's version, which includes olives and green peppers, is the most unusual.

Any published reference listed in the notes also appears in the Works Cited list.

Notes may come as footnotes at the bottom of the page on which the citation appears, or they may be included as endnotes, double spaced on a separate page at the end of your paper. Endnote pages should be placed between the body of the paper and the Works Cited list, with the title *Note* or *Notes.*

19 e   Conventions for the list of Works Cited

Every source mentioned in the body of your paper should be identified in a list of works cited attached to the end of the paper using the following format.

■   Center the title *Works Cited,* with no quotation marks, underlining, italicizing or boldface, one inch from the top of a separate page following the final page of the paper. (If you are asked to include works read but not cited, attach an additional page titled *Works Consulted.*)

■   Number this page, following in sequence from the last text page of your paper. If the list runs more than a page, continue the page numbering in sequence, but do not repeat the title *Works Cited.*

- Double space between the title and first entry and within and between entries.

- Begin each entry at the left-hand margin, and indent subsequent lines the equivalent of a paragraph indention (five spaces or one-half inch).

Order of Entries

Alphabetize entries according to authors' last names. If an author is unknown, alphabetize according to the first word of the title (but do not use an initial *A, An,* or *The*).

Entry Formats

Each item in the entry begins with a capital letter and is followed by a period. Each period is followed by one space. Capitalize all major words in the book and article titles. Italicize published titles (books, periodicals); put quotation marks around titles of chapters, articles, stories, and poems within published works. Do not italicize volume and issue numbers or end punctuation. Four variations on general formats are common.

BOOKS

ONE SPACE   ONE SPACE   ONE SPACE
Author(s). | *Book Title.* | Place of publication: |

INDENT 1/2 INCH—Publisher, | year of publication. | Medium of publication.
                  ONE SPACE   ONE SPACE

JOURNAL ARTICLES

ONE SPACE   ONE SPACE   ONE SPACE, NO PUNCTUATION
Author(s). | "Article Title." | *Journal Title* | volume
                                    ONE SPACE   ONE SPACE
INDENT 1/2 INCH—number.issue number (year of publication): | inclusive page numbers. |
Medium of publication.

MAGAZINE AND NEWSPAPER ARTICLES

ONE SPACE   ONE SPACE   ONE SPACE, NO PUNCTUATION
Author(s). | "Article Title." | *Publication Title* | date
                  ONE SPACE   ONE SPACE
INDENT 1/2 INCH—of publication: | inclusive page numbers. | Medium of publication.

ELECTRONIC SOURCES

ONE SPACE   ONE SPACE   ONE SPACE
Author(s). | "Title of the work." | *Title of the overall Web site.* |
                                    ONE SPACE
INDENT 1/2 INCH—Version or edition used. | Publisher or sponsor of the
          ONE SPACE   ONE SPACE
          site, | Date of publication. | Medium of
                      ONE SPACE
          publication. | Date of access.

AUTHORS

■ List the author's last name first, followed by a comma and then the rest of the name as it appears on the publication, followed by a period. Never alter an author's name by replacing full spellings with initials or by dropping middle initials.

■ For more than one author, use a comma rather than a period after the first author, and list the other authors' full names, first names first, separated by commas. Spell out the word *and* before the final author; do not use an ampersand (&). Put a period at the end.

■ For more than one work by the same author, use three hyphens followed by a period for all but the first entry.

TITLES

■ List full titles and subtitles as they appear on the title page of a book or in the credits for a film, videotape, or recording. Separate titles and subtitles with colons (followed by one space).

■ Italicize titles of books and periodicals. (See 61a.)

■ Use quotation marks around the titles of essays, poems, songs, short stories, and chapters or other parts of a larger work.

■ Put a period after the title of a book or an article. Use no punctuation after the title of a journal, magazine, or newspaper.

PLACES OF PUBLICATION

■ Places of publication are given for books and pamphlets, not for journals or magazines.

■ Give the city of publication from the title page or copyright page. If several cities are given, use only the first.

■ Use a colon to separate the place of publication from the publisher.

PUBLISHERS

■ The name of the publisher is given for books and pamphlets. Shorten the publisher's name as described below under "Abbreviations." If a title page indicates both an imprint and a publisher (for example, Arbor House, an imprint of William Morrow), list both shortened names, separated by a hyphen (*Arbor-Morrow*).

■ Use a comma to separate the publisher's name from the publication date.

DATE

■ For books, give the year of publication, followed by a period.

■ For other publications, give the year of publication within parentheses, followed by a colon.

- For newspapers, put the day before the month and year (*25 May 1954*) with no commas separating the elements.

- For magazines and newspapers, put a colon after the date.

- For electronic sources, include the date the site was accessed.

PAGE NUMBERS

- Page numbers are included for all publications other than books.

- Use a hyphen, not a dash, between inclusive page numbers, with no extra space on either side.

- Use all digits for ending page numbers up to 99 and the last two digits only for numbers above 99 (*130–38*) unless the full number is needed for clarity (*198–210*).

- If subsequent pages do not follow consecutively, use a plus sign after the last consecutive page number (*39+, 52–55+*).

- If no page numbers are available for electronic sources, include paragraph or section numbers.

ABBREVIATIONS

- To shorten a publisher's name, drop the words *Press, Company,* and so forth in the publisher's name (*Blair* for *Blair Press*). Use the abbreviation *UP* for *University Press* (*Columbia UP; U of Chicago P*).

- Use only the first name if the publisher's name is a series of names (*Farrar* for *Farrar, Straus & Giroux*). Use only the last name if the publisher's name is a person's name (*Abrams* for *Harry N. Abrams*).

- If no publisher or date of publication is given for a source, use the abbreviations *n.p.* ("no publisher") or *n.d.* ("no date").

- For periodicals, abbreviate months using the first three letters followed by a period (*Apr., Dec.*) except for *May, June,* and *July.* If an issue covers two months, use a hyphen to connect the months (*Apr.–May, June–Aug.*). (See model 20 below.)

19 f   Documenting books

1. Book by one author

Thomas, Lewis. *Lives of a Cell: Notes of a Biology Watcher.* New York: Viking,

1974. Print.

2. Book by two or three authors

Fulwiler, Toby, and Alan R. Hayakawa. *The Blair Handbook*, 5th ed. Upper

Saddle River: Prentice, 2007. Print.

MLA MLA MLA

GENERAL FORMAT FOR BOOK CITATIONS, MLA

one space   one space   one space one space
Author(s). *Book Title.* Place of publication: Publisher, year of publication.
Medium of publication.

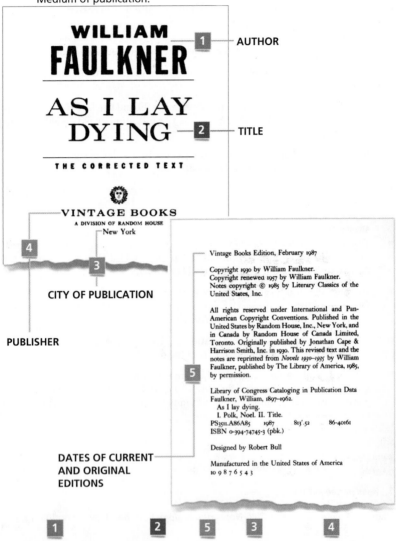

Faulkner, William. *As I Lay Dying*. 1930. New York: Vintage-Random,
1987. Print.

1 **AUTHOR OR EDITOR NAME.**
Last name first, comma, and rest of the name as it appears on the publication. Period. If a work has more than one author, second and later names are listed first name first, and separated by commas (for example, *Smith, Robert, Michael Jones, and Susan Morse*). Period. If more than one work by the same author, substitute three hyphens for the author's name after the first entry:

> Faulkner, William. *As I Lay Dying*. 1930. New York: Vintage-Random,
>
> 1987. Print.
>
> ---. *Light in August*. New York: Modern Library, 1932. Print.

2 **BOOK TITLE.**
List titles and subtitles fully, capitalizing them as in the original. *Italicize* the titles of entire books and put quotation marks around the titles of essays, poems, and short works within larger works. Period. Do not italicize the period that follows the title.

3 **CITY OF PUBLICATION.**
List first city of publication. If the name of a foreign city could be unfamiliar to readers, add abbreviation for the country. (See the section on abbreviations in Chapter 62.) Use a comma to separate city from country; use a colon to separate place from the publisher.

4 **PUBLISHER.**
Abbreviate publishers' names—for example, *Vintage* for *Vintage Books*. Omit words such as *press, publisher, inc.* Use *UP* for *University Press* (*Wisconsin UP*) or *P* (*U of Mississippi P*). If the title page indicates that a book is published under an imprint—for example, *Vintage Books* is an imprint of *Random House*—list both imprint and publisher, separated by a hyphen (*Vintage-Random*). Use a comma to separate the publisher from the publication date.

5 **DATE OF PUBLICATION.**
List year of publication as it appears on the copyright page. Period. If no publisher, place of publication, or date of publication is provided, use *n.p.* (for both publisher and place, to be clarified by its relation to the separating colon) or *n.d.* (for date).

6 **MEDIUM OF PUBLICATION.**
The MLA divides sources into three categories: print, Web, and other common sources. List the medium of publication, followed by a period.

Second and third authors are listed first name first. Do not alphabetize the authors' names within a single Works Cited entry. The final author's name is preceded by *and;* do not use an ampersand (&). A comma always follows the inverted ordering of the author's first name.

3. Book by more than three authors

Britton, James, et al. *The Development of Writing Abilities 11-18*. London:

Macmillan, 1975. Print.

With more than three authors, you have the option of using the abbreviation *et al.* (Latin for "and others") or listing all the authors' names, in full, as they appear on the title page of the book. Do not alphabetize the names within the Works Cited entry.

4. Book by a corporation, an organization, or an association

U.S. Coast Guard Auxiliary. *Boating Skills and Seamanship*. Washington: Coast

Guard Auxiliary National Board, 1997. Print.

Alphabetize by the name of the organization.

5. Revised edition of a book

Hayakawa, S. I. *Language in Thought and Action*. 4th ed. New York: Harcourt,

1978. Print.

6. Edited book

Hoy, Pat C., II, Esther H. Shor, and Robert DiYanni, eds. *Women's Voices: Visions
and Perspectives*. New York: McGraw, 1990. Print.

7. Book with an editor and author

Britton, James. *Prospect and Retrospect*. Ed. Gordon Pradl. Upper Montclair:

Boynton, 1982. Print.

The abbreviation *Ed.* when followed by a name replaces the phrase *Edited by* and cannot be made plural. (See models 13 and 14.)

8. Book in more than one volume

Waldrep, Tom, ed. *Writers on Writing*. 2 vols. New York: Random, 1985-88. Print.

When separate volumes were published in different years, use inclusive dates.

9. One volume of a multivolume book

Waldrep, Tom, ed. *Writers on Writing*, Vol. 2. New York: Random, 1988. Print.

When each volume has its own title, list the full publication information for the volume you used first, followed by information on the series (number of volumes, dates).

Churchill, Winston S. *Triumph and Tragedy*. Boston: Houghton, 1953. Vol. 6

of *The Second World War*. 6 vols. 1948-53. Print.

10. Translated book

Camus, Albert. *The Stranger*. Trans. Stuart Gilbert. New York: Random, 1946.

Print.

11. Book in a series

Magistrate, Anthony. *Stephen King, The Second Decade*: Danse Macabre *to* The

Dark Half. Twayne American Authors Series 599. New York: Twayne, 1992.

Print.

A book title appearing within another book's title is not italicized. Add series information just before the city of publication.

12. Reprinted book

Hurston, Zora Neale. *Their Eyes Were Watching God*. 1937. New York:

Perennial-Harper, 1990. Print.

Add the original publication date after the title; then cite information for the current edition.

13. Introduction, preface, foreword, or afterword in a book

Selfe, Cynthia. Foreword. *Electronic Communication Across the Curriculum*. Ed.

Donna Rice et al. Urbana: NCTE, 1998. ix-xiv. Print.

Atwell, Nancie. Introduction. *Coming to Know: Writing to Learn in the*

Intermediate Grades. Ed. Nancie Atwell. Portsmouth: Heinemann, 1990.

xi-xxiii. Print.

14. Work in an anthology or chapter in an edited collection

Donne, John. "The Canonization." *The Metaphysical Poets.* Ed. Helen Gardner.

Baltimore: Penguin, 1957. 61-62. Print.

Gay, John. *The Beggar's Opera.* 1728. *British Dramatists from Dryden to Sheridan.*

Ed. George H. Nettleton and Arthur E. Case. Carbondale: Southern Illinois

UP, 1975. 530-65. Print.

Lispector, Clarice. "The Departure of the Train." Trans. Alexis Levitin. *Latin*

American Writers: Thirty Stories. Ed. Gabriella Ibieta. New York: St.

Martin's, 1993. 245-58. Print.

Use quotation marks around the title of a poem, a short story, an essay, or a chapter. For a work originally published as a book, italicize the title. Add inclusive page numbers for the selection at the end of the entry.

When citing two or more selections from one anthology, you may list the anthology separately under the editor's name.

Gardner, Helen, ed. *The Metaphysical Poets.* Baltimore: Penguin, 1957. Print.

All entries within that anthology will then include only a cross-reference to the anthology entry.

Donne, John. "The Canonization." Gardner 61-62.

15. Essay or periodical article reprinted in a collection

Emig, Janet. "Writing as Mode of Learning." *College Composition and*

Communication 28 (1977): 122-28. Rpt. in *The Web of Meaning.* Ed. Janet

Emig. Upper Montclair: Boynton, 1983. 123-31. Print.

Gannet, Lewis. Introduction. *The Portable Steinbeck.* New York: Viking, 1946.

1-12. Rpt. as "John Steinbeck's Way of Writing" in *Steinbeck and His*

Critics: A Record of Twenty-five Years. Ed. E. W. Tedlock, Jr., and

C. V. Wicker. Albuquerque: U of New Mexico P, 1957. 23-37. Print.

Include the full citation for the original publication, followed by *Rpt. in* ("Reprinted in") and the publication information for the book. Add inclusive page numbers for the article or essay found in the collection; add inclusive page numbers for the original source when available.

16. Article in a reference book

"Behn, Aphra." *The Concise Columbia Encyclopedia.* 1998 ed. Print.

Miller, Peter L. "The Power of Flight." *The Encyclopedia of Insects.* Ed.

Christopher O'Toole. New York: Facts on File, 1986. 18-19. Print.

For a signed article, begin with the author's name. For commonly known reference works, full publication information and editors' names are not necessary. For entries arranged alphabetically, page and volume numbers are not necessary.

17. Anonymous book

The World Almanac and Book of Facts. New York: World Almanac-Funk, 2000. Print.

Alphabetize by title, ignoring an initial *A, An,* or *The.*

18. Government document

United States. Central Intelligence Agency. *National Basic Intelligence Fact Book.*
Washington: GPO, 1999. Print.

If the author is identified, begin with that name. If not, begin with the government (country or state), followed by the agency or organization. The U.S. Government Printing Office is abbreviated *GPO.*

19. Dissertation, unpublished or published

Kitzhaber, Albert R. "Rhetoric in American Colleges." Diss. U of Washington, 1953.
Print.

Use quotation marks for the title of an unpublished dissertation. Include the university name and the year. For a published dissertation, italicize the title and give publication information as you would for a book, including the order number if the publisher is University Microfilms International (UMI).

19 g Documenting periodicals

20. Article, story, or poem in a monthly or bimonthly magazine

"From Beans to Brew." *Consumer Reports* Nov. 1999: 43-46. Print.

Linn, Robert A., and Stephen B. Dunbar. "The Nation's Report Card Goes
Home." *Phi Delta Kappan* Jan. 2000: 127-43. Print.

Abbreviate all months except May, June, and July. Hyphenate months for bimonthlies (*July–Aug. 1993*). Do not list volume or issue numbers. If the article is unsigned, alphabetize by title.

21. Article, story, or poem in a weekly magazine

Ross, Alex. "The Wanderer." *New Yorker* 10 May 1999: 56-53. Print.

Note that when the day of the week is specified, the publication date is inverted.

GENERAL FORMAT FOR JOURNAL ARTICLES, MLA

one space   one space   one space   one space

Author(s). "Article Title." *Journal Title* volume number.issue number (year of

publication): page numbers. Medium of publication.

Indent second line five spaces.

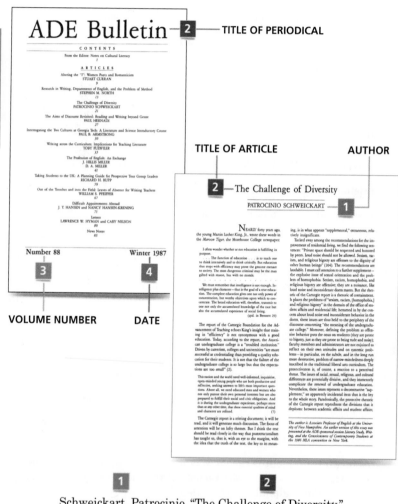

TITLE OF PERIODICAL

TITLE OF ARTICLE   **AUTHOR**

VOLUME NUMBER   **DATE**

Schweickart, Patrocinio. "The Challenge of Diversity."

ADE Bulletin 88 (1987): 21-26. Print.

1 AUTHOR NAME.

Last name first, comma, then rest of the name as it appears on the article. Period. If more than one author, second and later names are listed first name first, separated by commas, with *and* before last author (*Smith, Alan, Brian Jones, and Michelle Watts*). If four or more authors, you may list only first author followed by *et al.* (and others). If more than one work by the same author, substitute three hyphens for the author's name after the first entry:

> Schweickart, Patrocinio. "The Challenge of Diversity." *ADE Bulletin* 88.2
>
> (1987): 21-26. Print.
>
> ---. "Reading Ourselves." *Speaking of Gender*. Ed. Elaine Showalter.
>
> New York: Routledge, 1989. 88-98. Print.

2 TITLES.

List titles and subtitles fully, capitalizing as in the original and put quotation marks around the titles of articles, poems, and short works in the periodical. Period. Italicize book titles within **article titles** ("A Reassessment of Faulkner's *As I Lay Dying*"). Use single quotation marks around the titles of short works within article titles ("T.S. Eliot's 'Ash Wednesday' Revisited"). *Italicize periodical titles* (*ADE Bulletin*).

3 VOLUME, ISSUE, AND PAGE NUMBERS.

For journals, list volume number, period, and issue number (12.2), followed by year of publication (in parentheses) and a colon: then page numbers. Separate inclusive page numbers with a hyphen (*42-54*). Up to 99, use all the digits for the second page numbers, and above 99 list the last two digits only (*130-38*) unless the full sequence is needed for clarity (*198-210*). If page numbers are not consecutive, use the first page number, followed by a plus sign: 84+.

4 DATE OF PUBLICATION.

Place the year of publication for periodicals within parentheses, followed by a colon and a space to the page numbers. Never use season for a journal.

5 MEDIUM OF PUBLICATION.

The MLA divides sources into three categories: print, Web, and other common sources. List the medium of publication, followed by a period.

GENERAL FORMAT FOR MAGAZINE AND NEWSPAPER ARTICLES, MLA

one space   one space   one space   one space

Author(s). "Article Title." *Publication Title* Date of publication: page numbers.

Medium of publication.

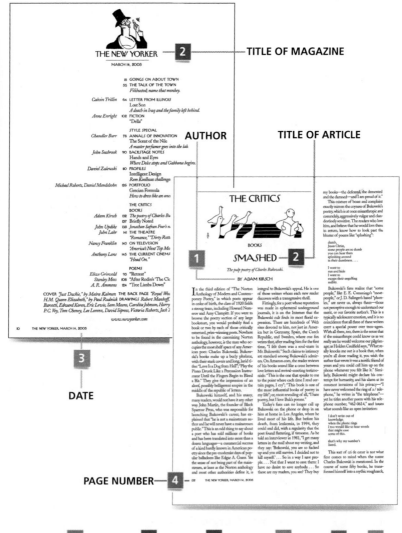

TITLE OF MAGAZINE

AUTHOR

TITLE OF ARTICLE

DATE

PAGE NUMBER

Kirsch, Adam. "Smashed." *New Yorker* 14 Mar. 2005: 132-36. Print.

1 **AUTHOR NAME.**

Last name first, comma, then rest of the name as it appears on the article. Period. If more than one author, second and later names are listed first name first, separated by commas, with *and* before last author (*Smith, Alan, Brian Jones, and Michelle Watts*). If more than one work by the same author, substitute three hyphens for the author's name after the first entry:

> Kirsch, Adam. "Smashed." *New Yorker* 14 Mar. 2005: 132-36. Print.
>
> ---. "The Lazy Gardener." *New York Sun* 28 Sept. 2005: A24. Print.

2 **TITLES.**

List titles and subtitles fully, capitalizing as in the original. Put quotation marks around the titles of articles, poems, and short works in the periodical. Period. Italicize book titles within **article titles** ("The Effect of Sunshine in Faulkner's *Light in August*"). Use single quotation marks around the titles of short works within article titles ("What's Cool in 'We Real Cool'?") *Italicize **periodical titles** and omit introductory articles (*New Yorker*, not *The New Yorker*).

3 **DATE.**

For daily, weekly, or biweekly magazines and newspapers, give day, month, and year of publication (*14 Mar. 2005*), but omit volume and issue numbers. Colon. Abbreviate all months except May, June, and July followed by a period (*Jan., Apr.*). If no date of publication, use *n.d.* in parentheses (*n.d.*).

4 **PAGE NUMBERS.**

Separate page numbers in a range with a hyphen (*42-54*). Up to 99, use all the digits for the second page numbers, and above 99 list the last two digits only (*130-38*) unless the full sequence is needed for clarity (*198-210*). If the page numbers are not consecutive (as in a newspaper), place a plus sign after the final consecutive page (39+, 52-55+). Period.

5 **MEDIUM OF PUBLICATION.**

The MLA divides sources into three categories; print, Web, and other common sources. List the medium of publication, followed by a period.

22. Article in a daily newspaper

Brody, Jane E. "Doctors Get Poor Marks for Nutrition Knowledge." *New York*

    Times 10 Feb. 1992: B7. Print.

"Redistricting Reconsidered." *Washington Post* 12 May 1999: B2. Print.

For an unsigned article, alphabetize by the title.

Give the full name of the newspaper as it appears on the masthead, but drop any introductory *A, An,* or *The.* If the city is not in the name, it should follow in brackets: *El Diario [Los Angeles].*

With the page number, include the letter that designates any separately numbered sections. If sections are numbered consecutively, list the section number (*sec. 2*) before the colon, preceded by a comma.

23. Article in a journal paginated by volume

Harris, Joseph. "The Other Reader." *Journal of Advanced Composition* 12.1

    (1992): 34-36. Print.

Do not give the month or season. Note that there is no space between the closing parenthesis and the colon.

24. Article in a journal paginated by issue

Tiffin, Helen. "Post-Colonialism, Post-Modernism, and the Rehabilitation of Post-

    Colonial History." *Journal of Commonwealth Literature* 23.1 (1998): 169-81.

    Print.

Include the volume number followed by a period and then the issue number (both in Arabic numerals, even if the journal uses Roman). Do not give the month of publication.

25. Editorial

"Gay Partnership Legislation a Mixed Bag." Editorial. *Burlington Free Press*

    5 April 2000: A10. Print.

If the editorial is signed, list the author's name first.

26. Letter to the editor and reply

Kempthorne, Charles. Letter. *Kansas City Star* 26 July 1999: A16. Print.

Massing, Michael. Reply to letter of Peter Dale Scott. *New York Review of Books*

    4 Mar. 1993: 57. Print.

27. Review

Kramer, Mimi. "Victims" Rev. of *'Tis Pity She's a Whore*. New York Shakespeare

Festival. *New Yorker* 20 Apr. 1992: 78-79. Print.

Lane, Anthony. Rev. of *The Mummy*. *New Yorker* 10 May 1999: 104. Print.

Databases

The Works Cited entries for electronic databases (newsletters, journals, and conferences) are similar to entries for articles in printed periodicals: cite the author's name; the article or document title, in quotation marks; the newsletter, journal, or conference title; the number of the volume and issue; the year or date of publication; and the number of pages, if available.

Portable databases are much like books and periodicals. Their entries in Works Cited lists are similar to those for printed material except that you must also include the following items.

■ The medium of publication (*CD-ROM, diskette, magnetic tape*).

■ The name of the vendor, if known. (This may be different from the name of the organization that compiled the information, which must also be included.)

■ The date of electronic publication, in addition to the date the material originally may have been published (as for a reprinted book or article).

28. Periodically updated CD-ROM database

James, Caryn. "An Army as Strong as Its Weakest Link." *New York Times* 16

Sep. 1994: C8. CD-ROM. *New York Times Ondisc*. UMI-Proquest. Oct. 1994.

If a database comes from a printed source such as a book, periodical, or collection of bibliographies or abstracts, cite this information first, followed by the medium of publication, the title of the database (italicized), the vendor name (if applicable), and the date of electronic publication. If no printed source is available, include the title of the material accessed (in quotation marks), the date of the material if given, the italicized title of the database, the medium of publication, the vendor name, and the date of electronic publication.

29. Nonperiodical CD-ROM publication

"Rhetoric." *The Oxford English Dictionary*. 2nd ed. Oxford: Oxford UP, 1992.

CD-ROM.

List a nonperiodical CD-ROM as you would a book, adding the medium of publication and information about the source, if applicable. If citing only part of a work, italicize the title of the selected portion or place it within quotation marks, as appropriate (as you would the title of a printed short story, poem, article, essay, or similar source).

30. Microform or microfiche article

Mayer, Caroline E. "Child-Resistant Caps to Be Made 'Adult-friendly.'"

    Washington Post 16 June 1995: A3. Newsbank. (1995) CON 16:B17.

    CD-ROM.

If the listing is derived from a computer-based reference source such as *Newsbank*, you may treat it exactly as you would any other periodical. To help your audience locate the source as quickly as possible, however, you should include the descriptor *CD-ROM*, the name of the service (*Newsbank*), and the available section/grid information.

19 h   Documenting electronic sources

Online Sources

Documenting a World Wide Web (WWW) or other Internet source follows the same basic guidelines as documenting other texts: cite *who* said *what, where,* and *when.* However, important differences need to be noted. In citing online sources from the World Wide Web or electronic mail, two dates are important: the date the text was created (published) and the date you found the information (accessed the site). When both publication and access dates are available, provide both.

Many WWW sources are often updated or changed, leaving no trace of the original version, so always provide the access date, which documents that this information was available on that particular date.

The following guidelines are derived from the seventh edition of the *MLA Handbook for Writers of Research Papers.* To identify a WWW or Internet source, include, if available, the following items in the following order, each punctuated by a period except the date of access.

- **Author** (or editor, compiler, translator, producer of work). Give the person's full name, if known, last name first; if the name is unknown, include any alias given.

- **Title of the work.** Italicize the title, unless it is part of a larger work. Put quotation marks around titles that are part of a larger work.

■ **Title of the overall Web site** (in italics) if it is different from the title of the work.

■ **Version or edition of the site**, if relevant.

■ **Publisher or sponsor of the site.** This information is often found at the bottom of the Web page. If this information is unavailable, use N.p. (for *no publisher*).

■ **Date of electronic publication.** Include the latest date of site revision if available. If no date is given, use *n.d.*

■ **Medium of publication.** For all online sources, the medium of publication is *Web*.

■ **Date of access.** Include the date you visited this site.

31. Work from an online database

Conniff, Richard. "Approaching Walden." *Yankee* 57.5 (May 1993): 84. *Article First*. Web. 2 June 2005.

Give the print publication information, name the database (italicized), medium of publication consulted (*Web*), and date of access.

32. Professional site

Yellow Wall-Paper Site. U of Texas. 1995. 4 Mar. 1998.

33. Government or institutional site

"Zebra Mussels in Vermont." *State of Vermont Agency of Natural Resources*. State of Vermont Agency of Natural Resources, n.d. Web. 3 May 1998.

34. Article in a journal

Erkkila, Betsy. "The Emily Dickinson Wars." *The Emily Dickinson Journal* 5.2 (1996): n.pag. Web. 2 Feb. 1998.

GENERAL FORMAT FOR ONLINE SOURCES, MLA

Author(s). "Article Title." *Title of Site*. Sponsoring body, Date of electronic publication. Medium of publication. Date of access.

MEDIUM (*WEB.*)

NAME OF WEB SITE

TITLE OF ARTICLE

AUTHOR OF ARTICLE ON WEB SITE (AT END OF 27 PARAGRAPHS)

SPONSORING ORGANIZATION

DATE SITE LAST REVISED (BOTTOM OF HOME PAGE)

Padgett, John B. "William Faulker." *Mississippi Writers Page*.

University of Mississippi English Department, 15 Apr. 2005.

Web. 8 June 2005.

1   **AUTHOR OF MATERIAL ON WEB SITE.**

Last name first, comma, then rest of the name. Follow rules for citing books and periodicals (*Padgett, John B.*). Period. If no author is listed, begin with page title (*Mississippi Writers Page*).

2   **TITLE OF MATERIAL ON WEB SITE.**

Enclose title of poem, short story, or other short work in quotation marks ("William Faulkner"). *Italicize* the site title and subtitle. Period. If no title is obvious, use home page name as title (found in URL).

3   **NAME OF SPONSORING ORGANIZATION.**

Usually found at bottom of site home page (*University of Mississippi English Department*). Comma,

4   **DATE OF ELECTRONIC PUBLICATION.**

Include latest date of site revision if available, followed by a period. If no date is given, use *n.d.*

5   **MEDIUM OF PUBLICATION.**

For all online sources, the medium of publication is *Web*.

6   **DATE OF ACCESS.**

Include the date you visited this site, followed by a period.

MLA MLA MLA

35. Book

Twain, Mark. *The Adventures of Tom Sawyer*. Internet Wiretap Online Library.
    Carnegie Mellon U, n.d. Web. 4 Mar. 1998.

36. Poem

Poe, Edgar Allan. "The Raven." *American Review*, 1845. *The Poetry Archives*.
    Web. 4 Mar. 1998.

37. Article in a reference database

"Jupiter." *Britannica Online*. Vers. 97.1. Encyclopaedia Britannica,
    1 Mar. 1997. Web. 29 Mar. 1998.

38. Posting to a discussion list

"New Virginia Woolf Discussion List." Online posting. 22 Feb. 1996. The Virginia
    Woolf Society, Ohio State U. 4 Mar. 1998 <gopher://
    dept.english.upenn.edu:70//OrO-1858-?Lists/20th/vwoolf>.

39. E-mail, listserv, or newsgroup (Usenet) message

Fulwiler, Toby. "A Question About Electronic Sources." Message to Alan
    Hayakawa. 23 Jan. 2004. E-mail.
Superman. <superman@200.uvm.edu>. "Writing Committee Meeting."
    University of Vermont. 24 Jan. 2001. Distribution list.

Include the author's name or Internet alias (if known, alias first, period)
followed by the subject line (in quotation marks) and the date of the posting. Identify the type of communication (*Personal e-mail, Distribution list,
Office communication*) before the access date. The source's e-mail address
is optional, following the name in angle brackets; secure permission before
including an e-mail address.

40. File transfer protocol (FTP), telnet, or gopher site

King, Jr., Martin Luther. "I Have a Dream Speech." University of Kansas. Telnet.
    28 Aug. 1963. Web. 30 Jan. 1996.

41. Synchronous communications (MUD, MOO, IRC)

StoneHenger. The Glass Dragon MOO. 6 Feb. 2004. Personal interview. 6 Feb.
    2004.

Synchronous communications take place in real time; when they are
over, an archive copy may remain, or they may simply be erased. After the
posting date, include the type of discussion (e.g., *Personal interview, Group
discussion*) followed by a period.

42. Home page—personal

Fulwiler, Anna. Home page. 1 Feb. 1998. Web. 3 Mar. 2003.

43. Home page—college course or academic department

Hughes, Jeffrey. Home page. *Fundamentals of Field Science*. Dept. of Botany, U of
    Vermont, Sep.–Dec. 2005. Web. 6 May 2008.

44. Online newspaper

Sandomir, Richard. "Yankees Talk Trades in Broadcast Booth." *New York Times*.
    New York Times, 4 Dec. 2001. Web. 5 Dec. 2001.

45. Online magazine

Epperson, Sharon. "A New Way to Shop for a College." *Time*. Time.com, 4 Dec.
    2001. Web. 5 Dec. 2001.

46. Online encyclopedia

Stanford Encyclopedia of Philosophy. Ed. Edward N. Zalta. Stanford U, 1995.
    Web. 5 Dec. 2001.

47. Online work of art

Van Gogh, Vincent. *The Olive Trees*. 1889. Museum of Modern Art, New York.
    MOMA. Web. 5 Dec. 2001.

48. Online interview

Plaxco, Jim. Interview. *Planetary Studies Foundation*. Planetary Studies
      Foundation, Oct. 1992. Web. 5 Dec. 2001.

49. Online film or film clip

Columbus, Chris, dir. *Harry Potter and the Sorcerer's Stone*. Trailer. Warner
      Brothers, 2001. *Hollywood.com*. Web. 5 Dec. 2001.

50. Online cartoon

Bell, Darrin. "Rudy Park." Cartoon. *New York Times*. New York Times, 5 Dec.
      2001. Web. 5 Dec. 2001.

51. Electronic television or radio program

Chayes, Sarah. "Concorde." *All Things Considered*. Natl. Public Radio, 26 July
      2000. Web. 7 Dec. 2001.

52. Blog entry

Ahern, Shauna James. "Buttermilk biscuits, gluten free." *Gluten-free Girl*.
      Blogspot.com, Oct. 2008. Web. 25 Nov. 2008.

19 i   Documenting other sources

53. Cartoon, titled or untitled

Davis, Jim. "Garfield." Cartoon. *Courier* [Findlay, OH] 17 Feb. 1996: E4. Print.

Roberts, Victoria. Cartoon. *New Yorker* 13 July 2000: 34. Print.

54. Film or videocassette

Casablanca. Dir. Michael Curtiz. Perf. Humphrey Bogart and Ingrid Bergman.
      Warner Bros., 1942. Film.

Fast Food: What's in It for You. Prod. Center for Science. Los Angeles: Churchill,
      1988. Videocassette.

Begin with the title, followed by the director, the studio, and the year
released. You may also include the names of lead actors, the producer, and

the like between the title and the distribution information. If your essay is concerned with a particular person's work on a film, lead with that person's name, arranging all other information accordingly.

Lewis, Joseph H., dir. *Gun Crazy*. Screenplay by Dalton Trumbo. King Bros.,

1950. Film.

55. Personal interview

Holden, James. Personal interview. 12 Jan. 2000.

Begin with the interviewee's name and specify the kind of interview and the date. You may identify the interviewee's position if relevant to the purpose of the interview.

Morser, John. Professor of Political Science, U of Wisconsin-Stevens Point.

Telephone interview. 15 Dec. 1999.

56. Published or broadcast interview

Sowell, Thomas. "Affirmative Action Programs." Interview. *All Things*

Considered. Natl. Public Radio. WGTE, Toledo. 5 June 1990. Radio.

Steingass, David. Interview. *Counterpoint* 7 May 1970: 3-4. Print.

For published or broadcast interviews, begin with the interviewee's name. Include appropriate publication information for a periodical or book and appropriate broadcast information for a radio or television program.

57. Print advertisement

Cadillac DeVille. Advertisement. *New York Times* 21 Feb. 1996, natl. ed.: A20.

Print.

Begin with the name of the product, followed by the description *Advertisement* and publication information for the source.

58. Unpublished lecture, public address, or speech

Graves, Donald. "When Bad Things Happen to Good Ideas." National Council of

Teachers of English Convention, St. Louis. 21 Nov. 1989. Address.

Begin with the speaker, followed by the title (if any), the meeting (and sponsoring organization, if needed), the location, and the date. If there is no title, use a descriptive label (such as *Speech*) with no quotation marks.

59. Personal or unpublished letter

Friedman, Paul. Letter to the author. 18 Mar. 1998. TS.

Personal letters and e-mail messages are handled nearly identically in Works Cited entries. Begin with the name of the writer, identify the type of communication (for example, *Letter*), and specify the audience. Include the date written, if known, or the date received.

To cite an unpublished letter from an archive or private collection, include information that locates the holding (for example, *Quinn-Adams Papers. Lexington Historical Society. Lexington, KY*).

60. Published letter

King, Jr., Martin Luther. "Letter from Birmingham Jail." 28 Aug. 1963. *Civil*

Disobedience in Focus. Ed. Hugo Adam Bedau. New York: Routledge, 1991.

68-84. Print.

Cite published letters as you would a selection from an anthology. Specify the audience in the letter title (if known). Include the date of the letter immediately after its title. Place the page number(s) after the publisher information. If you cite more than one letter from a collection, cite the entire collection in the Works Cited list, and indicate individual dates and page numbers in your text.

61. Map

Ohio River: Foster, KY, to New Martinsville, WV. Map. Huntington: U.S. Army

Corps of Engineers, 1985. Print.

Cite a map as you would a book by an unknown author. Italicize the title, and identify the source as a map or chart.

62. Performance

Bissex, Rachel. Folk Songs. Flynn Theater, VT. 14 May 1990. Performance.

Rumors. By Neil Simon. Dir. Gene Saks. Broadhurst Theater, New York. 17 Nov.

1988. Performance.

Identify the pertinent details such as title, place, and date of performance. If you focus on a particular person in your text, such as the director or conductor, lead with that person's name. For a recital or individual concert, lead with the performer's name.

63. Audio recording

Young, Neil, comp., perf. *Mirror Ball*. In part accompanied by members of Pearl
    Jam. Reprise, 1995. CD.

Marley, Bob, and the Wailers. "Buffalo Soldier." *Legend*. Island Records, 1984.
    Audiocassette.

Depending on the focus of your text, begin with the artist, composer, or
conductor. Enclose song titles in quotation marks, followed by the recording title, italicized. Do not italicize musical compositions identified only by
form, number, and key. Specify the recording format.

64. Television or radio broadcast

"Emissary." *Star Trek: Deep Space Nine*. Teleplay by Michael Pillar. Story by Rick
    Berman and Michael Pillar. Dir. David Carson. Fox. WFLX, West Palm
    Beach. 9 Jan. 1993. Television.

If the broadcast is not an episode of a series or the episode is untitled,
begin with the program title, italicized. Include the network, the station
and city, and the date of the broadcast. The inclusion of other information
such as narrator, writer, director, or performers depends on the purpose of
your citation.

65. Work of art

Holbein, Hans. *Portrait of Erasmus*. The Louvre, Paris. *The Louvre Museum*. By
    Germain Bazin. New York: Abrams, n.d. 148. Print.

Begin with the artist's name. Follow with the title, and conclude with
the location. If your source is a book, also give pertinent publication information.

19 j   Student paper: MLA style

The following paper was written by a first-year student, Andrew
Turner, in response to an open topic assignment for an American literature
survey course. The students were asked to present their research in MLA
style, including a title page, which is optional under the MLA system. The
title page is unnumbered.

MLA MLA MLA

TITLE IS
CENTERED,
LEFT TO RIGHT,   The Two Freedoms of Henry David Thoreau
ONE-THIRD
DOWN PAGE.

                                          by

NAME   Andrew Turner

INSTRUCTOR   Professor Stephany

COURSE   English 2

DATE   3 October 200x

                                          1"

Title page of a student essay in MLA format (optional). Note that margins shown are
adjusted to fit space limitations of this book. Follow actual dimensions shown and your
instructor's directions.

NAME — Andrew Turner

INSTRUCTOR — Professor Stephany

COURSE — English 2

DATE PAPER DUE — 3 October 200x

DOUBLE-SPACED

The Two Freedoms of Henry David Thoreau

Henry David Thoreau led millions of people throughout the world to think about individual freedom in a new way. During his lifetime, he attempted to live free of unjust governmental constraints as well as conventional social expectations. In his 1849 essay "On the Duty of Civil Disobedience," he makes his strongest case against governmental interference in the lives of citizens. In his 1854 book *Walden: Or, Life in the Woods*, he makes the case for living free from social conventions and expectations.

Thoreau opens "Civil Disobedience" with his statement that "that government is best which governs not at all" (222). He argues that a government should allow its people to be as free as possible, providing for the needs of the people without infringing on their daily lives. Thoreau explains: The government does not concern me much, and I shall bestow the fewest possible thoughts on it. It is not for many moments that I live under a government. ("Civil" 238)

Side notes:
WRITER OPENS WITH THESIS.
WRITER IDENTIFIES BY FULL TITLE THE TWO WORKS TO BE EXAMINED.
ONLY THE PAGE NUMBER IS NEEDED WHEN SOURCE IS INTRODUCED IN THE SENTENCE.
WRITER'S LAST NAME AND PAGE NUMBER APPEAR ON EACH PAGE.
DO NOT JUSTIFY RIGHT-HAND MARGIN.
ABBREVIATED TITLE IS USED AFTER WORK HAS BEEN IDENTIFIED BY FULL TITLE.
SHORT TITLE IS ADDED TO PAGE NUMBER BECAUSE TWO WORKS BY THE AUTHOR APPEAR ON THE WORKS CITED PAGE.

Turner 2

In other words, in his daily life he attends to his business of eating, sleeping, and earning a living and not dealing in any noticeable way with an entity called "a government."

Because Thoreau did not want his freedom overshadowed by governmental regulations, he tried to ignore them. However, the American government in 1845 would not let him. He was arrested and put in the Concord jail for failing to pay his poll tax—a tax he believed unjust because it supported the government's war with Mexico as well as the immoral institution of slavery. Instead of protesting his arrest, he celebrated it and explained its meaning by writing "Civil Disobedience," one of the most famous English-language essays ever written. In it, he argues persuasively that "under a government which imprisons any unjustly, the true place for a just man is also a prison" (230). Thus the doctrine of passive resistance was formed, a doctrine that advocated protest against the government by nonviolent means:

PAGE NUMBER ONLY (SENTENCE IDENTIFIES THE WORK)

USE 1 INCH INDENT FOR A QUOTATION LONGER THAN 4 LINES ◄—1"—► How does it become a man to behave toward this American government today? I answer that he cannot without disgrace be associated with it. I cannot for an instant recognize that political organization as my government which is the *slave's* government also. (224)

SIGNAL PHRASE INTRODUCES AUTHOR.

According to Charles R. Anderson, Thoreau's other writings, such as "Slavery in Massachusetts" and "A Plea for Captain John Brown," show his disdain of the "[N]ortherners for their cowardice on conniving with such an institution" (28). He wanted all free American citizens, North and South, to revolt and liberate the slaves.

In addition to inspiring his countrymen, Thoreau's view of the sanctity of individual freedom affected the lives of later generations who shared his beliefs (King). "Civil Disobedience" had the greatest impact because of its "worldwide influence on Mahatma Gandhi, the British Labour Party in its early years, the underground in Nazi-occupied Europe, and Negro leaders in the modern [S]outh" (Anderson 30). In other words, for nearly 150 years, Thoreau's formulation of passive resistance has been a part of the human struggle for freedom ("Gandhi").

PARTIAL QUOTATION IS WORKED INTO SENTENCE IN GRAMMATIC-ALLY SMOOTH WAY.

Thoreau also wanted to be free from the everyday pressure to conform to society's expectations. He believed in doing and possessing only the essential things in life. To demonstrate his case, in 1845 he moved to the outskirts of Concord,

MLA MLA MLA

Massachusetts, and lived by himself for two years on the shore of Walden Pond (Spiller et al. 396–97). Thoreau wrote *Walden* to explain the value of living simply, apart from the unnecessary complexity of society: "Simplicity, simplicity, simplicity! I say, let your affairs be as two or three, and not a hundred or a thousand" (66). At Walden, he lived as much as possible by this statement, building his own house and furniture, growing his own food, bartering for simple necessities, attending to his own business rather than seeking employment from others (*Walden* 16–17).

Living at Walden Pond gave Thoreau the chance to formulate many of his ideas about living the simple, economical life. At Walden, he lived simply in order to "front only the essential facts of life" (66) and to center his thoughts on living instead of on unnecessary details of mere livelihood. He developed survival skills that freed him from the constraints of city dwellers whose lives depended on a web of material things and services provided by others. He preferred to "take rank hold on life and spend [his] day more as animals do" (117).

While living at Walden Pond, Thoreau was free to occupy his time in any way that pleased him, which for him meant writing, tending his bean patch, and chasing loons. He was not troubled by a

Marginal notes:

IDENTIFICATION OF WORK WITH MORE THAN THREE AUTHORS.

ABBREVIATED SHORT TITLE AFTER FIRST REFERENCE

SHORT TITLE IS INCLUDED BECAUSE MORE THAN ONE TITLE APPEARS ON WORKS CITED PAGE.

PAGE NUMBERS SUFFICE WHEN CONTEXT MAKES SOURCE CLEAR.

BRACKETS INDICATE CHANGE IN WORDING SO PRONOUN CONFORMS TO SENTENCE GRAMMAR.

MLA MLA MLA

Turner 5

boss hounding him with deadlines or a wife and children who needed support. In other words, "he wasn't expected to be anywhere at any time for anybody except himself" (Franklin). His neighbors accused him of being selfish and did not understand that he sought most of all "to live deliberately" (*Walden* 66), as he felt all people should learn to do.

Then as now, most people had more responsibilities than Thoreau had, and they could not just pack up their belongings and go live in the woods—if they could find free woods to live in. Today, people are intrigued to read about Thoreau's experiences and are inspired by his thoughts, but few people can actually live or do as he suggests in *Walden*. In fact, most people, if faced with the prospect of spending two years removed from society—from modern plumbing, automobiles, television, telephone, and e-mail—would think of it as punishment or banishment rather than freedom (Poger).

WRITER'S CONCLUSION REPEATS THESIS.

Practical or not, Thoreau's writings have inspired countless people to reassess how they live and what they live for. Though unable to live exactly as he advocated, readers everywhere remain inspired by his vision of independence, equality, and, above all, freedom.

MLA MLA MLA

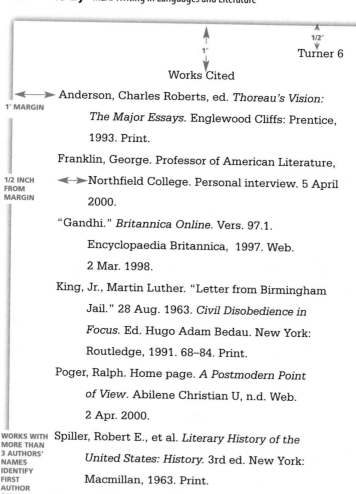

Turner 6

Works Cited

HEADING CENTERED

1" MARGIN

Anderson, Charles Roberts, ed. *Thoreau's Vision:*
The Major Essays. Englewood Cliffs: Prentice,
1993. Print.

Franklin, George. Professor of American Literature,
Northfield College. Personal interview. 5 April
2000.

1/2 INCH FROM MARGIN

ENTIRE PAGE DOUBLE SPACED

"Gandhi." *Britannica Online.* Vers. 97.1.
Encyclopaedia Britannica, 1997. Web.
2 Mar. 1998.

King, Jr., Martin Luther. "Letter from Birmingham
Jail." 28 Aug. 1963. *Civil Disobedience in*
Focus. Ed. Hugo Adam Bedau. New York:
Routledge, 1991. 68–84. Print.

Poger, Ralph. Home page. *A Postmodern Point*
of View. Abilene Christian U, n.d. Web.
2 Apr. 2000.

WORKS WITH MORE THAN 3 AUTHORS' NAMES IDENTIFY FIRST AUTHOR ONLY

Spiller, Robert E., et al. *Literary History of the*
United States: History. 3rd ed. New York:
Macmillan, 1963. Print.

Thoreau, Henry David. "On the Duty of Civil
Disobedience." 1849. *Walden and Civil*
Disobedience. 1854. New York: Signet-NAL,
1995. 222–40. Print.

AUTHOR'S NAME IS NOT REPEATED. NAME IS REPLACED BY 3 HYPHENS FOLLOWED BY A PERIOD.

---. *Walden: Or, Life in the Woods.* New York:
Signet-NAL, 1995. Print.

1" MARGIN

This chapter describes the aims, style, forms, and documentation conventions associated with disciplines in the social sciences: psychology, sociology, anthropology, political science, economics, social work, and education. The system of documentation described here is based on guidelines published by the American Psychological Association (APA).

20 a Aims

The social sciences examine the fundamental structures and processes that make up the social world. Sociology examines social groups; political science examines the methods of governance and social organizations; anthropology examines social cultures; economics examines the allocation and distribution of resources among social groups; and psychology examines the mind as both a biological and a social construction. The social sciences use methodical and systematic inquiry to examine and analyze human behavior, commonly asking questions such as the following:

- What is society? Can it be isolated and observed? How can it be described?

- How do social and psychological systems function? What forces hold them together or lead to their breakdown?

- Why do social organizations and individuals behave the way they do? Can governing laws be identified, explained, and understood?

Most writing in the social sciences explains findings based on factual research: either *empirical research*—based on firsthand observation and experimentation—or the wide reading that results in a *literature review*. Social scientists must also interpret their factual findings in a carefully reasoned manner, based on clear evidence objectively presented.

20 b Style

Writing in the social sciences must be clear, with connections among ideas explicitly stated. Language should be precise and informal diction discouraged. However, social science writing need not be dull or dry. Readers of the social sciences look for clarity, smoothness, and economy of expression. Writers should therefore avoid unnecessary jargon, wordiness, and redundancy.

As you write and revise in the social sciences, keep the following guidelines in mind:

- Write from a third-person point of view. (First-person experience is considered inappropriate for conveying empirical data because, in calling attention to the writer, it distracts from the information. First person is appropriate for conveying personal experience-based research.)

- Use the past tense to describe methods and results ("Individuals responded by . . ."); use the past or past perfect tense for literature reviews ("The study resulted in . . . ," "Jones has suggested . . ."); use the present tense to report established knowledge or to discuss conclusions ("The evidence indicates . . ."). Use tenses consistently.

- Include technical language of the discipline correctly, but avoid excessive jargon. Use plain, direct language. Choose synonyms with care.

- Attach graphs, charts, and illustrations when they convey information more readily than words. Label them clearly.

- Incorporate numbers, statistics, and equations clearly and accurately. Include explanations.

For more about the foundations and purposes of the APA system, see the *Publication Manual of the American Psychological Association,* 5th ed. (Washington: APA, 2001) or the APA Web site http://www.apastyle.org.

Guidelines for formatting manuscripts

The APA guidelines for submitting college papers are fairly conservative and do not reflect the wealth of visually interesting fonts, type sizes, graphics, and other options available with most modern word processing programs. If your instructor requests strict APA format, follow the guidelines below. If your instructor encourages more creative formats, use good judgment in displaying the information in your text. The following guidelines describe the preparation of the main body of your paper.

Paper and Printing

Print all academic assignments on 8½″ ×11″ white paper, in a standard serif font (for example, Times New Roman, Courier) and type size (11 or 12 points), using a good-quality printer.

Margins and Spacing

Allow margins of one inch all around. Justify the left margin only. Double space everything, including headings, quoted material, and the References page. Indent five spaces or one-half inch for paragraphs.

For prose quotations of more than forty words, indent five spaces or one-half inch from the left margin. Do not use quotation marks to mark the beginning and ending of long quotations; cite page numbers in parentheses (*pp. 34–36*) that end the passage.

Page Numbers

Print page numbers in the upper right margin of all pages one-half inch below the top of the paper (including the title page and abstract page). APA format requires a shortened title (2 or 3 words) five spaces before each page number to guarantee correct identification of stray pages (*Green Party 1, Green Party 2*).

Title Page

Attach a numbered title page to your paper. Center the title between the left and right margins and position about fifteen lines from the top (i.e., in the upper half of the page); immediately below the title, type your name, your instructor's name, the course name, and the date.

On the first full page of text, center the title, capitalizing the first letters of key words only. If your instructor asks for strict APA style, avoid using italics, underlining, quotation marks, boldface, or unusual fonts for the title. Double space to the first paragraph.

If you are not using a title page, include on page 1 your name, your instructor's name, the course title, and the date, double spaced on separate lines, flush with the upper left margin, one inch from the top of the page.

Abstract

Write a paragraph of seventy-five to one hundred words (120 words maximum) that states your thesis and the main supporting points in clear, concise, descriptive language. Avoid statements of personal opinion and inflammatory judgment. (See Chapter 36.) Center the word *Abstract* one inch from the top of the page; double space. Attach the abstract immediately following the title page. (Outlines are not required.)

Punctuation

One space is required after commas, semicolons, colons, periods, question marks, and exclamation points and between the periods in an ellipsis. Dashes are formed by two hyphens, with no extra spacing on either side.

Visual Information

APA style requires the labeling of all tables (charts, graphs), and figures (drawings, photographs) included in the text: *Table 1, Figure 2,* and so on. Include a clear caption for each, and place each table or figure in the text as near as possible to the passage referring to it. In your text, be sure to discuss the most important information or feature in each table or figure you include.

20 d   Guidelines for in-text citations

The following guidelines illustrate how to cite source information in the main body of your paper using APA style.

1. Single work by one or more authors

Whenever you paraphrase or summarize material in your text, give both the author's last name and the date of the source. For direct quotations, provide specific page numbers. Page references in the APA system are always preceded, in text or in the reference list, by the abbreviation *p.* to designate a single page or *pp.* to designate multiple pages.

Supply author names, publication dates, and page numbers (when listed) in parentheses following the cited material. Do not repeat any of these elements if you identify them in the text preceding the parenthetical citation.

> Exotoxins make some bacteria dangerous to humans (Thomas, 1974).

> According to Thomas (1974), "Some bacteria are only harmful to us if they make exotoxins" (p. 76).

> We need fear some bacteria only "if they make exotoxins" (Thomas, 1974, p. 76).

For a work by two authors, cite both names.

> Smith and Rogers (1990) note that all bacteria that produce exotoxins are harmful to humans.

> All known exotoxin-producing bacteria are harmful to humans (Smith & Rogers, 1990).

The authors' names are joined by *and* within your text, but APA convention requires an ampersand (&) to join authors' names in parentheses.

For a work by three to five authors, identify all the authors by last name the first time you cite a source. In subsequent references, list only the first author, followed by *et al.* ("and others").

> The most recent study supports the belief that alcohol abuse is on the rise (Dinkins, Dominic, & Smith, 1989).

> When homeless people were excluded from the study, the results were the same (Dinkins et al., 1989).

If you are citing a source by six or more authors, identify only the first author in all in-text references, followed by *et al.* (You must list the first six author names on the References page, however.)

2. Two or more works by an author published in the same year

To distinguish between two or more works published in the same year by the same author or team of authors, place a lowercase letter (*a, b, c,* and so on) immediately after the date. This letter should correspond to that in the reference list, where the entries are alphabetized by title. If two entries appear in one citation, repeat the year.

> (Smith, 1992a, 1992b)

3. Unknown author

To cite the work of an unknown author, use the first two or three words of the entry as listed on the References page in the author position. If the words are from the title, enclose them in quotation marks or italicize them, as appropriate.

> *Statistical Abstracts* (1991) reports the literacy rate for Mexico at 75% for 1990, up 4% from census figures 10 years earlier.

> Many researchers now believe that treatment should not begin until other factors have been dealt with ("New Evidence Suggests," 1987).

4. Corporate or organizational author

Spell out the name of the authoring agency for a work by a corporation, an association, an organization, or a foundation. If the name can be abbreviated and remain identifiable, you may spell out the name only the first time and put the abbreviation immediately after it, in brackets. For subsequent references, use only the abbreviation.

> (American Psychological Association [APA], 1993) (APA, 1994)

5. Authors with the same last name

To avoid confusion in citing two or more authors with the same last name, include each author's initials in every citation.

> (J. M. Clark, 1994)

> (C. L. Clark, 1995)

6. Quotation from an indirect source

Use the words *as cited in* to indicate quotations or information in your source that was originally from another source.

> Lester Brown of Worldwatch believes that international agriculture production has reached its limit and that "we're going to be in trouble on the food front before this decade is out" (as cited in Mann, 1993, p. 51).

7. More than one work in a citation

List two or more sources within a single parenthetical citation in the same order in which they appear in your reference list. If you refer to two or more works by the same author, list them in chronological order with the author's name mentioned once and the dates separated by commas.

> (Thomas, 1974, 1979)

List works by different authors in alphabetical order by the author's last name, separated by semicolons.

> (Miller, 1990; Webster & Rose, 1988)

8. Web site

When citing an entire Web site, not specific text or a figure, give the electronic address (URL) in your text.

> To locate information about faculty at the University of Vermont, visit the school's Web site (http://www.uvm.edu).

When the site's name and address are included in the text, no reference entry is needed.

9. Specific information from a Web site

Cite specific information (author, figure, table, paraphrased or quoted passage) from a Web site as you would a print source, by including the brief author/date information in the text or in parentheses, followed by complete information on the References page.

10. Long quotation set off from text

Start quotations of forty or more words on a new line, and indent the block five spaces or one-half inch from the left-hand margin. Indent the first line of the second or any subsequent paragraphs (but not the first paragraph) five additional spaces. Double space all such quotations, omit quotation marks, and place the parenthetical citation after any end punctuation, with no period following the citation.

11. Footnotes

Footnotes provide additional information of interest to some readers, but they are also likely to slow down the pace of your text or obscure your point for other readers. Make footnotes as brief as possible. When the information you wish to add is extensive, present it in an appendix.

Number footnotes consecutively on a separate page headed *Footnotes;* double space, and indent the first line of each footnote as you would a paragraph. The Footnotes page follows the References list.

20 e   Guidelines for the APA References page

All works mentioned in a paper should be identified in a reference list according to the following general rules of the APA documentation system.

Format

After the final page of the paper, title a separate page *References,* with no underlining, italics, or quotation marks. Center the title one inch from the top of the page. Number the page in sequence with the last page of the paper.

Double space between the title and the first entry. Also double space both between and within entries. Set the first line of each entry flush with the left-hand margin.

Indent the second and all subsequent lines of an entry five spaces from the left margin in a hanging indent.

If your reference list exceeds one page, continue in sequence on an additional page or pages, but do not repeat the title *References.*

Alphabetize the list of references according to authors' last names, using the first author's last name for works with multiple authors. For entries by an unknown author, alphabetize by the first word of the title, excluding insignificant words (*A, An, The*).

Entry Formats

Each item begins with a capital letter and is followed by a period and one space. Only the first word is capitalized in book and article titles, which are italicized or underlined. Follow these guidelines:

AUTHORS

- List the author's last name first, followed by a comma and the author's initials (not first name).

- When a work has more than one author, list all authors in this way, separating the names with commas.

- For multiple authors of a single work, place an ampersand (&) before the last author's name.

- Place a period after the last author's name.

TITLES

- List the complete titles and subtitles of books and articles, but capitalize only the first word of the title and any subtitle, as well as all proper nouns.

- Italicize the titles of books, magazines, and newspapers, but do not italicize article titles or place quotation marks around them. (Use underlining when you cannot produce italic typeface.)

- Place a period after the title. (When underlining, make sure punctuation is underscored, also.)

EDITION AND VOLUME NUMBERS

- For books, include the edition number, in parentheses, immediately following the title.

- For periodicals, include the volume number, italicized, immediately following the title.

PUBLISHERS

- List publishers' names in shortened form, omitting words such as *Company.*

- Spell out the names of university presses and organizations in full.

- For books, use a colon to separate the city of publication from the publisher's name.

DATES AND PAGE NUMBERS

■ For magazines and newspapers, use a comma to separate the year from the month and day, and enclose the publication date in parentheses (*1954, May 25*).

■ Give full sequences for pages and dates (*361–375,* not *361–75*), separating page numbers by a hyphen with no spaces.

■ If pages do not follow consecutively (as in newspapers), include subsequent page numbers after a comma: *pp. 1, 16.* Note that *pp.* precedes the page numbers for newspaper articles but not for journal articles.

ABBREVIATIONS

■ Abbreviate state and country names, but not months.

■ Use U.S. postal abbreviations (*NY, VT, WI*) for state abbreviations, but omit them for cities well known for publishing: Baltimore, Boston, Chicago, Los Angeles, New York, Philadelphia, and San Francisco.

20 f   Documenting books

Following are examples of the reference list format for a variety of source types using standard APA hanging indent format.

1. Book by one author

Benjamin, J. (1988). *The bonds of love: Psychoanalysis, feminism, and the problem of domination.* New York: Prometheus.

2. Book by two or more authors

Zweigenhaft, R. L., & Domhoff, G. W. (1991). *Blacks in the white establishment? A study of race and class in America.* New Haven, CT: Yale University Press.

Include all authors' names in the reference list, regardless of the number of authors associated with a particular work.

3. More than one book by the same author

List two or more works by the same author (or the same author team listed in the same order) chronologically by year, earliest work first. Arrange any such works published in the same year alphabetically by title, placing lowercase letters after the dates. In either case, give full identification of author(s) for each reference listing.

GENERAL FORMAT FOR BOOK, APA

Author/editor(s). (Year of publication). *Book title.* City of publication: Publisher.

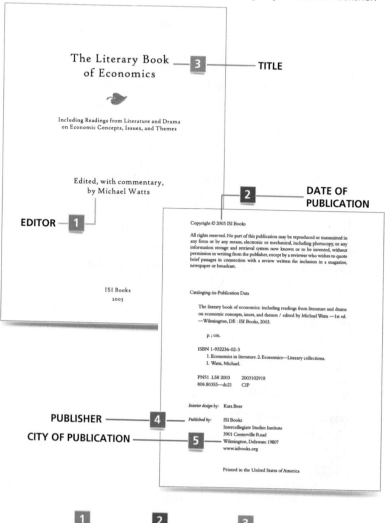

The Literary Book
of Economics — **3** —————— **TITLE**

Including Readings from Literature and Drama
on Economic Concepts, Issues, and Themes

Edited, with commentary,
by Michael Watts

2 ——————— **DATE OF
PUBLICATION**

EDITOR — **1**

ISI Books
2003

Cataloging-in-Publication Data

The literary book of economics: including readings from literature and drama on economic concepts, issues, and themes / edited by Michael Watts —1st ed. —Wilmington, DE : ISI Books, 2003.

p. ; cm.

ISBN 1-932236-02-3
    1. Economics in literature. 2. Economics—Literary collections.
    I. Watts, Michael.

PN51 .L58 2003   2003102918
808.80355—dc21   CIP

Interior design by: Kara Beer

PUBLISHER ———— **4** — *Published by:*   ISI Books
                                          Intercollegiate Studies Institute
                                          3901 Centerville Road
CITY OF PUBLICATION ——— **5** ——— Wilmington, Delaware 19807
                                          www.isibooks.org

Printed in the United States of America

1   **2**   **3**

Watts, M. (Ed.). (2003). *The literary book of economics.*

Wilmington, DE: Intercollegiate Studies Institute.

5   **4**

1 AUTHOR.

List the author's last name first, followed by a comma and the author's initials (not first name). When a work has more than one author, list all authors in this way, separating the names with a comma, placing an ampersand (&) before the last author's name, and ending with a period (*Smith, A. C., Jones, B., & Watts, M.*). If more than one work by the same author, list the earliest first.

> Watts. M. (1987). Student gender and school district differences
>
> affecting the stock and flow of economic knowledge. *Review of*
>
> *Economics and Statistics, 69,* 561–566.
>
> Watts. M. (Ed.). (2003). *The literary book of economics.* Wilmington, DE:
>
> Intercollegiate Studies Institute.

2 DATE.

Following author's name, give year of publication in parentheses.

3 TITLE.

List the complete titles and subtitles of books, but capitalize only the first word of the title and subtitle, as well as all proper nouns (*The literary book of African economics*). Italicize book titles and place a period after the title.

4 PUBLISHER.

List publishers' names in shortened form, omitting words such as *Publishers, Inc.,* or *Company.* Spell out the names of university presses and organizations in full (*New England University Press*). Use a colon to separate the place of publication from the publisher (*Wilmington, DE: Intercollegiate Studies Institute*).

5 CITY OF PUBLICATION.

Use U.S. postal abbreviations for state and country (*VT for Vermont, etc.*).

APA APA APA

Bandura, A. (1969). *Principles of behavior modification.* New York: Holt, Rinehart, and Winston.

Bandura, A. (1977a). Self-efficacy: Toward a unifying theory of behavioral change. *Psychological Review.* 191–215.

Bandura, A. (1977b). *Social learning theory.* Englewood Cliffs, NJ: Prentice Hall.

If the same author is named first but listed with different coauthors, alphabetize by the last name of the second author. Works by the first author alone are listed before works with coauthors.

4. Book by a corporation, an association, an organization, or a foundation

American Psychological Association. (2001). *Publication manual of the American Psychological Association* (5th ed.). Washington: Author.

Alphabetize corporate authors by the corporate name, excluding the articles *A, An,* and *The.* When the corporate author is also the publisher, designate the publisher as *Author.*

5. Revised edition of a book

Peek, S. (1993). *The game inventor's handbook* (Rev. ed.). Cincinnati, OH: Betterway.

6. Edited book

Schaefer, Charles E., & Reid, S. E. (Eds.). (1986). *Game play: Therapeutic use of childhood games.* New York: Wiley.

Place *Ed.* or *Eds.,* capitalized and in parentheses, after the editor(s) of an edited book.

7. Book in more than one volume

Waldrep, T. (Ed.). (1985–1988). *Writers on writing* (Vols. 1–2). New York: Random House.

For a work with volumes published in different years, indicate the range of dates of publication. If you referred to only one volume of a multivolume work, indicate only the volume cited.

Waldrep, T. (Ed.). (1988). *Writers on writing* (Vol. 2). New York: Random House.

8. Translated or reprinted book

Freud, S. (1950). *The interpretation of dreams* (A. A. Brill, Trans.). New York: Modern Library-Random House. (Original work published 1900)

The date of the translation or reprint is in parentheses after the author's name. Place the original publication date in parentheses at the end of the citation, with no period. In the parenthetical citation in your text, include both dates: (*Freud 1900 / 1950*).

9. Chapter or article in an edited book

Telander, R. (1996). Senseless crimes. In C. I. Schuster & W. V. Van Pelt (Eds.),

   Speculations: Readings in culture, identity, and values (2nd ed.,

   pp. 264–272). Upper Saddle River, NJ: Prentice Hall.

The chapter or article title is not underlined or in quotation marks. Editors' names are listed in normal reading order (surname last). Inclusive page numbers, in parentheses, follow the book title.

10. Anonymous book

Stereotypes, distortions and omissions in U.S. history textbooks. (1977). New York:

   Council on Interracial Books for Children.

11. Government document

U.S. House of Representatives, Committee on Energy and Commerce. (1986).

   Ensuring access to programming for the backyard satellite dish owner

   (Serial No. 99–127). Washington: U.S. Government Printing Office.

For government documents, provide the higher department or governing agency only when the office or agency that created the document is not readily recognizable. If a document number is available, list it in parentheses after the document title. Write out the name of the printing agency in full rather than using the abbreviation *GPO*.

20 g Documenting periodicals

In citing periodical articles, use the same format for listing author names as you use for citing books.

12. Article in a journal paginated by volume

Hartley, J. (1991). Psychology, writing, and computers: A review of research.

   Visible Language, 25, 339–375.

If page numbers are continuous throughout volumes in a year, use only the volume number, italicized, following the title of the periodical.

GENERAL FORMAT FOR JOURNAL ARTICLES, APA

Author(s). (Year of publication). Article title. *Journal Title, volume number*
(issue number), inclusive page numbers.

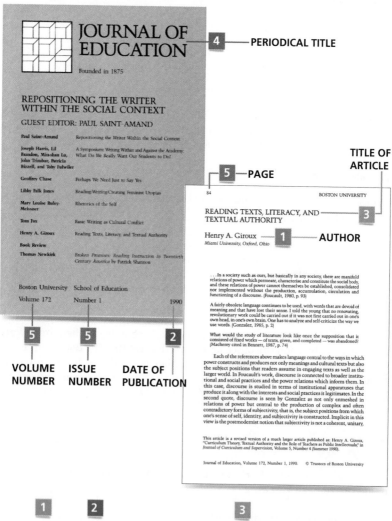

4 — PERIODICAL TITLE

5 — PAGE

TITLE OF ARTICLE — **3**

AUTHOR — **1**

VOLUME NUMBER — **5**

ISSUE NUMBER — **5**

DATE OF PUBLICATION — **2**

Henry A. Giroux
Miami University, Oxford, Ohio

Giroux, H. A. (1990). Reading texts, literacy, and textual authority.
Journal of Education, 172(1), 84–103.

4 **5**

1 AUTHOR.

List the author's last name first, followed by a comma and the author's initials (*Giroux, H. A.*). When a work has more than one author, list all authors in this way, separating the names with a comma and place an ampersand (&) before the last author's name (*Giroux, H. A., Smith, D., & Jones, M.*).

2 DATE OF PUBLICATION.

Following author's name, give year of publication in parentheses (*1990*). For magazines and newspapers, use a comma to separate the year from the month or month and day, and enclose in parentheses (*1954, May 25*). If no date is given in the document, write *n.d.* in parentheses followed by a period (*n.d.*).

3 TITLE OF ARTICLE.

List the complete titles and subtitles of articles, but capitalize only the first word of the title and subtitle, as well as all proper nouns. Period. Do not underline article titles or place quotation marks around them (*Reading texts, literacy, and textual authority: A study of American culture*).

4 TITLE OF PERIODICAL.

Italicize journal or publication titles. Capitalize the first letter of all words in the title, except articles, prepositions, and conjunctions less than four letters long.

5 VOLUME, ISSUE, AND PAGE NUMBERS.

In an article in a journal paginated by volume (continuous pagination), include only the volume number (*in italics*), not the issue. In an article in a journal paginated by issue, list the volume number (*in italics*) followed by the issue number in parentheses but not in italics: *172*(1). Comma. Inclusive page numbers for pages and dates should be written out in full, separated by a hyphen with no spaces (*361–375 not 361–75; 204–205, not 204–05*). If pages do not follow consecutively (as in newspapers), include subsequent page numbers after a comma (*pp. 1, 16*). Note that *pp.* precedes the page numbers for newspaper articles but not for journal articles.

APA APA APA

13. Article in a journal paginated by issue

Lowther, M. A. (1977). Career change in mid-life: Its impact on education.

Innovator, 8(7), 1, 9–11.

Include the issue number in parentheses if each issue of a journal is paginated separately; do not use the abbreviation *p.* or *pp.*

14. Magazine article

Garreau, J. (1995, December). Edgier cities. Wired, 158–163, 232–234.

For nonprofessional periodicals, include the year and month (not abbreviated) after the author's name; do not use the abbreviation *p.* or *pp.*

15. Newspaper article

Finn, P. (1995, September 27). Death of a U-Va. student raises scrutiny of off-

campus drinking. The Washington Post, pp. D1, D4.

If an author is listed for the article, begin with the author's name, then list the date (spell out the month); follow the article title with the title of the newspaper. If there is a section number or letter, combine it with the page or pages, including continued page numbers as well, using the abbreviation *p.* or *pp.* If the name of the newspaper includes the word *the,* capitalize and italicize it also.

APA conventions for documenting sources such as CD-ROMs, diskettes, and magnetic tapes list author, date, and title followed by the complete information for the corresponding print source, if available.

16. CD-ROM

Krauthammer, C. (1991). Why is America in a blue funk? Time, 138, 83. Retrieved

from UMIACH database (Periodical Abstracts, CD-ROM Item: 1126.00).

17. Computer software

HyperCard (Version 2.2) [Computer software]. (1993). Cupertino, CA: Apple

Computer.

Provide the version number, if available, in parentheses following the program or software name. Add the descriptive term *Computer software* in brackets, and follow it with a period. Do not italicize the names of computer programs.

20 h   Documenting online sources

Online Sources

An APA Internet citation should provide essentially the same information as any textual source: author (when identified), date of site creation, title (or description of document), date of retrieval, and a working address (URL).

Try to cite specific documents or links, whenever possible, rather than general home or menu pages since such pages commonly contain many links, only one of which you are citing.

To transcribe a URL correctly, keep your word processing file open and copy the URL directly from the Internet site to your paper. (Make sure your word processor's automatic hyphenation feature is turned off since an automatically inserted hyphen will change the URL; if you need to break a URL, do so after a slash or before a period.) APA does not recommend using angle brackets to indicate an Internet address.

If electronic sources don't provide page numbers, use paragraph numbers only if the paragraphs are numbered in the document: (*para 4*). If the source is divided into chapters, use chapter and paragraph numbers: (*chap 2. 12*). If the source is divided into sections, use section and paragraph numbers to identify the source location: (*section 6, 8*).

For more details than the following examples can provide, consult the APA's Web page at http://www.apa.org/journals/webref.html.

18. Online periodical article

Kapadia, S. (1995, November). A tribute to Mahatma Gandhi: His views on

women and social exchange. *Journal of South Asia Women's Studies*

[Online serial], 1(1). Retrieved December 2, 1995, from http://www

.shore.net/~india/jsaws

Indicate the number of paragraphs in brackets after the title, and add the term [*Online serial*] in brackets between the journal name and the volume number.

If you have viewed the article only in its electronic form, you should add *Electronic version* in brackets after the article title as in the following example:

Smithsonian Institution's Ocean Planet: A special report. (1995). [Electronic

version]. *Outdoor Life 3,* 13–22. Retrieved November 1, 1999, from

http://www.epinions.com/mags-Outdoor_Life

GENERAL FORMAT FOR ONLINE SOURCES, APA

Author(s). (Date of electronic publication). Title of site. Date of access, electronic
     address

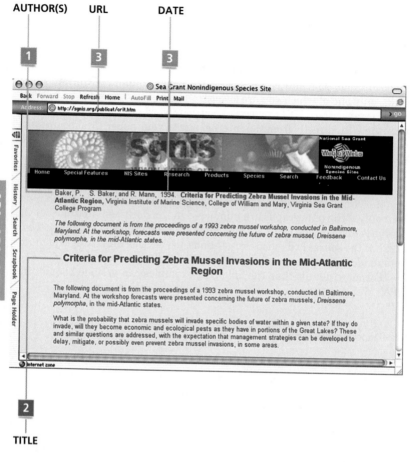

Baker, P., Baker, S., & Mann, R. (1994). Criteria for predicting zebra mussel

     invasions in the mid-Atlantic region. Retrieved June 8, 2005, from

     http://sgnis.org/publicat/crit.htm

1 AUTHOR OF MATERIAL ON WEB SITE.
Follow rules for citing books and periodicals. Last name, followed by initials for first and middle names (*Baker, P., Baker, S., & Mann, R.*). If no author is listed, begin with page title.

2 TITLE OF MATERIAL ON WEB SITE.
Capitalize first word in site title and subtitle and any proper names only. Period. Do not enclose in quotation marks (*Criteria for predicting zebra mussel invasions in the Mid-Atlantic region*). If no title is obvious, use home page name as title (found in URL).

3 PUBLICATION INFORMATION.
List two dates for each Internet site: first, the date the site was created or last revised (*1994*). Second, list the date you accessed the site with the words *Retrieved from* followed by the date and electronic address, no concluding period (*Retrieved June 8, 2005, from http://sgnis.org/publicat/papers/crit.htm*).

19. World Wide Web site

To document a specific file, list the author, the date of publication, the titles of the document and the complete work (if any). Add relevant information such as volume or page numbers of a print source. Conclude with a retrieval statement.

Williams, Scott. (1996, June 14). Back to school with the quilt. *AIDS Memorial*
Quilt Website. Retrieved June 14, 1996, from http://www.aidsquilt.org/
newsletter/stories/backto.html

Start with the title if no author is identified.

GVU's 8th WWW user survey. (n.d.). Retrieved August 8, 2000, from http://
www.cc.gatech.edu/gvu/usersurveys/survey1997-10/

20. Work from an online database

Conniff, R. (May 1993). Approaching *Walden. Yankee.* 57(5), 84. Retrieved June 2,
2005 from ArticleFirst database.

Give the print publication information and when it was retrieved from which database. No URL is required.

21. Weblog entry

Rickey, A. (8 June 2005). *Three years of hell to become the devil.* Retrieved June
10, 2005 from http://www.threeyearsofhell.com/

22. File transfer protocol (FTP), telnet, or gopher site

After the retrieval date, supply the FTP, telnet, or gopher search path.

Altar, T. W. (1993). *Vitamin B12 and vegans.* Retrieved May 28, 1996, from
ftp://ftp.cs.yale.edu Clinton, W. (1994, July 17). Remarks by the President
at the tribute dinner for Senator Byrd. Washington, DC: Office of the White
House Press Secretary. Retrieved February 12, 1996, from
gopher://info.tamu.edu.70/00/.data/ politics/1994/byrd.0717

23. Synchronous communications (MOO, MUD, IRC)

To document a *real-time communication,* such as those posted in MOOs, MUDs, and IRCs, describe the type of communication (e.g., *Group discussion, Personal interview*) if it is not indicated elsewhere in the entry.

Harnack, A. (1996, April 4). Words [Group discussion]. Retrieved April 5, 1996,

  from telnet://moo.du.org/port=8888

24. Web discussion forum

Holden, J. B. (2001, January 2). The failure of higher education [Formal

  discussion initiation]. Message posted to http://ifets.mtu.edu/archives

25. Listserv (electronic mailing list)

Weston, Heather (2002, June 12). Re: Registration schedule now available.

  Message posted to the Chamberlain Kronsage dormitory electronic mailing

  list, archived at http://listserv.registrar.uwsp.edu/archives/62.html

  Note that APA prefers the term *electronic mailing list* to *listserv.*

26. Newsgroup

Hotgirl (2002, January 12). Dowsing effort fails. Message posted to

  news://alt.science.esp3/html

27. Electronic newspaper article

Kolata, G. (2002, February 12). Why some people won't be fit despite exercise.

  New York Times. Retrieved February 12, 2002, from

  http://www.nytimes.com

28. Document available on university program or department Web site

McClintock, R. & Taipale, K.A. (1994). *Educating America for the 21st century: A*

  strategic plan for educational leadership 1993–2001. Retrieved February 12,

  2002, from Columbia University, Institute for Learning Technologies Web

  site: http://www.ilt.columbia.edu/ilt/docs/ILTplan.html

29. E-mail messages

  Under current APA guidelines, electronic conversations are not listed
on the References page. Cite e-mail messages in the text as you would personal letters or interviews.

R. W. Williams, personal communication, January 4, 1999.

Following is an in-text parenthetical reference to a personal e-mail message:

> James Tolley (personal communication, November 2, 2002) told me that the practice of dowsing has a scientific basis.

20   i   Documenting other sources

30. Motion picture, recording, and other nonprint media

Curtiz, M. (Director). (1942). *Casablanca* [Motion Picture]. United States: Warner Bros.

Alphabetize a motion picture listing by the name of the person or persons with primary responsibility for the product. Identifying information about this person or persons, such as the director, should appear in parentheses. Identify the medium in brackets following the title, and indicate both location (country of origin for motion picture) and name of the studio or distributor (as publisher).

31. Interviews and other field sources

These are identified in the text in parentheses (name, place, date) but are not listed on the References page. See model 29.

20   j   Informational research paper: APA style

The research essay "Green Is Only Skin Deep: False Environmental Advertising," by Elizabeth Bone, was written in response to an assignment to identify and explain one problem in contemporary American culture. She documented her essay according to the conventions of the American Psychological Association (APA). This sample includes a title page and an abstract; check with your instructor to find out whether an outline is required for course papers. Note that margins shown are adjusted to fit space limitations of book. Follow actual dimensions shown and your instructor's directions.

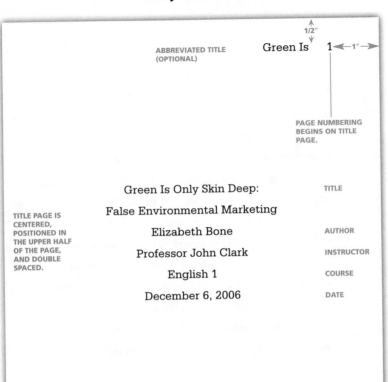

1/2″

ABBREVIATED TITLE
(OPTIONAL)

Green Is   1 ←— 1″ —→

PAGE NUMBERING
BEGINS ON TITLE
PAGE.

TITLE PAGE IS
CENTERED,
POSITIONED IN
THE UPPER HALF
OF THE PAGE,
AND DOUBLE
SPACED.

Green Is Only Skin Deep: TITLE

False Environmental Marketing

Elizabeth Bone   AUTHOR

Professor John Clark   INSTRUCTOR

English 1   COURSE

December 6, 2006   DATE

APA APA APA   APA APA

Title page for a student essay in APA format

ABSTRACT ON SEPARATE
PAGE FOLLOWING TITLE
PAGE

1″

1/2″

Green Is   2 ◄—1″—►

HEADING CENTERED

Abstract

NO
PARAGRAPH
INDENT

Most Americans consider themselves

DOUBLE
SPACE

environmentalists and favor supporting

environmentally friendly or "green" companies.

However, companies use a number of false

advertising practices to mislead the public

about their green practices and products by (1)

exaggerating claims, (2) masking false practices

behind technical terminology, (3) mis-sponsoring

green events, (4) not admitting responsibility for

real problems, (5) advertising green by association,

and (6) solving one problem while creating others.

Consumers must be skeptical of all commercial ads

and take the time to find out the truth behind

advertising.

THE
ABSTRACT
SUMMARIZES
THE MAIN
POINT OF
THE PAPER.

APA APA APA

Abstract for a student essay in APA format

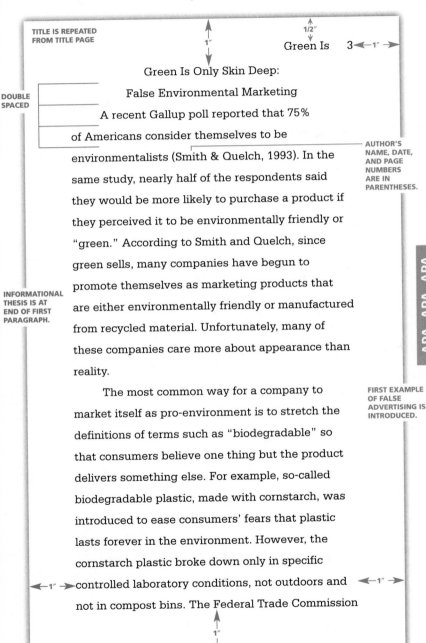

TITLE IS REPEATED FROM TITLE PAGE

1/2"

Green Is 3 ←—1"—→

1"

DOUBLE SPACED

Green Is Only Skin Deep:

False Environmental Marketing

A recent Gallup poll reported that 75%

of Americans consider themselves to be

environmentalists (Smith & Quelch, 1993). In the

AUTHOR'S NAME, DATE, AND PAGE NUMBERS ARE IN PARENTHESES.

same study, nearly half of the respondents said

they would be more likely to purchase a product if

they perceived it to be environmentally friendly or

"green." According to Smith and Quelch, since

green sells, many companies have begun to

promote themselves as marketing products that

INFORMATIONAL THESIS IS AT END OF FIRST PARAGRAPH.

are either environmentally friendly or manufactured

from recycled material. Unfortunately, many of

these companies care more about appearance than

reality.

The most common way for a company to

FIRST EXAMPLE OF FALSE ADVERTISING IS INTRODUCED.

market itself as pro-environment is to stretch the

definitions of terms such as "biodegradable" so

that consumers believe one thing but the product

delivers something else. For example, so-called

biodegradable plastic, made with cornstarch, was

introduced to ease consumers' fears that plastic

lasts forever in the environment. However, the

cornstarch plastic broke down only in specific

←—1"—→ controlled laboratory conditions, not outdoors and ←—1"—→

not in compost bins. The Federal Trade Commission

1"

APA APA APA

First text page of a student essay in APA format

Green Is   4

has updated its regulations to prevent such misrepresentations, so that now Glad and Hefty trash bags are no longer advertised as biodegradable (Carlson, Grove, & Kangun, 1993).

The use of technical terms can also mislead average consumers. For example, carbon fluoride compounds, called CFCs, are known to be hazardous to the protective layer of ozone that surrounds the earth, so their widespread use in air conditioners is considered an environmental hazard (Decker & Stammer, 1989). Chrysler Corporation advertises that it uses CFC-free refrigerant in its automobile air conditioners to appeal to environmentally concerned consumers ("Ozone layer," 1994). However, Weisskopf (1992) points out that the chemical compounds that replace CFCs in their air conditioners pose other environmental hazards that are not mentioned.

Another deceptive greening tactic is the sponsoring of highly publicized environmental events such as animal shows, concerts, cleanup programs, and educational exhibits. For example, Ocean Planet was a well-publicized exhibit put together by the Smithsonian Institution to educate people about ocean conservation. Ford Motor Company helped sponsor the event, which it then

SECOND EXAMPLE IS GIVEN.

AUTHOR QUOTED BY NAME IN THE TEXT IS FOLLOWED BY PUBLICATION YEAR IN PARENTHESES.

TRANSITIONS KEEP THE READER ON TRACK.

Green Is   5

used in its car advertisements: "At Ford, we feel
strongly that understanding, preserving, and
properly managing natural resources like our
oceans should be an essential commitment of
individuals and corporate citizens alike"

REFERENCE
CITED BY
TITLE WHEN
AUTHOR IS
UNKNOWN.

("Smithsonian Institution's Ocean Planet," 1995,
p. 14).

While sponsoring the exhibit may be a
worthwhile public service, such sponsorship has
nothing to do with how the manufacture and
operation of Ford automobiles affect the
environment. In fact, Ford was ranked as among
the worst polluters in the state of Michigan in 1995
(Parker, 1995).

Some companies court the public by
mentioning environmental problems and pointing
out that they do not contribute to those problems.
For example, the natural gas industry describes
natural gas as an alternative to the use of ozone-
depleting CFCs ("Don't you wish," 1994). However,

SHORTENED
TITLE IS USED
WHEN NO
AUTHOR IS
CREDITED ON
REFERENCES
PAGE.

according to Fogel (1985), the manufacture of
natural gas creates a host of other environmental
problems from land reclamation to carbon-dioxide
pollution, a major cause of global warming. By
mentioning problems they don't cause while
ignoring ones they do, companies present a

favorable environmental image that is at best a half truth, at worst an outright lie.

Other companies use a more subtle approach to misleading green advertising. Rather than make statements about environmental compatibility, these companies depict the product in unspoiled natural settings or use green quotations that have nothing to do with the product itself. For example, one Chevrolet advertisement shows a lake shrouded in mist and quotes an environmentalist: "From this day onward, I will restore the earth where I am and listen to what it is telling me" ("From this day," 1994, p. 19). Below the quotation is the Chevy logo with the words "Genuine Chevrolet." Despite this touching appeal to its love of nature, Chevrolet has a history of dumping toxic waste into the Great Lakes (Allen, 1991). Has this company seriously been listening to what the earth has been telling it?

The most common manner in which companies attempt to prove they have a strong environmental commitment is to give a single example of a policy or action that is considered environmentally sound. Chevron has had an environmental advertising campaign since the mid-1970s. In the 1990s the company's ads featured

QUOTATION OF FEWER THAN 40 WORDS IS INTEGRATED INTO THE TEXT.

APA APA APA

Green Is   7

Chevron employees doing environmental good deeds (Smith & Quelch, 1993). For example, one ad featured "a saltwater wetland in Mississippi at the edge of a pine forest . . . the kind of place nature might have made," going on to explain that this wetland was built by Chevron employees ("The shorebirds who found," 1990). However, LaGanga (1993) points out that during the time this advertisement was running in magazines such as *Audubon,* Chevron was dumping millions of gallons of nasty chemicals (carcinogens and heavy metals) into California's Santa Monica Bay, posing a health risk to swimmers. The building of the wetland in one part of the country does not absolve the company for polluting water somewhere else.

It should be clear that the environmental image a company projects does not necessarily match the realities of the company's practice. The products made by companies such as Chrysler, Ford, General Motors, and Chevron are among the major causes of air and water pollution: automobiles and gasoline. No amount of advertising can conceal the ultimately negative effect these products have on the environment (Kennedy & Grumbly, 1988). According to Shirley Lefevre,

ELLIPSIS POINTS INDICATE MISSING WORDS IN QUOTATION.

PAGE NUMBER IS NOT LISTED WHEN IT IS LISTED ON REFERENCES PAGE.

APA APA APA

president of the New York Truth in Advertising
League:

> It probably doesn't help to single out one
> automobile manufacturer or oil company as
> significantly worse than the others. Despite
> small efforts here and there, all of these
> giant corporations, as well as other large
> manufacturers of metal and plastic material
> goods, put profit before environment
> and cause more harm than good to the
> environment. (personal communication,
> May 1995)

Consumers who are genuinely interested in
buying environmentally safe products and
supporting environmentally responsible companies
need to look beyond the images projected by
commercial advertising in magazines, on billboards,
and on television. Organizations such as Earth
First! attempt to educate consumers to the realities
by writing about false advertising and exposing the
hypocrisy of such ads ("Do people allow," 1994),
while the Ecology Channel is committed to sharing
"impartial, unbiased, multiperspective
environmental information" with consumers on the
Internet (Ecology, 1996). Meanwhile the Federal
Trade Commission is in the process of continually

DOUBLE SPACED

INDENTED 5 SPACES OR 1/2 INCH

COLON IS USED TO INTRODUCE A LONG QUOTATION.

INTERVIEW CONDUCTED BY AUTHOR IS NOT LISTED ON THE REFERENCES PAGE.

APA APA APA

Green Is   9

upgrading truth-in-advertising regulations
(Carlson et al., 1993). Americans who are truly
environmentally conscious must remain skeptical
of simplistic and misleading commercial
advertisements while continuing to educate
themselves about the genuine needs of the
environment.

SECOND
CITATION
OF MORE
THAN THREE
AUTHORS IS
SHORTENED
TO FIRST
AUTHOR'S
NAME AND
ET AL.

THESIS IS
REPEATED IN
MORE DETAIL
AT END.

APA APA APA

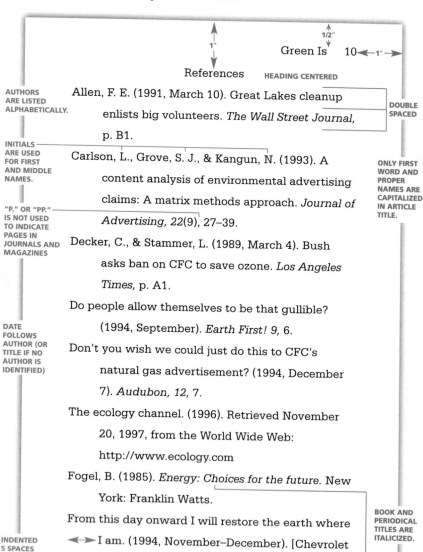

Green Is   10

1/2″

1″   ←1″→

References   HEADING CENTERED

AUTHORS
ARE LISTED
ALPHABETICALLY.

Allen, F. E. (1991, March 10). Great Lakes cleanup
enlists big volunteers. *The Wall Street Journal,*
p. B1.

DOUBLE
SPACED

INITIALS
ARE USED
FOR FIRST
AND MIDDLE
NAMES.

Carlson, L., Grove, S. J., & Kangun, N. (1993). A
content analysis of environmental advertising
claims: A matrix methods approach. *Journal of
Advertising, 22*(9), 27–39.

ONLY FIRST
WORD AND
PROPER
NAMES ARE
CAPITALIZED
IN ARTICLE
TITLE.

"P." OR "PP."
IS NOT USED
TO INDICATE
PAGES IN
JOURNALS AND
MAGAZINES

Decker, C., & Stammer, L. (1989, March 4). Bush
asks ban on CFC to save ozone. *Los Angeles
Times,* p. A1.

Do people allow themselves to be that gullible?
(1994, September). *Earth First! 9,* 6.

DATE
FOLLOWS
AUTHOR (OR
TITLE IF NO
AUTHOR IS
IDENTIFIED)

Don't you wish we could just do this to CFC's
natural gas advertisement? (1994, December
7). *Audubon, 12,* 7.

The ecology channel. (1996). Retrieved November
20, 1997, from the World Wide Web:
http://www.ecology.com

Fogel, B. (1985). *Energy: Choices for the future.* New
York: Franklin Watts.

From this day onward I will restore the earth where
I am. (1994, November–December). [Chevrolet
advertisement]. *Audubon, 11–12,* 18–19.

INDENTED
5 SPACES

BOOK AND
PERIODICAL
TITLES ARE
ITALICIZED.

Green Is   11

Kennedy, D., & Grumbly, T. P. (1988). Automotive emissions research. In Watson, A., Bates, R. R., & Kennedy, D. (Eds.), *Air pollution, the automobile, and public health* (pp. 3–9). Cambridge, MA: National Academy Press.

LaGanga, M. (1993, February 4). Chevron to stop dumping waste near shoreline. *Los Angeles Times,* pp. A1, A10.

The ozone layer has protected us for 1.5 billion years: It's time we returned the favor. (1994, November–December). [Chrysler advertisement]. *Audubon, 11–12,* 40–41.

Parker, L. (1995, March 28). GM, Ford among top polluters in state. *Detroit News,* p. A2.

The shorebirds who found a new wetland. (1990, July). *Audubon, 7,* 38.

Smith, N. C., & Quelch, J. A. (1993). *Ethics in marketing.* Boston: Richard D. Irwin.

Smithsonian Institution's Ocean Planet: A special report. (1995, March). *Outdoor Life, 3,* 13–22.

Weisskopf, M. (1992, February 23). Study finds CFC alternatives more damaging than believed. *The Washington Post,* p. A3.

"P." OR "PP." IS USED FOR PAGE NUMBERS IN BOOKS OR NEWSPAPERS.

TITLES OF PERIODICALS ARE NORMALLY CAPITALIZED.

TITLE IS USED WHEN NO AUTHOR IS IDENTIFIED IN THE SOURCE.

APA APA APA
APA APA

The most widely used documentation system in history, philosophy, religion, and the fine arts is found in *The Chicago Manual of Style,* 15th ed. (University of Chicago Press, 2003). The Chicago style (CMS) places numbers in the text that correspond to notes at either the bottom of the page (footnotes) or the end of the paper (endnotes). Since citations are signaled only by small raised numbers, CMS calls less attention to documentation than the parenthetical in-text systems of either MLA or APA. For move detailed information, consult www.press .uchicago.edu.

21 a Aims

The purpose of studies in the humanities is to understand the human experience as it is expressed and interpreted in a variety of media. History examines the many documents that a civilization produces that provide clues to how its people thought and lived. Philosophy and religion examine the nature of humanity by scrutinizing texts produced by past thinkers and prophets. Studies in art and communications examine texts that are often nonverbal, including paintings, sculptures, and films.

In the humanities, the study and practice of writing is a primary means of making meaning. Students of history and philosophy, for example, spend a lot of time reading texts, reading about texts, listening to lectures based on texts, and writing texts that demonstrate an understanding of historical or philosophical knowledge. However, unlike literary texts, those in history, philosophy, and religion, as well as art and musical history, are often steppingstones toward defining broader contexts and larger issues, toward a fuller understanding of human thought and expression. And unlike texts in the sciences and social sciences, those in the humanities involve matters of interpretation and debate rather than proofs and statistics. To be credible, interpretive papers need to be carefully reasoned, well supported, and clearly written.

21 b Style

In the humanities, thoughtfulness, variety, and vitality of expression are especially important. Though writing in the humanities is often explicitly argumentative, it is also fair and objective, presenting issues or positions reasonably and completely, and with a minimum of bias and subjectivity. The more neutral and analytical your tone, the more likely readers will take your ideas seriously. When you treat a text fairly, even one with which you disagree, readers are more likely to hear you out, which lays the foundation for strong and believable criticism. At the same time, the stylistic rules in the humanities are more variable than in most social science and science writing since individuality and uniqueness of expression are highly prized.

21 c Guidelines for formatting manuscripts

The CMS guidelines for submitting college papers do not reflect the wealth of visually interesting choices in fonts, type sizes, graphics, and other options available in modern word processing programs. If your instructor requests strict CMS format, follow the guidelines below. If your instructor encourages more creative formats, use good judgment in displaying the information in your text. The following guidelines describe the preparation of the main body of your paper.

Paper and Printing

Print all academic assignments on 8½″ ×11″ white paper, in a standard font (for example, Times New Roman or Courier) and point size (11 or 12), using a good-quality printer.

Margins and Spacing

Allow margins of one inch all around. Justify the left margin only. Indent five spaces or one-half inch for paragraphs.

For prose quotations of more than ten lines (or two lines of poetry), indent the entire quotation ten spaces. Do not use quotation marks to mark the beginning and ending of indented quoted passages.

Double space everything in the main body of the paper, including headings and quoted material, but single space individual entries in notes and on the bibliography page.

Page Numbers

Print page numbers in the upper right margin, one-half inch below the top of the paper; do not use the word *page* or the abbreviation *p.* It is optional to include your last name before each page number—a protection in case pages become separated from the manuscript. Count, but do not number, the title page, so that the text begins on page 2.

Title Page

Attach an unnumbered title page. Center the title fifteen lines from the top. Four lines below the title, center the word *By;* two lines below that, center your name, your instructor's name, the course title, and the date.

Body of Paper

Center the title on the first text page, capitalizing key words only. If your instructor asks for strict CMS style, avoid using italics, underlining, quotation marks, boldface, unusual fonts, or large type for the title. Double space to the first paragraph.

Punctuation

One space is required after commas, semicolons, colons, periods, question marks, and exclamation points and between the periods in an ellipsis. Dashes are formed by two hyphens, with no extra spacing on either side.

Visual Information

Label all tables (charts, graphs) and figures (drawings, photographs) included in the text: *Table 1, Fig. 2,* and so on. Include a clear caption for each, and place each visual element in the text as near as possible to the passage it refers to. In your text, be sure to discuss the most important information or feature in each table or figure you include.

21 d   Guidelines for CMS documentation

In the body of the paper, mark each quotation, paraphrase, and summary of source material by inserting a raised (superscript) Arabic number immediately after the sentence or clause. The superscript number follows all punctuation except dashes. Numbers run consecutively throughout the text.

> Frank Lloyd Wright's "prairie style" was characterized by the houses he built in and around Chicago "with low horizontal lines echoing the landscape."[1] Vincent Scully sees these suburban buildings as one of Wright's most important influences.[2]

For each superscript number, there is a corresponding endnote or footnote.

1. "Wright, Frank Lloyd," *The Concise Columbia Encyclopedia*, 1st ed.

2. Vincent Scully, *Architecture: The Natural and the Manmade* (New York: St. Martin's, 1991) 340.

Bibliography Page

A bibliography page is required at the end of a CMS-style paper. It lists all the works the writer consulted in writing the paper, whether or not the work was actually cited in a footnote or endnote. When endnotes are used, the bibliography page follows. Guidelines for assembling this page are as follows.

- Center the word *Bibliography* at the top of the page.

- Type the first line of each entry flush with the left margin; indent subsequent lines five spaces.

- List all authors or editors in alphabetical order, last name first.

- List the names of coauthors in normal order, first name first, separated by commas.

- If two or more authors share the same last name, alphabetize by first name.

- If two or more works are by the same author, alphabetize by the title of the work. After the first listing, use three hyphens to indicate the author's name.

- If neither an author nor an editor is listed, alphabetize by title.

- Use periods followed by one space to separate the author from the title and the title from the publication data.

- Capitalize all the important words in the title.

- Underline or italicize the titles of published books, periodicals, or films.

- Use quotation marks to indicate the titles of articles, chapters, poems, and stories within published books.

- The entries on a bibliography page appear the same way they do on the endnote page except that they are in alphabetical, not numerical, order.

Guidelines for Endnote or Footnote Citations

Endnotes are typed as one double-spaced list at the end of the text. The endnote format is easy to deal with, and it allows you to add or delete notes and change numbering with less fuss than modifying footnotes entails.

The endnote page follows the last page of text. It and subsequent pages are numbered in sequence. The title *Notes* appears centered without quotation marks, one inch from the top of the page. Double space before the first entry, within entries, and between entries. Entries appear in the order of the note numbers in your paper. Indent the first line five spaces; subsequent lines within an entry are flush with the left-hand margin.

Footnotes enable readers to find information at a glance. Footnotes appear in a single-spaced list at the bottom of the page, four lines below the last line of text. Numbers are aligned with the entry, followed by a period and one space before the first word. Indent the first line five spaces.

A bibliography page is normally required to provide readers with a convenient way of identifying an author's full set of sources (see Chapter 19). If you include only the sources you consulted, head the list *Works Consulted.* Use the same format given for a Works Cited list in the MLA documentation style.

21 e   Documenting books: First reference

1. Book by one author

1. Lewis Thomas, *Lives of a Cell: Notes of a Biology Watcher* (New York: Viking, 1974), 76.

2. Book by two or more authors

2. Toby Fulwiler and Alan R. Hayakawa, *The Blair Handbook*, 5th ed. (Upper Saddle River, NJ: Prentice Hall, 2007), 234.

3. Revised edition of a book

3. S. I. Hayakawa, *Language in Thought and Action,* 4th ed. (New York: Harcourt, 1978), 77.

4. Edited book and one volume of a multivolume book

4. Tom Waldrep, ed., *Writers on Writing,* vol. 2 (New York: Random House, 1988), 123.

5. Translated book

5. Albert Camus, *The Stranger,* trans. Stuart Gilbert (New York: Random House, 1946), 12.

6. Reprinted book

6. Zora Neale Hurston, *Their Eyes Were Watching God* (1937; reprint, New York: Perennial-Harper, 1990), 32.

7. Work in an anthology or edited collection

7. John Donne, "The Good-Morrow," in *The Metaphysical Poets,* ed. Helen Gardner (Baltimore: Penguin, 1957), 58.

8. Article in a reference book

8. *The Concise Columbia Encyclopedia,* 1998 ed., s.v. "Behn, Aphra."

An alphabetically arranged book requires no page numbers.

9. Anonymous book

9. *The World Almanac and Book of Facts* (New York: World Almanac-Funk & Wagnalls, 1995).

21 f Documenting periodicals: First reference

10. Article, story, or poem in a monthly or bimonthly magazine

10. Robert A. Linn and Stephen B. Dunbar, "The Nation's Report Card Goes Home," *Phi Delta Kappan,* October 2000, 127–43.

11. Article, story, or poem in a weekly magazine

11. Alex Ross, "The Wanderer," *New Yorker,* 10 May 1999, 56–63.

12. Article in a daily newspaper

12. Jane E. Brody, "Doctors Get Poor Marks for Nutrition Knowledge," *New York Times,* 10 February 1992, p. B7.

13. "Redistricting Reconsidered," *Washington Post,* 12 May 1992, p. B2.

13. Article in a journal paginated by volume

14. Joseph Harris, "The Other Reader," *Journal of Advanced Composition* 12 (1992): 34–36.

BIBLIOGRAPHY ENTRY FORMAT FOR BOOKS, CMS

Author(s) or Editor(s), *Book title.* City of publication: Publisher, Date of
publication.

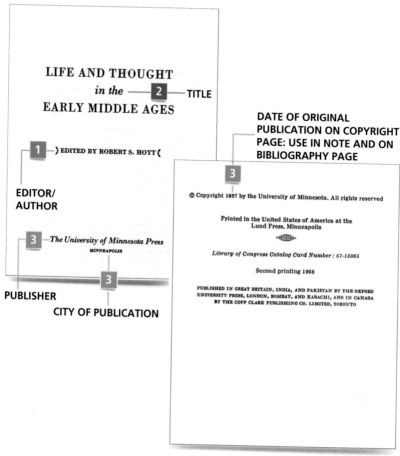

LIFE AND THOUGHT
in the — **2** — TITLE
EARLY MIDDLE AGES

1) EDITED BY ROBERT S. HOYT (

**EDITOR/
AUTHOR**

3 — *The University of Minnesota Press*
MINNEAPOLIS

PUBLISHER

3

CITY OF PUBLICATION

**DATE OF ORIGINAL
PUBLICATION ON COPYRIGHT
PAGE: USE IN NOTE AND ON
BIBLIOGRAPHY PAGE**

3

© Copyright 1967 by the University of Minnesota. All rights reserved

Printed in the United States of America at the
Lund Press, Minneapolis

Library of Congress Catalog Card Number: 67-15065

Second printing 1968

PUBLISHED IN GREAT BRITAIN, INDIA, AND PAKISTAN BY THE OXFORD
UNIVERSITY PRESS, LONDON, BOMBAY, AND KARACHI, AND IN CANADA
BY THE COPP CLARK PUBLISHING CO. LIMITED, TORONTO

CMS CMS CMS

1   **2**

Hoyt, Robert S., ed. *Life and Thought in the Early Middle Ages.*
Minneapolis: University of Minnesota Press, 1967.

3

1 AUTHOR OR EDITOR NAME.

Note: Name in normal order for individual or multiple authors or editors (*John Smith and Jim Jones*). Comma. In subsequent notes to same author, include last name only, shortened title, and page number (*Smith and Jones, Life and Thought, 78*). Add *ed.,* after name for editor.

Bibliography page (may also be called Works Cited or References): Follow MLA format for assembling this page, alphabetically, with last name first, and so on.

2 BOOK TITLE.

List titles and subtitles fully, capitalized and italicized (*Life and Thought in the Early Middle Ages.*). Comma. In subsequent notes, use shortened title. (*Life and Thought*).

In a bibliography entry, follow MLA style.

3 CITY, PUBLISHER, AND DATE OF PUBLICATION.

In the first note to a work, include all publication information as it appears on copyright page, in parentheses before the page number (*(Minneapolis: University of Minnesota Press, 1967), 103*). Period. In subsequent notes, omit publication information.

In a bibliography entry, follow MLA style.

GENERAL FORMAT FOR JOURNAL ARTICLES, CMS

Author(s). "Article Title." *Journal Title volume number, issue number* (Year of publication): inclusive page numbers.

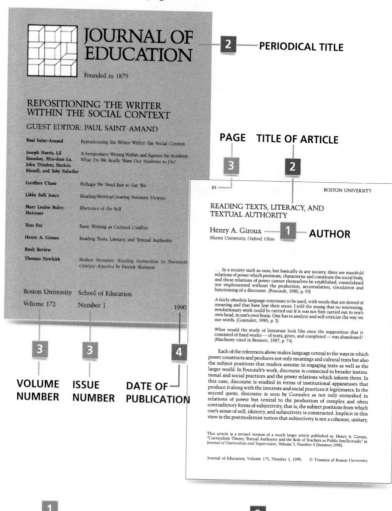

2 — PERIODICAL TITLE

PAGE   TITLE OF ARTICLE

3   **2**

AUTHOR **1**

VOLUME NUMBER **3**

ISSUE NUMBER **3**

DATE OF PUBLICATION **4**

1   **2**

Giroux, Henry A. "Reading Texts, Literacy, and Textual Authority."

Journal of Education 172, 1 (1990): 84–103.

2   3   4   3

1 **AUTHOR NAME.**

In a note, list name in normal order for one, two, or three authors, each separated by a comma, with *and* before last author (*Alan Charles Smith, Brian Jones, and Michelle Watts*). Comma. If four or more authors, list only first author followed by *and others*. In subsequent notes, cite author's last name, shortened title, and page number (*Giroux, "Reading Texts," 85*).

2 **TITLE.**

List titles and subtitles fully, capitalizing and put quotation marks around the titles of articles, poems, and short works within the periodical. Comma. Italicize book titles within **article titles** ("A Reassessment of Faulkner's *As I Lay Dying*"). Use single quotation marks around the titles of short works within article titles ("T.S. Eliot's 'Ash Wednesday' Revisited"). *Italicize* or underline **periodical titles** (*ADE Bulletin*).

3 **VOLUME, ISSUE, AND PAGE NUMBERS.**

For journals paginated separately by issue, list volume number, a comma, word "no.," and then issue number followed by date (in parentheses) and a colon: then page numbers: *(1990): 84–103*. Period. For journals paginated continuously, include volume number before the year and issue if available. Separate inclusive page numbers with an en dash (*42–54*). Only give the page numbers of pages referred to, or the first and last pages if referring to the article as a whole.

4 **DATE OF PUBLICATION.**

In magazines and newspapers, date of publication is placed within parentheses, followed by a colon and a space. For weekly or bi-weekly magazines give both day and month of publication in normal word order (Feb. 12, 2001). If no date of publication is given, put *n.d.* in parentheses (*n.d.*). Period.

14. Article in a journal paginated by issue

15. Helen Tiffin, "Post-Colonialism, Post-Modernism, and the Rehabilitation of Post-Colonial History," *Journal of Commonwealth Literature* 23, no. 1 (1988): 189–95.

15. Review

16. Mimi Kramer, "Victims." Review of *'Tis Pity She's a Whore,* as performed at the New York Shakespeare Festival, *New Yorker,* 20 April 1992, 78–79.

Documenting Online and Other Sources

To document a site on the World Wide Web, provide the following information.

- Author's name
- Title of document in quotation marks
- Title of complete work (if relevant) in italics or underlined
- Date of publication or latest revision (day/month/year) if available
- Date of access in parentheses (accessed day/month/year)
- Include end punctuation following a URL as needed.

16. Published Web site

17. Jonathan L. Beller, "What's Inside *The Insider?" Pop Matters Film,* 1999, http://popmatters.com/film/insider.html (accessed 21 May 2000).

17. Personal Web site

18. Toby Fulwiler, "Homepage," 2 April 2000, http://www.uvm.edu/~tfulwile (accessed 6 May 2000).

18. Professional Web site

19. *Yellow Wall-Paper Site,* University of Texas, 1995, http://www.cwrl.utexas.edu/~daniel/amlit/wallpaper/ (accessed 12 December 1999).

19. Publication reprinted on the web

    20. Betsy Erkkila, "The Emily Dickinson Wars," *The Emily Dickinson Journal* 5.2 (1996), 14 pars., 8 November 1998, http://www.colorado.edu/EDIS/Journal (accessed 2 June 1999).

20. Article in a reference database

    21. "Victorian," *Britannica Online,* Vers. 97.1, 1 March 1997, *Encyclopaedia Britannica,* http://www.eb.com:180 (accessed 3 May 1999).

21. E-mail or listserv message

    22. Toby Fulwiler, "A Question About Electronic Sources," E-mail to author, University of Vermont (23 May 2000).

DOCUMENTING OTHER SOURCES: FIRST REFERENCE

22. Personal interview

    23. John Morser, interview by author, 15 December 1999.

23. Personal or unpublished letter

    24. Paul Friedman, letter to author, 18 March 1998.

24. Work of art

    25. Hans Holbein, *Portrait of Erasmus,* The Louvre, Paris, page 148 in *The Louvre Museum,* by Germain Bazin (New York: Abrams, n.d.).

GENERAL NOTE FORMAT FOR ONLINE SOURCES, CMS

Number. Period. Author(s), "Title," Name of site or sponsoring body, Date of electronic publication, electronic address.

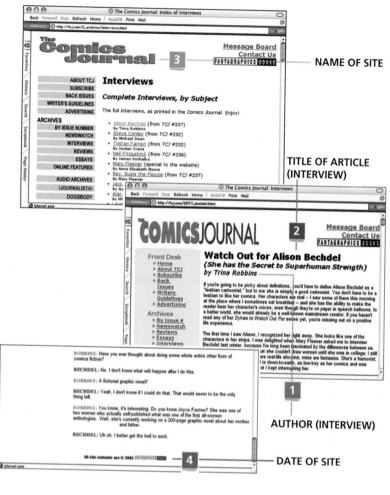

NAME OF SITE

TITLE OF ARTICLE (INTERVIEW)

AUTHOR (INTERVIEW)

DATE OF SITE

3. Trina Robbins, "Watch Out for Alison Bechdel (She has the Secret to Superhuman Strength)," *The Comics Journal,* 2001, http://tcj.com/237/ i_bechdel.html.

1 AUTHOR OF MATERIAL ON WEB SITE.

Note: Name in normal order for individual or multiple authors (*John Smith and Jim Jones*). Comma. In subsequent notes to same author, include last name only, shortened title, and page or paragraph number (*Smith and Jones, para. 12*). Add *ed.,* after name for editor.

Bibliography page (may also be called Works Cited or References): Follow MLA format for assembling this page, alphabetically, with last name first, and so on.

2 TITLE OF MATERIAL ON WEB SITE.

Enclose title and subtitle in quotation marks ("Watch Out for Alison Bechdel (She Has the Secret to Superhuman Strength)"). Comma. If no title is obvious, use the home page name as the title (found in URL). Use same guidelines as for periodicals.

3 NAME OF SITE OR SPONSORING ORGANIZATION.

Usually found at top or bottom of home page followed by date (*The Comics Journal, 2001*).

4 PUBLICATION INFORMATION.

List only the date the site was created or last revised (usually at bottom of page) followed by the electronic address without angle brackets (*http://tcj.com/237/i_bechdel.html*). Period. CMS does not request date of access unless material is time-sensitive.

CMS CMS CMS

Sample Page and Corresponding Endnote Page

Owsley 2

recorded "in exultant tones the universal neglect that had overtaken pagan learning."[2] It would be some time, however, before Christian education would replace classical training, and by the fourth century, a lack of interest in learning and culture among the elite of Roman society was apparent. Attempting to check the demise of education, the later emperors established municipal schools, and universities of rhetoric and law were also established in major cities throughout the Empire.[3]

The beginning of a page from the middle of a paper in CMS format. The superscript numbers 2 and 3 indicate that citations are documented in endnotes.

Owsley 12

Notes

1. Rosamond McKitterick, *The Carolingians and the Written Word* (Cambridge: Cambridge University Press, 1983), 61.

2. J. Bass Mullinger, *The Schools of Charles the Great* (New York: Stechert, 1911), 10.

3. James W. Thompson, *The Literacy of the Laity in the Middle Ages* (New York: Franklin, 1963), 17.

Endnote page with references in numerical order in CMS format

Sample Page with Footnotes

The Teatro Olimpico was completed in 1584, the statues, inscriptions, and basreliefs for the *fronsscena* being the last details completed. Meanwhile, careful plans were made for an inaugural, which was to be a production of *Oedipus* in a new translation.[10] Final decisions were made by the Academy in February 1585 for the seating of city officials, their wives, and others, with the ruling that "no masked men or women would be allowed in the theatre for the performance."[11]

The organization of the audience space was "unique among Renaissance theaters, suggesting . . . its function as the theater of a 'club of equals' rather than of a princely court."[12] The Academy is celebrated and related to Roman grandeur by the decoration over the monumental central opening, where its motto, "Hoc Opus," appears.[13] It is difficult to make out the entrances.

10. J. Thomas Oosting, *Andrea Palladio's Teatro Olimpico* (Ann Arbor: UMI Research Press, 1981), 118.

11. Oosting, *Palladio's Teatro,* 120.

12. Marvin Carlson, *Places of Performance: The Semiotics of Theater Architecture* (Ithaca: Cornell University Press, 1989), 5.

13. Simon Tidworth, *Theaters: An Architectural and Cultural History* (London: Praeger, 1973), 52.

A sample page from a paper using footnotes in CMS format

Documenting Subsequent References to the Same Work

25. Subsequent References to a Work

The second and any subsequent times you refer to a source, include the author's last name followed by a comma, a shortened version of the title, a comma, and the page number(s).

    26. Thomas, *Lives,* 99.

chapter **22** | *Writing in the Physical and Biological Sciences*

This chapter describes the general aims and styles of scientific writing and provides an overview of common forms and specialized documentation systems shared by the scientific community. If you write extensively in the sciences, consult one of the more detailed style manuals listed in this chapter.

22 a Aims

Scientific study examines the fundamental structures and processes of the natural world. In analyzing particular phenomena and organisms, scientists ask questions such as the following:

- What is it? Can it be isolated and observed? How can it be described?

- How does it function? What forces are in operation? How can these forces be explained?

- Why does it function the way it does? Can governing principles be identified, explained, and understood? Can predictions be made?

- What can be learned about other phenomena or organisms based on the evidence of particular studies?

Scientists approach and attempt to answer such questions using the *scientific method* of observation, prediction, experimentation, and analysis.

Observation. A chemist notices, for example, that when liquid A is mixed with liquid B, the solution of the two (C) has a higher temperature than either A or B alone.

Prediction. On the basis of this observation, the chemist predicts that whenever these amounts of A and B are mixed together, C will always have a higher temperature. This prediction is called a *hypothesis*—a preliminary generalization or explanation based on the observed phenomena.

Experimentation. To test the hypothesis, the chemist devises an experiment (in this example, the mixing of the two liquids under controlled conditions), watches the results, and carefully notes what happens.

Analysis and conclusions. The results of the experiment may lead the scientist to conclude, "Yes, when specific amounts of A and B are mixed, reaction C occurs." This finding can be shared with other scientists and could provide the basis for further hypotheses. If the results are different from the hypothesis, new questions must be asked and new hypotheses formulated to explain why the results differed from the initial observations.

Writing plays a central role throughout the investigative and experimental process. To develop a hypothesis, scientists record observations, questions, and possible explanations. In conducting an experiment, scientists take full and accurate notes to keep a running account of methods, procedures, and results. To understand the significance of the results, scientists report or publish the results so other scientists can read about them and respond.

Scientific writing does not report the writer's opinions, values, or feelings; it aims for objectivity and accuracy when reporting observations and findings. When you write in the sciences, try to separate your observations from your expectations or biases. Record only what you see and hear and what the instruments tell you, not what you hope to discover. Keep in mind that your primary purpose is to present information accurately—not to persuade, argue, or entertain.

22 b   Style

Most science writing seeks to convey information specifically, directly, economically, and accurately. But this common goal does not mean that the style of all science writing is uniform. For example, the form and style of a laboratory report is quite different from the laboratory notebook on which it is based. An article in *Scientific American* (written for a general readership) is quite different from one in *The Journal of Chemical Education* (written for college chemistry instructors).

SCI SCI SCI

Stylistic Guidelines for Writing in the Sciences

When writing in the sciences, keep the goals of clarity and directness in mind.

- Choose simple words rather than complex words when the meaning is the same, and use disciplinary terminology carefully and accurately.

- Prefer simple sentences to complex.

- Maintain a third-person point of view, to avoid the pronoun *I*. Use the passive voice when necessary to describe procedures: *The liquids were brought to a temperature of 35°C.*

- Use the present tense to refer to established knowledge or to discuss conclusions. Use the past tense to describe methods and results.

- Insert subheadings to help readers predict what is coming.

- Include tables and figures when they can help explain your methods or results. Label each of these clearly, and mention them at appropriate points in the text.

22 c   Number systems: Documenting sources

The life sciences (biology, botany, zoology), the applied sciences (chemistry, computer science, mathematics, physics), and the medical sciences (medicine, nursing, general health) all use a number system of documentation.

Conventions for Number Citation

In the number system of citation, writers alert readers to the use of other sources by citing a number, either in parentheses or with a *superscript,* a character raised a small space above the baseline of the surrounding text:[2] (as you can see, superscript numbers are also typically reduced in size for a neater appearance). This citation number corresponds to a numbered list of sources at the end of the paper. Math and life science disciplines generally prefer parenthetical numbers; chemistry, physics, the medical fields, and computer science disciplines generally prefer superscript numbers.

If, in using the number system, you use an author's name in a sentence, place the number immediately after the name, if possible.

> Linhoffer (3) reported similar results.
>
> Linhoffer[3] reported similar results.

If no author's name is used in the sentence, place the number immediately after the use of the source material. Science writers using parenthetical numbers have the option of including the author's last name before the number: (*Smith 3*).

According to the conventions of scientific writing, the numbers cited in the text can be organized either sequentially or alphabetically. In *sequential arrangement,* the first source cited in the text is numbered *1,* the second cited source is numbered *2,* and so on. Any subsequent reference to an already cited source is given the same number. Sequential reference is preferred by writers in chemistry, computer science, physics, the life sciences, and medicine.

In *alphabetic arrangement,* writers assign numbers according to the alphabetical order of the authors' last names as they appear on the reference page(s). For example, a reference to an author named Smith, even if it is the first source cited in the text, should be accompanied by the number *12* if Smith is the twelfth name on the alphabetical list of references. Alphabetical arrangement is preferred in mathematical writing.

When using the sequential system, number the bibliography sequentially as you write, and continue to use the same number each time you cite that authority. When using the alphabetical system, arrange your bibliography alphabetically and number accordingly.

Conventions for the List of References

The "Literature Cited" or "References" section provides publication information for all sources cited in the text.

Each scientific discipline has its own format for documenting sources; select the style appropriate to your discipline or consult your instructor. The following brief examples are illustrative only; they suggest that minor differences occur from discipline to discipline within scientific fields. If you need to write a substantial paper in any of these disciplines, consult the appropriate reference source listed below.

Life Sciences

Biology, botany, zoology, anatomy, and physiology follow the documentation system recommended in the *CBE Style Manual,* 6th ed. (New York: Cambridge University Press, 1994), published by the Council of Science Editors. CBE bases its standards for documentation on those presented in *National Library of Medicine Recommended Formats for Bibliographic Citation* (NLM 1991), the full text of which is available online at http://www.nlm.nih.gov/pubs/formats/internet.pdf.

In-text number citations are given sequentially in parentheses. Title the list of references "Literature Cited," "References Cited," or "References," and use the following general styles:

BOOK ENTRIES

1. Quammen, D. Natural acts: a sidelong view of science and nature. New York: Schocken Books; 1985. 221 p.

BOOK WITH MORE THAN ONE AUTHOR

2. Martini FH, Timmons MJ, McKinley MP. Human anatomy, third edition. Upper Saddle River, NJ: Prentice Hall; 1999. 886 p.

BOOK WITH AN EDITOR

3. Roberts GG, editor. The Prentice Hall anthology of science fiction and fantasy. Upper Saddle River, NJ: Prentice Hall; 2001. 1184 p.

Do not underline titles, and capitalize only the first word. Place a semicolon after the name of the publisher, and place a colon after the date if page range numbers are given. Leave no space(s) on either side of the colon that follows the date.

PERIODICAL ENTRIES

4. Brown, SG, Wagsten, MV. Socialization processes in a female lowland gorilla. Zoo Biol 1986;5(12):269-80.

NEWSPAPER ARTICLE

5. Garfinkel P. Medical students get taste of real-life doctoring. New York Times 2001 Oct 23;Sect F:7(col 2).

MAGAZINE ARTICLE

6. Kinsley M. In defense of denial. Time 2001 Dec 17:72-3.

Do not place in quotation marks or underline article or journal titles. Use no space(s) between year, volume, and page numbers, and place an issue number, if required, immediately after the volume number, in parentheses.

ELECTRONIC SOURCES

AN ONLINE JOURNAL ARTICLE

7. Alfred J. Fast fly maps at SNP. Nature reviews genetics [serial online] 2001 Dec. Available from: http://www.nature.com/cgitaf/DynaPage.taf?file=/nrg/journal/v2/n12/full/nrg1201-912b_fs.html. Accessed 2001 Dec 7.

AN ONLINE BOOK

8. Olson S. Shaping the future: biology and human values [book online]. Washington DC: National Academy Press; 1989. Available from: http://www.nap.edu/books/0309039479/html. Accessed 2001 Dec 7.

9. Plant Conservation Unit. Smithsonian Institute. [Internet]. c1997 [revised
2005, Jan.]. Available from: http://www.nmnh.si.edu/botany/projects/
pcu.htm. Accessed 2005, June 12.

Include three dates, if available, in a Web site reference: (1) the date of
publication or copyright; (2) the most recent revision (immediately after publication date [revised 2003, Jan.]); and (3) the date of access at the end of the
citation.

E-MAIL MESSAGE

10. Weaver, GT. Notice of meeting [electronic mail on the Internet]. Message to:
Mark Smith, 2005, June 1, 7:00 AM [cited 2005, June 2]. [two para].

Include author, subject line of message, the words [electronic mail on the
Internet], Message to: addressee's name, date of message, length of message.

Chemistry

Documentation style in chemistry is based on the American Chemical
Society's *The ACS Style Guide: A Manual for Authors and Editors,* 2nd edition. Edited by Janet S. Dodd (Washington, DC: American Chemical Society, 1997); online, see http://pubs.acs.org/books/references.shtml. In-text
citations should be superscript numbers and arranged either sequentially
or by author name and date. For entries on the reference list, which should
be titled "Literature Cited," use the following general styles.

BOOK ENTRIES

1. Siggia, S.; Hanna, J. G. Quantitative Organic Analysis via Functional Groups,
4th ed.; R. E. Krieger: Malabar, FL, 1988; pp. 55-60.

PERIODICAL ENTRIES

2. Scott, J. M. W. J. Chem. Ed. 1992(69)600-602.

For papers in the chemistry style, do not include article titles. If an issue
number is required, place it immediately after the volume number (*69* in
this example), in parentheses. Leave no spaces between date, volume, and
page numbers for periodicals, and use all digits for page sequences.

chapter 23 — *Writing in Business*

This chapter describes the aims, style, and common forms of writing in the business and professional world. Like writing in the social and physical sciences, business writing puts a premium on information; like writing in the humanities, it is highly influenced by the relationship between writer and reader.

23 a Aims

The guiding objectives of successful companies are efficiency, accuracy, and responsibility. Procedures are designed for minimal waste of time and energy, care is taken to avoid errors, and transactions are conducted fairly.

Communication in business mirrors these precepts. Business writing is primarily practical and instrumental, because its goal is to get things done. So knowing the purpose of the writing is paramount. For efficiency, it should be simple, direct, and brief; for accuracy, it should convey correct information and conform to standard conventions; and for responsibility, it should be honest and courteous.

Business writers must be aware of their audience. They must ask themselves: What is the purpose of this letter? To whom is it being written? What information do they already have? What else do they need to know? What does this communication need to include in order to have its intended effect? What, if any, secondary audience is likely to read this communication? Business writers must also be concerned about presentation. To make a good impression, any piece of writing must be neat, clean, and correct.

23 b Style

Because clear communication is highly valued, writing for business should be simple, direct, economical, and conventional. In general, the preferred tone is objective and fairly formal (although when you are addressing someone you know well, a more personal, informal tone might be appropriate). For most business writing, the following guidelines should be considered:

- **Start fast.** State your purpose—the main point—immediately, and avoid digression or repetition. In business, your reader's time as well as your own is valuable.

- **Write in a simple, direct style.** Keep your sentences as straightforward and readable as possible.

- **Choose the active voice (start fast)** rather than the passive voice. *(Fast starting is a principle to be followed.)*

- **Use technical terminology or jargon sparingly.** Write out complete names of companies, products, and titles. Explain any terms that could be misunderstood.

- **Avoid emotional or biased language** (sexist, racist) as well as stereotypes and clichés. Try to maintain a level of courtesy even when lodging a complaint.

- **Use numbers, bullets, or descriptive headings** to help readers locate information quickly.

- **Use graphs, charts, and other illustrations** when they convey information more clearly than verbal language.

23 c Common forms of writing in business

Memos

Memo is short for *memorandum,* meaning literally "a thing to be remembered." A memo is a note written to make a request, pass along information, or help either the sender or recipient remember something. Memos are less formal than business letters, partly because they are often sent between people who know one another and work together, usually in the same company. If you're writing to a stranger, a letter is more appropriate.

Format for Memos

> June 8, 2005
>
> From: Isabel Barahona
> To: Design team
> cc: Management group
> Subject: Commendation
>
> Everyone on the design staff made a terrific effort last week to put the finishing touches on the Rialto project. Janet, Kazuo, Sandy, and Jack, it's always a pleasure to make a presentation based on your work and to see its impact on customers. Thanks for going the extra mile under such a tight deadline.

1″ margins ─────

Subject: or Re: (regarding) ─────

no salutation ─────

block paragraph style ─────

very direct ─────

no closing ─────

E-mail within an organization often follows memo style in its directness and informality.

Business Letters

Know your purpose. Imagine your audience. Then think carefully about the manner in which you want to address this audience. Notice, for example, that your tone may change as your purpose changes.

- **Inquiring**—seeking information about a job opportunity or a product. "Can you tell me whether your company makes a mower that meets these specifications?"

- **Promoting**—providing information about a product or service and encouraging the reader to purchase it. "The Neighbor Kids lawn service will have your yard looking neat and trim on the very first visit. To schedule, call 555-5555."

- **Communicating**—transmitting the results of a decision or an information-gathering process. "I'm pleased to inform you that your company is the apparent low bidder. Please call my office so we can complete a contract."

- **Confirming**—documenting terms agreed to elsewhere. "As we discussed over lunch, I will work with you to identify suitable investment properties. My consulting rate is $120 per hour plus travel expenses. I look forward to being of assistance."

- **Complaining**—specifying a problem, documenting it, and requesting a solution. "Although you billed me for twelve ink cartridges, I received only six. I enclose copies of my order and your packing slip. Please forward the remaining items immediately or refund the balance."

- **Relating**—maintaining lines of communication. "I enjoyed visiting with you at the convention and look forward to doing business with you."

Your tone will also change depending on whether you're writing to a stranger, a business acquaintance, or someone with whom you have an established working relationship. Your relationship to your audience and how you want to present yourself and your company help determine your writing approach.

New contact: When making an initial contact by letter, identify yourself right away, then state your purpose. If you can identify yourself by referring to a mutual acquaintance or shared experience, so much the better.

> Dear Mr. Zenkov,
>
> My name is Rob Cirul. My partner, Chris Adams, and I operate the Neighbor Kids Lawn Care service. I live at 234 Hollow Hills Lane, and your neighbor Ellen Jones is one of our regular customers.

Format for Business Letter

Heading with business address and contact information. Can also appear below signature line. ——

1" margins, block paragraphs ——

inside address ——

Salutation. Note colon. ——

Identify yourself, relationship to addressee, and purpose of letter. ——

In body of letter, inquire, confirm, inform, or persuade. ——

Summarize, and ask for the action you seek. ——

Signature ——

Neighbor Kids Lawn Care
234 Hollow Hills Lane
Hamilton, OH 45014
(513) 555-5555
OhioYardboys@aol.com

March 18, 2005

Yvelisse da Silva
2352 Sixteenth Street
Hamilton, OH 45014

Dear Ms. da Silva:

I am Rob Cirul, one of the partners in Neighbor Kids lawn care service. You and I met at the Highland Garden Center last week and talked about yard work.

My partners, Cal Ortiz and Jillian Wong, and I have been mowing lawns and doing yard cleanup for three seasons, and we would be happy to have you as a customer. Our rates are reasonable, and we have more than a dozen repeat customers in the neighborhood who have been happy with our work.

We will be working on your block this weekend. I'll stop by to talk with you, or you can reach me at 555-5555. We hope to be able to work for you.

Sincerely yours,

Rob Cirul

Rob Cirul

State Abbreviations

Use the U.S. Postal Service abbreviations (capitalized, with no periods) for the names of the fifty states and the District of Columbia only on mail, in full addresses in text, or in documentation. Spell out these names in the text of a paper or letter.

STATE	ABBREVIATION	STATE	ABBREVIATION
Alabama	AL	Montana	MT
Alaska	AK	Nebraska	NE
Arizona	AZ	Nevada	NV
Arkansas	AR	New Hampshire	NH
California	CA	New Jersey	NJ
Colorado	CO	New Mexico	NM
Connecticut	CT	New York	NY
Delaware	DE	North Carolina	NC
District of Columbia	DC	North Dakota	ND
Florida	FL	Ohio	OH
Georgia	GA	Oklahoma	OK
Hawaii	HI	Oregon	OR
Idaho	ID	Pennsylvania	PA
Illinois	IL	Rhode Island	RI
Indiana	IN	South Carolina	SC
Iowa	IA	South Dakota	SD
Kansas	KS	Tennessee	TN
Kentucky	KY	Texas	TX
Louisiana	LA	Utah	UT
Maine	ME	Vermont	VT
Maryland	MD	Virginia	VA
Massachusetts	MA	Washington	WA
Michigan	MI	West Virginia	WV
Minnesota	MN	Wisconsin	WI
Mississippi	MS	Wyoming	WY
Missouri	MO		

Established relationship: A letter to an established customer can be more familiar, but keep the tone appropriate to business communication.

> Dear Mr. Clark,
>
> It's hard to imagine spring is just around the corner, but I see your daffodils budding and know that I'll soon be mowing lawns again. I'm writing to confirm that you'll want your regular Friday afternoon lawn spot in the schedule.

Form

Think of a business letter as a brief essay, with an opening, supporting detail, and a conclusion. First, identify yourself and your relationship to the recipient, and state your business purpose. Next, detail your proposal or request. Then summarize your case and request or specify the next action to be taken.

Resumés

A resumé is a brief summary of an applicant's qualifications for employment. It outlines education, work experience, and other activities and interests so a prospective employer can decide quickly whether or not an applicant is a good prospect for a particular job. Try to tailor your resumé for the position you are seeking by emphasizing experience that is most relevant to the position. Preparing a resumé on a computer lets you revise it easily and quickly.

Generally, a resumé is sent out with a cover letter that introduces the applicant, indicates the position the applicant is seeking, and offers additional information that cannot be accommodated on the resumé itself. Print out your resumé and cover letter on good-quality 8″ × 11″ stationery. Even if you fax these documents to prospective employers, you should have attractive copies to take with you to interviews. Examples of resumés appear on pages 253–255.

Resumés should be brief and to the point, preferably no more than a page long (if relevant experience is extensive, more than one page is acceptable). Resumé formats vary in minor ways, but most include the following information:

Personal Information. Resumés begin with the applicant's name, address, and phone number, usually centered at the top.

Objective. Many resumés include a line summarizing the applicant's objective, either naming the specific job sought or describing a larger career goal.

Education. Most first-time job applicants list their educational background first, since their employment history is likely to be fairly limited. Name the last two or three schools attended (including dates of attendance and degrees), starting with the most recent. Indicate major areas of study, and highlight any relevant courses. Also consider including your grade point average, awards, and anything else that shows you in a good light. When employment history is more detailed, educational background is often placed at the end of the resumé.

Work experience. Starting with the most recent, list all relevant jobs, including company name, dates of employment, and a brief job description. If you are applying for your first full-time job, listing summer jobs, work-study programs, and similar employment, even in a different industry, will show prospective employers that you have some work experience. Unpaid volunteer work may also be relevant. Use your judgment about listing jobs in which you had difficulties with your employer.

Special skills or interests. It is often useful to mention special skills, interests, or activities that provide additional clues about your abilities and personality.

References. The line "References available on request" indicates that you have obtained permission from two or three people—teachers, supervisors, employers—for prospective employers to contact them for a recommendation. To avoid embarrassment, select people who are likely to speak well of you, and secure their permission well in advance of your job search. Listing references on your resumé is acceptable but is not recommended. Most employers include a place to list references on their application form, and some have specific requirements, such as listing only people who know you through previous work experience and not using relatives as references.

Following are two sample resumés that contain essentially the same information. However, the traditional resumé emphasizes employment history, listing information in approximately the order outlined above, and would be appropriate for applying for any position. The skills-based resumé emphasizes capabilities more than past experience and would be advantageous for a candidate with wide, varied, or extensive skills that might be of special interest to a particular employer.

Chris Aleandro
405 Martin Street
Lexington, Kentucky 40508
(606) 555-XXXX
caleandro@XXX.XXX

Objective: Internship in arts administration.

Education

University of Kentucky: 2004 to present.

Currently a sophomore majoring in business administration with a
minor in art history. Degree expected May 2008.

Henry Clay High School (Lexington, KY.): 2000 to 2004.

College preparatory curriculum, with emphasis in art and music.

Related Work Experience

Community Concerts, Inc.: 2004 to present.

Part-time promotion assistant, reporting to local director.
Responsibilities include assisting with scheduling, publicity,
subscription/ticketing procedures, and fundraising. Position
involves general office duties as well as heavy contact with
subscribers and artists.

Habitat for Humanity: September to November 2004.

Co-chaired campus fundraising drive that included a benefit
concert, raising $55,000.

Art in the Schools Program: 2003–2004.

Volunteer, through the Education Division of the Lexington Center for
the Arts. Trained to conduct hands-on art appreciation presentations
in grade school classrooms, visiting one school a month.

Other Work Experience

Record City: 2000 to 2003 (part-time and summers).

Salesclerk and assistant manager in a music store.

Special skills: WordPerfect 5.1: desktop design of brochures, programs,
and other materials.

References: Available on request.

Figure 23–1   Traditional Resumé

Susan Anderson

CURRENT ADDRESS   222 Summit Street, Burlington, VT 05401
TELEPHONE AND E-MAIL   (802) 864-XXXX;
susan.anderson@XXX.XXX

OBJECTIVE: Researcher/writer for nonprofit environmental organization.

EDUCATION
> **University of Vermont.** School of Natural Resources, Geology
> and English double major. GPA: 3.6. Expected graduation,
> May 2008.
> **Fairfield High School.** Fairfield, OH. 2000–2004. Activities
> included debate team, Spanish club, student newspaper,
> field hockey, swimming.

SKILLS
> **Field research.** Extensive experience analyzing natural plant
> communities, quantifying data, surveying field sites, and
> drawing topographical site maps.
> **Newsletter publication.** Familiar with all aspects of editorial and
> feature writing, layout, production, and fundraising for
> nonprofit newsletters.
> **Computer literacy.** Fluent in MS Word, Excel, PowerPoint,
> Adobe Premier, Sigmaplot, INFORM, Quark Xpress.
> **Oral communication.** Confident public speaker to large and small
> audiences after three years on the university debate team.
> **Spanish.** Fluent after four years of secondary and college study,
> including AFS summer abroad in Quito, Ecuador.

RELEVANT ENVIROMENTAL COURSEWORK
> Field Ecology Methods
> Landscape and Ecosystem Ecology
> Fundamentals of Field Science
> Landscape Inventory and Assessment

Figure 23–2   Skills-Based Resumé

RESEARCH EXPERIENCE

    Southwest Earth Studies, June–August 2007. Internship to research public policy of acid mine drainage in the San Juan mountains, National Science Foundation.

    Field Research of the Newark Rift Basin, June 2006. Internship to study water flow in the Newark rift basin, Newark Environmental Foundation program.

COMMUNICATION EXPERIENCE

    Teaching Fellow, School of Natural Resources, University of Vermont, January 2007–present. Teach lab for a course, Environmental Problem Solving.

    Editorial Assistant, *Wild Gulf Journal,* The Chewonki Foundation, January 2006–December 2007. Edited a quarterly journal of environmental education.

    Tutor, Writing Center, University of Vermont, September 2005–December 2006. Counseled students in writing undergraduate papers in introductory and intermediate geology courses.

LEADERSHIP EXPERIENCE

    English Majors' Student Representative, University of Vermont, September 2005–May 2006. Elected to represent 200 English majors and participate as a voting member at faculty meetings and curriculum revision committee.

    Local Foods Coordinator, Onion River Co-op. Burlington, VT. January 2003–May 2004. Ordered and coordinated pick-ups from local farms.

REFERENCES: Available upon request.

Design is the process of arranging and presenting your writing for others to read. Whether you present your writing as a college paper, a newsletter, or a Web page, you are creating a *document* of one kind or another. Your objective is to present your work in a neat, attractive form that makes its organization apparent and your purpose clear.

24 a   Objectives of design

Good design is *transparent:* it calls attention to your work, not to itself. If a magazine cover catches your eye and you think, "That looks interesting—I want to read that," the design is doing its job.

Here are some objectives of good design and sample ways to achieve them.

1. **Attract attention.** Choose layout, type font, illustrations, and graphics to spark interest.

2. Create **flow.** Help readers move through your document. To remove obstacles, put background information or statistics in tables or boxes where they don't disrupt your narrative or argument.

3. Show **hierarchy.** Make items of similar importance resemble each other (this list is an example). In a college paper, set off major sections with subheadings, white space, or initial capitals.

4. Reinforce **contrast.** If your paper advances one side of an argument, consider summarizing the opposing view in a box or "sidebar."

5. Use **graphics.** Charts make numbers easier to understand. Drawings or photos can convey information more efficiently than words.

6. **Hold attention.** Break up long stretches with graphics or typographical devices such as subheadings or initial capitals. (See 24c.)

24 b   Layout

Most college instructors ask you to use 8½ ×11″ paper. Use paper heavy enough to prevent type on the following pages from showing through. Use an inkjet or laser printer.

Set page margins at one inch at the top, bottom, and sides of body text. In Microsoft Word, go to File, Page Setup. Click on View, Print Layout to see the proportion of type to white space. Double space text unless instructed otherwise.

If the title page is also the first page of your paper, put your name, your instructor's name, the course title, and the paper's due date at the top left-hand corner, each on a separate, double-spaced line using your regular type-face. Don't indent.

On the next double-spaced line, center the title of the paper. Use a type-face slightly larger than your body type. Don't underline or italicize your title or put it in quotation marks. Double space again, and begin the body of text. (For an example of this style, see 19j.)

If your instructor asks for a separate title page, follow his or her guidelines or those of your discipline. (See 19j and 20j for examples in MLA and APA formats.)

In the upper right-hand corner of each manuscript page, put your last name or an abbreviated title followed by the page number, separated by a single space. Do not use slashes, parentheses, periods, the abbreviation *p,* or the word *page.* (See 19j.) Your word processor can automatically insert your last name, title, and page number in a "header." The Word command is View, Header and Footer.

Rules for Indenting and Spacing

- Indent the first word of each paragraph five spaces.

- Space once after each word; space once after end punctuation if you write on a computer; otherwise check with your instructor.

- Space once after a comma, semicolon, or colon.

- Do not space between words and quotation marks, parentheses, or brackets. (See Chapters 53–54.)

- Do not space between quotation marks and end punctuation or between double and single quotation marks. (See 53a.)

- Do not space after a hyphen except in a suspended construction. *The rest of the staff are half- and quarter-time employees.* (See Chapter 58.)

- Do not space on either side of a dash, which consists of two hyphens. *Only two players remained—Jordan and Mario.* (See Chapter 55.)

- Space before and after a slash only when it separates lines of poetry. (See 55c.)

- To display quotations of more than four typed lines, use block format. (See Chapter 53.)

- Underlining spaces between underlined words is optional, but be consistent.

Once upon a time, most instructors preferred typewritten papers, and a few would accept handwritten ones. Today, the word processor has all but completely replaced the typewriter. Such programs let you present your work in a much more sophisticated and attractive form.

A type font consists of a typeface in various sizes with variations such as **bold** and *italic*. A serif font—like this one—has little strokes at the ends of each letterform. A sans serif font consists of type without serifs. For large blocks of text, serif type is easier to read. Use sans serif type in informal settings and for captions and labels.

For the body of your text, pick a serif font such as Times Roman, Marin, Bookman, Palatino, or New Century Schoolbook, unless your instructor specifies a typeface that looks like a typewriter's, such as Courier. Avoid unusual or unnecessary fonts. Choose a point size that is easy to read, usually 12 points. The wider each line of type, the larger the point size needed for easy reading.

```
12 point
Courier
(serif,
fixed
spacing)
```

12 point
Century
Schoolbook
(serif, propor-
tional spacing)

12 point
MS Gothic
(sans serif,
proportional)

Titles and Headings

After selecting the body type, pick a typeface for your title and for headings.

Designing Documents

(Chapter title, 16-point News Gothic bold)

Tools for designing

(First-level heading, 12-point News Gothic bold)

Typography

(Second-level heading, 12-point News Gothic)

Lists and Tables

(Third-level heading, 12-point Times New Roman bold)

An array or table can make numbers easier to understand. For a simple series of numbers, set up a simple table by using tab stops.

Median Income by Age of Householder

15–24 YEARS	25–34	35–44	45–54	55–64	65+	ALL HOUSEHOLDS
$27,699	44,473	53,240	58,218	44,992	23,048	42,148

Source: 2000 Census

To compare more than one series of numbers, use tab stops or your word processor's table function. (In Word, use the toolbar's Insert Table button.) The array of numbers in the following table is four columns wide by seven rows deep. Place the table near the text it illustrates.

Median Income by Age, 1993–2000

	1993	1999	2000
15–24	$22,740	26,017	27,689
25–34	36,793	43,591	44,473
35–44	48,063	52,582	53,240
45–54	54,350	58,829	58,218
55–64	39,373	46,095	44,992
65+	20,879	23,578	23,048

Source: 2000 Census

24 d   Graphics

The term graphics refers to ways of presenting information in nonverbal form, including charts, graphs, and illustrations.

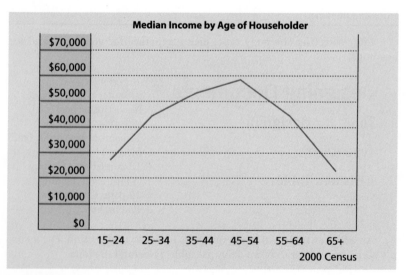

Line graph

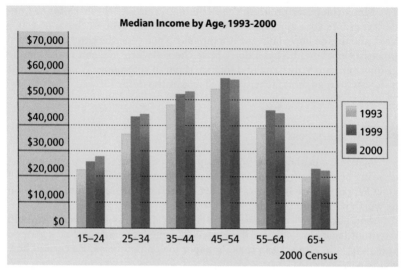

Bar graph

A line graph, sometimes called a fever graph, can make data easy to see.

A bar graph can compare multiple sets of data.

A pie chart translates proportions into sections of a circle to compare parts to the whole.

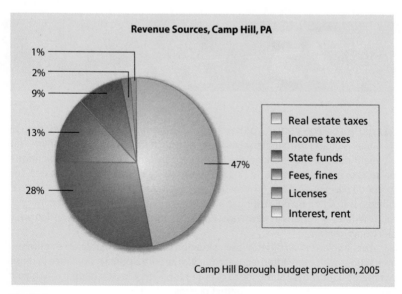

Pie chart

Many computer programs can create graphs like these. Enter the underlying data in a spreadsheet program, pick the type of chart, give it a title, and decide how you want it to appear. Then copy the chart into a word processor document. If you don't have the software, you can make simple graphs and charts by hand and include them in your paper. Keep them neat and easy to read, and identify the source of the data.

24 e Illustrations

A sketch can show how you set up the equipment for an experiment. A drawing or a snapshot can establish a mood, a sense of place, or a point of view. When you are writing about art or architecture, a picture really can be worth a thousand words.

Another source of illustration is clip art, simple illustrations once sold in cutout books but now available in electronic form. Because it is generic and simplistic, clip art can make a paper look amateurish. Be careful how you use it.

Use illustration not for decoration but for a purpose—to make something more understandable or easier to visualize or to convey information or emotion. A photo that relates specifically to your writing—"We followed Queen's Garden Trail through Bryce Canyon"—is more effective than a stock photograph—"We followed a trail that looked something like this."

chapter **25** *Writing for the Internet*

If you're a college student, you have grown up in a wired world, corresponding by e-mail, sending *instant messages* to friends, or *chatting* with groups online. You might publish your work on a *newsgroup* or an *e-mail list* for others to critique, or post an essay on the World Wide Web to seek feedback from classmates. You might display your writing for prospective employers or create an online journal, called a *weblog* or a *blog*. Writing is a big part of this new world, and the Internet raises writing questions in new ways. Why are you writing, for whom, and in what electronic format?

Your audience will differ in each situation, and each format enables different interactions with other Internet users. You'll write with a primary audience in mind, but there's a secondary audience to consider too—people who happen upon your writings and might need more context or explanation.

25 a   Writing for the Web

On a Web page, you can present text, charts, photographs, video clips, and audio recordings. But readers can't take in all these things at once, so you must construct paths for readers to choose.

Web Audiences

Readers on the Web often don't read in the same ways as print readers. They scan rather than read deeply. They skip from section to section, page to page, or site to site, looking for items that spark their interest. Others are seeking for specific information. If they don't find it quickly, they move on. If they think they might find what they need, they stick around a little longer. If they do find useful information, they linger.

A 2000 study by Stanford University and the Poynter Institute (a newspaper-industry think tank) found that even though many Web sites offer photos and graphics, a surprising number of readers focus first on words—headlines, captions, or stories. Readers' patterns of scanning suggest some strategies for Web writers. If the following ideas sound like design issues rather than writing strategies, that's because the Web makes the connection between organization, design, and writing even more important.

The first Web page readers encounter should provide most of the following items or, at least, links to them:

The subject—what's the site about?

Authorship—whose work is this?

Purpose—why was it created?

Contents—beyond the home page, what other content is available?

Context—is there information for readers new to the topic?

Organization—are there links to major sections? How does the reader navigate the site?

Paths—where did the information come from? Where can readers learn more?

Date—when was the site created and last modified?

Manageable Chunks

Make educated guesses about what your specific audience wants. Readers might seek specific information, or they might be interested in your perspective and opinions. Display prominently whatever you want readers to see and whatever you believe they will need or find interesting.

Break information into small, easily comprehensible *chunks*. Online readers prefer not to scroll through long screens. You can help by linking to separate pages of background information, answers to common questions, how or why you created the site, and other side issues.

Writing for Web Readers

How readers view a Web site	How to design for Web readers
Often begin with written text	Make captions, titles, and openings engaging and informative.
	Don't let graphics hinder reading.
Look for navigation signs	Use organization strategies common to other sites (such as a column of links repeated on the side of each page).
Read "shallow but wide"	Categorize. Don't hide important data "deep" in any one category. Write clear headings that tell what follows.
Scan rather than read	Create lists. Put keywords in boldface.
Read first sentences only	Make every word count.

Breaking Up Information

Lists make information accessible. Concise writing saves readers time. Compare these two examples:

Mission

The Chicago Opera Theater was founded in 1974. The mission of the Theater is to provide first-class productions, drawing from the operatic repertoire of some of the greatest works of the 17th, 18th, and 20th centuries. The Theater aims to produce intimate and innovative performances that are accessible to everyone and to discover and assist the development of the most talented young artists in the United States. The Theater further intends to make itself an integral part of the cultural landscape of Chicago.

Mission

Founded in 1974, the Chicago Opera Theater's mission is

- To provide first-class productions of operatic repertoire, including the greatest works of the 17th, 18th, and 20th centuries.

- To produce intimate and innovative performances that are accessible to everyone.

- To discover and develop the most talented young artists in the United States.

- To become an integral part of Chicago's cultural landscape.

Both examples contain the same information, but the second, which is what the opera company actually wrote, is easier to read and remember. This works in print, too!

Nonlinear Writing

Breaking information into chunks gives readers a choice of routes. They can read background information first or jump to your conclusions. They can examine your sources or look first at illustrations. But you must *anticipate* these moves and create paths for them.

Suppose you're writing for a history class about the roots of the Civil War. The Whig Party and the Compromise of 1850 will be familiar to your professor and classmates, but other readers will need more background. To find an organizational pattern, make a cluster diagram of main ideas.

Grouping and expanding these elements begins to suggest how a Web presentation of your research could be structured, a page or more for each section. These groupings will become the major elements of your presentation. You can use an embellished cluster diagram, like the one below, or outline each major element on a page of its own and arranged into sequence to create what is called a "storyboard" presentation.

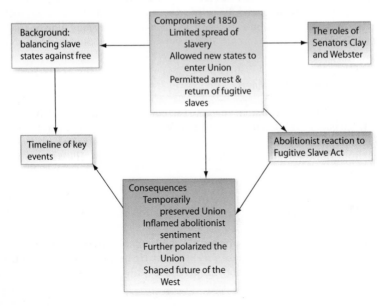

Links and Navigation Tools

Once you map the structure, you can begin to imagine the paths readers will need between sections. For example, a main reference to the Fugitive Slave Act should link to its impact among abolitionists. If you have a preferred sequence in mind, use a *next* link to connect each chunk to the next.

A navigation bar is a consistent set of links providing access to all pages in a site. Each page should include a link to other pages in its section, to other sections, and to the home page, so readers can see where they are at all times. The anchors for navigation links can be images such as buttons or pictures, or just words. A simple set of navigation links for the Compromise of 1850 paper might look like this.

Home: Compromise of 1850   Elements of Compromise   Timeline
Fugitive Slave Act   Clay and Webster   Consequences

Make navigation tools visually consistent, and keep them in the same position on every page.

Photos on Web Pages

If you include a photo that belongs to someone else, be sure you have permission, and give credit. File size is an important consideration. Digital photos are usually produced for print at a resolution of 300 dots per inch, or dpi, but that resolution can result in large files that load slowly. Use a photo-editing program to create 72 dpi versions of your photos.

Resources for Web Site Builders

Online tutorials can help you get started building Web sites. Check out the W3Schools HTML Tutorial at http://www.w3schools.com/html/. For a print reference, try *HTML 4 for the World Wide Web* by Elizabeth Castro (Peachpit, Berkeley, 2000). For others, search on the term "HTML tutorial."

25 b   E-mail and newsgroups

E-mail lists and newsgroups enable one-to-many interactions. This section focuses on writing in these formats. For tips on how to find and use e-mail lists and newsgroups for research, see 13d.

E-mail Do's and Don't's

Here are a few e-mail rules from the world of business, some learned by painful experience.

- In academic or business e-mail, write more formally than you would when corresponding with friends. Capitalize appropriately and spell conventionally. Don't use slang or informal abbreviations (great, not gr8). Don't assume the recipient will understand IMHO (in my humble opinion) or ROFL (rolling on the floor laughing).

- E-mail magnifies emotion. If you're angry, draft and wait before you send. If you have something negative to say—"Your answers seem to contradict one another. Why?"—make contact in person or by phone so that you can modulate your voice and not sound hostile.

- E-mail is forever. Even if you delete your files and the recipient does the same, copies can survive on servers at various points of Internet transmission. You might regret something you wrote, but you might not be able to erase it, so think before you send

- E-mail messages also can vanish if you don't take care to save them. To document an e-mail conversation for research or business, save and print a copy that includes dates and headers.

- Keep it simple. Be aware that many people will recognize and answer only one or two questions per e-mail.

Newsgroups and E-mail Lists

Information posted to a discussion group or *newsgroup* is collected on a computer "bulletin board." Readers interested in a group's topic download messages and submit their own. If you subscribe to an *e-mail list,* you receive and send messages by e-mail. Some lists and groups require you to become a member before posting or reading messages.

The e-mail do's and don't's (in 25b, above) also apply to lists and newsgroups. Before you post, read the group's frequently asked questions (FAQs, pronounced *fax*) and answers. They'll help you know whether you're in an appropriate group, list the key contacts, answer many preliminary questions, tell you how to post, and describe any special protocols. If there's an archive, search it for your specific topic before posting. Read some postings to determine the group's level of formality, and remember in academic or business correspondence to write in appropriately formal ways.

25 c   Weblogs

Weblogs, or blogs, are online, public journals. Blog postings frequently link to related material on other sites and permit readers to post comments. Thus blog authors—*bloggers*—connect with one another and with their readers. Over the last few years, blogging has moved from an obscure form of Internet scribbling to a collectively powerful force in commerce, journalism, and politics. How are bloggers causing this earthquake? They are *writing*.

There are nearly as many reasons for writing in a weblog as there are bloggers—as of spring 2006, the search site Technorati (www.technorati.com) was monitoring 37 million sites. What are all these people writing about? Whatever interests them—whatever they're thinking about, reacting to, struggling to understand, or trying to explain.

Blog Hosts and Blog Tools

Many host sites offer free blog accounts. A blog is basically a simple Web page, with the most recent journal entries at the top, but hosting software makes it possible to publish without knowing HTML. Other sites offer tools for editing or data gathering. There's a useful directory at Weblogs Compendium, www.lights.com/weblogs/hosting.html, or search on "blog host."

For weblog search tools, visit www.technorati.com, www.icerocket.com, or www.blogdigger.com, or search for "blog search."

RSS, or Really Simple Syndication, provides a way for readers to get summaries of their favorite blogs and for publishers to let readers know when sites are updated. Find tools and info at http://allrss.com/. There's an RSS search engine at www.feedster.com.

WRITING ACROSS THE CURRICULUM

Writing Across the Internet

Pick a Web site that you have found useful for research. How is it organized? What did you notice first, and how did you discover its organization? If you had difficulty finding anything, how did you resolve it? What would you do to improve the site's usefulness for visitors like you?

For a class other than your writing class, find a related e-mail list or newsgroup. Search the archives or current posts for information related to what you're studying. Compare the writing to the materials you've read in that class. What are the similarities and differences? How would you explain them?

Do you have a favorite blog? If not, browse until you find one that appeals to you. What do you like about it? What can you discern about the author's purpose? For what audience is the blog written? If comments are posted, what do they tell you about the site's readers?

If you were starting a weblog, what would you write about? Narrower question: What would you write about today? What three other blogs would you want to link to? What would your choice of links tell readers about you?

Beyond the classroom, a world of writing situations awaits. *Public writing* or *civic writing* includes persuasion in editorials, letters to the editor, and legal briefs. Writing reports is a key task in government and the social sciences. Journalism is a form of report writing, and even if you are not a journalist, understanding how journalists write can help you attract news coverage of issues or events.

In business, you might explain a proposed transaction, confirm an agreement, report on marketing prospects or propose a solution to a problem. You might write ads to persuade consumers to buy. As you meet these situations in business and public affairs, you'll recognize familiar writing purposes: *inform, explain, persuade, advocate*.

26 a   Reports

In a report, you are asked to describe a problem, process, or situation. Conventional news reporting often stops there. Business reporting often goes further, evaluating possible solutions and making recommendations.

First, understand the purpose, the audience, and the scope of your task. Next, gather information. Then write, organizing the information in ways that support your purpose.

Here are some common reporting purposes:

- Describe an event, its consequences, and people's reactions.

- Identify a problem and propose a solution.

- Document the process and results of a research project or an experiment.

- Describe a person's actions or behavior. This could be anything from a police report to a physician's statement to a nomination for a heroism award.

- Compare alternatives (an equipment purchase, a policy question) and recommend a course of action.

For whom are you writing? Journalists often imagine an individual or group whose characteristics are a composite of real readers they know. Within an organization, a *primary audience* is the people who will make decisions based on your report. A *secondary audience* comprises those who will be affected by that decision. An *immediate audience* consists of people—your editors or your immediate supervisors—who will read your report first.

Ask the journalist's questions—*who, what, when, where, why,* and *how.* Depending on the situation, some of these questions will be more important than others. *What* is the condition of city parks? *How much* will it cost to improve them? *Why* did a new product do poorly in the marketplace? *How many* voters think health care should be a private responsibility, and how many think it should be a public responsibility?

Here's a basic strategy for organizing a report:

- State the problem and the purpose (inform, analyze, recommend): *City parks have a backlog of deferred maintenance. Equipment is worn or unusable. Buildings need repair. What can or should be done?*

- Provide background information or context: *Spending has been cut over several years. Other budget areas had pressing needs.*

- Convey facts: *Further deferral of maintenance will damage some buildings past the point of repair. Growth in youth sports requires more maintenance of athletic fields.*

- List alternatives: *Close less-used parks; shift money from other budget areas; charge user fees; solicit donations; raise taxes.*

- Recommend action: *Form a group of park users and managers to budget repairs over five years and recommend a mix of shifted resources and new revenue. Bring recommendations to city council for next budget cycle.* (Some reports, including progress reports and news reports, need not include a recommendation or a conclusion.)

As you write, distinguish fact from opinion. Identify your own opinions. (In news reporting, your opinion is less important than the opinions of people affected by the events you describe.) In most reports, a fact or a prediction carries more weight than an emotional characterization: *The park maintenance supervisor says the roof of the pavilion needs to be replaced. If it leaks, repairs will be much more expensive.* That is more useful than *The park maintenance supervisor says the pavilion roof is in a "disgraceful condition."*

26 b   Pamphlets and brochures

A *pamphlet* or *brochure* provides quick, portable information about a product or service, usually following a simple format: a single 11 × 17″ or 8½ × 11″ sheet folded in sections and printed on both sides. The Mendocino Wine Country brochure reproduced here was designed to tell visitors where to find wineries on California's redwood coast.

With a word-processing computer, simple image-editing tools, and a printer, you can design and produce a basic brochure. Adapting the pamphlet format to the Web frees you from the restrictions of paper sizes.

MENDOCINO WINE COUNTRY

Fine Vines ∴ Great Wines on
California's Redwood Coast

525 So. Main St., Suite D
Ukiah, CA 95482
707-468-9886
www.mendowine.com

26 c   Newsletters

If you belong to an academic organization, a nonprofit group, or a club of people with a shared interest, chances are you receive a *newsletter.* Desktop publishing has allowed layout, illustration, and typographical chores that once required professional assistance to be performed at your own computer keyboard.

The editor of a special-interest newsletter has one key advantage: there's little need to guess about who is reading. The audience consists of people already familiar with the topic or newcomers curious enough to browse a while, so you need to balance introductory and advanced material.

A newsletter should list the key officers and contact information of the organization it represents. If the newsletter is published online or sent as e-mail, these elements can appear as links.

26 d   Press releases

To attract newspaper or television coverage, send a press release. There is no set format, but any release must tell *who, what, when,* and *where.* Background information can help explain *why* or *how.* To find out how long before an event to send a release, call a newspaper's *city, sports,* or *features desk;* the *assignment editor* of a television newsroom; or an online *content*

Press Release Guidelines

- If your organization has letterhead stationery or a logo, use it.

- Include basic contact information: officers' names, mailing address, phone number, e-mail addresses, Web address.

- Check for *who, what, when, where, why,* and *how.*

- Double-check your facts. Then check them again, especially times, dates, addresses, and phone numbers.

- Ask each news organization whether to send releases by postal mail, fax, or e-mail.

- Ask for the name of the person to contact for the type of information you're sending, and mark the release for that person's attention.

- *Always* include your name and phone number or that of someone in your organization who can provide more information.

- Follow up with a phone call to make sure the release was received and ask whether you can answer any questions.

DENISON UNIVERSITY

Library Links

Volume 5, Issue 3   *http://denison.edu/library/*   **Spring 2005**

National Library Week April 10 -16

It is National Library Week, a time to celebrate the contributions of libraries, librarians and library workers to their schools, campuses and communities.

As part of this annual event the William Howard Doane Library will be hosting the following events and displays.

National Library Workers' Day

Tuesday, April 14

Show your appreciation for your favorite library worker!

Spring Lemonade Stand

Thursday, April 14
10:30 a.m. - 12:00 p.m.
In front of the library. (Rain site - Library Atrium)

Senior Student Workers Display

New book area across from the Circulation Desk

Denison Faculty and Staff READ posters

Atrium Overlook Area

Granville Bicentennial Display

Located in the display case in the 3rd floor Gallery west of the office door

National Library Week 2005 marks the fifth year of The Campaign for America's Libraries, a multi-year public education campaign sponsored by the ALA and libraries across the country to speak loudly and clearly about the value of libraries and librarians in the 21st century.

Inside This Issue...

Local Celebrities Grace Read Posters

In the fall of 2004 the Denison Library launched it's first in a series of local celebrity READ posters. The purpose of the READ poster campaign is to promote the Denison libraries, literacy and reading. Denison University's celebrites were excited about donating their time to this cause.

Nedda Ahmed, Fine Arts Liaison Librarian, designed the posters. She and Star Andrews, Reserves Specialist, photographed the celebrities in their own environments with their favorite books.

Introduced at the "Welcome Back" Lemonade Stand last fall, the posters are currently on display in the library's Atrium area. The display includes posters of Library Director Scottie Cochrane and her husband Louis Middleman, President Dale Knobel, Provost

David Anderson, Studio Art Professor Ran Abram, Communication Professor Laurel Kennedy, Black Studies professor John Jackson, History Professor Catherine Dollard and husband Economics Professor Ted Burczak and their children, Spanish Professor Eduardo Jaramillio, and History Professor Don Schilling.

producer or *content editor.* Give as much advance notice as you can, since reporters, like college students, manage their time by planning ahead whenever possible.

Try to think like a reporter or an assigning editor, who upon reading your release will be thinking, "Why is this event newsworthy? What's happening? Who will be there? Who will want to read or hear about it? How can this event be illustrated?" Television relies heavily on film, and photography is increasingly important to newspapers. Online publications use still photos or video. If a "photo opportunity" will happen at a specific time, say so in the release. And remember, you're trying to catch people's attention, so keep your writing interesting.

26 e   Advocacy

Want to change the world? You need to reach people who might be able to help. You can publish your arguments on a weblog, e-mail them to friends, post them on a newsgroup, write to a public official, or send a letter to the editor of a magazine or newspaper.

In college, you have learned to assemble relevant facts and to employ logic, expecting your audience to respond in a fair-minded and reasonable way if approached in a similar manner. This strategy is a good starting point for public advocacy.

Letter to the Editor

Think of a letters column as a conversation. Readers write in to discuss what they have read, and other readers respond in turn. In many newspapers, pretty much any topic can be fair game, but it helps to refer to a recent, relevant article.

Brevity is essential to getting published. Identify the topic; state facts, and make as clear and as logical a point as you can. Close with an appeal to morality, patriotism, or emotion.

> To the Editor:
>
> The article "More homes become call centers" (May 5) states, "Most of the home-based agents work part-time or as independent contractors, so employers don't pay for . . . benefits. Unions, which represent employers at some large call centers, will be hard-pressed to reach workers spread across thousands of homes, analysts say."
>
> When did it become an undisguised employer objective to eliminate jobs that entail health insurance and benefits?

When did blatant anti-union strategy become part of the business plan?

So much for the rhetoric of employers, who keep insisting that our state needs business tax cuts to create good jobs.

Terry Stark
Harrisburg

This writer fit facts, an argument, and an emotional closing into just over 100 words.

Sign and date the letter, and include your address and telephone number. Most newspapers will not publish a letter without being able to contact the writer for verification.

Writing to Public Officials

Asking a government agency or nonprofit organization for action is a little different from writing to a newspaper. Public agencies have clearly defined missions that they are duty-bound to fulfill, so the first step is picking the responsible agency and persuading its officials that the problem you see is their responsibility.

May 12, 2006

The Honorable Judd Gregg
The Honorable Kent Conrad
Senate Office Building
Washington, D.C. 20510

Dear Senators Gregg and Conrad,

Following the passage of a budget outline for fiscal 2007, the approval of oil exploration in the Alaska National Wildlife Refuge seems increasingly likely.

In the past, I have written to oppose oil drilling in the refuge, as even the highest predicted levels of production will only postpone the coming energy crisis. However, I could accept oil development more readily if I could be assured that the nation would use the time it generates to solve an underlying problem—overdependence on fossil fuels. We should

- immediately raise fuel economy standards for all cars and trucks.

- encourage alternative sources by requiring utilities to credit consumers for solar energy contributed to the grid.

- support research and development in solar, wind, hydrogen, and cogeneration with grants and regulatory assistance.

The policy you craft in the Budget Committee in the coming months will go a long way to determining what our energy landscape looks like when the oil from the wildlife refuge has been consumed.

Sincerely yours,

Roosevelt Symington

43 Big Bend Road
Cave City, KY 42127

The letter is addressed to the chairman and ranking minority member of the Senate Budget Committee. The structure is familiar: State the situation; argue from facts; conclude by urging action.

WRITING ACROSS THE CURRICULUM

"6 RMS RIV VU"

In an unfamiliar writing situation, look for models you can emulate. If you've never written a real-estate brochure, a help-wanted ad, or a product review, a few minutes of study will get you started in the right direction.

Don't simply copy the examples you find. Look for unique conventions—"6 RMS RIV VU"—and decide how to freshen them. As you write, evaluate your own conventions. Should habits acquired in school be modified for business, professional, or social situations? For example, academic guidelines generally call for indented paragraphs; in business, the convention may favor block paragraphs separated by white space and no indentations. In other words, develop your "eye" and "ear" for writing in your new situation, and trust it.

Revised and edited final drafts are written to be read. At the minimum, your audience is your instructor; at the maximum, it's the whole world—an audience for student writing now made possible by access to the Internet. In writing classes, the most common audience, in addition to the instructor, is the class itself. This chapter explores two common avenues of presenting your work in final published form via writing portfolios and class books.

27 a Writing portfolios

In simplest terms, a writing portfolio is a collection of your writing contained within a single folder. This writing may have been done over a number of weeks, months, or even years. A writing portfolio may contain writing that you wish to keep for yourself; in this case you decide what's in it and what it looks like. Or a portfolio may contain work you intend to share with an audience to demonstrate your writing and reasoning abilities.

One kind of writing portfolio, accumulated during a college course, presents a record of your work over a semester and will be used to assign a grade. Another type of portfolio presents a condensed, edited story of your semester's progress in a more narrative form. In addition, portfolios are often requested by prospective employers in journalism and other fields of professional writing; these samples of your best work over several years may determine whether or not you are offered a job as a writer or editor.

27 b Course portfolios

The most common type of portfolio assigned in a writing course contains the cumulative work collected over the semester plus a cover letter in which you explain the nature and value of these papers. Sometimes you will be asked to assign yourself a grade based on your own assessment.

Guidelines for Preparing Course Portfolios

Make your portfolio speak for you. If your course portfolio is clean, complete, and carefully organized, that's how you will be seen. If it's unique, colorful, creative, and imaginative, that, too, is how you'll be judged. So, too, will you be judged if your folder is messy, incomplete, and haphazardly put together. Before giving your portfolio to somebody else for evaluation, consider whether it reflects how you want to be presented.

Attend to the mechanics of the portfolio. Make sure the folder containing your writing is the kind specified and that it is clean and attractive. In the absence of such specification, use a pocket folder, which is an inexpensive means of keeping the contents organized and secure. Put your name and address on the outside cover. Organize the material inside as requested. And turn it in on time.

- **Include exactly what is asked for.** If an instructor wants three finished papers and a dozen sample journal entries, that's the minimum your course portfolio should contain. If an employer wants to see five samples of different kinds of writing, be sure to include five samples.

- **Add supplemental material judiciously.** If you believe that supplemental writing will present you in a better light, include that, too, but only after the required material. If you include extra material, attach a note to explain why it is there. Supplemental writing might include journals, letters, sketches, or diagrams that suggest other useful dimensions of your thinking.

- **Include perfect final drafts.** Show that your own standard for finished work is high. Final drafts should be printed double-spaced on one side only of high-quality paper, be carefully proofread, and follow the language conventions appropriate to the task—unless another format is requested.

- **Demonstrate growth.** The signal value of portfolios in writing classes is that they allow you to demonstrate how a finished paper came into being. Consequently, instructors commonly ask for early drafts to be attached to final drafts, the most recent on top, so they can see how you followed revision suggestions, how much effort you invested, how many drafts you wrote, and how often you took risks. To build such a record of your work, date every draft of each paper.

- **Demonstrate work in progress.** Course portfolios allow writers to present partially finished work that suggests future directions and intentions. Both instructors and potential employers may find such preliminary drafts or outlines valuable. When you include such tentative drafts, be sure to attach a note explaining why it's not quite finished.

- **Attach a table of contents.** For portfolios containing more than three papers, attach a separate table of contents. For those containing only a few papers, embed your table of contents in the cover letter.

▪ **Include a cover letter.** The cover letter represents your own most recent assessment of the work you completed over the semester, serving two primary purposes: (1) as an introduction explaining the portfolio's contents and (2) as your own self-assessment of the quality of the work. Following is an excerpt from Kelly's letter describing the evolution of one paper:

> In writing the personal experience paper, I tried three different approaches, two different topics, and finally a combination of different approaches to my final topic. My first draft [about learning the value of money] was all summary and didn't show anything actually happening. My second draft wasn't focused because I was still trying to cover too much ground. At this point, I got frustrated and tried a new topic [the hospital] but that didn't work either. Finally, for my last draft, I returned to my original topic, and this time it worked. I described one scene in great detail and included dialogue, and I liked it better and so did you. I am pleased with the way this paper came out when I limited my focus and zeroed in close.

The following excerpt describes Chris's assessment of her work over the whole semester:

> As I look back through all the papers I've written this semester, I see how far my writing has come. At first I thought it was stupid to write so many different drafts of the same paper, as if I would beat the topic to death. But now I realize that all these different papers on the same topic went in different directions. This happened to some degree in the first paper, but I especially remember in my research project, when I interviewed the director of the Ronald McDonald House, I really got excited about the work they did there, and I really got involved in the other drafts of that paper.
>
> I have learned to shorten my papers by editing and cutting out needless words. I use more descriptive adjectives now when I'm describing a setting and try to find action verbs instead of "to be" verbs in all of my papers. I am writing more consciously now—I think that's the most important thing I learned this semester.

27 c Story portfolios

A story portfolio is shorter, more fully edited and more finely crafted than a cumulative course portfolio. Instead of including a cover letter and all papers and drafts written during the term as evidence for your self-assessment, a story portfolio presents the evolution of your work and thought over the course of the semester in narrative form. In a story portfolio, you include excerpts of your papers insofar as they illustrate points in your development as a writer. In addition, you include excerpts of supplemental written records accumulated at different times during the semester, including such items as 1) early and dead-end drafts of papers, 2) journal entries, 3) in-class writing and freewriting, 4) comments on papers from your instructor, and 5) comments from your instructor and classmates about your papers.

In other words, to write a story portfolio, you conduct something like an archeological dig through the written remains of your work in a class. By assembling this evidence in chronological order and choosing the most telling snippets from these various documents, you write the story that explains, amplifies, or interprets the documents included or quoted. The best story portfolios commonly reveal a theme or set of issues that runs from week to week or paper to paper throughout the semester. As you can see, a story portfolio is actually a small research paper, presenting a claim about your evolution as a writer with the evidence coming from your own written sources.

We encourage students to write their story portfolios using an informal voice as they might in a journal or letter. However, some students choose a more formal voice. Some prefer to write in the third person, analyzing the semester's work as if it were someone else's. We also encourage them to experiment with the form and structure of their story portfolios, so that some present their work as a series of dated journal entries or snapshots while others write a more fluid essay with written excerpts embedded as they illustrate this or that point. The following pages from Karen's portfolio exemplify the format and content of one type of story portfolio:

> When I entered English 1, I was not a confident writer and only felt comfortable writing factual reports for school assignments. Those were pretty straightforward, and personal opinion was not involved. But over the course of the semester I've learned that I enjoy including my own voice in my writing. The first day of class I wrote this in my journal:
>
> > 8/31 Writing has always been hard for me. I don't have a lot of experience writing papers except for straightforward things like

science reports. I never did very well in English classes, usually getting B's and C's on my papers.

But I began to feel a little more comfortable when we read and discussed the first chapter of the book—a lot of other students besides me felt the same way, pretty scared to be taking English in college.

I decided to write about our basketball season last year, especially the game that we lost. Here is a paragraph from my first draft:

> We lost badly to Walpole in what turned out to be our final game. I sat on the bench most of the time.

As I see now, that draft was all telling and summary—I didn't show anything happening that was interesting or alive. But in a later draft I used dialogue and wrote from the announcer's point of view. The result was fun to write and my group said fun to read:

> Well folks, it looks like Belmont has given up, the coach is preparing to send in his subs. It has been a rough game for Belmont. They stayed in it during the first quarter, but Walpole has run away with it since then. Down by twenty with only six minutes left, Belmont's first sub is now approaching the table.

You were excited about this draft too, and your comment helped me know where to go next. You wrote:

> Great draft, Karen! You really sound like a play-by-play announcer—you've either been one or listened closely to lots of basketball games. What would happen if in your next draft you alternated between your own voice and the announcer's voice? Want to try it?

This next excerpt comes from a story portfolio that included twelve pages of discussion and writing samples and concluded with this paragraph:

> I liked writing this story portfolio at the end of the term because I can really see how my writing and my attitude have changed. I came into class not liking to write, but now I can say that I really do. The structure was free and we had plenty of time to experiment with different approaches to each assignment. I still have a long way to go, especially on my argument writing, since neither you nor I liked my final draft, but now I think I know how to get there: rewrite, rewrite, rewrite.

27 d   Class books

Publishing a class book is a natural end to any class in which interesting writing has taken place. A class book is an edited, bound collection of student writing, usually featuring some work from each student in the class. When the book is published before the last class of the semester, a class discussion can be organized to examine the themes, style, and structure of the finished book. Responsibility for compiling and editing such a book is commonly assigned to class volunteers, who are given significant authority for design and production of the book.

Guidelines for Editing Class Books

- Establish manuscript guidelines. Discuss with the class what each submitted paper should look like: single- or double-spaced typing, typeface, font size, margins, justification, and title and author names.

- Set page limits. Since printing charges are usually made on a per-page basis, discussion of page length is related to final publication cost.

- Ask for camera-ready copy. To simplify and speed the publishing process, have each student prepare his or her own manuscript to submit to the editors.

- Set deadlines. Arrange for manuscript deadlines (when papers are due from contributors to editors) as well as final publication deadlines (when published books are available to students).

- Organize the essays. Arrange collected essays according to some logic—theme, content, quality, or author's last name.

- Establish a graphics policy. Discuss with the class how much space to leave in each essay for clip art, downloaded Web pictures, or taped-in photos.

- Write an introduction. Explain to readers the nature of the reading experience to follow. Introductions vary in length from a paragraph to several pages.

- Prepare a table of contents. Include author's name, essay title, and first page number for each essay.

- Ask the instructor to write an afterword. Instructors may write about the assignment objectives, impressions of the essays, or reactions to the class or add any other observation that seems relevant to the book.

- Collect student writer biographies. Conclude with short (50–100 word) serious, semiserious, or comical biographies of the student writers.

- Design a cover. Design the cover or commission a classmate to do so. (Color cardboard covers cost extra but are usually worth it.)

- Arrange for publication. Explore with local print shops the production costs and a timetable to produce copies for all students in the class.

■ Divide editorial responsibilities. Class books are best done by editorial teams consisting of two or more students who arrange among themselves the various duties described above.

WRITING ACROSS THE CURRICULUM

Discussing Class Books

Class books make excellent final projects for small classes such as first-year or senior seminars in which writing is required. Try the suggestions in this chapter, and plan to have all class books distributed (or purchased) and read by the final class. To prepare for a final class discussion, send out, in advance, a copy of the discussion questions below. Then invite the class book editors to lead a discussion in which students respond to these questions:

- Which are your favorite titles and why?
- What, besides your own, is your favorite essay and why?
- What ideas or techniques did you learn from classmates' essays?
- In your own essay, what are your favorite passages?
- In your own essay, what would you like to change?
- Which essay reveals the most substantial research?
- Which essay writer has the most interesting voice?
- In which essays are graphics used most effectively and why?

chapter **28** *Oral Presentations*

Public speaking is another way of "publishing" ideas that originate in written form. In speaking, as in writing, it's important to present ideas with confidence, clarity, accuracy, and grace: in the professions, in business, and in government, good writers and speakers get listened to, promoted, and rewarded; poor ones do not. While the art of public speaking can be addressed more comprehensively in speech class, we believe all writers should pay some attention to the oral publication of their ideas.

28 a Interpreting the assignment

The following suggestions have proved useful to successful public speakers:

Identify your purpose. What is your report supposed to accomplish? Is the purpose to present information, raise questions, argue a position, or lead the class in an activity? Regardless of your instructor's reason for making this assignment, to do a good job you'll need to believe in, understand, and know your subject. Choose a subject and a point of departure that you care about and believe in so you have the curiosity to do effective research and the passion to speak with conviction.

Know your audience. What you say and how you say it depends upon to whom you are speaking. In most class settings, your audience is composed of your instructor and classmates; the best oral report will reach both effectively. To keep them interested, plan to teach them something they don't already know. Don't cover material already covered in class or in the textbook, nor material unrelated to the course. Instead, build deliberately on issues, ideas, or information that stems from familiar class material, and present new information in that context.

Collaborate. If collaboration is called for or allowed the following guidelines might help: (1) Arrive at a consensus about what your task entails. (2) Divide tasks according to ability; do your own part promptly, and hold others accountable for doing theirs. (3) Meet often enough outside class so material is ready when the oral report is due. (4) Plan in advance who will report what and for how long.

28 b Preparing a speaking text

Texts that are spoken need to be simple, clear, and direct. The following ideas follow such a process:

Invent. Allow time for thinking, planning, inventing, discovering—don't try to prepare your whole oral report the night before it is due.

Compose. Even if you don't intend to read your report out loud, write it out in full to see how it looks and where it's going. Once a talk is composed, even roughly, it's easy to make an outline from which to speak.

Research. Find current and detailed information to convey. Cite textual sources, quote local experts, report survey results, explain on-site visits.

Outline. Effective oral reports are spoken rather than read, with the speaker making eye contact with the audience as much as possible. Consequently, the "final draft" of an oral report is a "speaking outline" or notes to be glanced at as needed.

Create listening signposts. The old advice for making speeches goes like this: *"Tell what you're gonna tell 'em. Tell 'em. Then tell 'em what you've told 'em."* It makes sense to be repetitious in oral presentations because it's hard for audiences to remember all they hear. *Listening signposts*—words that signal what's coming—help do this. For example, tell your audience you are going to make three points about gun control legislation, then enumerate each to help them remember.

Prepare note cards. In a short report, a one-page speaking outline is all you need. For longer or more complex reports that include quotations and statistics, use index cards to follow as you move from point to point in your talk.

Start strong. In oral delivery it's especially important to get everyone listening at the same time, so speakers commonly use questions, stories, or jokes to catch quick attention. If you tell a story or joke, make sure it pertains to your subject.

Finish strong. Many speakers map out their conclusion first, then work backward to make sure the text leads them there. With only five, ten, or fifteen minutes, be sure that when time is up, you've made the point you intended.

Write simply for oral delivery. Simple jargon-free language is easiest to understand at a single hearing; repeating key words and phrases helps reinforce the listening memory.

Edit your reading text. If your material is complex and your time short, you may choose to read your report out loud. While it's less engaging, unless you're an excellent reader, it does guarantee that you say exactly what you meant precisely and economically. Triple space your reading copy, use a large font, leave wide margins to pencil in extra notes, and start new paragraphs on new pages. For timing purposes, plan two-and-a-half minutes for each page of double-spaced text ($8\frac{1}{2} \times 11''$).

28 c   Speaking in public

Presenting to a group means leaving your comfortable seat and moving front and center for attention. A recent poll identified public speaking as the greatest fear of most Americans. Even famous actors and speakers feel anxiety before performing before live audiences, and they learn to use their nervous energy to keep a sharp edge while performing. Nervousness is unavoidable; accept it, and try to harness this energy to help your performance. The following suggestions may help to alleviate this fear.

Rehearse. Run through your oral presentation in the privacy of your room to check your understanding and to set your pace to make sure you can deliver the talk in the time allotted. Rehearsing your talk out loud several times beforehand will help you understand your own material better as well as give you confidence when you walk to the front of the room.

Rehearsing in front of a mirror and recording your rehearsals can help you to see your presentation from the perspective of a listener.

Make the room your own. Set up the room to suit the purpose of your presentation. If that means rearranging desks, tables, screens, or lecterns, don't hesitate to do so. If there is a lectern front and center but you don't plan to use it, move it to one side. If you use the lectern, stand still and rest your hands on it—that will help you control any shaking. If you prefer your audience in a semicircle or in groups instead of straight rows, ask them to sit that way. Taking control of your space makes you comfortable and gives you ownership of your time in front of the class.

Maintain eye contact with friendly audience members. While it's important to look around at the whole audience and make everyone feel as if you are addressing him or her, return periodically to the faces most receptive to your words—to smiles or nods or friends—for these will boost your confidence and keep you going smoothly.

Speak point by point. The reason for sticking to your outline or note cards is to present information in an economical and orderly fashion. If your report is supposed to last ten minutes, jot the starting time on your notes and stick to ten minutes. If you speak too quickly, the audience can't follow you; if you speak too slowly, people get restless—so strive for balance.

Leave time for questions. When giving oral reports, it is customary to allow your audience time to ask questions. Plan for this time, show your willingness to discuss further what you know, and always answer succinctly and honestly; if you don't know an answer, say so.

28　d　Creative options

Depending on your task and time, you may want to enhance your presentation with some of the following materials or activities:

Use handouts. Many talks are augmented by handouts (outlines, poems, stories, ads, articles) illustrating points made in the talk or as a text to attend to at some time during the presentation. Prepare handouts carefully; make sure they are legible; document them if they are borrowed from another source, and make enough for everyone in your audience.

Use prepared visual aids. Many talks are made more powerful when accompanied by illustrations or examples of what is being talked about. Visual aids include videos, films, maps, charts, sketches, photographs, posters, computer graphics, or transparencies shown on overhead projectors. With computer programs such as PowerPoint (see the WAC Box on pages 289–290), it is easy to prepare professional-quality visual aids.

Use process visual aids. It often helps to illustrate something on the spot in front of your audience, something often called for during a question-and-answer session. Media that help you write or sketch things out include blackboards, flip charts, and overhead projectors. Arrange for these aids in advance and bring chalk or markers.

Use audio aids. Some talks are best advanced when accompanied by music or oral recordings. Audience attention picks up noticeably when you introduce sounds or voices other than your own into your presentation. A sound or visual recording may be the featured text in your presentation, or it may provide useful accompaniment.

***Be* a visual and audio aid.** For some topics, a live demonstration may be appropriate. Be sure to have all the props, supplies, and equipment you need for your demonstration, whether it involves how to play the trombone or how to dress for in-line skating. Even if you do not demonstrate a process, you can use *body language* to your advantage. Smiling at your audience, in addition to making eye contact, will help to establish a friendly connection. Natural gestures can help you maintain your audience's interest and can reinforce what you are saying. Body language also includes the sound of your voice; volume, speed of delivery, emphasis, tone, and pitch all add meaning to the words you say.

Ask your audience to write. If you want to engage your audience quickly and relax yourself at the same time, ask people to write briefly before you speak. For example, on the subject of "alcohol on campus," ask people to jot down their own experience with or knowledge of the subject on scratch paper, telling them their notes will remain private. After a few minutes, ask them to talk about—not read—their ideas with a neighbor for several more minutes. Talking aloud to seatmates pulls them in deeper still, and the oral buzz in the room makes everyone—especially you—more comfortable. To resume control, ask for several volunteer opinions and use these as a bridge to your own presentation.

WRITING ACROSS THE CURRICULUM

Guidelines for PowerPoint Presentations

PowerPoint has become the standard visual aid program for making presentations across the curriculum. In classrooms equipped with computer projectors, it allows you to show text, slides, graphics, and photos, as well as moving images, to help you supplement oral presentations in any course of study. The following tips will help you create an effective presentation and avoid both cuteness and clichés.

- **Prepare good material.** No slick slide show can enhance shallow ideas: do your homework, back up claims with substantial evidence, and keep eye contact with your audience.

- **Keep it simple.** Follow an outline of your presentation, using slides to highlight major points. Fill in details orally, by careful explanation, not by reading the material on your slides.

- **Make organization visible.** If your outline has three main sections, consider beginning with a slide listing points I, II, and III. Then show the main points of Section I in one or more slides, followed by the main points of Section II, and so on.

- **Check out** the space in advance. Make sure the room can be darkened and that the screen isn't facing the light. Check sight lines to be sure the whole audience can see.

- **Estimate the distance** from the farthest seat to the screen. Use the sign-painter's rule of thumb: one-inch letters can be read from ten feet, two-inch letters from twenty feet, etc. Adjust type accordingly. (On a monitor, 72-point type is about one inch high.)

- **Consider readability** when choosing colors for background and type. Complementary colors (red on green) may be hard to see while other combinations (black on yellow) may need to be toned down. Choose light colors for backgrounds.

- **Use art carefully.** If a photo or graphic is the best way to convey information, use it. Most clip art cartoon figures convey little information and look amateurish.

- **Avoid unnecessary animation.** Moving type, elements that fade into or out of view, and/or animated graphics tend to distract from what you're saying.

- **Consider a printed handout** for important information you want your audience to carry away from your presentation.

- **Rehearse** with a tape recorder and a computer so you can watch and listen to your presentation at the same time.

A Caution About PowerPoint

Be aware that the use of slide programs such as PowerPoint can have a downside as well, sometimes causing presenters to bore audiences with overly glitzy slides, too many slides, and a tendency to read from the screen rather than speak directly to listeners. (For more on the risks of using packaged prepared slides, see "PowerPoint Is Evil" by Edward Tufte, wired.com/archive/11.09/ppt2.)

While drafting and revising, you have focused primarily on your purpose—what you're trying to say. At some point, you will begin to examine your work with a more critical eye and to think about the reactions of readers. How will your words come across? How well will fellow students and instructors understand what you intend to say? What more do you need to explain? To change?

When you make this shift of focus, you have begun the process called editing, which means putting your work into a polished, final form. As you can tell from this description, there are no sharp boundaries that divide composing from revising and revising from editing. Almost all writers are mindful of their audience and of writing conventions throughout the stages of writing. We make the distinctions partly because it's impossible to talk about every aspect of writing simultaneously, but we also encourage you to set aside time and energy for editing in addition to your time for drafting and revising.

The next four parts of this book discuss different aspects of editing, proceeding from larger scale to smaller. In Part 6, we focus on making meanings clear within paragraphs and sentences. What we refer to as "clarity" also can be called "style." We mean style not in the sense of fashion but as the manner in which a writer's use of language communicates ideas clearly and effectively. Part 7 addresses grammatical correctness and the conventional use of language at the level of sentences and individual words. Marks of punctuation, discussed in Part 8, help readers recognize sentences and the structures within them. Part 9 discusses spelling and the mechanics of presenting language in finished form.

In editing a college paper, keep in mind that everything in it should help to support or advance the thesis or central idea. If it is not clear how a piece of information supports your thesis, take time to explain. If you have included information that does not serve that purpose, consider deleting it.

The basic process of editing consists of three steps.

1. **Identify potential problems.** Do this by asking yourself repeatedly, "Will readers understand this as I intend?"

2. **Generate alternatives.** Rewrite the passage in question, perhaps in more than one way, to improve understanding.

3. **Choose.** In light of your purpose and audience, which alternative is best?

Good paragraphing groups related thoughts into visual blocks. When a new paragraph begins, readers expect a new step in the development of your ideas.

Within a paragraph, readers expect each sentence to develop a main idea—that the paragraph will be unified. Readers also expect each paragraph to display an internal order that makes sense—that it will be organized. And they expect that each sentence within a paragraph will relate clearly to the sentences around it—that it will be coherent.

Paragraphs give readers a chance to pause. Writers often start new paragraphs intuitively at places where they leave one thought and begin another or where a break seems needed. So, while there are no rules that cover every reason to paragraph, it's a good idea to review your intuitive paragraphing to see that it helps rather than confuses readers. The following principles can help.

30 a   Unity

The topic sentence of a paragraph states its unifying principle in one sentence. In a paper that argues or explains, a topic sentence usually appears as an explicit statement at the beginning or end of a paragraph. In reflective writing or writing about personal experience, paragraph topics are sometimes more implied than stated. (For instance, try identifying the topic sentences in the reflective essay "Writing in Safety" in 6g.)

To edit for unity, first determine the paragraph's topic. Keep words and sentences that support or clarify that idea, and delete or move those that do not.

In the following passage from a research paper, the writer identified the first sentence as her topic sentence. When she read the other sentences, she realized that her fourth sentence did not illustrate the topic sentence, so she moved it to the next paragraph, where it fit better.

For various reasons, some unhappy couples remain married. Some are forbidden to divorce by religion, others by social custom. Still

others stay together "for the sake of the children," In recent years, psychologists and sociologists have studied families to determine whether more harm is done to children by divorce or by parents who stay together despite conflict. But by staying together, such parents feel believing they are sparing their children the pain of divorce.

In his study of family conflict, Robert S. Weiss found that children in such families were often happiest "when Daddy is at work."

<h2>30 b   Internal organization</h2>

A recognizable pattern of organization within a paragraph helps readers follow your thinking. The strategy you choose depends on what you are trying to do. The following patterns are well known, so readers will follow them easily, but many other patterns work as well.

General to Specific

This common paragraph pattern begins with a general statement of the main idea. Subsequent sentences contain examples that support, explain, and expand that statement.

GENERAL STATEMENT

SPECIFIC EXAMPLES

The evolution of the horse can be inferred from fossil evidence of related animals with progressively more sophisticated leg structure. The earliest horse, *eohippus,* ran on four toes like many mammals. A later species, *mesohippus,* or middle horse, ran on three toes. The modern horse runs on one toe; its hoof is the toenail of the digit that corresponds to a middle finger. Vestiges of the second and fourth toes can be found above the hoof.

Specific to General

This pattern begins with a series of details or examples and culminates in a general statement. Placing your general statement, or topic sentence, at the end of the paragraph allows you to build toward and emphasize your conclusion.

SPECIFIC
EXAMPLES

As early horse species changed, so did their environment, from forest to open grasslands. The tougher hooves were better on hard ground. Longer legs provided speed where there was nowhere to hide. Along with the changes in the feet came changes in teeth to shift from chewing leaves to grinding

GENERAL
STATEMENT

grasses and grain. *The fossil record shows the horse's ancestors adapting to their changing habitat.*

Chronological Order

Events are sometimes best presented in the order in which they happened. The topic sentence, or general statement, can appear at the beginning or the end of the paragraph.

EVENT 1
EVENT 2

Before the arrival of Europeans, Haiti was populated by the Arawak tribes. Within fifty years after Columbus set foot on the island in 1492, the Arawaks had nearly died out, victims of

EVENT 3

disease and enslavement. The Spanish colonists imported blacks from Africa to replace the natives as slaves on their plantations.

EVENT 4

Late in the seventeenth century, the island was ceded to France but was the subject of dispute among England, Spain, and France for decades before achieving independence. *The popula-*

GENERAL
STATEMENT

tion of Haiti today, predominantly black and French-speaking, reflects that history.

Reverse chronological order—moving backward from the most recent events to the most distant—can be an effective way to reflect on the past.

Climactic Order

To draw readers in and build toward a conclusion, present specific details in order of increasing importance, and end with a dramatic statement or prediction.

GENERAL
STATEMENT

Consider the effects of increases in Earth's atmospheric temperature. Global mean surface temperatures have risen 0.5 to 1.0 degrees over the past 100 years. By 2050, the Environ-

SPECIFICS OF
INCREASING
IMPORTANCE

mental Protection Agency says that temperatures could rise three times that much and that sea levels are likely to rise by up to one foot. The Federal Emergency Management Agency estimates 25 percent of buildings within 500 feet of the U.S. coastline could be destroyed by coastal erosion within 60 years.

CLIMAX

As sea level continues to rise, dozens of coastal cities could be destroyed, and life as we know it would be changed utterly.

Spatial Order

In a physical description, details can be ordered so that the mind's eye moves from one object to the next. The topic sentence, here a general statement summarizing and interpreting the details, can appear at the beginning or the end.

SPECIFICS
ARRANGED
SPATIALLY

Above the mantelpiece hung an ancient flintlock musket that gave every indication of being in working order. A small collection of pewter, most of it dating from the colonial period, was arrayed across the mantel. To the left of the hearth stood wrought-iron fireplace tools and a bellows of wood and leather with brass fittings. At the right, a brass hopper held several cut limbs of what might have been an apple tree. On an iron hook above the coals hung a copper kettle, blackened with age and smoke. *The fireplace looked as though it had changed little since the Revolution.*

GENERAL
STATEMENT

30 c   Coherence

Paragraphs are coherent—literally, they "stick together"—when each sentence relates appropriately to the surrounding ones. Your writing will be more coherent if you join choppy paragraphs by using transitional expressions, shorten overly long paragraphs, and deliberately repeat key words.

Transitional Expressions

Some words and phrases indicate how one thing relates to another. Other terms can compare or contrast ideas or show relationships in time and space. Transitions smooth out shifts in ideas. Without its transitional expressions, the following paragraph would be a string of seemingly unrelated facts.

Newspaper and magazine publishing is not usually regarded as cyclic, *but* the recent recession cut deeply into advertising revenue. As the economy gathers steam, classified-ad buyers should return, *although* display advertising will lag. *Meanwhile,* publications that have already sharply cut their costs should see profits taking a strong upturn as advertisers return. *For them,* the coming year looks rosy.

The changes you make when restructuring paragraphs for unity, organization, or length often mean adding new transitions. In this paper on divorce, the writer added two sentences, the first to mark a change in the direction of her argument, the second to let readers know she was ready to sum up this portion of it.

> **During a divorce, parents have the ability to shield a child from potential harm. Many couples who stay together believe that the two-parent structure is crucial to the child's well-being.**
> This, however, appears not to be the case.
> **A child's secuity is based on his or her relationship with each parent individually, according to studies by Judith Wallerstein, who found that a stable, caring relationship between a child and each parent is the most significant ingredient in a child's emotional health. Maintaining even one stable relationship appears to reduce the effect of divorce on a child's emotions.**
> The issue during a divorce, then, is how well a child can maintain at least
> **During the early stages of a breakup, both parents are often distracted by other issues. The child may suffer as a result.**
> one secure relationship.

Transitions between paragraphs or sections

Generally, transitions between or within sentences should be very brief. Transitions between paragraphs often merit longer explanations—sometimes a full sentence. Between major sections of a paper, a transition can be as long as a paragraph, perhaps summarizing what has gone before and explaining where you are headed next and why.

Deliberate Repetition

Words or phrases repeated sparingly can link sentences and help your ideas stick together. Deliberately repeating key words keeps the writing focused, making it easier for readers to follow your thoughts. Notice how the key words, in italics, echo the topic of this paragraph.

> The *controversy* over the proposed Northgate Mall has continued for at least five years. The *dispute* has divided the city into two camps. A small group seems *opposed* to the mall, but its members are vocal and energetic. The *opponents* maintain that the mall would rob trade from existing businesses downtown and contribute to traffic congestion. *Proponents* say that the growth it would bring would be easily manageable.

Substituting similar words (*dispute* for *controversy*) prevents the repetition from becoming monotonous.

A deliberate repetition can also create a rhythmic effect.

~~When~~ ^S^ she read to me, I ^and^ ~~could~~ ^saw^ ~~see~~ faraway islands fringed with coconut palms. ~~With~~ ^She read to me, and with^ Jim Hawkins, I shivered in the apple barrel while the pirates plotted. ^She read to me, and^ I ran with Maori warriors to raid the villages of neighboring tribes. ^She read to me, and^ I heard Ahab's peg leg thumping on the deck overhead, and I marveled at the whiteness of the whale.

Transitional Expressions

These brief transitional expressions are appropriate for use between or within sentences. Choose carefully to express the precise nature of the transition.

To Expand

also, and, besides, finally, further, in addition, moreover, then

To Exemplify

as an illustration, for example, for instance, in fact, specifically, thus

To Qualify

but, certainly, however, to be sure

To Summarize or Conclude

and so, finally, in conclusion, in short, in sum, therefore, this shows, thus we see

To Show Logical Relationships

as a result, because, by implication, for this reason, if, since, so, thus, therefore, this shows that

To Compare

also, as well, likewise, similarly

To Contrast

although, but, despite, even though, nevertheless, on the other hand, yet

To Show Relationships in Time

after, before, between, earlier, formerly, later, longer than, meanwhile, since

To Show Relationships in Space

above, adjacent to, behind, below, beyond, in front of, nearby, next to, north (south, east, west) of, opposite to, over, through, within

Suggestions for Using Transitional Expressions

Here are some guidelines for deciding when to use a transitional expression.

- Use transitions to warn readers of shifts in thought that they may not expect. For example, an unexpected contrast might need a transitional phrase.

  The film's plot is very predictable, and the characters are not especially likable. *Nevertheless,* the movie is worth seeing.

- Between paragraphs or larger sections of your writing, a transition might require a sentence or even a whole paragraph.

  To these criticisms, the author has a ready response.

  [Meaning, "We've heard the criticisms; it's the author's turn to reply."]

- If you use a series of transitional expressions to mark a sequence or to list points, make them parallel in form. For example, use *first, second,* and *last* to introduce three points, but not *first, in the second place,* and *lastly.*

- Avoid beginning a series of sentences with transitions, such as *Also, Moreover,* or *And in addition.* Find a way to eliminate some transitions, or put some of the transitional expressions in the middle of sentences.

  ~~Moreover, the~~ The researchers discovered that *further* ...

- Incorporate a variety of transitional expressions. Rather than rely exclusively on *but* to show contrast, consider an equivalent: *by contrast, however,* or *nevertheless.*

Revising Paragraph Length

A very long paragraph can strain readers' attention. Look for places where dividing a long paragraph into two or more can contribute to clarity. On the other hand, a string of very short paragraphs can seem choppy and make ideas appear disconnected. Look for places where several small paragraphs develop what is really one idea, and combine them.

The first words of your paper may be the most important. Your opening must engage your readers, introduce your topic and your main idea, and point toward what you intend to say. In a two- or three-page essay, one paragraph may suffice to open; in longer papers, you may have a page or two to play with. If your instructor specifies an opening strategy for an assignment, be sure to use that approach. If not, here are some techniques you can adapt to your writing situation as appropriate.

31 a Opening strategies

Begin with a Thesis Statement

Many opening paragraphs in college papers start with a broad statement, narrow the focus, and end by stating the thesis, as in the following paragraph (thesis statement in italics).

> Anxiety, stress, and tension exist in us all. Stress can jeopardize our health. At its worst, it can kill. *The most effective way to control stress and live more comfortable lives is to use techniques for relaxation.*

Make a striking assertion

Make a statement so improbable or far-reaching that the reader will demand to see how you support such an assertion. Here Lawrence Shanies makes an outrageous claim about one of the greatest poets of the English language.

> *John Milton was a failure.* In writing *Paradise Lost,* his stated aim was to "justify the ways of God to men." Inevitably, he fell short of accomplishing that goal and only wrote a monumental poem. Beethoven, whose music was conceived to transcend fate, was a failure, as was Socrates, whose ambition was to make people happy by making them reasonable and just. The inescapable conclusion seems to be that the surest, noblest way to fail is to set one's own standards titanically high.
> —LAWRENCE SHANIES, "THE SWEET SMELL OF SUCCESS ISN'T ALL THAT SWEET"

Open with an Anecdote

Tell a brief story, no more than a paragraph or two, about someone or something that introduces, sets up, or illustrates the thesis of the whole paper.

> Once I met a woman who grew up in the small North Carolina town to which Chang and Eng, the original Siamese twins, retired after their circus careers. When I asked her how the town reacted to the twins marrying local girls and setting up adjacent households, she laughed and said: "Honey, that was nothing compared to what happened before the twins got there." *Get the good gossip on any little mountain town, scratch the surface and you'll find a snake pit!*
>
> —FRANCINE PROSE, "GOSSIP"

Open with an Intriguing Detail

Plunge readers into an unfamiliar but provocative situation to pique their curiosity.

> "Mrs. Tolstoy is your basic L.O.L. in N.A.D., admitted for a soft rule-out M.I.," the intern announces. I scribble that on my patient list. In other words, Mrs. Tolstoy is a Little Old Lady in No Apparent Distress who is in the hospital to make sure she hasn't had a heart attack (rule out a myocardial infarction). And we think it's unlikely that she has had a heart attack (a soft rule-out).
>
> If I had learned nothing else during my first three months of working in the hospital as a medical student, I learned endless jargon and abbreviations.
>
> —PERRI KLASS, "SHE'S YOUR BASIC L.O.L. IN N.A.D."

Begin with a Striking Quotation or Statistic

I asked my physician to estimate the death rate for my particular condition. "One per person," she said, faintly smiling. While I struggled to contain my reaction, she continued. "You're a human being. The question is not whether you'll die, but of what." I've been thinking about my own mortality from time to time ever since.

Most quotations need context to make sense. Present them as part of your text, not standing on their own.

> "Taxation without representation is tyranny," Patrick Henry famously said of the British crown's revenue-raising methods. His words are frequently borrowed by Springfield residents upset over rising property taxes, but beyond the shared sense of outrage, how accurate is the charge of undemocratic methods?

Focus on One Person

"Issues" that affect faceless numbers of people can turn readers off. Which of the following openings works better for you? This?

> Statistics show that an increasing number of students graduate from college with a debt load that will limit their purchasing power and perhaps even dictate their career choices. . . . Approximately two-thirds of all students use loans to pay for their higher education, according to the Center for Economic and Policy Research using data from the College Board. The average debt for students graduating in 2003–2004, the latest data available, was $15,622 for public schools and $22,581 for private; many students rack up even more on their credit cards.
>
> ADAPTED FROM CNNMONEY.COM

Or this?

> Mayrose Wegmann, 25, should have been starting her . . . career as a political consultant by now and saving toward her first home. Instead, Wegmann, who graduated . . . in political science and journalism . . . and moved to Washington, D.C., is working at a non-profit because it pays significantly more than entry-level politics work. And she won't consider buying a home for several more years. In fact, she won't consider much except how to meet the $300 a month she owes on her $34,000 student loan balance.
>
> CNNMONEY.COM, MAY 2, 2006

When moving from the individual case to the general, be careful to point out ways in which your individual is or is not typical of the situation or trend you're writing about.

Pose a Provocative Question

Establish the topic, then pose the question that you will answer, explore, or reflect upon.

> Many children spend more than five hours a day watching television when they could be reading or playing outside. What effect does television have on these kids? At what levels do those effects appear? In other words, how much TV is too much?

31 b   Sharper openings

Pay attention to every sentence and every word. Eliminate unnecessary words (*it is a fact that, it is interesting to note that*), empty phrases (*first and foremost, last but not least*), and clichés (*the crack of dawn, the sands of*

WRITING ACROSS THE CURRICULUM

Different Audience, Different Opening

Here are two opening paragraphs on the same topic by the same author. The first is from an article in the magazine *Scientific American,* a magazine written and edited primarily for sophisticated general readers. The second is from *Science,* the journal of the American Association for the Advancement of Science. How has the author adjusted his approach for each publication and its audience?

> People are often surprised, even alarmed, to learn that many of their cells crawl around inside them. Yet cell crawling is essential to our survival. Without it, our wounds would not heal; blood would not clot to seal off cuts; the immune system could not fight infections. Unfortunately, crawling contributes to some disease processes, too, such as destructive inflammation and the formation of atherosclerotic plaques in blood vessels. Cancer cells crawl to spread themselves throughout the body: were cancer just a matter of uncontrolled cell growth, all tumors would be amenable to surgical removal.
>
> Thomas P. Stossel, "The Machinery of Cell Crawling,"
> *Scientific American,* 1994

> Ungainly in comparison to flying, swimming, or running, the crawling motions of single animal cells are nevertheless profoundly important.... [M]ovements of single cells are fundamental for the life of multicellular beings. After conception, selected cells of the developing mammalian zygote invade the uterine wall to establish the placenta, while the intricately programmed migration of other cells within the embryo changes the complex form of the emerging organism. Legions of white blood cells patrol body tissues to engage hostile microorganisms. Locomotion of fibroblastic and epithelial cells heals wounds, and osteoblasts and osteoclasts crawl about as they remodel bone.
>
> Thomas P. Stossel, "On the Crawling of Animal Cells," *Science,* 1993

Take a paper you have written for a specialized audience, such as a class in economics or political science. What changes would be required to prepare it for a general academic audience? For a general-interest magazine?

---

time). Avoid worn-out generalizations (*society is a rat race; the liberal arts provide a well-rounded education*).

■ **Narrow the focus.** Opening statements that are too broad or obvious may fail to engage readers. Readers want to learn quickly what you are talking about.

Isaac Asimov was among the first to write about robotics. *I, Robot* is a collection of short stories on the subject, the first of which is from 1940. Even when going to the moon was science fiction, Asimov predicted that people would come to fear their own creations, a concept that dates back at least as far as Mary Shelly's *Frankenstein.* . . . The film *Terminator,* in which a computer attempts to eradicate the human race, illustrates the paranoia Asimov predicted.

A robot is defined as "any mechanical device operated automatically, especially with autonomous internal control." The subject I will be addressing is the argument that robots are stealing jobs from humans: that skilled laborers of all kinds are being replaced by machines.

Rereading his opening, Ernie decided he had taken too long to get to his subject, but he wanted to keep his literary examples. Here's his more focused opening.

The claim that robots are stealing jobs from humans is nothing new; it is an old fear in a new form. Many writers and filmmakers have explored the underlying anxiety.

Isaac Asimov was among the first to write about the interaction of robots and humans. . . .

■ **Sharpen your focus.** Notice the difference between "the first to write about robotics" and "the first to write about the interaction between robots and humans." The reader immediately learns the piece is not just about technology.

■ **Be direct.** Delete phrases that needlessly slow the reader: *it is a fact that, it appears that,* and *it has come to my attention that.* If you must qualify a statement, consider "flagging" it with a general qualifier (*sometimes, almost always*) and returning later to the specifics.

chapter **32**   *Thoughtful Closings*

I magine that, after reading all your evidence and arguments, readers will remember only one paragraph. What would you want that paragraph to say? That's your conclusion—the strongest statement of your case that you can make based on the evidence you've assembled. More than simply summarizing what your paper has shown or restating its thesis, a good conclusion suggests what it might mean.

32 a Rhetorical questions

A rhetorical question is really an answer framed as a question. In posing such a question, the writer believes all reasonable readers will arrive at the same answer—which, of course, the paper has outlined in full. It's a strong, persuasive strategy, posing a question to which there's only one answer.

Drug violence will continue as long as citizens tolerate the easy availability of guns on the streets; as long as the public shells out money for violence glorified in music and film; as long as drug users, deprived of effective treatment, pour money into disadvantaged neighborhoods. *How can society sit by and do nothing?*

32 b Genuine questions

In papers that pose real problems or ask difficult questions, it's fair to end by acknowledging that you don't have all the answers.

Drug addiction and the violence it creates seem almost impossible to stop. As soon as one dealer is put away, two come to take his (or her) place. Why do so many young people risk their lives in this dirty business? It's because there's money to be made and because making it seems so easy. *So, do we solve this problem with better enforcement of existing laws? Do we spend more on education? Do we make drugs legal and try regulate them? As we've seen, each approach has limited benefits and potentially steep costs, and each involves tradeoffs, not all of which can be predicted.*

32 c Concise summary

Recap the main points in the paper, and say what you think they mean.

The tasks are urgent and difficult. Realistically, we know we cannot abolish crime. But we can abolish—as a nation, not just state by state—capital punishment. We can accept the fact that prisoners, convicted criminals, are hostages to our own human failures to develop and support a decent way of living. And we can accept the fact that we are responsible to them, as to all living beings, for the protection of society, and especially responsible for those among us who need protection for the sake of society.

—MARGARET MEAD, "A LIFE FOR A LIFE"

32 d Call to action

Use your powers of persuasion to mobilize readers to action.

Until the SAT is reformed or abolished, those students who score low on the test will suffer. They will have a hard time getting into many colleges, even though they might have what it takes to succeed there. The emphasis on the test distracts high school students from things that are also important to admission decisions, such as writing ability, grades, course load, and extracurricular activities. *It is time for those who care about justice to see that this system is fixed.*

32 e Implications

Imagine the future if the action you propose is—or is not—taken.

The government gathers data on telephone calling patterns. It conducts closed trials with limited avenues of appeal. It wants to know what we search for on the Internet. A national identity card has been proposed. Prosecutors want to jail reporters who expose government secrets. Of course, the government reassures us that its purpose is benign. But if we forfeit the rights our Constitution provides, that reassurance will provide small comfort if—or when—it is not.

Writing Stronger Conclusions

An effective conclusion summarizes, but it should do something more. This is your last chance to speak to your readers. What do you most want them to remember? When editing, focus on the single most important idea and try to take it a step further.

- **Be direct.** Wordiness can undermine the authority of your final sentences and weaken your message. Use transitional phrases—*in conclusion, all in all,* or *to sum up*—sparingly, if at all; your readers should recognize your conclusion without them. Many qualifying phrases—*I think* or *I believe,* for example—are also unnecessary because readers assume the ideas in your paper are your own. Use such phrases only when you need to distinguish your conclusions from someone else's.

- **Focus.** When editing, see that your concluding statements or questions do, in fact, fulfill the promises you made at the beginning of your paper. Also make sure you have not asked or answered a question your paper didn't pose in the first place.

- **Review.** If you have revised parts of your paper by adding new research or branching out in directions that differ from your first draft, make sure the opening and conclusion you may have written earlier still hold. You might be able to sharpen the opening or strengthen your conclusion.

cademic, business, and technical writing should convey information efficiently. Avoiding wordy, obscure, or confusing language takes careful editing, a process that some writers call "boiling down," the way a cook turns large quantities of thin broth into a smaller quantity of hearty soup.

33 a Generalities

From specific data—*That radiator burned my hand when I touched it*—we fashion generalizations: *Hot radiators can be dangerous.* Generalizations are useful to express abstract ideas or general principles. Sometimes, however, writers lapse into generalities, statements so vague that they mean little: *It is our duty to take responsibility for our actions.* (When was that not the case?)

A generality can be something so widely accepted that stating it seems silly: *Shakespeare is a great writer.* (And . . . ?) Other generalities indulge in circular reasoning: *During the harsh winters of the 1870s, the weather was very cold.* (*Harsh* implies that.) Some writers announce that a point is going to be made but don't make it: *Many factors played a part in the Bush victory.* (What factors?)

Particularly in openings and conclusions, you may be trying hard to impress. Look for the obvious and edit it out.

Fetal alcohol syndrome affects one of every 750 newborn babies~~.~~, ~~It is clearly not good for them,~~ causing coordination difficulties, malformed organs, small brains, short attention spans, and behavioral problems.

33 b Idle words

Eliminate idle words. To test whether a word is working or idle, remove it: if no meaning is lost, leave it out. Look out for "automatic phrases" that seem to write themselves. Often one word can take the place of several.

Today,   _often_
~~In this day and age,~~ children ~~in many instances~~ know more about
 ^   ^
chemistry than they do about baking.

Some imprecise words—*area, aspect, factor, kind, manner, nature, tendency, thing,* and *type*—can contribute to wordiness.

WORDY	One of the factors that gave them problems in the lab was a tendency toward contamination.
MORE CONCISE	Contamination was sometimes a problem in the lab.
OR	The lab sometimes was contaminated.

Writers sometimes use words like *clearly, obviously, interestingly, undoubtedly, absolutely, fortunately, hopefully, really, totally,* and *very* to make a sentence sound forceful or authoritative, but a sentence can sound stronger without them.

These intensifiers ~~clearly~~ add ~~very~~ little, and they can ~~hopefully~~ be deleted.

Wordy Phrases

WORDY	MORE CONCISE
most of the people	most people
all of the work	all the work
due to the fact that	because, since
despite the fact that	although
at that (*or* this) point in time	then, now
communicate to (*or* with)	tell
impact on	affect, influence
in this day and age	today, now
in any case	anyway
in the case of	regarding, about
in most instances	usually
in some instances	sometimes
subsequent to	after
in case	if
in the final analysis	finally, at last
proceeded to enter	entered

33 c   Redundancy

True facts? Round circles? Phrases that are in and of themselves repetitious are called redundant. In speaking, some repetition helps listeners understand. Public speakers are often advised, "Tell them what you're going to say; say it; then tell them what you said." In writing, however, where readers are able to slow down, pause and reread, repetition is redundant unless it serves other purposes—to create emphasis or rhythm, for instance. As you edit, evaluate each instance of repetition. Ask whether the repetition links ideas, sustains a rhythm, or prevents confusion. If not, cut it.

> The ~~general~~ consensus ~~of opinion~~ among students was that the chancellor had exceeded her authority.

Consensus *means a generally held opinion.*

> About ninety percent
> ~~A very high percentage~~ of the prison's inmates take advantage of
> the special education program,. ~~about ninety percent.~~

Redundant Phrases

first ever	refer back
first and foremost	basic fundamentals
full and complete	initial preparation
past history	terrible tragedy
round in shape	final result
red in color	free gift
general consensus of opinion	true facts
a faulty miscalculation	completely destroyed

33 d   Pretentious language

When you want to sound authoritative, it's tempting to use big words. Writing that sounds as if it's puffed up to impress is called pretentious. Pretentious language also relies unnecessarily on the third-person point of view and often uses the passive voice. Edit in favor of plain language.

ORIGINAL   The range of diagnostic audiovisual services provided includes examinations to determine optical or auditory impairment.

EDITED   We offer eye and ear examinations.

Checklist of Pretentious Language

Here are some pretentious phrases and possible plain-language substitutes. Can you think of others?

PRETENTIOUS	MORE CONCISE
incarcerated offenders	prisoners
client populations	people served
voiced concern that	said, worried
range of selections	choices
minimizes expenditures	saves money
of crucial importance	important, crucial
institution of higher learning	college, university

33 e   Euphemisms

A euphemism is an inoffensive word or phrase deliberately substituted for one considered harsh or indelicate. Our conversations are full of euphemisms, especially in reference to money, death, sex, and body functions. We might say, "I lost my grandmother" or "She has passed away" instead of "My grandmother died." Workers are fired in massive layoffs, but companies speak of "downsizing."

In academic writing, you strive to inform, not to obscure, but you must balance directness with your audience's comfort. If in doubt, ask a peer or an instructor to check your choices.

Think of each sentence as a story, with actors (nouns and pronouns) and actions (verbs). Help your readers imagine the story unfolding before their eyes. To do this, let the main actor of the sentence be its grammatical subject as well. Express the principal action of the sentence in its main verb.

Not

> *Festivities were held* by Derry Street residents and their children to celebrate the opening of a new community playground.

but

>   ┌──── MAIN ACTORS ────┐   ┌─ MAIN ACTION ─┐
> *Children and residents* of Derry Street *celebrated* the opening of a new community playground.

or perhaps

>   ┌── MAIN ACTORS ──┐ ┌─ MAIN ACTION ─┐
> *Dozens of toddlers christened* a new *playground* on Derry Street today,
> ┌── MORE ACTION ──┐   ┌── MORE ACTION ──┐
> *clambering* on the climbing structures and *teetering* on the teeter-totters.

What do you see when you hear festivities, children, residents, *or* were held? *Not much. But* toddlers, celebrated, christened, clambering, teetering—*those words awaken the imagination.*

34 a   Specific subjects

A sentence shouldn't be a who-done-it mystery. If you know who did it, say so.

WEAK	At a hearing before the selection committee, three sites were taken out of consideration, and a fourth was placed under further study.
STRONGER	At a hearing, *the selection committee took* three sites out of consideration and said it would study a fourth.
STILL STRONGER	*The selection committee eliminated* three sites *and agreed to study* a fourth.

Using the principal character (the committee) as the grammatical subject and putting the key actions in the main verbs (eliminated, agreed) brings the sentence to life—and shortens it!

34 b Concrete terms

Abstract words refer to ideas and concepts: *transportation, wealth, childhood, nutrition.* Concrete words name things that can be felt, seen, heard, smelled, or tasted: *car, dime, child, broccoli.*

General words refer to a category or group: *pet, building, educator, car.* Specific words identify objects or people: *Rover, the Chrysler Building, history teacher, five-door hatchback.*

We would be unable to discuss literature, constitutionality, or music without terms for abstract ideas. However, writing that relies exclusively on abstractions seems to have no substance. To give form, shape, and life to abstract and general ideas, look for concrete details and specific examples to support them.

We built a fire on the beach and stayed to watch the moon set.
~~The party was awesome. It was really fun.~~
^

34 c Action verbs

Action verbs denote specific actions. **Static verbs** that show no action—*be, appear, become, seem, exist*—can leave your sentences underpowered. Look for places to replace static verbs with action verbs.

sprawl across
The outer suburbs of Los Angeles ~~are in~~ the hills beyond the San
^
Fernando Valley.

erupt
Voter anger will soon ~~become evident.~~
^

A sentence with *is, are, was* or *were* as its main verb sometimes contains a stronger verb in a lesser role. Make that verb the main verb of the sentence.

The most effective writers ~~are ones who~~ *write* as though they are
simply talking.

Constructions such as *there are, there is,* and *it is* often bury a strong verb elsewhere in the sentence. To turn that verb into a main verb, sometimes you can just delete a few words.

Many
~~There are many~~ people ~~who~~ believe that Elvis Presley is still alive,
even though ~~it is~~ only the tabloids ~~that~~ take such "news" seriously.

Not all verbs that describe action spark clear images. Verbs such as *do, get, go, have, make,* and *think* inspire few mental pictures. Substitute stronger verbs where possible.

bakes
He ~~makes~~ good sourdough bread.

sings wonderfully.
She ~~has a wonderful singing voice.~~

If a verb relies on other words for its descriptive power, find a more effective one.

scurried
He ~~walked quickly~~ from the room.

34 d   Change nouns back to verbs

Many English verbs can become useful nouns with the help of a suffix—*announce* to *announcement* or *tempt* to *temptation,* for example. But nouns made from verbs (called nominalizations) can bury the real action of a sentence. To make matters worse, such a sentence usually employs a weak verb—*have, do, make,* or *be.* As you edit, dig up the buried verbs.

still fascinates
Pickett's Charge ~~has a continuing fascination for~~ historians of the battle of Gettysburg.

Changing Nouns to Verbs

Replacing these expressions with the action verbs buried within them can improve your sentences.

NOMINALIZATION	BURIED VERB
put forth a proposal	propose
hold a discussion	discuss
formulate a plan	plan
reach a decision	decide
arrive at a conclusion	conclude
hammer out an agreement	agree
hold a meeting	meet
go on strike	strike
make a choice	choose
perform a dance	dance

34   e   **Active voice**

A common type of English sentence consists of subject, verb, and object. The person or thing performing the action is the subject; the action word is the verb; the receiver of the action is the object. In this kind of sentence, the verb is said to be in the active voice. (See 42g.)

ACTOR/SUBJECT   ACTIVE-VOICE VERB   DIRECT OBJECT (RECIPIENT OF ACTION)

Juana   collects   the tickets.

When a verb is in the passive voice, the recipient of the action becomes the subject. Passive-voice sentences are less economical and less direct, and they take longer to understand.

SUBJECT   PASSIVE-VOICE VERB   AGENT OF ACTION

The tickets   are taken   by Juana.

Advantages of the Active Voice

Use the active voice unless you have a specific reason not to. By focusing on the actor, the active voice helps readers visualize what happens and who does it. Active-voice sentences usually use fewer words and have a more direct effect than passive-voice sentences. (The sentences in this paragraph and the majority throughout this book are in the active voice.)

Advantages of the Passive Voice

The passive voice de-emphasizes the actor and highlights the recipient of the verb's action—an effect you may choose for selected occasions.

To stress results

A $500 million reduction in the national debt was approved by Congress.

To leave the agent unstated

The city's first homeless shelter was established in a vacant warehouse.

To assert objectivity

The samples were tested for bacteria.

Disadvantages of the Passive Voice

The common advice "Avoid the passive voice" is based on the following problems.

Wordiness

Compare

> The fish were eaten by the birds.
>
> The birds ate the fish.

Vagueness

> The samples were tested for bacteria.
>
> *By whom?*

Possible deceptiveness

Compare

> Mistakes were made.
>
> I made mistakes.

But sometimes the passive voice is just the right technique for your writing situation. If you keep the possible disadvantages in mind, you'll be able to make an appropriate choice.

(For more on structuring sentences to support meaning, see Chapter 38.)

chapter **35** *The Right Word*

In the rich vocabulary of English, the place you live, for instance, might be your *house, home, residence, abode, dwelling, domicile, habitation, quarters, lodging, apartment, pad, place, shack, spot,* or *digs.* It's your job as a writer to find the right word to convey your meaning.

35 a   Dictionaries, thesauruses, and usage guides

Many writers rely on dictionaries and thesauruses to supplement their vocabularies and to guide them in their use of language. If you consult these books regularly, your word skills will grow.

Dictionaries

An unabridged dictionary offers the most comprehensive listing of words in American English, plus information on word origins, definitions, and usage. Examples include *Webster's Third New International Dictionary,* with 470,000 entries, and the 615,000-word *Oxford English Dictionary* (commonly called the *OED*). A searchable edition of the *OED* is available on CD-ROM.

An abridged dictionary omits less frequently used words and some obsolete or archaic definitions. The *American Heritage College Dictionary* (4th ed.), *Merriam-Webster's Collegiate Dictionary* (11th ed.), and the *Random House Webster's College Dictionary* are good for everyday use. The *Merriam-Webster Collegiate* is available online at <http://www.m-w.com>. The fourth edition of the *American Heritage Dictionary of the English Language* can be found online at <http://www.bartleby.com/61/>.

Thesauruses

A thesaurus (the word comes from the Greek for "treasure") lists synonyms for each entry. Many thesauruses list antonyms as well. *Roget's International Thesaurus of English Words and Phrases* lists words by concept. *Roget's II: The New Thesaurus* lists words alphabetically, with a concept index. Both of these are available online at http://www.bartleby.com/62/. At those times when you know there's a word for what you want to say but can't think of it, a thesaurus might help. Looking for an older word for *epidemic?* A thesaurus might help you come up with *plague.*

Never pick a word from a thesaurus just because you think it might sound more authoritative or impressive. A thesaurus offers little guidance on using the words it suggests, and you could end up with embarrasing results. For example, if you have described someone as *easygoing* and are looking for another, similar word, you might find *lackadaisical, spontaneous, uncultivated* or *wild,* each of which has very different meanings (see 35c). When the thesaurus suggests a word you are unfamiliar with, look it up in the dictionary or in a guide to usage.

Usage Guides

Should you use *appraise* or *apprise? Compose* or *comprise? Affect* or *effect? Much* or *many?* These are questions of usage, the choice of the appropriate word. A guide to usage offers what a thesaurus does not: advice on which word is appropriate or customary in which context. Some choices include *A Dictionary of Modern American Usage* (Oxford: Oxford University Press, 2003); *Choose the Right Word,* 2nd edition (New York: Harper Collins, 1994); and *The American Heritage Book of English Usage* (Boston: Houghton Mifflin, 1996). For a quick reference, consult the Glossary of Usage at the end of this book.

35 b   Roots, prefixes, and suffixes

Roots, prefixes, and suffixes provide substantial clues to a word's meaning. A *root* is a base word, or part of a word, from which other words are formed: *mile* in the word *mileage*.

A *prefix* is a group of letters attached to the beginning of a root that changes its meaning: *un-* in *unfinished.* The word *prefix* itself consists of a root, *-fix,* which means "attach," and a prefix, *pre-,* meaning "before." A *suffix* is a group of letters attached to the end of a root: *-age* in *mileage.*

Both prefixes and suffixes change the meaning of the root to which they are attached. For example, the words *antebellum, bellicose,* and *belligerent* share the root *bellum,* Latin for "war." If you already know that *belligerent* means "warlike or at war," you might guess that *antebellum* means "before war."

What's in a Dictionary Entry?

Most dictionaries follow the format found in the tenth edition of *Merriam-Webster's Collegiate Dictionary.*

③ PART OF SPEECH LABEL
① ENTRY WORD   ② PRONUNCIATION   ④ INFLECTED FORMS

com•mu•ni•cate \ kə-'myü-nə-,kāt \ *vb* **-cat-ed; -cat-ing** [L *com-municatus,* pp. of *communicare* to impart, participate, fr. *communis* common — more at MEAN] *vt* (1526) **1** *archaic* : SHARE **2 a** : to convey knowledge of or information about : make known ⟨ ~ a story⟩ **b** : to reveal by clear signs ⟨ his fear *communicated* itself to his friends⟩ **3** : to cause to pass from one to another ⟨some diseases are easily *com-municated*⟩ ~ *vi* **1** : to receive Communion **2** : to transmit infor-mation, thought, or feeling so that it is satisfactorily received or under-stood **3** : to open into each other : CONNECT ⟨the rooms ~⟩ — **com•mu•ni•ca•tee** \ -,myü-ni-kə-'tē \ *n* — **com•mu•ni•ca•tor** \ -'myü-nə-,kā-tər \ *n*
⎬ ⑤ DERIVATION
⎬ ⑥ DEFINITIONS

1. The **entry word** appears in bold type. Bars, spaces, or dots between syllables show where the word can be hyphenated. If two spellings are shown, the first is more common, although both are acceptable. If two spellings are dissimilar, entries are cross-referenced: **gaol** (jāl) *n Brit. sp.* of jail. A superscript numeral before an entry indicates that two or more words have identical spellings.

2. **Pronunciation** is spelled phonetically, set in parentheses or between slashes. (The pho-netic key is at the bottom of the page.) If two pronunciations are given, the first is more common, although both are acceptable.

3. **Parts-of-speech labels** are set in italic type. The abbreviations are *n* for noun, *vb* for verb, *vt* for transitive verb, and so forth.

4. **Inflected forms** are shown, including plurals for nouns and pronouns, comparatives and superlatives, and principal parts for verbs. Irregular spellings also appear here.

5. The **derivation** of a word that has roots in other languages is set between brackets or slashes (*OE* and *ME* = Old English and Middle English, *L* = Latin, *Gr* = Greek, *OFr* = Old French, *Fr* = French, *G* = German).

6. **Definitions** appear with major meanings numbered and arranged from the oldest to the most recent or from the most common to the least common. An example using the word may be enclosed in brackets.

   ■ **Synonyms** or **antonyms** may be listed, often with comments on how the words are similar or different.

   ■ **Usage labels** are used for nonstandard words or meanings.
   archaic: from a historic period; now used rarely if at all
   colloquial (coll.): used informally in speech or writing
   dialect (dial.): used only in some geographical areas
   obsolete (obs.): no longer used
   slang: highly informal, or an unusual usage
   substandard (substand.): widely used but not accepted in formal usage
   British (Brit.), Irish, Scottish (Scot.), and so on: a word used primarily in an area other than the United States
   Some dictionaries use an asterisk to mark Americanisms.

   ■ **Usage notes** may follow definitions. They may also comment on acceptability or un-acceptability.

35 c   Denotations and connotations

The denotation of a word is its direct, literal meaning. *Fragrance, odor, smell,* and *stench* denote the same thing: something perceived by your olfactory sense. But the associated meanings, or connotations, differ. *You have a distinct fragrance* suggests a pleasant smell while *You have a distinct odor* suggests an unpleasant one.

Connotations affect meaning, so consider them when you edit. You might say that the filmmaker Ingmar Bergman is *concerned* or *fascinated* with childhood, but you might not want to say that he is *obsessed* with it. Edit carefully to eliminate unintended connotations. If in doubt, consult a dictionary or a usage guide.

35 d   Idiomatic expressions

Why do we ride *in* a car but *on* a train? Why do we *take* a picture but *make* a recording? Such conventional—that is, widely accepted—speech patterns are called idioms, patterns that may not follow rules of logic or grammar.

Prepositions—*at, by, for, in, on, out, to,* and so on—show a relationship between a noun or a pronoun and other words in the sentence.

> This novel shows a great similarity *to* that one. The similarity *of* [or *between*] the stories is remarkable.

> I will meet *with* you *in* the evening, *at* sunset.

Particles—such as *up, down, out, in, off,* and *on*—look like prepositions, but they combine with verbs to form phrasal verbs, or two-word verbs. Both the verb and the particle are needed to convey the meaning of a phrasal verb, which can be quite different from the meaning of the verb alone.

> How did this *come about?*   *(happen)*

> When did the question *come up?*   *(When was it raised?)*

> Of course, I expected things to *come out* all right.   *(end)*

> I was unconscious for a moment, but I soon *came to.*   *(revived)*

Common Phrasal Verbs and Their More Formal Alternatives

Remember, while informal spoken English may utilize phrasal (verb plus particle) forms, academic writing is more formal. Use the single-word verb whenever possible.

PHRASAL VERB	EQUIVALENT SINGLE VERB
bring up	raise or educate someone
build up	make stronger
call off	cancel
catch up (with)	overtake or exchange news and/or gossip
check out	do research or appraise someone's looks
come up with	create
cut down	reduce
figure out	discover or determine something
find out	discover
get away	leave, escape
get back	return
get in	arrive or enter
get out	leave
get over	recover from
get rid of	eliminate

get up	arise *or* stand
give up	quit, stop *or* discontinue
go up and down	fluctuate
go up	increase
grow up	become an adult, be mature
help out	assist
keep up	continue *or* stay in pace with someone
let down	disappoint *or* break a promise
look into	investigate
look up	find facts (for example, a phone number) *or* plan to visit someone
make up	pretend or invent *or* apologize after a fight *or* offer a replacement for plans canceled
pick up	get or collect *or* meet someone at a party or bar
point out	tell *or* inform
run out	come to the end
set up	establish, arrange
settle down	relax
show off	look for attention *or* admiration
show up	appear *or* embarrass
sign up	register, enlist
slow down	relax *or* become slower
take off	start (flying) *or* make free time
try out	test something *or* audition (for example, for a role in a play)
turn down	refuse a suggestion or invitation *or* decrease (for example, the volume on a radio or television)
turn off	stop operating *or* displease
turn on	start operating *or* arouse
turn up	increase (for example, volume on a radio or television) *or* to visit unexpectedly
work out	exercise *or* solve a problem

35 e   Slang, regionalisms, and colloquialisms

Everyone uses slang, informal language that originates in and is unique to small groups such as students, musicians, athletes, or politicians. Some slang words eventually enter the mainstream and become part of standard English. A *jeep* was originally slang for a *general purpose (g. p.)* military vehicle used in World War II. Now it is a brand name.

Regionalisms are expressions used in one part of the country but are not common elsewhere. The name for a carbonated beverage, for example, varies by region from *pop* to *soda* to *soft drink* to *seltzer*. Some bits of regional dialect are regarded as nonstandard, that is, not widely used in academic writing.

A colloquialism is an expression common to spoken language but seldom used in formal writing. For example, the noun *pot* has a standard meaning as "a cooking vessel" and colloquial meanings of "marijuana," "the amount of money bet on a hand of cards," and "ruination" (as in "go to pot").

Use slang words, regionalisms, and colloquialisms sparingly. They may not be understood, and their informality may imply a lack of rigor, discrimination, or care on your part. They can, however, convey immediacy and authenticity in descriptions and dialogue.

 Prescriptive Versus Descriptive Grammar

Much of the grammar you have studied reflects the *prescriptive* approach to language, that is, a set of rules that prescribes or tells a speaker or writer how to use the language correctly. However, there is a large gap between the prescriptive *grammar* you have studied and the language as you hear it used around you, called *descriptive* grammar—grammar that describes the way people actually interact and use the language.

Thus, you will hear people saying things like <u>*There's*</u> some donuts on the table instead of <u>*There are*</u> some donuts on the table. This discrepancy simply reflects the difference between the way people speak (informal and colloquial language) and the way they write (more formal and careful wording).

Focus on keeping your writing formal even as you learn some of the informal uses of spoken language.

35 f Jargon

Every profession or field develops its own jargon, terms to express its special ideas. As you edit, decide whether your audience will understand your terms. Avoiding technical terms helps you communicate with a general audience, but a specialized audience expects you to use technical language appropriately. Your choices will be influenced by the discipline in which you are writing. For example, writing in the natural sciences, you might substitute *femur* for *thigh bone*. In the humanities, you might make the opposite choice. Avoid jargon added merely to make your writing sound important. (For an example of material presented in different terms for different audiences, see the WAC box in 31a.)

Here's a passage from a magazine about custom pickup trucks. As you read it, note the unfamiliar terms. Do you have any idea what the writer is talking about? If not, what effect does the jargon have on you as a nonenthusiast reader? If you do recognize the terms, how do they affect your view of the writer?

> Tall tires equal significantly added weight, more rotating mass, and you guessed it, dwindling power. The first remedy that comes to mind is to toss a bunch of power parts at the problem. . . . While it's never a bad plan to dig up some additional ponies with items like headers, exhaust systems, programmers, air intakes, and even superchargers, if your wallet has the ammo, harnessing all of those power bolt-ons to their true potential requires cracking open the differential and lowering the gear ratio to restore throttle response and all-out pavement-shredding torque. Many enthusiasts with lifted trucks install tires in excess of 35 inches tall and never bother to re-gear the differential. The result is poor throttle response, significantly decreased torque behavior, and weak passing power.
>
> TRAVIS NOACK, "POWER TO THE PAVEMENT," *STREET TRUCKS,* JUNE 2006

If you were editing this passage for an audience of, say, "average" car owners, what changes would you make?

35 g Figurative language

Figurative language, which likens one thing to another in imaginative ways, brings freshness and resonance to writing.

> But let judgment *run down as waters,* and righteousness *as a mighty stream.*
>
> AMOS 5:24

One common problem writers have is inadvertently juxtaposing incongruous images. A mixed metaphor combines two or more unrelated images, often with unintended effects. When you find a mixed metaphor in your writing, eliminate the weaker one and extend the more appropriate one.

> drown
> **We must *swim* against the *tide* of cynicism that threatens to ~~cloud~~**
> our hope
> ~~our vision~~ **of a world without hunger.**

Swim/tide/drown/hope *make a more consistent metaphor and therefore a clearer image than do* swim/tide/cloud/vision.

Figurative Language

- A **simile** that explicitly likens one thing to another.

  German submarines swam the seas *like* sharks, striking without warning.

- A **metaphor** implicitly equates one thing with another.

  Her life *became a whirlwind* of design meetings, client conferences, and last-minute decisions.

- An **analogy** is an extended comparison.

  The course catalog at a large university *resembles a smorgasbord*. Courses range from differential calculus to American film, from Confucianism to liberation theology. Students receive little advice as to which classes are the salads, which the desserts, and which the entrees of a college education. Even amid this feast, a student risks malnutrition.

- **Personification** is the technique of attributing human qualities or behavior to a non-human phenomenon.

  The ship sailed into the *teeth* of the hurricane.

- Deliberate exaggeration is called **hyperbole.**

  No book in the world is more difficult than this economics text. Reading it is *absolute torture.*

- The opposite of hyperbole is deliberate **understatement.**

  With temperatures remaining below zero all day, it will seem *just a bit chilly* outside tomorrow.

- **Irony** is a contrast, especially a humorous or tragic one. *Sarcasm* is one form of irony in which a speaker says the opposite of what he or she means: "Lovely weather, isn't it?" amid a raging blizzard. *Situational irony* is a contrast between intentions and results. In Percy Bysshe Shelley's poem "Ozymandias," the inscription on the ruined statue of a once-mighty ruler reads, "Look upon my works, ye Mighty, and despair." Words that once urged the mighty to tremble now speak of the transience of power.

35 h   Clichés

Our language is full of worn-out expressions called clichés. Interestingly, *cliché* is a French word for the sound of a stamping press making multiple, identical images. In other words, something has become a cliché if it no longer causes the audience to think.

the last straw	needle in a haystack
as strong as an ox	handwriting on the wall
better late than never	tried and true
lay your cards on the table	hit the nail on the head
a drop in the bucket	best thing since sliced bread

To edit a cliché, try improving on it. Go back to the original image and describe it in new words or add fresh details.

Outside, the wind ~~howled.~~ keened as though it had lost a child
                                    ^

If you can't revive it, replace the cliché with a direct statement of what you are trying to say.

                    so   that we waited in vain for our eyes to adjust
It was dark ~~as night~~ **inside the cave.**
              ^   ^

Writing that relies on careless generalization as a substitute for specific description reflects mental laziness. Furthermore, using a generalization about a group of people to predict, describe, or interpret the behavior or characteristics of an individual in that group is both insensitive and illogical.

Careless generalizations based on race, ethnicity, gender, cultural background, age, physical characteristics, or lifestyles are called stereotypes. Whether they refer to gender, race, ethnicity, or sexual preference, stereotypes are oversimplified generalizations. Positive or negative, they substitute a simplistic formula for an appreciation of individual differences and the richness of human variation.

36 a Stereotypes

Many stereotypes stem from ignorance and from fear of people who are perceived as "different." These stereotypes often penetrate our language, both in descriptions of people (*spineless liberal, right-wing nutcase*) and in descriptive images (*sleepy Southern town*). Calling a doctor or a lawyer *he* reinforces the stereotype that all doctors and lawyers are men.

Edit to eliminate stereotypes. Qualify broad generalizations, and support or replace sweeping statements with specific factual evidence. In some cases, drop the stereotypical observation altogether.

many inexperienced

Like ~~most teenage~~ drivers, he drove too fast.

~~Like so many of his race,~~ Allen Iverson is a superbly gifted athlete.

Frank Peters, now in his late eighties 'but still alert, remembers the dry, hot summer of the Tillamook Burn.

Eliminating Stereotypes

As you edit, ask these four questions.

1. Have I relied more on stereotypes than on evidence to make my point? Are all African Americans "good dancers"?
2. Do my generalizations follow from factual evidence? Is it true that "students these days can't write"?
3. Do my generalizations about a group improperly label individuals? Can I assume that my Canadian classmate "must be a hockey fan" simply because hockey is popular in Canada?
4. Have I used euphemism to mask a stereotype? Is a woman "a wonderful asset to her husband" or something more in her own right?

36 b Group labels

People often label themselves in terms of the groups to which they belong. However, labels inevitably emphasize a single feature of a person's identity, ignoring other characteristics. They may also offend people who do not want to be so characterized. Furthermore, many labels go beyond simple identification and become explicitly or implicitly derogatory. As you edit, examine any labels you have used; try to use only those acceptable to the members of the group themselves, and avoid labels with negative connotations.

Using a Group's Own Labels

Even though members of a particular group may not agree on what they should be called, whenever possible, refer to such a group by the label most of its members prefer. Labels sometimes move quickly into or out of favor as they acquire unintended connotations, so be sure to check current practice.

Designations of Race, Ethnicity, and Nationality

Terms for race and ethnicity change over time as their political and social context changes. *Colored* has fallen into disuse, partly because of its association with Southern segregation. *Negro,* once the term proudly demanded as an alternative to *colored* by the civil-rights advocates of the 1940s through the early 1960s, has since been supplanted by *black* and *African American. People of color* is another currently accepted term, but it is sometimes used more broadly to include other groups.

The terms *Asian* and *Asian American* have widely replaced *Oriental* for people of Asian ancestry. To some people, *Oriental* carries a note of condescension. For others, both *Asian* and *Oriental* lump groups together in a way that ignores national and cultural differences. To refer to national origin or ancestry, using a specific country is always correct: *Japanese, Korean, Malaysian, Chinese.*

Today some Americans of Spanish-speaking heritage refer to themselves as *Hispanics,* while others prefer *Latino* and *Latina,* and some Mexican Americans prefer *Chicano* and *Chicana,* a term that refers specifically to Mexican origins. Some *Native Americans* prefer that term to *Indian,* but using the name of the tribe or nation is often a better choice: *Navajo, Lakota Sioux, Seneca.* Many *Inuit* prefer that term to *Eskimo.*

If the religion of a person or group has relevance, use the preferred terms. For example, a follower of Islam is a *Muslim;* a person of the Jewish faith is a *Jew.*

Designations of Gender and Sexual Orientation

Most adult women prefer to be called *women* rather than *girls* or *ladies. Girls* is particularly inappropriate in reference to salespeople and administrative staff.

When writing about sexual orientation, keep in mind that people have widely different views about the role of sexuality in our personal and public lives. Be aware that not everyone may share your perspective, and consider using a group's own chosen term. *Heterosexual, homosexual, bisexual,* and *transgendered* are descriptive rather than evaluative words that are generally accepted.

Designations of Ability

People with physical limitations often prefer *disabled* to *handicapped.*

Designations of Age

Modern American culture does not extol old age, and even accepted terms can seem blunt or condescending. Think about using *senior citizens* rather than *the elderly.* If a person's age is critical to what you want to say, cite the actual age: *68-year-old.*

Checking Labels for Negative Connotations

Some labels that might at first seem neutral can have negative connotations. For example, the term *AIDS victims* implies that such people are blameless, which you may intend, but also that they are helpless, which you may not. As you edit, watch for such unnecessary or unintended negative connotations, and substitute more neutral alternatives. Because neutral phrases can be cumbersome, they are easily mocked as too "politically correct." Here are two general rules.

- Focus on people's strengths: people *live with* cancer, or they are cancer *survivors,* rather than *suffering* from the disease.

- Focus on the person first and the characteristic or condition second: *a woman who is quadriplegic,* not *a quadriplegic.*

36 c   Gender-neutral language

When you use words that embody sexual stereotypes, you run the risk of alienating at least half of your potential audience. Gender bias can arise from unexamined habits of thought and language.

Pronoun Choice

Until recently, *he, him,* and *his* were used generically to refer to singular nouns or pronouns when the gender of the antecedent was unknown, unstated, or irrelevant: *Anyone who believes those promises should have his head examined.* Such usage is disappearing because many people believe that the general *he* excludes women.

However, English does not have a singular personal pronoun of indefinite gender to match the gender-neutral plural pronoun *they.* In speaking, people often use plural pronouns to avoid the masculine forms: *Everybody had fun on their vacation.* But since *everybody* is singular, any pronoun that refers to it should be singular, so you have to choose between *his* and *her.*

If you know the gender of the first reference, match it with the pronoun of the same gender: *Each nun makes her own bed.*

If you don't know the gender, choose one of these strategies.

- Make the antecedent plural and adjust other agreement problems: *All the residents make their own beds.*

- Use *his or her* or *he or she: Each resident makes his or her own bed.* Use this strategy sparingly to avoid distracting repetition.

- Restructure: Instead of *Everyone has done <u>his</u> part,* write *Everyone has <u>helped</u>.*

Universal Terms

The use of *man* and *mankind* to refer to the whole of humanity seems to ignore the female half of the species. As you edit, substitute more inclusive terms such as *humanity, the human race, humankind,* or *people.*

Occupational Terms

Focus on the occupation, not on the gender of the person who holds it. There are almost no jobs that are "naturally" held by either men or women. Avoid language that implicitly identifies an occupation with gender, that assumes all flight attendants, nurses, secretaries, or teachers to be female or all airline pilots, business executives, streetcar conductors, or bronco busters to be male.

Avoid using occupational terms with feminine suffixes: *actress, authoress, poetess, executrix,* which unnecessarily call attention to gender. Such feminine forms have become obsolete, and the formerly male form has become neutral: *actor, author, poet, executor.* Others, such as *waitress,* are changing to more inclusive terms: *server.*

Checklist of Neutral Occupational Labels

Occupational terms that end in *-man* imply that everyone who holds that job is male. Gender-neutral substitutes for many occupations are readily available.

SEXIST	NEUTRAL
statesman	diplomat
congressman	representative in Congress, congressional representative, representative
mailman	letter carrier, mail carrier
policeman	police officer
fireman	firefighter
businessman	executive, businessperson
salesman	sales representative, salesperson

Proofreading is the process of finding and correcting errors before submitting your final manuscript for publication or grading. The key to proofreading is to see what is actually on the page, not what you meant to put there.

The main business of proofreading is correcting typographical errors and errors in spelling, punctuation, and mechanics. If you make the same errors often, list them in your journal or notebook, and check for them in subsequent papers. The following guidelines help ensure accurate proofreading:

- **Proofread on hard copy.** If you have been composing on a computer, print out a hard (paper) copy to proofread more effectively. Errors and awkward passages are much easier to see in print on paper. Make each correction immediately on the computer, or enter them all at once when you finish, whichever works better for you.

- **Read aloud.** Reading aloud will help you hear anything that isn't clear and natural. It also will help you to find dropped words and incorrect punctuation.

- **Ask someone else to read your paper.** A fresh pair of eyes often will spot errors that you might overlook because you're so close to the writing. If that person also reads your work aloud, you may hear problems in rhythm, construction, and meaning. If English is not your first language, a native speaker might be able to spot issues you are not aware of.

- **Read backward.** It's easy to be distracted by meaning and thus miss technical or mechanical mistakes. One way around this problem is to start with the last word on each page and work back toward the beginning of the page, one word at a time. Use a ruler to help you focus on a single line, or point a pencil at each word.

- **Use—but don't trust—your computer's spelling checker.** A spelling checker is really not much help. It won't reveal a dropped word or a misspelling that creates another legitimate word—such as typing *of* when you meant to type *off* or *on*. It may alert you unnecessarily when you deliberately use unconventional spelling (*ain't, gotta*), unusual plurals (*underlinings*), or foreign words. But the spell checker does not know the correct spelling of many proper nouns, nor will it catch errors in numbers. Therefore, proofread again *after* your computer has checked for spelling. Make sure that you have typed the words you intended, and use a dictionary to check questionable spellings.

- **Use—but don't trust—your computer's grammar checker.** A grammar checker is usually even less useful than a spell-checker. It may miss many major errors, and it also will identify minor ones, such as extra spaces, while usually overlooking missing words. It might flag items that are not errors (very long sentences or unusual syntax). Its main value is in alerting you to double-check.

Proofreading Marks

Standard symbols (see list on inside back cover) provide an efficient way to mark up your paper for correction later. Don't leave proofreading marks or corrections on final copy; reprint individual pages as necessary, making sure that the replacement pages begin and end with the same words as the original.

A string of sentences whose relationship to one another is unclear can be confusing. If each fact has its own sentence, it might not be clear what those facts add up to. Early drafts sometimes display this problem as writers concentrate on what they're saying but not on how effectively they're saying it. To provide tools for showing relationships among ideas, this chapter introduces the basic sentence types (see 47c for more details). Then it offers suggestions on emphasizing the equality of ideas (coordination), the relative importance of ideas (subordination), or their similarities (parallel structure).

38 a   Types of sentences

A typical simple sentence is short. It contains few words. It is direct. It doesn't wander. It contains a single thought. Technically, a simple sentence has a single independent clause. That is, it has a subject and a verb and expresses a complete idea.

SUBJECT VERB
John   ran.

SUBJECT VERB   OBJECT
John   hit   a home run.

While simple sentences are easy to follow, a string of them can be tedious to read (see the paragraph above). But following a series of longer sentences, a simple sentence can make readers slow down and pay attention.

Fortunately, although they have lost their leaves, deciduous trees aren't dead in winter. They still maintain life, although little growth occurs. It's just too cold.

A compound sentence contains two or more simple sentences (or independent clauses) joined by words such as *and, but,* and *or* (see also Chapter 40). Technically, compound sentences contain two or more independent clauses joined either by a comma and a coordinating conjunction (see 38b and 40a) or by a semicolon.

INDEPENDENT CLAUSE   INDEPENDENT CLAUSE

John ran far,   but he didn't run very fast.

INDEPENDENT CLAUSE   INDEPENDENT CLAUSE

Pollution is a problem; however, it won't go away soon.

Compound sentences imply a relationship between the ideas within the sentence. A compound sentence keeps readers moving faster than a pair of simple sentences.

A complex sentence contains at least two clauses, one of which can't stand on its own. Technically, a complex sentence has one independent clause and one or more dependent clauses.

INDEPENDENT CLAUSE   DEPENDENT CLAUSE

John ran   as though he were dreaming or lost in thought.

A compound-complex sentence contains at least two independent clauses and one dependent clause.

INDEPENDENT CLAUSE   DEPENDENT CLAUSE

John ran   as though he were dreaming or lost in thought,

INDEPENDENT CLAUSE

but actually he was carefully counting the cracks in the sidewalk.

38 b   Relationships between equal ideas (coordination)

If two related ideas are of roughly equal importance, you can coordinate them by putting them together in a compound sentence. To join two or more thoughts together in a compound sentence, use one of the following techniques.

Coordinating Conjunctions

The most common method of joining independent clauses uses a co-ordinating conjunction—*and, or, nor, for, but, yet, so*—and a comma. Each co-ordinating conjunction expresses a different relationship, so be sure to choose the right one.

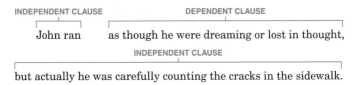

Incoming students must pass a placement examination to meet the foreign language requirement, , or they ~~Those who fail the test~~ **must take an introductory language course.**

not only   _, but he_
Lavar won high honors in mathematics and physics. ~~He~~ also was
                                                                            ^   ^
recognized for achievement in biology.

Semicolons

When the relationship between two ideas is apparent, a semicolon alone
can join two independent clauses.

Taking an introductory language course will fulfill the foreign
                                                    ; the
language requirement. ~~The~~ courses are offered during the fall
                                                      ^
semester.

If you use a transitional expression such as _however, moreover,_ or _never-_
theless between two independent clauses, a semicolon is required. A comma
is not sufficient in this situation (see 48a and 48b).

                                                                                    _;_
An advanced placement score will be accepted, however, the test
                                                                                  ^
must have been taken within the last year.

As you edit, look for places where combining sentences using coordination can smooth the flow of ideas.

Specifying Relationships Between Ideas

RELATIONSHIP	COORDINATING CONJUNCTIONS	TRANSITIONAL EXPRESSION
addition	and	also, besides, moreover
contrast	but, yet	instead, however
choice	or	otherwise
causation	so, for	therefore, accordingly, consequently
substitution		alternatively

Illogical Coordination

If two ideas aren't related, don't use coordination, which implies that
they are. If you do use coordination, be sure to choose the right kind.

I made eggs for breakfast, and I missed the bus.

If the breakfast preparations did not cause the writer to miss the bus, the two sen-
tences are not related and should not be joined. If there is a cause-and-effect re-
lationship, make it more clear.

I took time to make eggs for breakfast, *so* I missed the bus.

Faulty coordination can be confusing or inaccurate.

The project was a huge undertaking, ~~yet~~ _so_ I was exhausted at the end.

The conjunction yet *implies contrast, but that is not what the sentence means. The conjunction* so *states the proper cause-and-effect relationship.*

Overused Coordination

Too much coordination begins to sound childish. How much is too much? If a sentence with several coordinate structures seems weak, decide which elements belong together and which should stand alone. The following paragraph, for example, could be edited like this:

Coordination can be overdone, *. When* ~~and when~~ it is used too much, it begins to sound repetitive, *. Readers* ~~and readers~~ may begin to imagine the voice of a child speaking in sentences that go on and on, strung together with *and*, ~~and~~ soon they may get confused or bored, *As* ~~so as~~ a writer you should try to prevent that.

| **38** | **c** | **Hierarchy of ideas (subordination)** |

Use subordination to emphasize one idea and de-emphasize (subordinate) another within a single sentence. Place the most important idea in the main clause of the sentence. Place less important information in a dependent (subordinate) clause. To illustrate, look at these two ideas presented as separate simple sentences, with neither given more weight than the other.

John Playford collected seventeenth-century music. He was an English musician.

To emphasize Playford's activity as a collector (first sentence), subordinate his identity (second sentence) by putting it in a dependent clause.

John Playford, who was an English musician, collected seventeenth-century music.

To emphasize Playford's identity, make that element the main clause.

John Playford, who collected seventeenth-century music, was an English musician.

When editing, if you find two related sentences with one more important than the other, put the less important sentence into a subordinate structure.

NO SUBORDINATION	John Playford was an English musician. He collected seventeenth-century music and descriptions of popular dances. He published them in a book called *The English Dancing Master.*

The absence of subordination presents a string of facts without showing hierarchy or relationships.

SUBORDINATION	John Playford was an English musician who collected seventeenth-century music and descriptions of popular dances in a book called *The English Dancing Master.*

Emphasizes the identification of Playford.

SUBORDINATION	John Playford, an English musician, collected seventeenth-century music and descriptions of popular dances in a book called *The English Dancing Master.*

Emphasizes what Playford did.

A subordinate element may appear as a clause, a phrase, or a single word. The less important the element is grammatically, the less attention it demands.

NO SUBORDINATION	The campaign manager wrote a plan. It seemed to cover every major contingency.
CLAUSE	The plan *that the campaign manager wrote* seemed to cover every major contingency.
PHRASE	The plan *written by the campaign manager* seemed to cover every major contingency.
WORD	The *campaign manager's* plan seemed to cover every major contingency.

A dependent or subordinate clause, one that contains a subject and a verb but cannot stand alone as a full sentence, is usually introduced by a relative pronoun such as *who, whom, which, what,* or *that* or a subordinating conjunction such as *although, because, if, since, whether,* or *while.*

, which has been widening for twenty years,

The gap between rich and poor has caused great concern among
                                                       ^
social thinkers. ~~The gap has been widening for over twenty years.~~

What we know today   is

~~There are a few basic facts~~ about AIDS ~~we know today. They are~~
        ^   ^
the result of years of painstaking research.

Another important use of subordination is to condition one statement
on another.

                                        if it receives
The plan has a chance of success. ~~It needs~~ **support from certain**
                                           ^
key people.

Using an if *clause makes it more clear that the support is a necessary condition
of success.*

Subordinating the wrong element in a sentence changes the meaning
of what you want to say. Watch for illogical subordination that can confuse
readers.

INDEPENDENT   Scientists have carefully examined this theory. Some have
SENTENCES   criticized it.

INCORRECT   Some scientists who have criticized this theory have carefully
SUBORDINATION   examined it.

*This sentence inadvertently implies that some opponents have not been so
careful.*

CORRECT   Some of the scientists who have carefully examined this
SUBORDINATION   theory have criticized it.

Look also for subordination that suggests causal relationships you do
not intend.

                                        that began shortly after
The nation was plunged into a deep recession ~~when~~ **Ronald Reagan**
                                                      ^
took office in 1981.

The writer did not mean to imply that Reagan's election caused the recession.

Overused Subordination

Sometimes you can rely too much on subordination, which can
                         . Every
sound insipid ~~because every~~ **point seems to be qualified, while**
          ^
nothing is said directly.

More Words That Specify Relationships

RELATIONSHIP	CONJUNCTION
cause/effect	as, because, since, so, so that, in order that
condition	if, even if, if only, unless
contrast	although, even though, though
comparison	as if, as though, than, whereas, while
choice	rather than, than, whether
sequence	after, as, as long as, as soon as, before, once, since, until, when, whenever, while
space	where, wherever, whence

(Also see Relationships between equal ideas in 38b.)

 Using Subordinating Conjunctions

- A clause that begins with a subordinating conjunction (*after* in this example) can't be regarded as a complete sentence. Be sure to connect such a clause to another sentence.

  After the ballots were counted, everyone Everyone was surprised at the results.

- When you start a sentence with *whereas, while, although, though,* or *even though,* do not begin the next clause with *but.*

  Although a smile shows happiness in most cultures, ~~but~~ in some it may be a sign of embarrassment.

- When you use *because* or *since* to describe a reason or cause, do not use *so* in the following clause.

  Because Rudolf Nureyev defected from Russia, ~~so~~ for many years he could not return to dance in his native country.

- *Because* and *because of* are not interchangeable. Use *because* when what follows is expressed as a clause, with a subject and a verb.

  SUBJECT VERB
  Because snow peas die in hot weather, you should plant them in early spring.

  Use *because of* when your subordinate idea is expressed as a *phrase,* with no verb.

  PHRASE
  Because of the hot weather, the snow peas did not grow well.

- Used by itself, *even* is not a subordinating conjunction. Use *even though* to mean "despite the fact that."

  though
  Even I don't play well, I still enjoy taking piano lessons.

  Use *even if* to mean "whether or not."

  if
  Even it rains tomorrow, the race will be held.

341

Combining Sentences to Let Ideas Flow

If every idea requires a separate simple sentence, your writing will be disjointed. Carefully choosing coordination or subordination can make your ideas flow better.

Giving Ideas Equal Weight

Use coordination to connect equally important ideas.

To generate electricity, utilities burn huge quantities of coal. ~~Another fuel widely~~ *and* , but many ~~used is~~ oil. ~~Many~~ utilities also operate hydroelectric dams.

Subordination to Combine Sentences

Use subordination to emphasize central ideas.

Although they are quite different restaurants, Zoë and Match have both become popular within the past year. ~~They are quite~~ ~~different restaurants.~~ To succeed in New York, a restaurant should not emulate a certain style. ~~It must set its own style and excel~~ *Customers will respond best if it sets its own style and excels* at it. ~~Customers will respond best~~ ~~to that.~~ Zoë and Match accomplish this goal. ~~They~~ *, even though they* do it in different ways.

38 d   **Parallel structures**

Parallelism refers to the repetition of a grammatical structure. Parallel constructions are rhythmic and memorable. In the following examples, notice how parallelism creates a pleasing rhythm when you say the sentence aloud.

WORDS   We saw the frogs swimming, jumping, and splashing.

PHRASES   Of the people, by the people, for the people

CLAUSES   Do as I say, not as I do.

Elements joined *and, or, nor, for, but, yet,* or *so* should be grammatically parallel.

They spent their time praying and ~~work~~ with the poor.
working

So should elements joined by *either . . . or, neither . . . nor, not only . . . but also,* and *both . . . and.*

Wind-generated electric power is not only difficult to capture but also ~~it must be stored at great expense.~~
expensive to store.

Comparisons

In comparisons, set up equivalent alternatives that are parallel in grammatical form.

Laura likes painting as much as ~~to read.~~ *reading.*

He always believed that effective communication was more a matter of thinking clearly than ~~to try to write~~ *writing* **well.**

Elements in a series or list joined must also be parallel in grammatical form.

She enjoyed music, dancing, and ~~played~~ *playing* **the piano.**

Uses for Parallelism

Few devices achieve greater power, gravity, and impact than a good parallel construction. Use parallelism for emphasis.

With local leaders afraid of the "no growth" label, the quality of local decision making has clearly declined. The question facing towns like Mayberry is *not whether they will plan to have no growth but whether they will face growth with no plan.* ~~whether they will do enough planning to avoid uncontrolled development.~~

The addition of not whether . . . but whether *and* no growth . . . no plan *makes the conclusion more resonant.*

Many writers repeat parallel structures to create a rhythmic effect.

To die, to sleep. To sleep, perchance to dream.
—WILLIAM SHAKESPEARE, *HAMLET*

Good parallelism makes comparisons clear. Watch for words omitted from parallel structures: prepositions (*to, for, at*), subordinating conjunctions (*although, since, because*), and relative pronouns (*who, which, what*).

The researchers tried to ensure that interviewees were representative of the campus population and *that* **their opinions reflected those of the whole student body.**

Without the additional that, *it is unclear whether the clause beginning with* their opinions *refers to the researchers or the interviewees.*

A sentence is a group of words that expresses a complete idea. A group of words punctuated as a sentence that does not express a complete thought is called a fragment. Although fragments occur in everyday speech, they are usually seen as errors in academic writing.

One kind of fragment neglects to tell what the sentence is about (the subject) or what happened (the verb). Other fragments have a subject and a verb but don't make sense standing alone.

Before you can fix a fragment, you have to identify it. To recognize a fragment, ask yourself the following questions.

- Does the group of words contain a verb? If not, it is a fragment.

  A controlled experiment $\overset{\text{was conducted}}{\wedge}$ to compare the effect of light on plants.

  An infinitive such as to compare *(or a participle such as* comparing*) cannot serve as the main verb of a sentence (see Verbs, 42a).*

- Does it contain a subject? If not, it is a fragment.

  During the night, the protesters talked quietly and slept$\overset{\text{and}}{\cancel{\wedge}}$ ~~And~~ prayed.

  The fragment And prayed *has no subject. Including it in the previous sentence allows* protesters *to serve as its subject.*

  (*Sentences in the imperative mood—commands, orders, and requests—do not require explicit subjects:* Come at noon.)

- Can it stand alone?

  Clarify ambiguities$\overset{\text{wherever}}{\cancel{\wedge}}$ ~~Wherever~~ you find them.

  Wherever you find them *isn't a complete sentence. It must become part of another sentence to make sense.*

39 a Missing verbs or subjects

To turn fragments into complete sentences, follow these strategies.

- Supply a missing subject or verb.

- Incorporate the fragment into a nearby sentence.

344

Adding the Missing Elements

If a fragment lacks a verb or subject, you can simply add one.

A fleet of colorful fishing boats ~~rocking~~ was at anchor in the bay.

The -ing form of a verb can't serve as the main verb of a sentence without another verb called an auxiliary (see 42d).

The snowboarder cleared the rock ledge and flew into space. ~~Spun~~ , spun twice in midair and sliced into the clean powder below.

Spun *doesn't have a subject unless it's in the same sentence with* snowboarder.

Joining the Fragment

Another solution is to make the fragment part of a nearby sentence.

Few employees held the president in high regard. ~~Or~~ or believed he could make the company profitable.

Employees *works as the subject for* believed *as well as for* held.

Symbolism is an important technique in Alice Walker's "Everyday ~~Use." A~~ Use," a story of cultural differences between generations.

| 39 | b | **Dependent clause fragments** |

This is my cousin Jacob. Who has never missed a day of school.

Even though it contains a subject and a verb, the clause *who has never missed a day of school* isn't a complete sentence. A clause that doesn't make sense standing alone is called a subordinate or dependent clause (see 39b). You can recognize a dependent clause by its first word, such as *after, although, since, if, because, when, where,* or *whether*—these are called subordinating conjunctions—or *who, which, whoever,* or *that*—these are relative pronouns.

To fix a this kind of fragment, remove the subordinating word or attach the dependent clause to the sentence it modifies.

This is my cousin Jacob. ~~Who~~ He has never missed a day of school.

This is my cousin Jacob. ~~Who~~ , who has never missed a day of school.

39 c   Intentional fragments

Writers occasionally use fragments to create special effects—to reproduce the sound of spoken language or to create dramatic emphasis. Intentional fragments appear in fiction, personal essays, and narratives, and wherever dialogue is reproduced.

> I knew that I was no legitimate resident of any world of ideas. I knew I couldn't think. All I knew then was what I couldn't do. All I knew then was what I wasn't, and it took me some years to discover what I was. *Which was a writer.*
>
> *By which I mean not a "good" writer or a "bad" writer, but simply a writer, a person whose most absorbed and passionate hours are spent arranging words on pieces of paper.*
>
> —JOAN DIDION, "WHY I WRITE"

If you use a fragment, think carefully about its effect. Make sure that it seems intentional. When emphasizing your point warrants disrupting readers' expectations, consider using a fragment. If it works.

---

chapter **40** | *Comma Splices and Run-On Sentences*

The errors called "comma splices" and "run-on sentences" can draw sharp reactions from instructors who feel that such "sentence errors" are serious writing offenses. Once you learn to spot them, however, they're easy to repair or to avoid. In fact, many of these errors occur when writers are combining two sentences into one, as discussed in Chapter 38. Some of the remedies discussed here also appear in Chapter 48, Commas, and Chapter 49, Semicolons.

The error called a comma splice occurs when two sentences are joined (or "spliced") into one by only a comma.

INDEPENDENT CLAUSE

COMMA SPLICE   Professional athletes can earn huge salaries,

INDEPENDENT CLAUSE

some are paid millions of dollars a year.

Seeing the comma after salaries *without a coordinating conjunction, readers might expect what follows to be part of the first clause rather than a new clause. Either of the following alternatives is correct.*

Professional athletes can earn huge salaries. Some are paid millions of dollars a year.

Professional athletes can earn huge salaries; some are paid millions of dollars a year.

A run-on sentence occurs when two independent clauses are joined without any marker.

RUN-ON SENTENCE   Athletes' salaries drive up costs and ticket price increases can make fans angry.

And ticket price increases sounds as if it might belong with the first part of the sentence. A reader might expect the sentence to read Athletes salaries drive up costs and ticket prices. *A comma after* costs *prevents that misreading.*

Athletes' salaries drive up costs, and ticket price increases can make fans angry.

Here are ways to correct comma splices and fused sentences.

■ Use a comma and a coordinating conjunction (*and, but, or, for, so, or, nor* or *yet*).

■ Use a semicolon, alone or with a conjunctive adverb or a transitional phrase.

■ Use a colon when the second clause illustrates the first.

Recognizing Comma Splices and Run-On Sentences

Comma splices and fused sentences sometimes occur when two ideas are closely linked and the writer forgets to signal appropriately where one ends and the next begins. Here are some common situations.

■ The second clause offers an example, explanation, or elaboration of the first.

The tribes gathered every summer along the banks of the river ~~they~~ ·They fished and hunted and picked berries.

■ The second clause contains a meaning that contrasts with the first.

Everyone was asked to express an opinion on the plans, *but* Mr. Johnson had to leave early.

■ The subject of the second clause is the same as the subject of the first.

She asked us to write down our thoughts ~~she~~ ·She said to write whatever came to mind.

■ A transitional phrase is incorrectly used to join two sentences.

I remember playing with Ernest and Mike ; in fact , I barely remember playing with anyone else.

- Divide the sentence into two sentences.

- Subordinate one clause to the other.

- Rewrite the sentence as one independent clause.

40 a   Using a comma and a coordinating conjunction

The words *and, but, yet, so, for, or* and *nor* are coordinting conjunctions—they're *conjunctions* because they join together (con-join) grammatical elements; they're *coordinating* conjunctions because they specify a
relationship between equal grammatical elements: *and* for addition; *but*
and *yet* for contrast; *so* and *for* for cause; *or* and *nor* for choice.

To join independent clauses, use an appropriate coordinating conjunction preceded by a comma.

> **Maya Angelou has worked as an actress and director, ^but^ her greatest
>
> success came as an autobiographer and poet.**

40 b   Adding a semicolon

A semicolon after an independent clause signals that the following independent clause is just as important as the first one. Two independent
clauses may be joined with a semicolon alone if the ideas in the clauses are
closely and clearly related. (For more situations that call for semicolons,
see Chapter 49.)

> **For years the Federal Communications Commission has advocated
>
> legislation to allow competitive auctions for broadcast licenses ^;^ so
>
> far, Congress has refused.**

Semicolons are useful in sentences with more than two independent
clauses.

> **The sculpture was monstrous ^;^ its surface was rough and pitted,
>
> and its colors were garish.**

Words like *finally* and *however* and phrases such as *in fact, for example,* and *among others* are called transitional expressions. When they are
used to join independent clauses, a semicolon is also required.

The rebel forces were never defeated $\overset{;}{\underset{\wedge}{/}}$ moreover, they still controlled several highland passes.

Our friends helped us do a lot of work on Saturday $\overset{;}{\underset{\wedge}{/}}$ in fact, we stacked two cords of wood.

40 c Adding a colon

Use a colon to join two independent clauses when the second clause explains, elaborates, or illustrates the first.

My mother gave me one important piece of advice $\overset{:}{\underset{\wedge}{/}}$ never wear stripes with plaids.

40 d Writing separate sentences

Sometimes the best solution is to create separate sentences.

My last year of high school was an eventful one $\underset{\wedge}{/}$ ~~everything~~ ^{. Everything} seemed to be happening all at once.

40 e Using subordination

To emphasize the main idea in your sentence, place the less important idea in a dependent clause. Dependent clauses are introduced by subordinating conjunctions (*because, if, than, after, although, whenever, while,* and so on) or relative pronouns (*who, which, that*).

^{Because the}
$\underset{\wedge}{\text{~~The~~}}$ rain had frozen as it hit the ground $\underset{\wedge}{,}$ the streets were slick with ice.

Inserting because *makes the connection between events more clear.*

^{that}
The panel studied the issue $\underset{\wedge}{\text{~~it~~}}$ decided to recommend allowing the group to participate.

40 f Creating one independent clause

If the two clauses in a fused sentence or comma splice are close in meaning, collapse them into one clause. If they have the same subject, create a compound predicate.

> **This book held my attention *and* ~~it~~ gave a lot of information about the Renaissance.**

Here the subject, book, *has two predicates:* held my attention *and* gave a lot of information.

You can also turn one clause into a modifier phrase.

> **Mary Stewart steeps her stories in historical detail*, my favorite author,* ~~she is my favorite author.~~**

---

chapter **41** *Shifts and Mixed Constructions*

R eaders are like bus riders: They like to know where they are being taken. Good writers keep their passengers comfortable by avoiding unplanned detours.

Throughout a piece of writing, readers expect continuity in point of view and references to time. Within sentences, they expect consistency, with no puzzling shifts in person or the number of subjects (see 41a), the forms of verbs (see 42e–42g), or the way quotations are reproduced. There should also be no unwarranted twists and turns in grammar, logic, or sense.

41 a In person and number

Unnecessary shifts in person often occur when pronouns are used in sentences about groups or about unidentified people.

> **When the researchers mixed the two chemicals, ~~you~~ *they* saw a surprising reaction.**

Some writers shift needlessly from third person (*he, she, it, one, they*) to second person (*you*) when trying to make a comprehensive statement.

With the cost of prescription drugs spiraling upward every day,
                                                                     one
y̶o̶u̶ can expect attempts to regulate the pharmaceutical industry.
      ^

Unnecessary shifts in number often occur with the use of pronouns. This error may occur when the writer is trying to avoid sexist use of the pronoun *he* or *his*.

                                         his or her
Every employee sets t̶h̶e̶i̶r̶ own work pace.
                         ^

Here employee *is singular, so the plural pronoun* their *does not match. A singular pronoun is required.*

41 b In tense

Tense places the action of a verb in time.

While a writer may use different tenses to show actions occurring at different times (*We will play* tennis before we *eat* breakfast but after we *have had* coffee), it is important to maintain a governing tense (the main tense of a piece of writing). Departures from the governing tense can be confusing (*When the letter* <u>arrived,</u> *it* <u>says</u> *nothing about the contract*). (See 42e.)

The literary present tense is used to discuss literature or art. Once the literary present tense is established as your governing tense, be sure to maintain it.

In *The Glass Menagerie,* Tom <u>realizes</u> how trapped he <u>is</u> after the
                                  departs.
Gentleman Caller d̶e̶p̶a̶r̶t̶e̶d̶.
                     ^

41 c In mood

English verbs have three moods: the *indicative mood,* used for statements and questions; the *imperative mood,* used for commands, orders, and directions, and the *subjunctive mood,* used for wishes and for statements that are known to be not factual. (See 42f.)

Watch for unnecessary shifts from the imperative to the indicative, particularly in instructions.

First cover your work surface with newspapers, and then y̶o̶u̶ make

sure your materials are within easy reach.

Watch out for unnecessary shifts from the subjunctive to the indicative or the imperative.

> that
> **The contract requires that you *be* in Denver on July 1, and you**
> ^
> ~~**must**~~ **be in Houston on August 1.**

41 d   In voice and subject

The subject of an active-voice verb performs the verb's action: *He hit the ball.* The subject of a passive voice verb is acted upon: *The ball was hit by him.* (See 42g.)

If a sentence has two verbs that share the same subject, it is acceptable to shift voice.

> The students *completed* the project first and *were awarded* the prize.

> *Here* completed *is the active verb and* were awarded *is the passive verb, but both share the same subject,* students.

Avoid shifting from the active to the passive voice (or passive to active) if it requires a change of subject.

> we saw
> **As we peered out of the tent, the waning moon** ~~**was seen**~~ **through**
> ^
> **the trees.**

41 e   Between direct and indirect quotation

Direct quotations reproduce someone's *exact* words and are enclosed in quotation marks: *"I love my wife," he said.* (See 57a–57b.)

Indirect quotations paraphrase someone else's words and do not appear in quotation marks: *He insisted that he loved his wife.* Be consistent when using these.

> wondered why   had   him.
> **He said that he loved his wife and** ~~**"Why did she have to leave me?"**~~
> ^   cried, "Why ^   ^
> **He insisted that he loved his wife and** ~~**"why**~~ **did she have to**
> me?"
> **leave** ~~**him?**~~
> ^

There are several ways to revise a sentence whose clarity is jeopardized by an awkward mix of indirect and direct quotations. Either use indirect quotation in both instances, quote less than the full sentence directly, or start a new sentence.

Dr. Ryan claims that the play was composed before 1600 and
~~that it was written by~~
~~"It shows the clear hand of~~ Shakespeare."
⌃

Dr. Ryan claims that the play was composed before 1600 and
that it "shows
~~"It shows~~ the clear hand of Shakespeare."
⌃

                                                    . He
Dr. Ryan claims that the play was composed before 1600 ~~and~~
says,
                                                       ⌃
"It shows the clear hand of Shakespeare."
⌃

41　f　Mixed constructions

A sentence that begins one way and then takes a turn in another is
called a mixed construction.

Using a grammatically unacceptable element as a subject or predicate
causes a mixed construction. Prepositional phrases, for example, cannot
serve as subjects of a sentence.

Listening
~~By listening~~ closely and paying attention to nonverbal signals
  ⌃
helps a doctor make a better diagnosis.

A doctor can make a better diagnosis by
~~By~~ listening closely and paying attention to nonverbal signals　　.
⌃   ⌃
~~helps a doctor make a better diagnosis.~~

Clauses beginning with subordinating conjunctions (*after, before, when,
where, while, because, if, although,* or *unless*) cannot be the subject of a sentence. Revise the sentence by providing a new subject.

The doctor's status as
~~Because the doctor is~~ an expert does not mean a patient should
      ⌃
never question a diagnosis.

Mixed constructions also can occur with verbs. A dependent clause, for
example, cannot contain the main verb of a sentence.

The fact that most patients are afraid to ask questions,/ ~~which~~ gives

doctors complete control.

Here gives *becomes the main verb.*

41 g   Illogical construction

Though your meaning might seem very clear to you, the writer, it might not be clear to the reader. If you find that some elements don't make sense, reduce your sentence to its most basic elements—subject and verb—to see where the problem lies.

Most

~~The opinion of most~~ people believe that dogs make better pets than cats.

Reducing the sentence to its basic subject and verb, we realize that opinion *cannot be the subject for* believe; *therefore, the sentence needs revision to make* people *the subject for* believe.

have their licenses

Repeat offenders whose licenses have been suspended for drunk driving will ~~be~~ revoked.

It is not offenders who will be revoked *but rather* their licenses.

A subject complement, which follows a linking verb (*is, seems, appears,* and so on), must rename or comment on the subject. If it does not, you must revise the mixed construction.

My father's favorite kitchen appliance is ~~using~~ the microwave oven.

Think of the sentence as an equation; appliance ≠ using.

41 h   Faulty predication

Look out for a construction such as *is where* or *is when*.

based on

Pop art is ~~where an artist reproduces~~ images from commercial products and the popular media.

In sudden-death   ,

~~Sudden death~~ overtime ~~is when~~ the game is extended until one team scores.

Though often spoken, "The reason is because . . ." creates faulty constructions in writing. You must change one part of the sentence to match the other.

Little

~~The reason little~~ has been done to solve the problem ~~is~~ because

Congress is deadlocked.

that

The reason little has been done to solve the problem is ~~because~~

Congress is deadlocked.

While verbs show action, they also can provide other information, much of which is described in the following box. When drafting and revising your work, select correct verb forms that best convey the meaning you intend. Common verb problems are discussed here. More description of standard verb forms appears in 47b.

42 a   Standard verb forms

Except for the verb *be,* all English verbs have five forms. They are used to express the tense of a verb.

■ To express present action

BASE FORM   I *act.*

-S FORM   He *acts.* She *acts.* It *acts.*

■ To express past action

PAST TENSE (BASE FORM + -D OR -ED)

I *acted.*

PAST PARTICIPLE (FORM OF *BE* OR *HAVE* + PAST PARTICIPLE)

I *have acted.*

PRESENT PARTICIPLE (BASE FORM + -*ING*) EXPRESSES CONTINUING ACTION (IN PRESENT AND PAST TENSE)

I *am acting.*

I *was acting.*

Information Conveyed by Verbs

Person indicates who or what performs an action.

1st person	the one speaking	*I read.*
2nd person	the one spoken to	*You read.*
3rd person	the one spoken about	*He reads.*

Number indicates how many people or things perform the action.

| singular | one | *I think.* |
| plural | more than one | *We think.* |

Tense indicates the time of the action.

present	at this time	*I learn.*
past	before this time	*I learned.*
future	after this time	*I will learn.*

Mood expresses the speaker's attitude toward or relation to the action.

indicative	states a fact or asks a question	*You are quiet.*
imperative	gives a command or a direction	*Be quiet!*
subjunctive	expresses a desire or requirement or states a condition contrary to fact	*I would be happier if you were quiet.*

Voice presents the "doer" as subject (active) or as agent (passive).

| active | *She read the book.* |
| passive | *The book was read by her.* |

Using -s and -ed Forms

Except for the verbs *be* and *have,* -s or -es is the ending for third person singular regular verbs in the present tense.

The baby *sleeps.*

Everyone at the party *dances.*

Though nonstandard usage is sometimes heard in dialects or informal speech, academic writing ordinarily requires standard verb usage.

^{doesn't}
He ~~don't~~ need to study.
     ^

The past tense of all regular verbs is created by adding *-d* or *-ed* to the base form.

walked
She ~~walk~~ her dog even though it was raining.
^

Irregular verbs form the past tense and past participle in other ways.

42 b   Irregular verb forms

While regular verbs form the past tense and part participle by adding *-d* or *-ed,* irregular verbs do not follow this pattern. Some irregular verbs (including *bet, bid, burst, cost, cut, hit, quit*) do not change in any form.

Summary of Verb Forms

BASE FORM	-S FORM	PAST TENSE	PAST PARTICIPLE	PRESENT PARTICIPLE
REGULAR				
act	acts	acted	acted	acting
seem	seems	seemed	seemed	seeming
IRREGULAR				
know	knows	knew	known	knowing
eat	eats	ate	eaten	eating
hit	hits	hit	hit	hitting

I *hit* the ball now, but I *hit* it better yesterday. In the past, I have *hit* it even better.

Others have a pattern of vowel changes.

I *ring* the bell today, and I *rang* it yesterday as I have *rung* it every morning.

However, these patterns are not predictable. Consult the following box when you revise and edit your work.

Forms of Irregular Verbs

BASE FORM	PAST TENSE	PAST PARTICIPLE
arise	arose	arisen
awake	awoke, awakened	awakened, awoken
be	was, were	been
bear	bore	borne
beat	beat	beaten, beat

become	became	become
begin	began	begun
bend	bent	bent
bet	bet	bet
bid	bid	bid
bind	bound	bound
bite	bit	bitten
blow	blew	blown
break	broke	broken
bring	brought	brought
build	built	built
burst	burst	burst
buy	bought	bought
catch	caught	caught
choose	chose	chosen
cling	clung	clung
come	came	come
cost	cost	cost
creep	crept	crept
cut	cut	cut
deal	dealt	dealt
dig	dug	dug
dive	dived, dove	dived
do	did	done
draw	drew	drawn
dream	dreamed, dreamt	dreamed, dreamt
drink	drank	drunk
drive	drove	driven
eat	ate	eaten
fall	fell	fallen
feed	fed	fed
fell	felt	felt
fight	fought	fought
find	found	found
flee	fled	fled
fly	flew	flown
forbid	forbade	forbidden
forget	forgot	forgotten, forgot
forgive	forgave	forgiven
freeze	froze	frozen
get	got	gotten, got
give	gave	given
go	went	gone
grow	grew	grown
hang (suspend)	hung	hung
have	had	had
hear	heard	heard
hide	hid	hidden
hit	hit	hit
hold	held	held
hurt	hurt	hurt

keep	kept	kept
know	knew	known
lay (put)	laid	laid
lead	led	led
leap	leapt, leaped	leapt, leaped
leave	left	left
lend	lent	lent
let (allow)	let	let
lie (recline)	lay	lain
light	lit, lighted	lit, lighted
lose	lost	lost
make	made	made
mean	meant	meant
meet	met	met
mistake	mistook	mistaken
pay	paid	paid
prove	proved	proved, proven
quit	quit	quit
read	read	read
rid	rid	rid
ride	rode	ridden
ring	rang	rung
rise	rose	risen
run	ran	run
say	said	said
see	saw	seen
seek	sought	sought
send	sent	sent
set	set	set
shake	shook	shaken
shoot	shot	shot
show	showed	shown, showed
shrink	shrank	shrunk
sing	sang	sung
sink	sank	sunk
sit	sat	sat
slay	slew	slain
sleep	slept	slept
speak	spoke	spoken
spin	spun	spun
spit	spit, spat	spit, spat
spring	sprang	sprung
stand	stood	stood
steal	stole	stolen
stick	stuck	stuck
sting	stung	stung
stink	stank, stunk	stunk
strike	struck	struck, stricken
swear	swore	sworn
swim	swam	swum
swing	swung	swung

take	took	taken
teach	taught	taught
tear	tore	torn
tell	told	told
think	thought	thought
throw	threw	thrown
wake	woke, waked	woken, waked, woke
wear	wore	worn
win	won	won
write	wrote	written

42 c   *Sit* and *set*, *lie* and *lay*

Because the forms of *sit* and *set* and *lie* and *lay* sound similar and are related in meaning, they are often confused. They are really very different.

Set and *lay* mean "to place" and need an object to complete their meaning (what are they placing?). They are transitive verbs and take a direct object. (See Verbs, 47b.)

     DIRECT OBJECT   DIRECT OBJECT

I *set* the newspaper on the table each morning before I *lay* the mail on the desk.

Sit ("to be seated") and *lie* ("to recline") need no object to complete their meaning and are intransitive verbs. (See 47b.)

I will *sit* outside for a while, but soon I'll want to *lie* down.

Lie and *lay* often are confused because the past tense of *lie* is *lay*. To use the correct verb, first establish your meaning: Are you setting or laying *something*? (Or are you just enjoying yourself sitting and lying down?). Refer to the following chart for help.

                    lying
The books were ~~laying~~ on the table.
                  ^

                            sit
She asked me to come in and ~~set~~ with her a while.
                                ^

Sit/set and *lie/lay*

BASE FORM	PAST TENSE	PAST PARTICIPLE	PRESENT PARTICIPLE
sit (intransitive verb)	sat	sat	sitting
set (transitive verb)	set	set	setting
lie (intransitive verb)	lay	lain	lying
lay (transitive verb)	laid	laid	laying

42 d   Auxiliary verbs

Main verbs often require auxiliary or helping verbs, commonly forms of *be, have,* or *do.* (See 47b). Together, the auxiliary verb and main verb form a verb phrase.

```
        VERB PHRASE
   ┌──────────┴──────────┐
  AUXILIARY   MAIN VERB
   ┌────┴───┐ ┌────┴────┐
Tyler has been working.
```

Auxiliary verbs do various jobs in sentences.

The student council *is considering* what to do.   *(present progressive tense)*

They *do want* to go to the conference.   *(emphasis)*

Has he *received* the blueprints?   *(question)*

He *does* not *intend* to leave without them.   *(negative statement)*

The blueprints *were delivered* on Friday.   *(passive voice)*

Forms of *have, do,* and *be* change to indicate tense.

have, has, had

do, does, did

be, am, is, are, was, were, being, been

I *have mended* a jacket that *had been* torn.

Modal Auxiliaries

Can, could, may, might, must, shall, should, will, and *would* are used with a main verb to express condition, intent, permission, possibility, obligation, or desire (and certain tenses; see 42e). These modal auxiliaries cannot stand alone as a main verb; they always appear with the base form of the verb unless the context creates necessary meaning. They *do not* change form to show person, tense, number, or mood.

Staying in touch with friends *can become* difficult as we grow older.

Can she *dance?* Yes, she can.   *(Dance is understood here.)*

Using Auxiliary Verbs Correctly

Standard English requires the auxiliary verb *be* or *have* with present participles and irregular past participles.

> is
> **Gina running for student council.**
>   ^

> has
> **She spoken to everyone about it.**
>   ^

A form of *be—is, are, was, were*—along with the main verb is needed to create the passive voice.

> Each student *is given* a book at graduation.

42 e   Tense

English has three simple tenses, three perfect tenses, and a progressive form for each of them.

The simple present tense describes regular actions or those occurring at the same time as the speaking.

> He *looks* happy today. He usually *looks* content.

The simple present also is used to state general facts or truths and when writing about literature.

> In *The Tempest,* the wizard Prospero *seems* to control the heavens.

The simple past tense describes actions completed in the past.

> He *looked* a little depressed yesterday.

The simple future tense describes actions that will occur in the future or predictable events.

> He *will look* different tomorrow.

> Flowers *will* wilt if left unattended.

The three perfect tenses indicate *action completed by a specific time.* Using forms of *have* plus the past participle, they place that action in the present, past, or future.

The present perfect describes action completed in the past or a completed action still occurring.

She *has looked* for the file today.

She *has looked* for it every day this week.

The past perfect describes action completed before another past action took place.

She *had looked* for the file ten times before she found it.

The future perfect describes an action that will be completed at some specific time in the future.

Once she goes through the last drawer, she *will have looked* everywhere.

The three progressive tenses describe *continuing action* in the present, past, or future.

The present progressive describes ongoing action in the present.

She *is anticipating* the holidays.

The past progressive describes continuous action in the past with no specified end.

Before her father's illness, she *was anticipating* the holidays.

The future progressive describes continuous or ongoing action in the future, which often depends on some other action or circumstance.

Once her father is better, she *will be anticipating* the holidays again.

The three perfect progressive tenses describe action that continues up to a specific time of completion in the present, past, or future.

The present perfect progressive describes action that began in the past and still continues.

He *has been looking* for a job since August.

The past perfect progressive describes ongoing action that was completed before some other action.

Before he found work, he *had been looking* for a job since August.

The future perfect progressive describes continuous action that will be completed at some future time.

By August, he *will have been looking* for a job for six months.

Sequence of Tenses

Verb tenses throughout a piece of writing must relate logically to one another. The dominant tense of a piece is its governing tense, which affects the choice of tense for every verb.

In sentences, many combinations of verb tenses are possible, but the *sequence of tenses*—the way in which one verb's tense relates to the tense of others nearby—needs to describe events accurately and to make sense.

PRESENT   FUTURE
I think that you will enjoy this movie.

I am thinking *this before you* enjoy *the movie.*

PRESENT   PRESENT
I know that you like foreign films.

I know *this at the same time as you* like *them.*

PRESENT   PAST
I believe that you misunderstood me.

I believe *this after you* misunderstood *me.*

Changing the tense of any verb can change the meaning of a sentence, so edit carefully for verb tense.

Sequence with Infinitives and Participles

The tense of an infinitive or participle must be in sequence with the tense of the main verb. (See 47b for more on infinitives and participles.)

The present infinitive (*to* plus the base form of verb) can show action occurring at the same time as, or later than, the action of the main verb.

Some children *like to play* with educational toys.

Liking *and* playing *take place at the same time.*

The committee *plans to vote* on the proposal next week.

Voting *takes place later than* planning.

The perfect infinitive (*to have* plus the past participle) generally indicates action that occurred before the action of the main verb.

I *seem to have misplaced* my credit card.

Misplacing *it has already happened.*

The present participle (the *-ing* form of the verb) shows action occurring at the same time as the action of the main verb.

Working obsessively, he *wrote* late into the night.

He wrote *while obsessed.*

The present perfect participle (*having* plus the past participle) shows action completed before that of the main verb.

Having worked feverishly all night, at dawn he *saw* the sunrise.

The past participle shows action taking place at the same time as, or completed before, the action of the main verb.

Guided by instinct, the swallows *returned* as usual on March 19.

Guiding *and* returning *take place at the same time.*

Born in 1917, John F. Kennedy *became* the country's youngest president in 1961.

He was born *before he* became *president.*

Sequence for Habitual Actions and Universal Truths

When a dependent clause expresses a habitual action or a universal truth, the verb in the dependent clause stays in the present tense regardless of the tense in the independent clause. (See also 42f.)

He *told* me he *works* for Teledyne.

Copernicus *demonstrated* that the Earth *revolves* around the sun.

Notice that shifting to the past tense in a dependent clause can suggest that something is not true or habitual.

He *told* me that he *worked* for Teledyne, but the company *had* no record of him.

Ptolemy *believed* the Earth *was* the center of the universe.

Verbs That Do Not Have a Progressive Form

Verbs that express action, processes, or events can usually be used in a progressive -*ing* form to express an action in progress.

I am *walking* through the park.

Other verbs express attitudes, conditions, or relationships are not usually used in a progressive -*ing* form. The technical term for these is **stative verbs.**

believe
I am <s>believing</s> your story.
^

Common Stative Verbs

admire	dislike	like	see
agree	doubt	look	seem
appear	hate	love	smell
believe	have	need	sound
belong	hear	own	taste
contain	imagine	possess	think
cost	include	prefer	understand
disagree	know	remember	want

Occasionally these verbs are used as dynamic verbs to describe an activity or a process. In these cases, the progressive form may be used.

Don't bother me while I *am thinking.*

I *was agreeing* with you until you started the argument.

42 f   Mood

English verbs have three different moods, each of which serves a different purpose.

The indicative mood states facts, opinions, or questions and notes things that have happened, are happening, or will happen.

He *believes* that the theory is valid.

The imperative mood commands and gives directives. It appears as the base form of the verb and omits the subject, which is understood to be *you.*

Sit down and *complete* these forms.

Knead the dough until it forms a ball.

The subjunctive mood expresses wishes, requirements, and conditions that the speaker knows not to be so. Different forms exist for present, past, and perfect subjunctive.

The present subjective is the same *base form of the verb* for all persons and number.

I asked that we *leave* early to avoid traffic.

I asked that she *leave* me alone.

The past subjunctive uses the *simple past tense* for all verbs except *be,* which always uses *were.*

If you *donated* more than a million dollars, your college would name a hall after you.

If he ~~was~~ willing to help, what would we ask him to do?

(with "were" written above "was")

The perfect subjunctive uses *had* plus the past participle (the past perfect tense of a verb).

If he *had caught* the ball, the run would not have scored.

Using the Subjunctive

Use the subjunctive in some idiomatic expressions.

Long live the queen!	as it were
if I were you	far be it from me

After *as if, as though,* or *if*

Use the subjunctive in dependent clauses beginning with *if, as if,* and *as though* that note conditions contrary to fact. Use the past or perfect subjunctive in these cases.

He screamed as though the house *were* on fire.

If it *were* sunny, he could go out.

When the *if* clause expresses an *actual* condition, use the indicative mood.

If the baseball game *has begun,* we will know where to find him.

Do not use conditional auxiliaries—*could* or *would*—in *both* the dependent clause and the main clause.

If I ~~would have~~ left earlier, I would have been on time.

(with "had" written above "would have")

Use the subjunctive mood to express a wish, a requirement, or a request.

Use the past or perfect subjunctive in dependent clauses expressing wishes. (Sometimes the relative pronoun *that* is omitted.)

I wish there ~~was~~ ^were^ some way to help them.

Use present subjunctive after verbs that require *(ask, demand, insist, recommend, request, require, specify, suggest)*

Courtesy requires that he ~~arrives~~ ^arrive^ on time.

Barbara insisted she ~~goes~~ ^go^ alone.

42 g   Voice

The voice of a verb tells you whether the subject is the actor (active voice) or the receiver of the action (passive voice). Use the active voice for simpler, more direct language.

She *read* the book. *(active voice)*

The book *was read* by her. *(passive voice)*

chapter 43 | *Subject–Verb Agreement*

Verbs must agree with their subjects in number (Are you talking about one or more than one?) and person (Who is the subject? I? You? She? He? It? We? They?).

43 a   In person and number

In the present tense, agreement between the subject and verb usually involves the addition of the letter *s* to the third person singular. (See 42a and 42b.)

	SINGULAR	**PLURAL**
1ST PERSON	I think.	We think.
2ND PERSON	You think.	You think.
3RD PERSON	He, she, it thinks.	They think.

Though the addition of the letter *s* in the third person singular works for many verbs in common usage, the verb *to be* has different forms in the present and past tenses.

PRESENT TENSE		**PAST TENSE**	
I am.	We are.	I was.	We were.
You are.	You are.	You were.	You were.
He/she/it is.	They are.	He/she/it was.	They were.

Some general rules:

- If the *subject* ends in *-s* or *-es* (usually indicating a plural noun), the verb probably shouldn't end in *-s*.

  The *mansions seem* elegant.

- If the *verb* ends in *-s* or *-es* (usually indicating a singular verb), the subject probably shouldn't end in *-s* or *-es*.

  The *mansion seems* elegant.

Nouns with irregular plurals—*children, men*—don't follow these rules, of course. These plurals still require a verb without an *-s* or *-es*.

  The *children walk* home.

Another exception is nouns that end in *-s* but are singular.

  Genetics is the study of the mechanisms of heredity.

There are also some verbs that end in *s* in their base form. These verbs add *-es* for the third person singular in the present tense.

  They *pass* my house on their way to school.

  She *passes* my house on her way to school.

43 b   Interruptions between subject and verb

Words placed between the subject and verb can be confusing. To determine what verb is needed, eliminate the interrupting words and test for the proper match.

The bowl of apples <s>are</s> on the table. *is*

Reduce the sentence to The bowl . . . is on the table. *The singular subject* bowl *takes the singular verb* is.

Mr. Johnson, along with his children, <s>were</s> waiting outside. *was*

Reduce the sentence to Mr. Johnson . . . was waiting outside. *The singular subject* Mr. Johnson *takes the singular verb* was.

43 c   Subject following the verb

When subjects follow verbs in sentences, it is sometimes hard to find the subject and determine the proper agreement. Restore normal word order to help find the subject.

Underneath the freeway overpass (*huddle / huddles?*) a ramshackle collection of cardboard shelters.

Reverse the sentence to A ramshackle collection of cardboard shelters *huddles* underneath the freeway overpass. *The singular subject* collection *takes the singular verb* huddles.

Questions

In questions, part of the verb almost always precedes the subject. Find the subject and check for proper agreement.

Are those seats next to you empty?

Change the sentence to Those seats next to you *are* empty.

There is and *it is*

In sentences that begin with *it is* or *there is, it* and *there* are not really subjects; they are simply filling a spot in the sentence (see also 34c). These space-fillers are called expletives. The real subject of the verb, which determines its number, appears later in the sentence.

There *are* many *ways* to roast a turkey.

There *is* but one *way* to get there from here.

43 d   With linking verbs

Linking verbs, such as *be, become, seem,* and *appear,* connect or link the subject of the sentence to a complement that renames or describes it. As you edit sentences containing a subject complement, make sure the verb agrees with the subject, not the complement.

Her hobbies ~~is~~ *are* the one thing that makes her happy.

His promises to change ~~appears~~ *appear* to be a waste of breath.

43 e   With subjects joined by *and*

Two or more subjects linked by *and* (compound subjects) are almost always *plural* and take a plural verb.

Peter and Patrick <u>play</u> on the lacrosse team.

Exceptions:

■ When the two joined words comprise a single entity, use a singular verb.

Red beans and rice <u>is</u> my favorite dish.

■ When all the parts of a compound subject refer to the same person or thing, use a singular verb.

My *friend, partner, and mentor <u>has</u>* brought expertise to the firm.

■ When *each* or *every* precedes singular subjects joined by *and,* use a singular verb.

Each river, brook, and stream in the country <u>*has*</u> suffered pollution.

■ When *each* follows a compound subject, the subject and verb are plural.

The *pianist and the singer each <u>deserve</u>* special praise.

43 f   With subjects joined by *or* and *nor*

When parts of a subject are joined by *or, nor, either . . . or, neither . . . nor,* or *not only,* make the verb agree with the subject closest to it.

Neither the *researchers nor* the *professor <u>accepts</u>* the results.

The singular noun professor *is closer to the verb; use the singular verb* accepts.

Neither the professor *nor* the *researchers* <u>*accept*</u> the results.

The plural noun researchers *is closer to the verb; use the plural verb* accept.

43 g   With collective nouns

Words that refer to groups of people, animals, or things (*couple, flock, crowd, herd, committee*) are called collective nouns. When a collective noun refers to a group as a singular unit, it generally takes a singular verb.

The *jury has* reached a verdict.

Here the group, jury, *is considered one unit and takes the singular verb* has.

When the members of the group are acting individually,

The *couple disagree* about which movie to see.

The members of the couple are acting separately, so the plural verb is aprropriate.

Media, data, curricula, criteria, and *phenomena* look like singular words in English, but in fact they are the plural forms of *medium, datum, curriculum, criterion* and *phenomenon.* These words usually take *plural* verbs. Check your dictionary to see whether a noun that ends in *a* is a singular or plural.

The media ~~has~~ **continued to focus on crime even as data** ~~shows~~
have
cities are becoming safer.
show

The collective noun *number,* preceded by *the,* refers to a group as a single unit and takes a singular verb.

The number of visitors *has* been small.

When *number* is preceded by the article *a,* it implies "more than one" or "several," and it takes a plural verb.

A number of visitors *have* been enthusiastic about the new exhibits.

Verb Agreement with Noncount Nouns

Count nouns name persons, places, or things that can be counted—*one apple, two oranges.* Noncount nouns refer to things that can't be counted—*oil*—or refer to things in a sense that does not imply counting—*money, sand.* (See 47b.)

NONCOUNT NOUNS	ABSTRACTIONS	EMOTIONS	QUALITIES
equipment	behavior	anger	confidence
water	education	happiness	honesty
homework	health	love	integrity
money	knowledge	surprise	sincerity

A few noncount nouns appear to be plural because they end in the letter *s,* but they are actually singular. Examples are *mathematics, news,* and *physics* (see 43j).

Noncount nouns are usually used in the singular—most have no plural form—and take singular verbs.

Public <u>transportation</u> in Atlanta <u>makes</u> getting around easy.

This <u>information</u> <u>is</u> intended to help you when you edit.

43 h   With indefinite pronouns

Indefinite pronouns do not refer to *specific* persons or things. Some indefinite pronouns (*someone, nobody, everything, everyone*) are always considered *singular* (and take a singular verb).

Someone <u>has been sleeping</u> in my bed.

Everybody <u>wears</u> a heavy coat in such cold weather.

Some indefinite pronouns (*few, many, others,* and so on) are always considered *plural* (and take a plural verb).

Luckily, *few* of the passengers <u>*were injured*</u>.

Several of the children <u>*want*</u> to be included.

Still other pronouns (*all, any, some,* and so on) can be either singular or plural, depending on their meaning and the nouns to which they refer. (See the box Common Indefinite Pronouns.)

All <u>are</u> required to take the exam.

All I have <u>*is*</u> a rough idea.

All is plural when it means "the entire group." It is singular when it means "everything" or "the only thing."

The word *none* takes a singular verb.

The birds all escaped, and *none* of them <u>was</u> recaptured.

Common Indefinite Pronouns

ALWAYS SINGULAR

another	everybody	nobody	somebody	either
anybody	everyone	no one	someone	neither
anyone	everything	nothing	something	each
anything				much
				none
				one

EITHER SINGULAR OR PLURAL

all	any	more	most	some	what

ALWAYS PLURAL

both	few	many	others	several

---

43 i With *who, which,* and *that*

To determine whether a verb following one of the relative pronouns *who, which,* or *that* should be singular or plural, consider the word to which the pronoun refers (its antecedent; see 44a).

Barb and Robin, *who* want to join the project, <u>have applied</u>.

Who refers to the plural Barb and Robin *and therefore takes the plural verb* have applied.

A bale of shingles *that* <u>slips</u> off the roof could hurt someone.

That refers to bale *and therefore takes the singular verb* slips.

Relative pronouns following *one of the* or *the only one of the* can be tricky. As a rule, *one of the* takes a plural verb and *the only one of the* takes a singular verb.

His wonderful laugh is one of the *qualities* that <u>endear</u> him to us.

plural

The voters believed that Tom was the only *one* of the candidates who <u>*was*</u> qualified.

singular

Verb Agreement with Quantifiers

Few and *A Few*

> *Few:* "not many," "not enough"
>
> *A few:* "some," "several," "a small number"

Both take plural verbs.

> Many students are taking exams today. *A few* <u>*are*</u> out sick.
>
> Few <u>*have failed*</u> in past years.

Little and *A Little*

> *Little:* "not much"
>
> *A little:* "some," "a small amount"

Both take singular verbs.

> Little <u>*has been done*</u> to address the problem of poverty.
>
> When it comes to jalapeños, *a little* <u>*goes*</u> a long way.

Most and *Most of the*

> *Most:* "the majority"

Use a singular or plural verb, depending on the noun or pronoun it modifies or refers to.

> *Most* violence on TV <u>*is*</u> unnecessary.
>
> *Most* dogs <u>*are tied up*</u> when their owners are away.
>
> *Most of, most of the:* "the majority of"

Use a plural verb when followed by a plural noun or pronoun; use a singular verb when followed by a noncount noun or a singular pronoun.

> *Most of* our friends <u>*encourage*</u> their children to read.
>
> *Most of the* neighborhood <u>*wants*</u> a bicycle path.

Nouns Ending in *-s*

Statistics, politics, economics, athletics, measles, news, acoustics, and *aesthetics* appear to be plural nouns, but all take singular verbs.

Economics is sometimes *called* "the dismal science."

Exception: When these nouns refer to specific instances or characteristics, they are considered plural and take a plural verb.

The *economics* of the project *make* no sense.

Nouns that Specify Amounts

Words describing amounts of *time* or *money, distances, measurements,* or *percentages* can take singular or plural verbs, depending on whether they refer to a singular unit (or sum) or a group of individuals (plural).

Fifteen *minutes is* too long to keep a class waiting.

Minutes here is considered a block of time. The singular unit takes a singular verb.

Fifteen *minutes fly* when you're having fun.

The plural minutes *takes a plural verb.*

Names or Titles Used as Words

Names or titles involving more than one word are considered singular and take a singular verb.

Divine Secrets of the Ya-Ya Sisterhood was written by Rebecca Wells.

General Motors is an important employer in Michigan.

When a plural word is used as *a particular term,* use a singular verb.

Hyenas was what my father lovingly called us children.

A pronoun is a stand-in for a noun that has been mentioned previously.

Sam lent me his *sweater,* but *it* was wrinkled.

His refers to *Sam,* and *it* refers to *sweater.* The noun to which a pronoun refers is called the pronoun's antecedent.

While pronouns are frequently used in spoken and written language, they are also often the cause of confusion. This is partly because there are so many kinds of pronouns.

Personal pronouns substitute for specific persons or things.

Sally usually goes to the gym, but today *she* won't be able to.

Possessive pronouns show ownership.

That backpack is *mine.*

Reflexive pronouns return the reference to the person "doing" something.

John cut *himself* with the scissors.

Relative pronouns introduce dependent (modifier) clauses.

Josh and Sandra are the students *who* are leading the class this morning.

Interrogative pronouns introduce questions.

Who is going to the movies tonight?

Demonstrative pronouns indicate specific nouns and can also function as adjectives.

Don't pick *those* apples; *these* are riper.

Indefinite pronouns refer to nonspecific persons or things.

Everyone is working on this project.

Reciprocal pronouns refer to an action shared between two people, things, or ideas.

The investigators helped *one another* with the research.

(See 47b for more on pronouns.)

Pronoun problems often surface in the following ways.

Reference: Is it clear to whom or what the pronoun refers?

Agreement: Does the pronoun agree with the noun to which it refers?

Case: Should I use *I* or *me? Who* or *whom?*

44 a Reference

The word to which a pronoun refers is called its antecedent. If it's unclear what a pronoun refers to, misunderstanding can occur. To clarify, state the antecedent explicitly.

Ambiguous reference (sentence can be read two ways)

Marco met Roger as he arrived at the gym. *(When* who *arrived at the gym?)*

Clear reference

As Marco arrived at the gym, he met Roger.

Marco met Roger as Roger arrived at the gym.

Implied reference

                                                                        reporting
Interviews with several television newspeople made it seem like
                                                                          ^
a fascinating career.

In the original, it *has no appropriate antecdent.*

Vague Reference for *this, that,* and *which*

Make sure that *this, which,* and *that* have specific, grammatically appropriate antecedents.

                                                              tax
No one has suggested taxing health care. This is unlikely.
                                                               ^

Without the added word, it's not clear whether the suggestion or the tax is unlikely.

a response

She took the situation seriously, which I found laughable.

Without the explicit reference, it's not clear whether I found the situation or her response laughable.

Vague Reference for *it, they,* or *you*

In casual speech, people often use *it, they,* or *you* without explicit antecedents. Academic writing requires explicit reference.

According to

~~It said on~~ the news this morning ~~that~~ the game has been canceled.

The club doesn't

~~They don't~~ let anyone in without shoes.

Choosing between that *and* which

- Use *that* only in a restrictive clause, that is needed to identify what it modifies. A *that* clause is never set off by commas.

  The money *that was in Ann's trust fund* has been embezzled.

  The modifier that was in Ann's trust fund *is needed to specify which money.*

- Use *which* in a nonrestrictive clause, one that adds more information but is not necessary to identify or limit. A nonrestrictive clause must be set off by commas.

  Ann's money, *which was in a trust fund,* has been embezzled.

  The modifier which was in a trust fund *is not needed to specify whose money it was.*

- *Which* also can be used in restrictive clauses. If you do so, use no commas.

  When in the course of human events it becomes necessary for one people to dissolve the political bonds *which* have connected them with another ... a decent respect for the opinions of mankind requires that they should declare the reasons *which* impel them to the separation. [Italics added.]

  DECLARATION OF INDEPENDENCE

  Just to avoid confusion, some writers choose to use *which* only for nonrestrictive modifiers.

- *Who* may introduce either restrictive or nonrestrictive modifiers.

  NONRESTRICTIVE   Americans, *who* eat a richer diet than Europeans, have higher rates of heart disease.

  RESTRICTIVE   Americans *who* cut down on fatty foods may live longer than those *who* don't.

(For more on identifying and punctuating nonrestrictive modifiers, see 48c.)

Choosing *who, which,* or *that*

Use *who* for people or animals with names.

Black Beauty is a horse *who* lives in vanished world.

Use *which* or *that* for objects, ideas, and unnamed people or animals.

This is the policy *that* the administration wants.

He tried to rope the last steer, *which* twisted to avoid him.

44 b   Pronoun–antecedent agreement

Personal pronouns should agree with (that is, match) their antecedents in number, person, and gender.

Number

A *pronoun* is singular if *it* has a singular antecedent.
Pronouns are plural if *they* have plural antecedents.

Person

I ask you to call *me* Ishmael.

Gender

Mrs. Shaw held the door for *her* guest.

Gender-neutral Pronouns

Agreement becomes a problem when pronouns refer to indefinite antecedents such as *anyone, someone,* and *everyone.* Since these pronouns can refer to either males or females, you must be careful in your use of pronouns that refer to these indefinite antecedents. (See 36c.)

he or she
If anyone needs to miss class, ~~he~~ will have to contact the instructor.
^

This use of *he* is *not* acceptable since *he* refers only to males. To address this problem, consider the following alternatives.

Use the phrase *he or she* or *his or her.* Do not use *they* to refer to a singular antecedent.

he or she
If anyone needs to miss class, ~~they~~ will have to contact the
                                    ^
instructor.

Use the plural *students* in place of the singular *anyone*.

students need   they
If ~~anyone needs~~ to miss class, ~~he~~ will have to contact the instructor.
   ^   ^

Eliminate personal pronouns altogether.

Students who need
~~If anyone needs~~ to miss class,~~ he~~ will have to contact the instructor.
^

Agreement with Antecedents Joined by *and*

Pronouns with a compound antecedent should be *plural*.

The book and the folder are in *their* places on the shelf.

Use a *singular* pronoun in the following cases.

- The compound antecedent is preceded by *each* or *every*.

   Each book and folder is in *its* place on the shelf.

- The parts of the compound antecedent refer to the same person or thing.

   As my *sociology professor and thesis advisor, she* helped me choose this semester's courses.

- The compound antecedent refers to a single entity.

   My favorite dish is rice and beans; *it* always tastes good on cold days.

Agreement with Antecedents Joined by *or* and *nor*

When all parts of an antecedent joined by *or* or *nor* are *singular,* the pronoun referring to it is *singular.*

Either the assessor's *office* or the *court* will have to cut *its* budget.

When one part of the compound antecedent is singular and one is plural, make the pronoun agree with the antecedent closer to it.

Either the equipment failures or the bad *weather* will take *its* toll.

The singular pronoun its *refers to the singular—and closer—antecedent* weather.

Agreement with Collective Nouns

Use a single pronoun to refer to collective nouns (*couple, flock, crowd*) that are seen as a single group or unit.

The flock rose suddenly from the pond and took up ~~their~~ usual
                                                  its ^

formation.

Use a plural pronoun to refer to collective nouns if members of the group are acting separately.

The crew gathered ~~its~~ belongings and prepared to leave the ship.
                         their ^

Agreement with Indefinite Pronouns

Indefinite pronouns such as *anyone, everyone, someone, anybody, everybody, somebody, anything, everything, something, either, neither, each, nothing, much, one, none,* and *no one* do not refer to a specific person, place, or thing. They are always singular and should take a singular pronoun.

Someone has left *his or her* notebook.

None of these books has *its* original cover.

The indefinite pronouns *few, many, both,* and *several* are always plural and therefore require a plural pronoun.

Few of the students have completed *their* work.

The indefinite pronouns *some, any, all, more, most,* and *none* can be singular or plural depending on their context.

In a survey of young voters, *some* said *they* were conservative.

The money is still in the safe. *Some* is still in *its* bags.

<table>
<tr><td>**44**</td><td>**c**</td><td>**Case**</td></tr>
</table>

In speaking, we say *I saw him* rather than *me saw him,* and *my car* rather than *I car,* without ever thinking about it. These changes of form, called case, help indicate a pronoun's role in a sentence.

Use the subjective case for the person or thing that performs the action of the sentence.

She plays piano.

Use the objective case when a pronoun receives the action.

The music impressed *me* greatly.

Use the possessive case to show ownership.

My grandmother lives in Ohio.

	SUBJECTIVE	**OBJECTIVE**	**POSSESSIVE**
SINGULAR	I	me	my
	you	you	your
	he, she, it	him, her, it	his, her, its
PLURAL	we	us	our
	you	you	your
	they	them	their

Preceding a noun, use the possessive pronouns above.

This is *her* book; that one is *my* book

However, use these possessive pronouns when no noun follows: *mine, yours, his, hers, its, ours, yours, theirs.*

This book is *hers;* that one is *mine.*

Compound Subjects

Choosing the correct pronoun can be tricky when two or more words are joined. Test the sentence with only the pronoun.

Todd and ~~me~~ pruned the tall white pine.
                    I

When you test the sentence as Me pruned the tall white pine, *it is clear that pronoun should be* I.

                          he
Ralph, Otto, and ~~him~~ planned to go bowling.

Remove Ralph *and* Otto. <u>Him</u> planned to go bowling *is not correct;* <u>he</u> planned to go bowling *is correct.*

Subject Complements

Subject complements follow linking verbs (see 47a) and rename the subject or complete its meaning: *The winner was my dad.* *Winner* and *dad* are the same person, linked by the verb *was.* In a compound complement, use the subjective case for the pronoun.

It is *I* who is sorry.

**The real winners were my father and ~~me~~. ** *(I)*

Compound Objects

Objects joined by *and, or,* or *nor* take the objective case for each part of the construction.

Just between you and ~~I~~, it's a fake. *(me)*

Give your donations to Nancy or ~~I~~. *(me)*

Appositives

Appositives rename nouns or pronouns and must have the same case as the words they rename.

The victors, Paul and *he,* wanted to leave.

Paul and he *renames* victors, *the subject, and is therefore in subjective case.*

They asked the teachers, Barbara and *me,* to help out.

Barbara and me *renames* teachers, *the object of* asked, *and is therefore in the objective case.*

We or *us* before a Noun

To determine which case to use, omit the noun and test for appropriate use.

~~Us~~ hikers were worried about the weather. *(We)*

You wouldn't say, "Us were worried about the weather."

They told ~~we~~ ^us^ hikers not to worry.

You wouldn't say, "They told we *not to worry."*

With Verbals

Participles, gerunds, and infinitives are called verbals because they are derived from verbs (see 47b), and like verbs, they can have objects. When a pronoun is the object of a verbal, use the objective case.

I saw Robert greeting *him.*

Him *is the object of the participle* greeting.

Seeing *her* made the holiday complete.

Her *is the object of the gerund* seeing.

To know *him* well took many years.

Him *is the object of the infinitive to* know.

Before Gerunds

Use possessive pronouns preceding verbals used as nouns (gerunds).

~~Me~~ ^My^ leaving made them all sad.

Before Infinitives

Use the objective case for pronouns preceding infinitives.

They want *her* to help.

It was hard for *him* to agree.

After *than* or *as*

If you are uncertain what case pronoun to use, construct test sentences to see which you mean.

She likes her dog better than (me/I?).

She likes her dog better than *I* (like her dog).

She likes her dog better than (she likes) *me.*

The choice of pronoun can affect the meaning of this sentence, so choose carefully.

Who or *whom*?

The distinction between *who* and *whom* has all but disappeared from everyday speech, but in formal writing use *who* for subjects and *whom* for objects.

In Questions

To decide whether to use *who* or *whom* in a question, answer the question, substituting *he* or *she* or *him* or *her* as the answer. If *he* or *she* fits, use *who*. If *him* or *her* fits, use *whom*.

Who had the authority to enter the building at night?

She *had the authority, so use* who.

To *whom* are you speaking?

You are speaking to him, *so use* whom.

In Dependent Clauses

When deciding whether to use *who* or *whom* in a dependent clause, check for the word's function within the clause.

That woman, ~~who~~ ^{whom} I met last week, won the Nobel prize for chemistry.

Whom is the object of the verb *met, even though it renames the subject of the main clause,* woman.

I want to meet the woman ~~whom~~ ^{who} won the prize.

Within the clause, who *is the subject of* won.

I want to meet the woman ~~who~~ ^{whom} the committee honored.

Within the clause, whom *is the object of* honored.

She tells that same story to ~~whomever~~ ^{whoever} will listen.

Whoever is the subject of *will listen.*

Using Reflexive Pronouns

Reflexive pronouns reflect the action of the sentence back to the subject.

John cut *himself* with the scissors.

I speak only for *myself,* not for my research partner.

Do not use reflexive pronouns as subjects.

My partner and ~~myself~~ were invited to the reception.

---

chapter **45** | *Adjectives and Adverbs*

A djectives and adverbs modify—they describe, identify, or limit the meaning of—other words. Modifiers can enrich description, transforming a simple sentence like *The hikers were lost* into a more engaging one like *The exhausted hikers were hopelessly lost.*

45 a   Adjective or adverb?

Adjectives modify (describe, identify, or limit) nouns or pronouns.

NOUN   NOUN   NOUN

Hector is a *fine* father who has *gentle* hands and *abundant* patience

NOUN

with *crying* babies.

PRONOUN

He is *loving, careful,* and *dependable.*

Adverbs modify verbs, adjectives, other adverbs, and sometimes whole clauses.

VERB   ADJECTIVE   ADVERB

He *often* takes care of the baby at *truly* late hours and *nearly* always

VERB

quiets her *quickly.*

When attached to verbs, adverbs tell *when, where, how, why,* and *under what conditions* something happens. *Often, always,* and *quickly* modify verbs in the sentence above. When adverbs modify adjectives and other adverbs, they intensify or qualify the words they modify. *Truly* modifies *late* (adjective); *nearly* modifies *always* (adverb) in the sentence.

Suffixes

Adjectives are sometimes formed by adding endings such as *-able, -ful,* and *-ish* to nouns and verbs: *acceptable, beautiful, foolish.* Adverbs are often formed by adding *-ly* to an adjective: *nearly, amazingly, brilliantly.* However, an *-ly* suffix does not always mean that a word is an adverb. A number of adjectives end in *-ly: brotherly, friendly, lovely.* And many adverbs do not end in *-ly: always, here.*

45 b   After verbs

Following a verb, do you use an adjective or an adverb? If the modifier describes the action, use an adverb.

The ghost of Hamlet's father appears *suddenly.*

If you are describing a *state of being,* as opposed to an action, use an adjective.

The ghost of Hamlet's father appears *anxious.*

(In the second example, *appears* is a linking verb. See 47b for more on linking verbs and modifiers.)

45 c   Commonly confused modifiers

In casual speech, adjectives are sometimes used to modify verbs: *It fit real well* instead of *It fit really well.* Be sure to use the correct form of the following pairs in academic writing.

Bad and *badly*

Bad is an adjective and should be used only to modify nouns and pronouns: *bad food, bad assignment. Bad* is used as an adjective with linking verbs (see 47b), while *badly* is used to modify other verbs.

She looked as though she felt ~~badly~~. *bad*

They were playing so ~~bad~~ *badly* that I left at halftime.

Good and *well*

In speech, *good* and *well* are often confused. *Good* is always an adjective. *Well* can be either an adjective meaning "healthy" or an adverb meaning "skillfully." *Good* and *well* also share comparative and superlative forms: *good, better, best; well, better, best.*

She is a very good singer, but can she sing ~~good~~ *well* enough to get the lead?

The hat looks ~~well~~ *good* on you.

ESL *Order of Adjectives*

The order of adjectives preceding nouns is somewhat flexible, but some types of adjectives typically occur before others. For example, an adjective describing size occurs before one describing color: *the large white house* rather than *the white large house.*

The following list shows the typical order of adjectives before nouns.

1 Determiner: *a, the, her, Bob's, that, these, a few*

2 Order: *first, next, third*

3 Evaluation: *good, pretty, happy, interesting*

4 Appearance—size: *big, small, minuscule*

5 Appearance—shape: *oblong, squarish, round*

6 Appearance—condition: *broken, shiny*

7 Appearance—age: *old, young, new*

8 Appearance—color: *blue, green, magenta*

9 Material: *wooden, cotton*

10 Noun used as adjective: *flower garden*

>   1   2   6   7   10
> One never forgets that first shiny new sports car.

> 1   4   5   9
> A few large square wooden boxes were stacked on the floor.

Real and *really*

Real is an adjective meaning "genuine, true, not illusory." *Really* is an adverb meaning "truly" or "very."

Andrew is a *real* friend.

                                                        really
After the interview, he was ~~real~~ excited about his job prospects.
                                            ^

Less and *fewer*

Less describes something considered as a whole unit: *less hope, less money. Fewer* signifies quantities that can be counted: *fewer hopes, fewer dollars.* (See noncount nouns, 43g, 47b)

                                        fewer
The house would lose *less* heat if ~~less~~ windows were open.
                                  ^

Less can also be an adverb.

Sam was *less* successful as an actor than Brad because Sam delivered his lines *less* convincingly.

45 d   Comparatives and superlatives

Adjectives and adverbs have three forms: the positive, the comparative, and the superlative. The positive form of describes a particular property (*smart, funny*). The comparative compares that property between *two* people or things (*smarter, funnier*). The superlative form makes a comparison among *three or more* people or things (*smartest, funniest*). Some lengthy adjectives and most adverbs ending in *-ly* use *more* and *most* to form comparative and superlative forms. Negative comparisons are formed by using *less* and *least*.

POSITIVE	COMPARATIVE	SUPERLATIVE
big	bigger	biggest
fast	faster	fastest
good	better	best
careful	more careful	most careful
sharply	more sharply	most sharply
hopeful	less hopeful	least hopeful

Irregular Adjectives and Adverbs

POSITIVE	COMPARATIVE	SUPERLATIVE
good	better	best
well	better	best
bad	worse	worst
badly	worse	worst
ill	worse	worst
many	more	most
much	more	most
some	more	most
little*	less	least

*Little meaning "not much" is irregular. *Little* meaning "small" is regular: *little, littler, littlest.*

Which modifier you choose can tell a lot about what you're comparing.

Of the brothers, Joe was the *stronger* athlete. *(There are two brothers.)*

Of the brothers, Joe was the *strongest* athlete. *(There are at least three brothers.)*

Do not use double comparatives or superlatives. When forming comparatives, use either *-er* or *more,* not both.

When forming superlatives, use either *-est* or *most,* not both.

After eating, he felt ~~more~~ better.

45 e Avoiding double negatives

In English, one negative modifier (*no, not, never*) is sufficient to change the meaning of a sentence. When two negatives appear in the same sentence, they cancel each other out: I <u>didn't</u> have <u>no</u> money literally means *I did have some money.*

       had

I ~~didn't have~~ no money.

or

       any

I didn't have ~~no~~ money.

I n English, word order can change meaning. For example, it makes a difference whether you say *the man ate the fish* or *the fish ate the man*.

Word order problems in writing often involve modifiers or phrases or clauses used as modifiers. Since there can be more than one place in a sentence to put a modifier, it is important to connect the modifier clearly with what it is intended to describe or qualify.

46 a Misplaced

A misplaced modifier can seem to modify words or phrases other than the ones the writer intends.

We wanted our ordeal to end desperately.

Chances are the writer did not want things to turn out badly, but rather he or she wanted very much (desperately) *that the ordeal would end:* We desperately wanted our ordeal to end.

Limiting Modifiers

Put limiting modifiers such as *almost, even, hardly, just, merely, nearly, only, scarcely,* or *simply* directly before the words they modify. Notice how the meaning changes in the following sentences if the limiting modifier, *just,* is placed in front of different words.

They *just* want her to sing this song.   *(and they want nothing else.)*

They want *just* her to sing this song.   *(and no one else.)*

They want her *just* to sing this song.   *(and not to do anything else.)*

They want her to sing *just* this song.   *(and not to sing anything else.)*

Which position is right? What do you want the sentence to mean?

46 b Squinting

Squinting modifiers seem to modify two things at once.

Students who follow directions *consistently* score well on tests.

Are we talking about people *who consistently follow directions* or *who consistently score well*? Rewrite the sentence to clarify your intended meaning.

> consistently
> **Students who follow directions ~~consistently~~ score well on tests.**

> **Students who follow directions ~~consistently~~ score well on tests.**
> consistently

46 c Dangling

A dangling modifier causes confusion, since there is no clearly recognizable element for it to modify. Consequently, the reader is left dangling as well.

> Running through the rain, our clothes got soaked.

This sentence reads as if *our clothes* were *running through the rain*. What's missing is the subject—who was running? Place the new subject directly after the modifier, and edit appropriately.

> we got
> **Running through the rain, our clothes ~~got~~ soaked.**

> she earned an A on .
> **Having completed her research, the paper ~~earned her an A.~~**

Who completed the research? Not the paper.

> residents prepared for
> **Still digging out from Thursday's snowfall, another storm ~~is due~~**
> **on Sunday.**

The passive voice can leave introductory phrases floating with no subject to modify. Try changing to active voice.

> researchers have forced
> **In studying the effects of cigarette smoking, monkeys ~~have been~~**
> **~~forced~~ to inhale the equivalent of a hundred cigarettes a day.**

Since monkeys have not been studying cigarette smoking, the meaning needs to be clarified.

46 d Disruptive

Disruptive modifiers interrupt the flow of a sentence. Check any modifier that needlessly separates major sentence elements.

Split Infinitives

An infinitive consists of *to* plus the base form of a verb: *to fly, to grow, to achieve.* When a modifier comes between these two words, it is called a split infinitive: *to completely agree.* While we may often use such phrases in speech, they are considered awkward in formal writing.

He promised to ~~whenever possible~~ avoid splitting infinitives. *whenever possible*

The director ~~wanted to vividly recreate~~ a bullfight for the second act. *planned a vivid re-creation of*

Split Verb Phrases

A verb phrase consists of one or more auxiliary verbs—a form of *be, do,* or *have*—and a participle or the base form of a verb: *have been formed, does mention.* Lengthy interruptions between the two parts of a verb phrase can become unwieldy.

~~The Roanoke colony had, by~~ the time a supply ship arrived four years later, disappeared without a trace. *By* *the Roanoke colony had*

ESL Placing Adverbs

- When an adverb is used between elements of a verb phrase, it usually appears after the first auxiliary verb.

  Our baseball stadium has *rarely* been filled to capacity.

  Rarely has been filled *is also correct.*

- In questions, the adverb appears after the first auxiliary verb and the subject, but before the other parts of the verb.

  Have you *always* prepared for tests by cramming the night before?

- When *not* negates another adverb, it should appear directly after the first auxiliary verb and before the other adverb.

  This newspaper does *not often* put sports on the front page.

- *Not* should appear after the adverb when it negates the action expressed by the main verb.

  The managers have *often not* followed this policy.

Separated Sentence Elements

Major sentence elements—subjects, verbs, objects, and complements—need to be near each other to make their relationships clear. At the same time, modifiers need to be near the sentence elements they modify. When these needs conflict, you have to make some choices. Since there are few hard-and-fast rules about modifier placement, let the goals of clarity and precision guide your decisions.

~~Kentucky was, even~~ *Even* though many of its residents fought on the side of the Confederacy during the Civil War, *Kentucky was* never a stronghold of slavery.

or

Kentucky was, *never a stronghold of slavery,* even though many of its residents fought on the side of the Confederacy during the Civil War, ~~never a stronghold of slavery.~~

---

chapter **47** *Grammar Terms*

The **sentence,** a group of words expressing a complete thought, is the basic unit of speech and writing. Sentence grammar describes how sentences are organized and structured. It also describes the function of each word in a sentence. An understanding of grammar helps you identify and improve places where your writing may be confusing. It also can help you find nonstandard structures or usages that may distract readers.

One approach to grammar asks "What is the word's role in the sentence?" This leads to a discussion of phrases and clauses, subjects, predicates, objects, and complements. Another approach asks, "What kind of word is this?" This approach classifies words as nouns, pronouns, verbs, adjectives, adverbs, prepositions, conjunctions, and interjections. The question "What kind of sentence is this?" leads to the classification of sentences by their structure.

47 a Elements of a sentence

This section asks, "How is the word used in the sentence?" Sentences contain a subject (what or who performs the action of the sentence) and a predicate (what the subject does). A subject consists of a noun, a pronoun, or a phrase functioning as a noun, along with modifiers. A predicate contains the verb of the sentence along with its objects, its modifiers, and any complements or modifiers that refer to the subject.

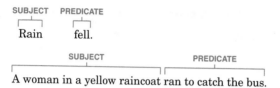

Subjects

The simple subject is the person or thing that performs the action of the predicate. Usually a noun or pronoun, it can also be a verbal, phrase, or clause used as a noun.

Long *shadows* crept along the lawn.   *(A noun as the subject)*

He looked exactly like a cowboy.   *(A pronoun)*

Her *singing* pleases me.   *(A verbal—gerund—as the subject)*

To work hard is our lot in life.   *(An infinitive phrase as the subject)*

That Lily could dance so well amazed us all.   *(A clause as the subject)*

The complete subject consists of the simple subject and all words that modify or directly relate to it.

Winning the last game of a dreadful season that included injuries, losing streaks, and a strike was small consolation to the team.

A compound subject includes two or more subjects linked by a coordinating conjunction such as *and* or *or*.

Books, recordings, <u>and</u> videotapes filled the room.

An implied subject is one that is not stated directly but may be understood. The most common example is a command with the implied subject *you*.

(You) Come to the meeting to learn about the preschool program.

Predicates

The simple predicate consists of the main verb of the sentence and any auxiliaries.

The candidate who wins the debate *will win* the election.

The complete predicate consists of the simple predicate and all words that modify or directly relate to it. Objects and complements are part of the complete predicate, along with any modifiers, including phrases, clauses, and single words.

The farmer *gave the pigs enough food to last the weekend.*

A compound predicate includes two or more verbs for the same subject.

At the beach we *ate* our picnic lunch, *swam* in the surf, *read* to each other, and *walked* on the sand.

The four verbs—ate, swam, read, *and* walked—*share the same subject,* we.

Objects of Verbs

A direct object receives the action of a transitive verb.

The company paid its *workers* a day early.   *(Workers is the object of* paid.*)*

She studied her *notes* all afternoon.   *(Notes is the object of* studied.*)*

Direct objects often fill in the missing *who* or *what* of the transitive verb: *Whom did the company pay? What did she study all afternoon?*

An indirect object is a person or thing to (or for) whom the verb's action is directed. It is either a noun or a pronoun that *precedes the direct object of the sentence.* (If this element is accompanied by a preposition, it becomes the object of the preposition and cannot be the object of the verb.)

| INDIRECT | DIRECT |
| OBJECT | OBJECT |

The company paid the workers their money.

Indirect objects answer the question *To whom?* or *For whom?*: *To whom did the company pay the money?*

Complements

A complement renames or modifies a subject or an object; it can be a noun, a pronoun, or an adjective.

A subject complement renames or describes the subject of a sentence. It follows a linking verb—*be, become, seem, appear,* and so on—that joins two equivalent terms. (See 47b.) Whatever appears before the linking verb is the subject; whatever appears after it is the subject complement.

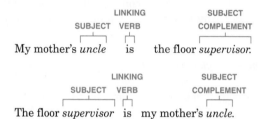

An object complement follows a direct object and renames or modifies it.

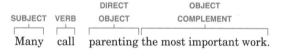

Phrases

A phrase is a group of related words lacking a subject, a predicate, or both.

Verb Phrase

A verb phrase consists of the main verb of a clause and its auxiliaries. It functions as the verb of a sentence.

VERB PHRASE

The college *has been having* a difficult year.

Noun Phrase

A noun phrase includes a noun or a pronoun together with all its modifiers.

NOUN PHRASE

The famous and venerable institution is bankrupt.

Noun phrases may function as subjects, objects, or complements.

The college's president is distraught. *(subject)*

He addressed *the board of trustees.* *(object)*

They became *a terrified mob.* *(subject complement)*

Prepositional Phrase

A prepositional phrase consists of a preposition, its object, and any related modifiers.

PREPOSITIONAL PHRASE

The new book was hailed *with great fanfare.*

A prepositional phrase may function as an adjective or an adverb.

He knows the difficulty *of the task.* *(prepositional phrase modifies difficulty)*

She arrived *at work* a little early. *(prepositional phrase modifies arrived)*

Appositive Phrase

An appositive phrase appears directly after a noun or pronoun and renames or further identifies it.

APPOSITIVE PHRASE

Ralph Nader, *a longtime consumer advocate,* supports the new mileage standard.

Clauses

A group of related words with a subject and a predicate is a clause. A clause that *can* stand alone as a complete sentence is called an independent clause or main clause of the sentence.

The moon rose.

MAIN CLAUSE

The winner will be the candidate who best communicates with the voters.

A clause that *cannot* stand by itself as a complete sentence is called a dependent clause or subordinate clause. Such a clause usually begins with a subordinating conjunction (*because, when, unless,* and so on) or a relative pronoun (*who, which, that,* and so on).

The little girl laughed *when the moon rose.*

The little girl laughed *can stand alone as a complete sentence, but* when the moon rose *cannot.*

I assume *that the best candidate will win the election.*

The clause that the best candidate will win the election *cannot stand alone.*

To make sense, dependent clauses must be joined to independent clauses. (See 39b.)

What I want is a good job.

(noun clause as subject of the sentence)

In class we learned *how we can improve our writing.*

(noun clause as direct object of verb)

We wondered to *whom we should send them.*

(noun clause as object of preposition)

The book *that you reserved* is now available.

(adjective clause modifies book)

The fish ride the tide *as far as it will carry them.*

(adverb clause modifies ride)

47 b   Parts of speech

A word's meaning and position in a sentence determine what part of speech it is. Some words change depending on the context in which they appear. For example, *ride* can function as a verb or a noun.

They went for a *ride.*   *(noun)*

They *ride* their horses.   *(verb)*

Nouns

Nouns are words that name persons, animals, places, things, or ideas: *woman, Flipper, Grand Canyon,* and *wealth* are all nouns.

Proper nouns name particular people, animals, places, or things: *Ralph Nader, Black Beauty, Kentucky, Catholicism.* They are almost always capitalized. (See 57c.) Generic nouns, or common nouns, can apply to any member of a class or group: *scientist, horse, state, ship, religion.* They are generally not capitalized.

Concrete nouns refer to things that can be seen, heard, touched, smelled, or tasted: *butterfly, telephone, ice, fudge.* Abstract nouns refer to ideas or concepts that cannot be directly sensed: *nature, communication, temperature, temptation.* (For the uses of concrete and abstract nouns, see 34b.)

Count nouns refer to items that can be counted: *books, ideas, stars.* Count nouns have singular and plural forms: *banana, bananas.* Noncount nouns refer to entities that either cannot be counted individually (*water, oil*) or are used in a sense that does not imply counting (*sand, money*). They are seldom made plural.

Collective nouns, such as *crowd, couple,* and *flock,* refer to groups of similar things.

SOME NONCOUNT NOUNS

air	energy	love	smoke
alcohol	equipment	machinery	snow
art	fog	mail	stuff
beef	food	make-up	sugar
biology	freedom	mathematics	temperature
candy	fruit	milk	traffic
cash	furniture	money	travel
cereal	garbage	news	truth
cheese	gasoline	noise	wind
clothing	homework	peace	wine
coffee	information	rain	wood
cold	jewelry	research	work
courage	knowledge	rice	writing
darkness	life	scenery	

Remember that some nouns that are noncount when used in a general sense can be count nouns in a specific sense.

Food is essential to life.

We sampled many wondrous new *foods.*

Singular and Plural Nouns

Singular nouns refer to one person, place, or thing: *student, dormitory, box.* Plural nouns refer to more than one: *students, dormitories, boxes.*

Adding *-s* or *-es* to the singular usually creates plural forms. However, some nouns change more radically from singular to plural: *goose, geese; child, children; man, men; medium, media.* Other nouns remain the same regardless of number: *sheep, sheep.* (For more on forming plurals, see 55b.)

ESL Using Articles with Nouns

Whether to use *a, an,* or *the* before a noun depends on the type of noun and the context in which it is used. Count nouns, which name things that can be counted, can be singular (*island, child, ratio*) or plural (*islands, children, ratios*). Noncount nouns, naming things that generally cannot be counted or quantified, are almost always singular (*information, homework, justice, success*).

With singular count nouns,

■ Use an article—*a, an* or *the*—unless the noun has a number (*one*) or a possessive (*my, her*) before it.

an island   the child   a ratio

In most cases, singular proper nouns do not require an article.

Italy   Pearl Street   Lake Erie

Plural proper nouns usually take the article *the*

the Dakotas   the Washingtons

■ Use *a* or *an* when you have not specified one particular thing or individual.

There is *a problem* with this approach.

Readers don't know what the problem is yet.

We all appreciate *an understanding friend.*

Any understanding friend, not a particular one.

Use *the* in the following cases.

■ The noun has already been mentioned.

There is a problem with this approach. *The problem* is a subtle one.

■ The noun is made specific by elements that follow it.

The problem that arose in the experiment is a subtle one.

The writer is referring to one specific problem.

■ The noun is made specific by the context.

I entered a large lecture hall. *The teacher* was standing behind a lectern. *The blackboard* seemed very far away.

In a lecture hall, there is likely to be only one teacher and only one blackboard.

Possessive Forms of Nouns

To indicate possession, ownership, or connections, add an apostrophe and an *-s* to a noun: *the student's paper, the school's mission.* (For guidelines on forming possessives of plural nouns and nouns that end in *-s*, see 52a.)

Pronouns

A pronoun is a substitute for a noun (or for another pronoun). The word that the pronoun replaces is called its antecedent.

```
      ANTECEDENT          PRONOUN
     ┌──────────┐          ┌─┐
If the assignment is long, it will require some planning.
```

Antecedents usually appear before the pronoun, but they may also follow the pronoun.

```
       PRONOUN              ANTECEDENT
        ┌─┐               ┌──────────┐
Because of its length, the assignment was a challenge.
```

(For description of pronoun reference to clear antecedents, see 44a.)

Personal Pronouns

Personal pronouns (*me, you, it, they,* and so on) refer to specific people, animals, places, things, or ideas.

Possessive pronouns (*my, your, theirs*) indicate ownership.

She asked *me* to visit *her* family.

Personal pronouns are categorized according to person, number, and gender (in third person singular).

	SINGULAR		PLURAL	
1ST PERSON	I, me	my, mine	we, us	our, ours
2ND PERSON	you	your, yours	you	you, yours
3RD PERSON			they, them	their, theirs
MASCULINE	he, him	his		
FEMININE	she, her	her, hers		
NEUTER	it	its		

Pronouns

Personal

I, me, my, mine   we, us, our, ours

you, your, yours

she, her, hers

he, him, his   they, them, their, theirs

it, its

Demonstrative

this   that   these   those

Relative

that   whatever   whichever   whoever   whomever

what   which   who   whom   whose

Interrogative

what   which   who   whom   whose

whatever   whichever   whoever   whomever

Reflexive and Intensive

myself   yourself   himself   herself   itself

ourselves   yourselves   themselves   oneself

Reciprocal

each other   one another

Indefinite

all	each	many	none	somebody
any	either	more	no one	someone
anybody	everybody	most	nothing	something
anyone	everyone	much	one	what
anything	everything	neither	several	
both	few	nobody	some	

Demonstrative Pronouns

Demonstrative pronouns (*this, that, these, those*) point to a specific person, place, or thing.

This is the best classroom! (This = *classroom*.)

Relative Pronouns

Relative pronouns (*who, whom, whose, which,* and *that*) introduce clauses that act as adjectives.

She chose the knife *that cut best.* (That cut best *modifies* knife.)

Other relative pronouns (*whoever, whomever, whatever, what,* and *whichever*) introduce noun clauses.

He'll do *whatever he wants.* (Whatever he wants *acts as the object of* do.)

Some relative pronouns change form to show case. (See 44c.)

Interrogative Pronouns

Interrogative pronouns (*who, what, whose,* and so on) ask questions.

Who is there?

Whose essay is this?

Reflexive and Intensive Pronouns

Reflexive and intensive pronouns end in *-self* or *-selves (myself, yourself, themselves,* and so on). Reflexive pronouns show that the "doer" and the "done to" are the same person.

Dave cut *himself* while shaving. (Dave *and* himself *refer to the same person.*)

Intensive pronouns are used to emphasize, or "intensify," an antecedent.

I talked to the president *herself.*

Unlike reflexive pronouns, intensive pronouns can be omitted without changing the sense of the sentence: *I talked to the president.* Reflexive and intensive pronouns change form to show person, number, and gender, just as personal pronouns do.

Indefinite Pronouns

Indefinite pronouns (*all, each, many, none,* and so on) refer to nonspecific persons, places, or things and therefore do not require an antecedent. Most are either always singular (*someone*) or always plural (*many*). They do not change form to show person, number, or gender.

Pronoun Case

Case indicates the role a word plays in a sentence, whether it is a subject, an object, or a possessive.

When pronouns act as subjects, use subjective case.

We should leave now.   *(We is the subject.)*

It was *she* who wanted to leave.   *(She is the subject complement.)*

When pronouns act as objects, use objective case.

Whom did they choose?   *(Whom is the object of the verb* choose.*)*

The judging seemed unfair to *us*.   *(Us is the object of the preposition* to.*)*

Seeing *her* made the holiday complete.   *(Her is the object of the verbal* seeing.*)*

When pronouns indicate possession or connection, use possessive case. Some possessive pronouns act as adjectives (modifying nouns) while others act as nouns (as subjects or complements).

That is *my* book bag.

(My modifies book bag.*)*

That book bag is *mine*.

(Mine is the same as, or subject complement to, book bag.*)*

SUBJECTIVE		OBJECTIVE		POSSESSIVE	
SINGULAR	**PLURAL**	**SINGULAR**	**PLURAL**	**SINGULAR**	**PLURAL**
I	we	me	us	my, mine	our, ours
you	you	you	you	your, yours,	your, yours
he, she, it	they	him, her,	them	his, her,	their, theirs
		it		hers, its	
who		whom		whose	
whoever		whomever			

(For more on pronoun case, see 44c.)

Verbs

A verb describes an action or state of being.

The course *will cover* three centuries of Persian art.

The students *are* seniors this year.

Verbs change form to show person, number, tense, voice, and mood. (See Chapter 42.)

- **Person** indicates who performed the action: *I write; she writes.*

- **Number** indicates whether one or more performed the action: *he sings; they sing.*

- **Tense** indicates when the action was performed: *she argues; she argued.*

- **Voice** shows whether the subject acts or is acted upon: *she paid the bill; the bill was paid.*

- **Mood** indicates the speaker's relation toward the action: *I am a millionaire; if I were a millionaire.*

Auxiliary Verbs

In addition to a main verb in a sentence, auxiliary or helping verbs (forms of *be, do, have,* and so on) may appear to create a verb phrase.

MAIN VERB

After swimming for an hour, he decided to go home.

VERB PHRASE

My oldest sister was doing a crossword puzzle.

The verb phrase consists of the main verb doing *and the auxiliary verb* was.

When used as auxiliaries, these verbs change to show person, number, and tense.

Other auxiliary verbs, known as one-word modals (*can, could, may, must, might, shall, should, would, will*) and multiple-word modals (*be able to, be going to, have got to, have to,* and so on) are also used as auxiliaries. One-word modals do not change form.

I can sing, and you can dance.

I *am* able to sing, and you *are* able to dance.

Transitive and Intransitive Verbs

In a sentence like *Joe hit the ball, ball* is the direct object of the verb *hit:* it receives the action of the verb. A verb that has a direct object is called a transitive verb. A verb without a direct object is called an intransitive verb: *Rain falls.* Many verbs can work either way, depending on the context.

TRANSITIVE VERB

Joey *grew* tomatoes last summer.

INTRANSITIVE VERB

The tomatoes *grew* rapidly.

Linking Verbs

Linking verbs (*be, become, seem, appear, look, feel, taste, smell, sound*) link the subject of a sentence to a subject complement, an element that renames or identifies the subject (see 47a). Like an equal sign, linking verbs connect two equivalent terms.

Sue *is* nice.	Sue = nice
They *felt* tired.	They = tired
Jake *was* a recent graduate.	Jake = graduate

Voice

Verbs can show action in the active voice, in which the subject of the sentence is the "doer."

The engine *propels* the train.

When the subject of the sentence is "done to," the verb is in the passive voice.

The train *is propelled* by the engine.

The "spotlight" is different in these two sentences; *engine* is the subject in the first, *train* in the second (see 42g).

Verbals

Certain verb forms can function as other parts of speech. These forms are called verbals. There are three kinds of verbals, which have different forms and functions.

Gerund: the *-ing* form of a verb functioning as a noun.

I love *jogging* early in the morning.

(Jogging *serves as the direct object of* love.)

Participle: present participle (ending in *-ing*) or past participle (ending in *-d, -ed, -en,* and so on) of a verb used as an adjective.

We explored several *hiking* trails.

Exhausted, the hikers decided to camp.

Infinitive: *to* plus the base form of a verb, usually used as a noun.

Her ambition is *to sing* at Carnegie Hall.

*(*To sing *is a subject complement.)*

To have sung so well last night is something you should be proud of.

(Notice that the infinitive changes form to show tense.)

After prepositions and certain verbs, the *to* of an infinitive does not appear; *to* is implied.

He did everything except *wash* the floor.

She *let* them *visit* their cousins.

(For more on verb selection, see Chapter 42. For subject-verb agreement, see Chapter 43.)

Adjectives and Adverbs

Adjectives and adverbs modify other words; they specify or say more about other words in sentences. To identify them, look at the words they modify.

Adjectives modify nouns and pronouns (and phrases and clauses used as nouns).

The hikers wanted *waterproof* parkas for the trip.

The adjective answers the question, "What kind of parkas?" and says more about the parkas.

Adverbs modify verbs, adjectives, and adverbs (and verbals, clauses, and full sentences).

His judgment was made *hastily.*   *The adverb modifies* was made.

The feathers are *quite* beautiful.   *The adverb modifies* beautiful.

Adjectives and adverbs can communicate degrees of comparison.

POSITIVE   He lives in an *old* house.

   (Makes no comparison.)

COMPARATIVE   It is *older* than mine.

   (Compares two things.)

SUPERLATIVE   It is the *oldest* house in the county.

   (Distinguishes among three or more things.)

(For more on forming comparatives and superlatives, see 45d.)

Kinds of Adjectives

Adjectives that describe attributes of something are called descriptive: *gray sky, beautiful garden*. Adjectives that specify are called limiting: *this sky, my garden*. Limiting adjectives include the indefinite articles (*a* and *an*) and the definite article (*the*). Use *a* when the following word begins with a consonant or long *u* sound (*a monster, a university*) and *an* when the following word begins with other vowel sounds (*an apron*).

Several types of pronouns can also serve as limiting adjectives when they are directly followed by a noun.

PERSONAL PRONOUN   She is going to buy *her* dog today.

RELATIVE PRONOUN   She hasn't decided *which* dog she will pick.

DEMONSTRATIVE PRONOUN   She likes *that* dog very much.

INDEFINITE   But *all* [the dogs] look cute to her.

Numbers, nouns, and proper nouns can also be used as adjectives when followed directly by nouns: *two dogs, masonry contractor,* and *Alaskan crab* (note capitalization). (See 57c.)

Kinds of Adverbs

In addition to the adverbs noted above, which modify verbs, adjectives, and other adverbs, several special groups of words are also classified as adverbs.

No, not, and *nor* are adverbs called negators.

We are *not* ready.

Conjunctive adverbs, such as *however* and *nevertheless,* link two independent clauses that are separated by a semicolon. (See 38b and 48b.)

Sally wanted to say goodbye to Tom; *however,* the train was leaving.

Relative adverbs, such as *where, why,* and *when,* introduce dependent clauses. (See 47a.)

We were visiting the house *where* I grew up.

(For editing tips on using adjectives and adverbs, see Chapter 45. For tips on positioning modifiers, see Chapter 46.)

Prepositions

Prepositions show the relationship of a noun or pronoun to another part of a sentence. Pronouns "take objects" and, together with their objects, form prepositional phrases. (See 47a.)

The cow jumped <u>*over the moon.*</u>

Over *is a preposition,* the moon *is its object.*

Common Prepositions

aboard	below	in case of	past
about	beneath	including	regarding
above	beside	in front of	since
according to	besides	inside	through
across	between	in spite of	throughout
after	beyond	into	till
against	but	like	to
ahead of	by	near	together with
along	concerning	next to	toward
along with	despite	notwithstanding	under
among	down	of	underneath
apart from	due to	off	unlike
around	during	on	until
as	except	onto	up
as for	except for	on top of	upon
at	for	other than	up to
away from	from	out	via
because of	in	out of	with
before	in addition to	outside	within
behind	in back of	over	without

Choosing the Right Preposition

Prepositional phrases can indicate time, location, place, or direction. Here is a list of common prepositions that begin such phrases.

Time

at noon, *at* night, *at* breakfast time

in a year or month, *in* 1999, *in* the twenty-first century, *in* the afternoon, *in* the morning, *in* an hour or a specified time period

on a specific date or day: *on* Monday, *on* October 3

by a specific date or time and not later: *by* next Thursday, *by* Thanksgiving

during (within a particular time period): *during* the day, *during* the month, *during* this century

until (any time before and up to a specified point): *until* today, *until* 8:00, *until* now

Location or Place

at the table, *at* home, *at* school, *at* the corner, *at* the subway station

in an enclosed space, *in* Canada, *in* the world, *in* class, *in* the car

on the desk, *on* the radio, *on* the wall, *on* a plane

Direction

arrive *from* somewhere: *from* Australia, *from* your house, *from* another planet

go *to* a place: *to* Canada, *to* school, *to* church

fall *off* something: *off* a bike, *off* the roof

travel *around* an area: *around* Europe, *around* town

snowboard *down* something: *down* the hill

Conjunctions

Conjunctions join two or more words, phrases, or clauses.

Coordinating conjunctions (*and, or, nor, for, but, yet,* and *so*) join equal or similar elements.

Bill *and* I went shopping.

The bus will take you to the market *or* to the theater.

Bill went to the market, *but* Clara went to the theater.

Correlative conjunctions (*either . . . or, neither . . . nor, both . . . and, not only . . . but also, whether . . . or*) appear in pairs and join pairs of similar words.

Neither Jack *nor* his brother was in school this morning.

She *not only* sings *but also* dances.

Subordinating conjunctions (*after, although, because, before, if unless, when, where,* and *while*) introduce ideas in dependent clauses that are less important than (or subordinate to) the ideas in main (or independent) clauses. (See 38c.)

DEPENDENT CLAUSE   INDEPENDENT CLAUSE

While you finish your writing, I will start dinner.

INDEPENDENT CLAUSE   DEPENDENT CLAUSE

I left *because* I had to catch a train.

Conjunctive adverbs (*however, therefore, furthermore,* and so on) show transitions between independent clauses that are separated by a semicolon. (See 48b.)

We have completed the experiment; *therefore,* we should tabulate the results.

Interjections

Interjections are words that show surprise, dismay, or strong emotion. They are often "interjected" in speech or dialogue and typically require an exclamation point.

Ouch! That coffee is hot!

47 c Classifying sentences

Sentences can be classified by function and by grammatical structure.

Classifying Sentences by Function

Declarative sentences make statements. The normal word order for a declarative sentence is subject followed by predicate.

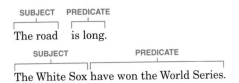

SUBJECT   PREDICATE

The road   is long.

SUBJECT   PREDICATE

The White Sox have won the World Series.

Word order is occasionally inverted.

PREDICATE   SUBJECT

At the top of the hill stood a tree.

Interrogative sentences ask questions using either an interrogative pronoun or inverted word order.

Who goes there?

Can pigs really fly?   *(The verb is* can fly.*)*

Imperative sentences make commands or requests. The subject, *you,* is typically not stated but implied. The verb form used for the imperative is always the base form.

Drive slowly.

Signal before changing lanes.

Exclamatory sentences exclaim (and usually end with an exclamation point).

Oh, how I hate to get up in the morning!

Classifying Sentences by Grammatical Structure

Sentences are classified by grammatical structure according to how many dependent and independent clauses they contain.

A simple sentence consists of a single independent clause and no dependent clause. Some simple sentences are brief.

Marmosets eat bananas.

Others, if they contain modifier phrases or compound subjects, verbs, or objects, can be quite long.

Benny and Griselda, marmosets at our local zoo, eat at least fifteen bananas a day, in addition to lettuce, nuts, oranges, and apples.

A compound sentence has two or more independent clauses and no dependent clause. The independent clauses are usually joined by a comma and a coordinating conjunction.

INDEPENDENT CLAUSE   INDEPENDENT CLAUSE

They grew tired of waiting, so they finally hailed a taxi.

A complex sentence contains one independent clause and at least one dependent clause.

INDEPENDENT CLAUSE   DEPENDENT CLAUSE

The students assemble outside when the bell rings.

A **c**ompound-complex sentence contains at least two independent clauses and at least one dependent clause.

Commas are the most frequently used punctuation in English. In speech, pauses sometimes indicate grammatical changes in a sentence. Commas serve a similar function in writing, letting readers know when a new grammatical structure begins. They help signal many of the different ways in which sentences are divided into parts and how those parts are related.

48 a To connect independent clauses

Use a comma between two or more independent clauses (clauses that could stand alone as complete sentences) when they are joined by *and, or, nor, for, but, yet,* or *so* (coordinating conjunctions) to form a compound sentence.

We must act quickly, *or* the problem will get worse.

The farmers ate lunch at 10:00, *and* they rested in the shade whenever they got too hot.

The comma before the conjunction may be omitted when the two sentences are very short and closely related.

The sun rose *and* the fog lifted.

Do not use a comma without a coordinating conjunction to join independent clauses. This error is called a comma splice. (See Chapter 40.)

and
His hobby is raising geese, he proudly displays the ribbons his
^
birds have won.

48 b After introductory elements

An element at the beginning of a sentence that is not part of the sentence's main clause should be followed by a comma. Here are examples of such introductory elements that should be followed by commas.

When Elizabeth I assumed the throne of England in 1569, the country was in turmoil.

In every taste test, the subjects chose the new flavor over the old.

His dream of glory destroyed, the boxer died an embittered man.

Yes, we need to improve our parks.

As a matter of fact, John does know the answer.

The comma is optional when an introductory phrase is brief and when its absence will not cause confusion.

In 1963 an assassin's bullet shocked the world.

Unfortunately Jane will be late.

---

48 c   To set off nonessential information

Elements that are essential to the meaning of a sentence are called restrictive. Elements that are nonessential or nonrestrictive can be removed without destroying the meaning of a sentence. Use commas to set off nonrestrictive elements.

Restrictive (necessary)

The team *that scores the most points* will receive a bronze trophy.

The clause identifies the team that gets the trophy; therefore, no commas.

Nonrestrictive (not necessary)

The dinner party, *which had been carefully planned,* went smoothly.

Commas are needed since the careful planning is optional information.

A clause that modifies a proper noun is almost always nonrestrictive (optional), so commas are needed.

John Glenn, *who was one of the first astronauts,* later was elected to the United States Senate from Ohio.

To test whether an element is essential, leave it out. If the meaning does not change, the modifier is not necessary, but commas are.

The moon *which we could see from our window* **was full and bright.**

Without the clause beginning with which, *the words* The moon was full and bright *makes sense, so insert commas.*

The four objects *that Galileo saw "wandering around Jupiter"* were moons.

Without the clause beginning with that, *the sentence has lost its meaning, so no commas are needed.*

Appositives

A noun or phrase that immediately follows a noun and renames it is called an appositive. It can be essential to meaning (restrictive) or not (nonrestrictive). The same comma rule applies.

Restrictive appositive

Former president *Theodore Roosevelt* was an avid big-game hunter.

There are many former presidents; the appositive Theodore Roosevelt *restricts the statement to one; no commas.*

Nonrestrictive appositive

Theodore Roosevelt, *who served in the Spanish-American War,* was an avid big-game hunter.

The additional information is not necessary to identify Roosevelt, so use commas.

48 d   To set off parenthetical elements

A parenthetical element, or an aside, comments on a sentence but does not change its meaning, so it is nonrestrictive and should be set off with a comma or commas. It can appear anywhere in the sentence without greatly changing the meaning.

Surprisingly, none of the bicycles was damaged.

None of the bicycles, *I noticed,* was damaged.

None of the bicycles was damaged, *to my surprise.*

48 e   Between items in a series

A series consists of a list of three or more elements in similar grammatical form. Use a comma after each element in a series, including the element that precedes *and, or,* or *but.*

He studied all the notes, memos, and reports.

A good driver accelerates smoothly, stops without jerking, and makes gradual turns.

He reported that some economists believed the recession was over, that some believed it continued, but that most agreed recovery would be slow.

(For punctuating a series whose elements contain commas, see 49c.)

48 f Between equal modifiers

Commas separate two or more adjectives of equal weight (coordinate adjectives)—*a warm, sunny day*. To test, try inserting *and* between them or reversing their order. If the resulting sentence still makes sense, you need a comma. (See "Order of Adjectives," 45c.)

He put on a *clean, pressed* shirt.

Pressed, clean *works as well as* clean, pressed, *so use a comma.* Pressed and clean *also makes sense.*

I found *five copper* coins.

Neither copper five coins *nor* five and copper coins *makes sense; no comma.*

48 g To set off contrast elements, tag sentences, and direct address

Use commas in all these instances where a pause would seem natural in spoken English.

Use commas around elements of contrast, which describe something by emphasizing what it is not or by citing some opposite condition.

The experience was illuminating, *but unnerving,* for everyone.

Jeremiah was a bullfrog, *not a toad.*

Use a comma before tag sentences, which are short statements or questions at the ends of sentences.

You received my application in time, *I hope.*

They meet every Monday, *don't they?*

Words that name the person or persons spoken to should be set off with commas. These are called words of direct address.

Lilith, it was good to see you.

That, *my friends,* is not the end of the story.

48 h With quotations

Use commas to set off direct quotations from the words that identify speakers. The comma appears inside the closing quotation mark if the speaker's attribution follows the quotation.

"When I went to kindergarten and had to speak English for the first time, I became silent," writes Maxine Hong Kingston.

If the speaker is identified first, the comma precedes the opening quotation mark.

Mark Twain is widely quoted as saying, "The report of my death was an exaggeration."

Use commas before and after the attribution if it interrupts a complete sentence, with the first comma within the quotation marks.

"The fossil shells of this district . . . such as have fallen within my observation," writes Gilbert White, "must not be passed over in silence."

Use a question mark or an exclamation point, without a comma, at the end of a quoted question or exclamation.

"What does the latest survey show?" Marion asked.

Do not use commas when a quotation is preceded by *that* or when the quotation is worked naturally into the sentence.

He closed by saying that time "will prove us right."

Time "will prove us right."

Do not use commas with *indirect* discourse that uses no quotation marks.

Emerson wrote that we should trust ourselves.

(For more on direct quotations, see 53a–53b.)

48 i With numbers, dates, names, and places

Counting from the right, use a comma after every three digits in numbers with five or more digits. The comma is optional in four-digit numbers.

2700 (or 2,700)   79,087   467,391

Do not use a comma in page numbers, street numbers, zip codes, or years.

21001 Southern Boulevard

Use commas before and after the year when a date giving month, date, and year is part of a sentence.

Louis Armstrong always said he was born on July 4, 1900, in
New Orleans.

When only the month and year are given or when the day precedes the month, do not use a comma.

The Great War broke out in August 1914 and ended on 11 November 1918.

Use commas to set off a title or abbreviation following a name.

Joyce B. Wong, MD, supervised the training.

Use commas to set off the name of a state from the name of a city.

She moved to Dayton, Ohio, for a new job.

Commas separate each element of a full address given in a sentence. The zip code does not have a comma before or after it.

Please note that my address will be 169 Elm Street, Apartment 4, Boston, MA 02116 as of July 6.

48 j To prevent misreading

Even when no specific rule requires one, a comma is sometimes added to guarantee a cue or pause to prevent a misreading.

We will all pitch in, in the event of a problem.

Guidelines for Using Commas

As you edit, make sure you have used commas in the following places.

■ Before conjunctions that join independent clauses
■ After introductory elements at the beginning of sentences
■ To set off nonessential modifiers
■ To set off parenthetical elements
■ Between all items in a series
■ Between coordinate adjectives
■ To set off elements of contrast, tag sentences, and words of direct address
■ With quotations
■ To separate numbers, dates, names, and addresses
■ To prevent misreading

Editing Misused Commas

Commas are the most used mark of punctuation and the most frequently misused. Look out for these common comma errors.

Eliminate single commas between subjects and verbs, between verbs and their objects, between linking verbs and their complements, or between objects and their complements.

SUBJECT   VERB

A season of drought/ worried the farmers.

VERB   OBJECT

The agreement entails/ training the part-time staff.

LINKING VERB   COMPLEMENT

The laid-off workers   seem/   surprisingly calm.

OBJECT   COMPLEMENT

The extra pay made him/ quite happy.

Eliminate commas between the parts of compound elements.

Compound Subject (two subjects of same verb)

The members of the senior class/ and their parents were invited.

Compound Verb (two verbs with same subject)

Maria quickly turned off the lights/ and locked the door.

Compound Object (two objects of same verb, in this case, *put*)

Shawan put the books on the shelf/ and the pens in the drawer.

Gina tried to save more/ and spend less.

Compound Complement (two elements renaming or describing the same subject, here, *weather*)

The weather was unbearably hot/ and much too humid.

Compound Modifier (in this case, two modifier clauses beginning with *who*)

The rule applies to students who have maintained their grades/ and who have paid all their fees.

When the word order of a sentence is inverted, do not use a comma after an introductory phrase.

With the changing colors of fall/ comes the time for cider.

Don't use a comma after a phrase that functions as the subject of the sentence.

Hearing that song/ evokes warm memories.

Eliminate commas before and after restrictive modifiers or appositives.

The information/ that we requested/ has arrived.

Noted bluesman/ Keb' Mo'/ will perform.

(*But* Keb' Mo', a noted bluesman, will perform.)

Do not use a comma to separate a relative pronoun or a subordinating conjunction from the clauses they introduce.

He wrote that/ home accidents are the cause of most childhood injuries.

Our negotiators have no idea how to proceed because/ we have not come to a consensus.

Eliminate a comma before the first element or after the last element in a series unless another rule requires one.

The primary colors are/ red, yellow, and blue.

They went to London, Paris, and Rome/ on their last trip.

Eliminate a comma between an adjective and the noun it modifies.

His trim, tidy/ boat was finally ready for the water.

Do not use a comma between adjectives that are not coordinate.

Andy bought a new/ black leather motorcycle jacket.

O ne use of the semicolon is to signal that one independent clause is closely related to another. Another is in a series in which some of the items contain commas. Semicolons are common in formal academic writing, less common in informal writing.

49 a Between clauses

Use a semicolon to join two independent clauses, especially when the second clause qualifies, complements, or contradicts the first. In such cases, a semicolon substitutes for a period but suggests a stronger relationship between the two thoughts.

It rained in August; the leaves turned bright red in September.

Most dogs aim to please their owners; cats don't behave that way.

If you connect related sentences with a coordinating conjunction (*and, or, nor, for, but, yet, so*), use a comma instead of a semicolon. (See 47a.)

Most dogs aim to please their owners, but cats don't behave that way.

A semicolon may be used with a coordinating conjunction when the sentences connected contain commas.

If the weather clears, we'll leave at dawn; but if it doesn't, we won't leave at all.

49 b With transitional expressions to join two independent clauses

Use a semicolon between independent clauses joined by transitional expressions (*indeed, for example, on the other hand*) or conjunctive adverbs (*however, furthermore, therefore*). (See 39b.)

The cat jumped out of the hat; indeed, it was an amazing leap.

Many in the community were angry; however, they lacked a strong leader.

49 c   Between items in a series containing commas

Use semicolons between elements in a series when at least one element of the series includes a comma.

> The candidates for the award are Darnell, who won the essay competition; Elaine, the top debater; and Kiesha, the theater director.

Semicolon Guidelines

- Semicolons substitute for periods, implying that two sentences are closely related.
- Semicolons substitute for commas when too many commas would cause confusion.

Editing Misused Semicolons

Eliminate semicolons between an independent clause and a dependent clause.

He ran down the block to the old mailbox; where he dropped his letter into the slot.

Do not use a semicolon between a phrase and an independent clause.

Having failed in my exasperating search of the old files and dusty records; I longed for a simpler research assignment.

Do not use a semicolon to introduce a list. Use a colon instead (see 50a).

It was a fine old house, but it needed work; plaster repairs, wallpaper, rewiring, paint, and a thorough cleaning.

chapter **50** *Colons*

A colon is a more forceful stop within a sentence than a semicolon. As a mark of introduction, a colon alerts the reader that the information following it will provide further explanation. The colon also has specialized uses, as explained in the following sections. The colon is a powerful and somewhat formal mark of punctuation, so use it carefully.

50 a   As marks of introduction

Use a colon to introduce an explanation, an example, a list, or a quotation. What precedes the colon must be an independent clause (full sentence). The explanation or example that follows the colon can be a single word, a phrase, or a clause.

He has but one objective: success.

He has three objectives: fame, money, and power.

Do not use a colon when what precedes the list is not a complete independent clause.

His three objectives are⁄ fame, money, and power.

Do not use a colon when the list is preceded by a phrase such as *for example, such as,* or *including.*

She has reasonable goals, such as⁄ sales, revenue growth, and market penetration.

A colon may be used in place of a period or semicolon between two independent clauses to imply that the second clause helps make sense of the first.

The agreement erected a wall between the mayor and the city council: the council controlled the money, and the mayor set policy.

Following a colon, some writers capitalize the first word when that word begins an independent clause. However, a lowercase letter after a colon is always correct. Whichever you choose, be consistent.

This year's team is surprisingly inexperienced: seven of the players are juniors, and six are sophomores.

If a list introduced with a colon is set off with each item on a separate line, capitalizing the first line of each item is optional, but be consistent.

The following issues need to be taken into account before the building site is selected:

Climate variations

Geographical context

Site access

Procedure for securing building permits

Cost of building supplies

For the trip I packed the following items:

    down sleeping bag, air mattress

    tent, ground cloth, rope

    extra blue jeans

    shorts, swimsuit

    sneakers, sandals.

Commas are generally used to introduce quotations and identify speakers. (See 53a.)

As the song from *South Pacific* puts it, "You've got to be carefully taught."

However, when an independent clause precedes and introduces a quotation, use a colon.

The song from *South Pacific* puts it well: "You've got to be carefully taught."

Use a colon to introduce a long quotation (five lines or more, according to MLA) set off from the main text in block format. (See 53a.)

50 b   In time references, biblical citations, titles, and business communication

Here are some conventional uses for colons.

Between hours, minutes, and seconds

Court convened promptly at 9:00 a.m.

The official elapsed time for the race was 2:45:57.

In biblical citations

Isaiah 14:10

(In MLA style, use a period: Isaiah 14.10)

Between main titles and subtitles

Blue Highways: A Journey into America

Salutations and memo headings in formal correspondence

Dear Mr. Ramirez:

To: Doris DiGiovanni
From: Paul Nkwami
Subject: 2005 budget

Editing Misused Colons

Delete a colon between a verb and its object or complement.

The menu included: fruit, salads, and soups.

Delete a colon between a preposition and its object.

This trip took her to: New Orleans, San Francisco, and Chicago.

Delete a colon after an introductory or transitional expression: *for example, such as, like, especially,* and *so on.*

The show included a number of unusual pets, such as: iguanas, raccoons, a civet, and a black widow spider.

---

chapter **51**   *End Punctuation*

Periods, question marks, and exclamation points tell you that a complete thought, a sentence, has ended.

51 a   Periods

Use a period at the end of a statement, a command, or a request.

The view from the tower was worth the climb.

Stand on the right or walk on the left.

Would you please sit down.

Use a period, not a question mark, after an indirect question (a question that is reported but not asked directly).

I wonder who chose that pattern.

When an abbreviation ending with a period ends a sentence, use only one period.

Her flight leaves at 6:15 a.m.

Use a period in certain abbreviations.

Mr., Mrs., Ms., in., ft., etc., e.g., i.e., vs.

Dr., Rev., Msgr., Mon., Tues., Wed., Atty., Gov., Sen.

Jan., Feb., St., Ave., Rd., p., para., fig., vol.

But titles and degrees, such as *MD, PhD, Esq,* or *LLD,* use no periods. See 60a.
Include a space between the abbreviated letters for an author's name,
especially in documenting citations according to APA style.

E. B. White

Do not use a space after the periods within abbreviations that stand for
more than one word.

B.C.   A.D.   a.m.

Do not use periods with acronyms (words formed from initials and pronounced as words) or with abbreviated names of government agencies, cor-
porations, and other entities.

NASA, NATO, AIDS, CNN, SAT, FBI, CIA, EPA, IRS, IRA, NCAA

Names of countries abbreviated all in capital letters do not use periods
(see 60e).

US   UK

51 b   Question marks

Use question marks at the end of direct questions. (Direct questions
are usually signaled either by *what, where,* or *why* or by inverted word
order, with the verb before the subject.)

Where is Times Square?

Use a question mark or a period at the end of a request to emphasize
politeness.

Would you please sit down?

Compare *Would you please sit down.*

Use a question mark when a sentence ends with a tag question.

> This train goes to Times Square, doesn't it?

Use a question mark for a direct question in quotation marks. Put the question mark before the closing quotation mark, and use no other end punctuation. (See 53e.) Do not capitalize the first word identifying the speaker after a quotation unless that word is a proper name.

> "Have we missed the train?" she asked.

Use question marks after each question in a series of questions, even if they are not all complete sentences. (Capitalization is optional, but be consistent.)

> Where did Mario go? To the library? To the cafeteria? To class?

Use a question mark after a direct question set off by dashes.

> When the alarm rang—was it 7 a.m. already?— I jumped out of bed.

51 c Exclamation points

Use an exclamation point to convey emphasis and strong emotion in sentences that are exclamations, strong commands, or interjections.

> Wow! It's late!   Stop the train!

In direct quotes, place the exclamation point inside the quotation marks and do not use any other end punctuation.

> "Ouch!" he cried. "That hurts!"

Use an exclamation point after an exclamation set off by dashes.

> They told me—I couldn't believe it!—that I'd won.

In most college writing, understatement is preferred to overstatement, so use exclamation points sparingly, if at all.

The apostrophe indicates the possessive form of a noun or pronoun, marks certain plural forms, and indicates where a letter has been dropped in contractions.

52 a   To show possession

To form the possessive case, add either an apostrophe and -*s* or just an apostrophe to nouns and some indefinite pronouns.

Singular Nouns

Use an apostrophe and -*s* to form the possessive of any singular noun that does not end in -*s*.

Sean Penn's new movie is his best yet.

Use an apostrophe and -*s* to form the possessive of a singular noun ending in -*s*. (If pronouncing the additional syllable is awkward, you may use the apostrophe alone.)

Don't waste the *class's* time.

The company produced *Yeats'* cycle of plays.

Plural Nouns

Use an apostrophe alone to form the possessive of a plural noun ending in -*s*.

They wrote to the *boys'* parents.

Use an apostrophe and -*s* to form the possessive of any plural noun that does not end in -*s*.

She has long been an advocate for *children's* rights.

Compound Nouns

To form the possessive of a compound noun, use an apostrophe and *-s* on only the last word.

He borrowed his *mother-in-law's* car.

The *secretary of state's* office certified the results.

Joint Possession

When nouns joined by *and* form a unit that has joint possession, use an apostrophe and *-s* on only the last noun.

My aunt's and uncle's party was a disaster.

However, when nouns joined by *and* are individuals with separate possession, add an apostrophe and *-s* to each noun.

The documentary compared Aretha ~~Franklin~~ Franklin and Diana Ross's

early careers.

Possessive Apostrophes with Indefinite Pronouns

Use an apostrophe to show possession with the pronouns that refer to people in general (*someone, anybody, no one, one,* and *another*).

Someone's umbrella was left at the bank.

That is *no one's* business but my own.

The possessive pronoun *its* does not take an apostrophe.

The horse found its way home.

Do not use an apostrophe and *-s* with *all, any, both, each, few, many, most, much, none, several, some,* or *such* (the indefinite pronouns). To show possession, use *of,* or use a pronoun that has a possessive form.

We will read the works *of* both.

We will read both *of their* works

52 b   In plurals of words used as words, letters, numbers, and symbols

Use an apostrophe and *-s* to form the plural of a word discussed as a word or term and to form the plural of letters and symbols.

There are two *perhaps*'s in that sentence.

The word *occurrence* is spelled with two *r*'s.

A row of ***'s marks the spot where I'm having trouble.

Note that words and letters referred to as themselves are italicized (or underlined) (see 61d). The apostrophe and the final *s*, however, are not italicized.

You may use an apostrophe and *-s* for the plural of centuries and decades expressed in figures; however, the Modern Language Association recommends the letter *-s* with no apostrophe. Do not use an apostrophe when the century or decade is expressed in words.

the 1800s (or the 1800's)   the '60s (or the '60's)   the sixties

Use an apostrophe and *-s* for plurals of abbreviations ending with periods. Use *-s* alone for abbreviations without periods.

We edited to delete all the *Mr.*'s and *Mrs.*'s.

She has some *IOUs* to call in.

52 c   To form contractions

A contraction is a word in which one or more letters are intentionally omitted and replaced by an apostrophe, such as *can't, it's, they're, 'bye*. An apostrophe also can show that digits have been dropped from a year: *the class of '99, the '90s*.

Common Contractions

cannot	can't	she would	she'd
do not	don't	there is	there's
does not	doesn't	they are	they're
has not	hasn't	was not	wasn't
have not	haven't	we have	we've
I am	I'm	who is	who's
it is	it's	will not	won't
let us	let's	would not	wouldn't
she is, she has	she's	you are	you're

Editing Misused Apostrophes

Possessives and contractions often sound alike—*whose* and *who's, its* and *it's, your* and *you're*. So do plurals and plural possessives. As you edit, be especially careful to check the placement and appropriateness of the apostrophes you use.

Eliminate apostrophes from possessive pronouns.

Theirs~~'~~ is the glory, theirs~~'~~ the fame.

Do not use an apostrophe to form the plural of a noun.

Although they seem like a happy family, the ~~Simpson's~~ Simpsons do not always behave that way.

Make sure you have not confused a possessive with a contraction. When you see a word with an apostrophe, spell out the contraction. If it is a true contraction, the sentence will still make sense.

You're late.

You are late *makes sense.*

~~You're~~ Your hat is on the hook.

Spell out the contraction. You are hat *is nonsense.*

When you see *its, your,* or *their,* substitute *of it, of you,* or *of them.* If the possessive is correct, the sentence will make sense.

The accused are innocent until proven guilty, ~~its~~ it's said.

Of it said *doesn't make sense.*

What is its name?

The name of it *does make sense.*

chapter **53** *Quotation Marks*

Quotation marks indicate that you are reproducing a direct quotation, the exact words written or spoken by someone else. (See 16b.)

In written texts, quotation marks also distinguish certain titles, foreign expressions, and special terms from the main body of the work. American English uses double quotation marks (" ") for quotations and certain titles, but single quotation marks (' ')—apostrophes on most computer keyboards—for quotations within quotations (or titles within titles).

53 a   For direct quotations

When quoting another person's exact words directly, keep in mind the conventions for short or long passages.

Short Passages

Use quotation marks to enclose brief direct quotations of up to four typed lines of prose or up to three lines of poetry. Any parenthetical citation of a source goes after the closing quotation marks but before the period.

In *Lives under Siege,* Ratzenburger argues that "most adolescents are far too worried about the next six months and far too unconcerned about the next sixty years" (84).

Use single quotation marks for a quotation within a quotation.

After the election, the incumbent said, "My opponent will soon learn, as Lincoln said, 'You cannot fool all the people all the time.'"

Long Passages

Set off longer quotations from the main text in block format. Start a new line for the quotation, indent all lines of the quotation ten spaces, and *do not use quotation marks.* If the words that introduce a block quotation are a complete sentence, use a colon or a period after them. If they are not a complete sentence, use either a comma or no punctuation, depending on the structure (see 48h). Place a source in parentheses one space after the end punctuation of the quotation. Here is an example of a block quotation.

A recent editorial describes the problem.

In countries like the United States, breast-feeding, though always desirable, doesn't mean the difference between good and poor nutrition—or life and death. But it does in developing countries, where for decades infant food manufacturers have been distributing free samples of infant formulas to hospitals and birthing centers. (*Daily Times* 17)

The editorial goes on to argue that the samples last only long enough for the mother's own milk to dry up; then the mothers find they cannot afford to buy the formula.

Use double quotation marks for a quotation within a block quotation, since the outer quotation has none.

Note that paragraph indents are not used for quoting single paragraphs or parts of paragraphs. For two or more paragraphs, indent the first line of each new paragraph after the first (use three additional spaces).

For poetry, copy as precisely as possible the line breaks, indents, spacing, and capitalization of the original, but do not use quotation marks, as the indentation signals quoted material.

> In *Patience,* W. S. Gilbert has the character Reginald Bunthorne proclaim,
>
> > This air severe
> > Is but a mere
> > Veneer!
> >
> > This cynic smile
> > Is but a wile
> > Of guile! (5–10)

53 b For dialogue

Use quotation marks to set off dialogue. Using a new paragraph every time the speaker changes indicates who is speaking even without attribution.

> "Early parole is not the solution to overcrowding," the prosecutor said. "We need a new jail."
>
> The chairman of the county commission asked, "How do you propose we pay for it?"
>
> "Increase taxes if you must, but act quickly."

If one speaker's words continue for more than a single paragraph, use quotation marks at the beginning of each new paragraph but at the end of only the last paragraph.

53 c For certain titles

Use quotation marks for the titles of brief poems, book chapters and parts, magazine and journal articles, episodes of television series, and songs. (Use italics or underlining for titles of longer works, such as books, magazines and journals, recordings, films, plays, and television series.)

"Araby" is the third story in James Joyce's book *Dubliners.*

This chart appeared with the article "Will Your Telephone Last?" in November's <u>Consumer Reports.</u>

In my favorite episode of *I Love Lucy,* "Job Switching," Lucy and Ethel work in a chocolate factory.

The Beatles' <u>Sgt. Pepper's Lonely Hearts Club Band</u> includes one of the most famous songs of the twentieth century, "A Day in the Life."

Do *not* use quotation marks or italics for the following.

Generic Titles of Parts of a Work or Series
Chapter 6   Part II   Episode 43

Titles of Sacred Works and Ancient Manuscripts
the Talmud   the Bible   the Koran

Documents
the Constitution   the Gettysburg Address

Use single quotation marks for quoted material that is part of a title enclosed in double quotation marks.

We read "'This Is the End of the World': The Black Death" by historian Barbara Tuchman.

53 d   For special purposes

Translations

Use quotation marks around the translation of a foreign word or phrase into English. The foreign word or phrase itself is italicized.

I've always called Antonio *fratellino,* or "little brother," because he is six years younger than I.

Special Terms

Use quotation marks around specialized terms when they are first introduced and defined.

The ecology of this "cryocore"—a region of perpetual ice and snow—has been studied very little.

Titles Within Titles

Use the following models when presenting titles within titles. These guidelines also apply to other words normally indicated by quotation marks or by italics, such as quotations and foreign words, when they appear in titles.

1. A title enclosed in quotation marks within an italicized (or underscored) title

    "A Curtain of Green" and Other Stories

2. An italicized title within a title enclosed in quotation marks

    "Morality in *Death of a Salesman*"

3. A title enclosed in quotation marks within another title enclosed in quotation marks

    "Symbolism in 'Everyday Use'"

4. A published title within another published title (italics for first title, underline for second title)

    Modern Critics on <u>Hamlet</u> *and Other Plays*

Irony

Quotation marks may be used around a word or phrase used ironically—that is, with a meaning opposed to its literal one.

Jonathan Swift's essay "A Modest Proposal" offers a quick "solution" to Ireland's poverty and overpopulation: eat the children.

Unusual Nicknames

Use quotation marks around unusual nicknames at first mention.

The president was a man named Garnett E. "Ding" Cannon.

53 e With other punctuation

Which punctuation mark comes first when a word is followed by a quotation mark and another mark of punctuation? Both logic and convention govern the order.

Periods and Commas

Put periods and commas inside quotation marks.

After Gina sang "People," Joe began to hum "The Way We Were."

"Denver is usually cool in the spring," he said, "but this year it's positively hot."

Colons and Semicolons

Put colons and semicolons outside quotation marks.

The sign read "Closed": there would be no soda today.

In 1982, Bobbie Ann Mason wrote "Shiloh"; it is considered one of her finest works.

Question Marks, Exclamation Points, and Dashes

Put question marks, exclamation points, and dashes inside the quotation marks if they are part of the quotation, outside the quotation marks if they are not.

She asked, "Have you read 'The Tiger'?"

Was it you who asked, "Who's there?"

That song is from "Oklahoma!"

I can't believe you've never read "The Lottery"!

"Hold on a minute. I can't hear—"

Emma's first word—"Dada"—caused Tom to beam.

Editing Misused Quotation Marks

Quotation marks are like shoes: use them in pairs. (The only exception is in extended dialogue; see 53b.)

"There are always a few students who boycott the assembly," he said, "but that's no reason for us to call it off."

When quoting passages, make sure the material enclosed within the quotation marks is only quoted words. (For modifying quoted material, see uses of brackets, 54b.)

If the logic of a sentence dictates that a quotation end with a question mark or an exclamation point but sentence grammar calls for a period or comma as well, use the stronger mark (the question mark or exclamation point) and delete the weaker one (the period or comma).

As soon as we heard someone shout "fire!," we began to run.

Do not use quotation marks to indicate emphasis. Use italics for emphasis when necessary.

He was guilty of a "felony," not a misdemeanor.

Do not use quotation marks for slang or for terms you think are overused. Instead, consider substituting another word or phrase.

Several of these companies should go into a "hall of shame" for their employment practices.

Parentheses and brackets are marks that set off the writer's language from the normal flow of thought within a sentence.

54 a Parentheses

Enclose in parentheses any elements that would otherwise interrupt a sentence: explanations, examples, asides, digressions, and supplementary information. (Since parentheses de-emphasize the material they enclose, use them carefully.)

Explanations, Examples, and Asides

Enclose explanations, examples, and asides within sentences or paragraphs.

Relatives of famous people now famous themselves include Angelica Huston (daughter of John) and Michael Douglas (son of Kirk).

Some vegetables resist light frost (pumpkins, squash) while others do not (tomatoes, peppers).

Define the term *postmodern.* (Good luck!)

Enclose the translation of a specialized term or foreign word.

English also borrowed the Dutch word *koekje* ("cookie").

Dates, Cross-References, and Citations

Set off the date of an event or the dates of a person's birth and death.

The Oxford English Dictionary was first published under the editorship of James A. H. Murray (1888–1933).

Use parentheses to enclose cross-references to other parts of your paper or to enclose documentation. (For more on documentation, see Chapters 19–23.)

> The map (p. 4) shows the areas of heaviest rainfall.

> Nick Carraway felt unsettled to see Gatsby at the end of his dock beckoning in the direction of a "single green light" (21).

Enclose numbers or letters that introduce items in a list within a sentence.

> The dictionary provides (1) pronunciation, (2) etymology, (3) past meanings, and (4) usage for almost 300,000 words.

Place commas directly *after* a set of parentheses.

> His favorite American author is Emily Dickinson (he refers to her as "my favorite recluse"), but he also appreciates Walt Whitman.

When a parenthetical sentence is not enclosed within another sentence, capitalize the first word and use end punctuation inside the closing parenthesis.

> The countess of Dia is almost forgotten today. (She was quite well known in her own time.)

When a parenthetical sentence falls within another sentence, do not capitalize the first word, and use no period.

> Uncle Henry (he is my mother's brother) has won two awards for his poetry.

54 b   Brackets

Brackets are used to enclose words that are added to or changed within direct quotations or, in certain cases, to substitute for parentheses.

Use brackets to enclose small changes that clarify the meaning of a reference or of a word or to make quoted words read correctly within the context of a sentence.

> E. B. White describes a sparrow on a spring day. "Any noon in Madison Square [in New York City], you may see one pick up a straw in his beak, and put on an air of great business, twisting his head and glancing at the sky."

Brackets are used to provide supplemental information to clarify the sentence.

E. B. White describes a spring day. "Any noon in Madison Square, you may see [a sparrow] pick up a straw in his beak, and put on an air of great business, twisting his head and glancing at the sky."

Brackets are used to change a pronoun (one) *to a more specific word* (sparrow) *since the writer has taken the sentence out of its original context.*

White concludes by noting that the bird "[hopped] three or four times and [dropped] both the straw and the incident."

Brackets indicate a change of tense from present to past to fit the writer's sentence grammatically.

Use the Latin word *sic* ("thus") within brackets to indicate that an error in quoted material was present in the original.

In its statement, the commission said its new health insurance program "will not effect [*sic*] the quality of medical care for county employees."

Use brackets within parentheses to avoid double parentheses.

Theodore Bernstein explains that a person who feels sick is nauseated: "A person who feels sick is not *nauseous* any more than a person who has been poisoned is *poisonous*" (*Dos, Don'ts and Maybes of English Usage* [New York: *Times,* 1977]).

Parentheses, Commas, or Dashes?

Parentheses, commas, or dashes can set off nonessential material within a sentence. Which you use depends on how far you wish to remove the information from central attention. In many cases, the choice amounts to a writer's judgment call.

■ Use commas when the material being set off is closely related in meaning to the rest of the sentence.

A dusty plow, the kind the early Amish settlers used, hung on the wall of the old barn.

Dashes would also work well with this example.

■ Use parentheses when the material being set off is not closely related and when you want to de-emphasize it.

Two young boys found an old plow (perhaps as old as the first Amish settlement) hidden in an unused corner of the barn.

Dashes or commas would also work well with this example.

■ Use dashes when the material being set off is not closely related to the main sentence and you want to emphasize it. (See 55a.)

The old plow—the one his great-grandfather had used—was still in good working order.

Use brackets when you change the capitalization to lowercase (or vice versa) from a quotation to fit correctly into your sentences.

When Henry David Thoreau said that "[t]he mass of men lead lives of quiet desperation," he actually knew little about the conditions under which most Americans lived.

Use brackets with ellipsis points to show the omission of an entire line or lines in quoted poetry (see 55b).

chapter **55** *Dashes, Slashes, and Ellipsis Points*

D ashes, slashes, and ellipses provide ways of representing breaks, pauses, and omissions within prose sentences or poetic verses.

55 a Dashes

Dashes set off explanations, definitions, examples, appositives, and other supplementary information as well as interruptions and pauses in speech. In contrast to parentheses, they call attention to the material they set off and thus emphasize contrasts.

Dashes set off explanations, definitions, examples, or appositives within and at the end of sentences.

True democrats—small "d" democrats—believe in majority rule.

We did not notice the rain—it began so softly.

Dashes emphasize contrasts.

I haven't read many novels by European writers—not to mention those by Asian or African writers.

Dashes indicate a pause, interruption, or abrupt shift in thought.

"It's exciting to see an eagle—there's one now!"

Dashes with Other Punctuation

Do not capitalize the first word of a sentence enclosed by dashes within another sentence. If the enclosed sentence is a question or an exclamation, use a question mark or an exclamation point at the end.

> The twenty-first century is here—who would have thought so little would be changed?

> The twenty-first century—and what a century it promises to be!—is here.

Do not use commas or periods immediately before or after a dash.

Dashes are especially flexible punctuation marks, capable of substituting for periods and semicolons as well as commas and parentheses in fast, informal writing. But since informality is sometimes frowned upon in academic writing, use them judiciously.

55 b   Ellipsis points

Ellipsis points are three periods, each preceded and followed by a space. They are used to mark the deliberate omission of words or sentences from direct quotations.

Use ellipsis points to indicate an omission within a sentence.

> In *Drawing on the Right Side of the Brain,* Betty Edwards tells the reader, "You may feel that . . . it's the drawing that is hard."

If you are omitting the end of a sentence, use a period or other end punctuation before an ellipsis. Do not insert a space between the last word before the omission and the period.

> Edwards says, "Drawing is not really very hard. . . . You may not believe me at this moment."

Use a whole line of spaced ellipsis points when you omit a line or more of poetry. Note the use of brackets.

> She walks in beauty, like the night
> [. . . . .]
> And all that's best of dark and bright
> Meet in her aspect and her eyes.

Use ellipsis points to indicate a pause or interruption in dialogue.

> "The panther tracks come from that direction . . . but where do they go after that?" he wondered.

55 c   Slashes

The slash (/) is used to separate lines of poetry quoted in text, to indicate alternative choices, and to separate figures in certain situations.

Use a slash, preceded and followed by a space, to mark the end of a line of poetry incorporated in text.

> Shakespeare opens "The Passionate Pilgrim" with a seeming paradox: "When my love swears that she is made of truth, / I do believe her, though I know she lies."

Use a slash with no space before or after to separate alternatives.

> an either/or situation   a pass/fail grading system

Use a slash to separate month, day, and year in a date and to separate numerator and denominator in a fraction.

> 7/16/04   2/3

English spelling sometimes seems to defy reason. As the language has borrowed and absorbed words from other languages, it has assumed or adapted the spellings of the originals. Thus, pronunciation is often not a good key to spelling. The same sound may be represented in different letter combinations—such as with the long *e* sound in *meet, seat, concrete, petite, conceit,* and *piece.* Conversely, the same letter or letter combination can represent different sounds—such as the *a*'s in *amaze,* the *g*'s in *gorgeous,* and the *ough* in *tough, though,* and *through.*

56 a Commonly confused words

Homonyms

Homonyms are words with the same sound but different meanings: *great/grate, fair/fare.* Be especially careful when spelling similar-sounding words. It is particularly easy to confuse contractions with their homonyms—*it's* for *its* and *their* for *there* or *they're.*

Similar Spellings

Words with similar pronunciations or spellings are easy to confuse.

advice (noun)	loss (noun)
advise (verb)	lose (verb)
breath (noun)	personal (pertaining to a person)
breathe (verb)	personnel (employees; staff)
chose (past tense)	perspective (angle of view)
choose (present tense)	prospective (in the future)
device (noun)	prophecy (noun)
devise (verb)	prophesy (verb)
human (of people)	
humane (merciful)	

Homonyms and Similar-Sounding Words

accept (receive)
except (leave out)

access (approach)
excess (too much)

adapt (change)
adopt (choose)

affect (influence)
effect (result; bring about)

allot (assign, distribute)
a lot (a large amount)

allude (suggest)
elude (escape)

allusion (suggestion)
illusion (deception)

already (previously)
all ready (completely prepared)

altar (church table)
alter (change)

altogether (entirely)
all together (all in one place)

always (at all times)
all ways (all methods)

ascent (climb)
assent (agree)

assure (convince)
ensure (make certain)
insure (indemnify)

bare (uncovered)
bear (carry; the animal)

bazaar (market)
bizarre (weird)

birth (childbearing)
berth (place of rest)

board (plank; food)
bored (drilled; uninterested)

born (given birth to)
borne (carried)

break (smash, split)
brake (stopping device)

canvas (fabric)
canvass (examine)

capital (city; wealth)
capitol (building)

censor (prohibit)
censure (blame)
sensor (measuring device)

cite (mention)
site (place)
sight (vision)

coarse (rough)
course (way, path)

complement (make complete)
compliment (praise)

conscience (moral sense)
conscious (aware)

council (committee)
counsel (advice; adviser)

cursor (computer marker)
curser (swearer)

dairy (milk-producing farm)
diary (daily book)

dessert (sweet food)
desert (dry land)

dissent (disagreement)
descent (movement downward)

dual (having two parts)
duel (fight between two people)

dye (color)
die (perish)

elicit (draw forth)
illicit (improper)

eminent (noteworthy)
imminent (impending)

everyday (ordinary)
every day (each day)

exercise (activity)
exorcise (drive out)

fair (just; average; bazaar)
fare (food; fee)

faze (disturb)
phase (stage)

formerly (at an earlier time)
formally (according to a pattern)

forth (forward)
fourth (follows *third*)

forward (to the front)
foreword (preface)

gorilla (ape)
guerrilla (fighter)

hear (perceive)
here (in this place)

heard (perceived)
herd (group of animals)

heroin (drug)
heroine (principal female character)

hole (opening)
whole (entire)

holy (sacred)
wholly (entirely)

immigrate (come in)
emigrate (leave)

its (possessive of *it*)
it's (contraction of *it is*)

know (be aware)
no (negative, not yes)

lead (metal)
led (guided)

lesson (instruction)
lessen (reduce)

lightning (electric flash)
lightening (making less heavy)

maybe (perhaps)
may be (could be)

meat (food)
meet (encounter)

miner (excavator)
minor (person under a given age)

pair (two)
pear (fruit)
pare (peel; reduce)

passed (went by)
past (an earlier time)

peace (absence of war)
piece (part, portion)

peer (look; equal)
pier (pillar)

plain (simple; flat land)
plane (flat surface; smooth off; airplane)

pray (ask, implore)
prey (hunt down; what is hunted)

principle (rule)
principal (chief, chief person; sum of money)

quiet (silent)
quite (really, positively, very much)

rain (precipitation)
reign (rule)

right (proper; entitlement)
rite (ritual)

road (path)
rode (past tense of *ride*)

scene (setting, stage setting)
seen (perceived)

sense (perception)
since (from that time)

shone (past tense of *shine*)
shown (displayed)

sometime (at some time)
some time (an amount of time)

stationary (not moving)
stationery (writing paper)

straight (not curved)
strait (narrow place)

tack (angle of approach)
tact (sensitivity, diplomacy)

taut (tight)
taught (past tense of *teach*)

than (word of comparison)
then (at that time)

their (possessive of *them*)
there (in that place)
they're (contraction of *they are*)

threw (past tense of *throw*)
through (by way of)

to (in the direction of)
too (also)
two (the number)

waist (middle of the torso)
waste (squander)

weak (feeble)
week (seven days)

wear (carry on the body)
where (in what place)

weather (atmospheric conditions)
whether (if, in case)

which (what one)
witch (sorceress)

whose (possessive of *who*)
who's (contraction of *who is*)

write (inscribe, record)
wright (builder)
right (correct)

your (possessive of *you*)
you're (contraction of *you are*)
yore (long ago)

ESL *American versus British Spellings*

Use American spellings rather than British ones: *center*, not *centre*; *labor*, not *labour*.
If you are accustomed to British spellings, notice American variants as you read U.S. publications, and keep a list.

56 b   Spelling rules

The *ie/ei* Rule and Its Exceptions

The familiar rule that "*i* comes before *e* except after *c,* or when sounded like *ay* as in *neighbor* and *weigh*" holds true in most cases.

i **before *e*:** belief, field, friend, piece, priest

ei **after *c*:** ceiling, conceive, deceit, deceive, receipt

ei **sounding like "ay":** eight, feign, freight, sleigh

Exceptions

ie **after *c*:** ancient, conscience, science, species

ei **not after *c*:** caffeine, counterfeit, either, feisty, foreign, forfeit, height, leisure, neither, seize, weird

Spelling Tips

Misspellings can undermine your credibility. In some cases, a reader might misunderstand you.

- **Always** consult a dictionary or source materials when in doubt about spelling.

- **Note the etymology**—the origin and the usage history—of an unfamiliar word. This information will help you understand why a word is spelled in a particular way and help you remember.

- **Keep a list** in a notebook, journal, or computer of difficult words you encounter.

- **Use the spelling checker** on your word-processing program. It locates many misspellings, duplicated words, and transposed or dropped letters.

- **Don't trust a spell-checking program.** If you use a spelling checker, don't automatically accept its suggestions; make your own decisions. After spell checking, proofread carefully, because these programs only catch misspellings, not dropped words or wrong words. If you confuse *to, too,* and *two* or *its* and *it's,* the spelling checker won't notice because it can't recognize the context in which the word is used. That's up to you.

Spelling Rules for Suffixes

A suffix is a letter or a group of letters added to the end of a word that changes its meaning and sometimes its spelling.

The Suffixes -*cede,* -*ceed,* and -*sede*

The syllables -*cede,* -*ceed,* and -*sede* sound alike and are often confused.

-*cede* (most common): concede, intercede, precede

-*ceed:* exceed, proceed, succeed

-*sede* (appears in only one word): supersede

Suffixes after Words Ending in *y*

If the letter before the final *y* is a consonant, change the *y* to *i* before adding the suffix unless the suffix begins with *i.*

friendly, friendlier   happy, happily   apply, applying

Exceptions: dryly, shyly, wryly.
Keep the *y* if the letter before the *y* is a vowel.

convey, conveyed   annoy, annoyed   pay, payment

Suffixes after Words Ending in *e*

When the suffix begins with a consonant, keep the final *e* before the suffix.

sure, surely   polite, politeness   hate, hateful

Exceptions: acknowledgment, argument, judgment, truly, wholly, awful, ninth.

Pronunciation and Spelling

If you spell some words exactly as you pronounce them, you will probably misspell them. As you edit, try to pronounce each word in your mind the way it is spelled, not the way you normally say it. The following words can be troublesome.

accidentally	literature	recognize
arctic	mathematics	relevant
arithmetic	memento	roommate
athlete	mischievous	sandwich
candidate	nuclear	similar
congratulations	possibly	surprise
environment	prejudice (noun)	temperature
extraordinary	prejudiced (adjective)	tentative
February	probably	usually
interference	pronunciation	veteran
laboratory	quantity	Wednesday
library	realtor	wintry

Suffixes after Words Ending in a Consonant

When adding a suffix to a word ending in a consonant, do not change the spelling, even if a double consonant results.

benefit, benefited   girl, girllike   fuel, fueling

Final -*ly* or -*ally*

The suffixes -*ly* and -*ally* turn nouns into adjectives or adjectives into adverbs.

Add -*ly* to words that do not end in -*ic:* absolutely, really.

Add -*ally* to words that end in -*ic:* basically, automatically.

Spelling Rules for Plurals

Most English nouns are made plural by adding -*s.* The following are exceptions to this rule.

Nouns Ending in *ch, s, sh,* or *x*

Add -*es* to form the plural of most nouns ending in *ch, s, sh,* or *x:*

church, churches   glass, glasses   box, boxes

Nouns Ending in *y*

Add -*s* to form the plural of nouns ending in *y* if the letter before the *y* is a vowel. Change the *y* to *i* and add -*es* if the letter before the *y* is a consonant.

day, days   alloy, alloys   melody, melodies

Nouns Ending in *o*

Add -*s* to form the plural of most nouns ending in *o.*

video, videos   trio, trios   inferno, infernos

For a few nouns that end in an *o* preceded by a consonant, form the plural by adding -*es.*

hero, heroes   potato, potatoes

For other nouns that end in *o,* the plural can be formed either way.

zero, zeros, zeroes   tornado, tornados, tornadoes

Nouns Ending in *f* and *fe*

Change the *f* to *v* and add *-es* to form the plural of some nouns ending in *f*.

leaf, leaves   self, selves   half, halves

Add *-s* to form the plural of other nouns ending in *f*.

brief, briefs   belief, beliefs   proof, proofs

For some but not all nouns ending in *fe,* change the *f* to *v* before adding *-s*.

wife, wives   knife, knives   safe, safes

Irregular and Unusual Plural Forms

A few nouns form plurals without adding *-s* or *-es*.

woman, women   man, men   goose, geese
child, children   foot, feet   mouse, mice

A few words have the same form for singular and plural.

moose, moose   sheep, sheep   series, series

Plurals of Proper Nouns

Add *-s* to form the plural of most proper nouns.

the Chungs   the Kennedys   several Jennifers

Add *-es* when the plural ending is pronounced as a separate syllable.

the Bushes   the Lopezes   the Joneses

Plurals of Compound Nouns

When a compound noun is written as one word, make only the last part of the compound plural: *newspapers, notebooks.*

When a compound noun is written as separate words or hyphenated, make the word plural that expresses the main idea, usually a noun: *attorneys general, brothers-in-law, bath towels.*

apital letters mark the beginning of sentences and the first letters of names, titles, and certain other words. The pronoun *I* (*I will, I'm, I'd*) and the interjection *O* (*O best beloved* and *forgive us, O Lord*) are also capitalized.

57 a First word of a sentence

Use a capital letter at the beginning of a sentence or an intentional sentence fragment. Like this.

Capitalization is optional in a series of questions, but be consistent.

What was the occasion? A holiday? A birthday?

57 b Quotations and lines of poetry

Capitalize the first word of a quoted sentence.

"We'd like to talk to you," she said.

Do not capitalize the first word of the continuation of a quotation that is interrupted.

"Unfortunately," he said, "we don't sell coffee."

When you change the capitalization from a source to fit your sentences, enclose such changes in square brackets. (See 54b.)

When quoting poetry, always follow the capitalization of the original.

Frost's poem opens formally: "Whose woods these are, I think I know. / His house is in the village, though."

Lucille Clifton's opens informally: "boys / i don't promise you nothing. . . ."

57 c Proper nouns

Capitalize the names of particular persons, places, or things.

Mercedes Benz   Persian Gulf   Gulf of Mexico

Do not capitalize the articles, conjunctions, or prepositions that appear within such names.

457

Individual People and Animals

Capitalize the names and nicknames of individual people and animals.

Carmelo Anthony   Buffalo Bill   Smarty Jones

Capitalize words describing family members when they are used as names

Mother   Aunt Carol

but not when used as common nouns.

my mother   his aunt Carol

Religions and Their Members, Deities, and Sacred Texts

Capitalize the names of religions, members of a religion, religious sects, deities, and sacred texts.

Judaism, Jews   Protestant

Allah   the Bible

Nationalities, Ethnic Groups, and Languages

Capitalize the names of nationalities, ethnic groups, and languages.

English   French   African American

Slavic   Hindustani   Caucasian

Titles

Capitalize formal and courtesy titles and their abbreviations when they are used before a name and not set off by commas.

Gen. George S. Patton,   Professor Cox,   Ms. Wu,   President Lincoln

But the vice president of the United States, Dick Cheney, . . .

Months, Days of the Week, and Holidays

Capitalize the names of months, days of the week, and holidays.

August 12, 1914   Tuesday   Labor Day

Fourth of July   Thanksgiving

Do not capitalize numbers written out or the names of seasons.

the twentieth of April   spring

Geographic Names, Place Names, and Directions

Capitalize the names of cities, states, countries, provinces, regions, bodies of water, and other geographic features.

Little Rock, Arkansas   Mexico   Quebec   the Midwest

the Western Hemisphere   Lake Erie   the Grand Canyon

Capitalize common nouns like *river, street,* and *square* when they are part of a place name.

Rodeo Drive   Hudson River   Washington Square

Do not capitalize common nouns when two or more proper nouns precede them.

the Tigris and Euphrates rivers   Haight and Ashbury streets

Capitalize direction words when they indicate regions, but not when they indicate compass directions.

the West, westerly   the Southwest, toward the south

Institutions, Organizations, and Businesses

Capitalize the names of organizations and businesses.

Oberlin College   Federal Reserve Bank of New York

Nashville Chamber of Commerce

Historical Documents, Events, Periods, and Movements

Capitalize the names of historical documents and well-known events or periods.

the Constitution   the Bill of Rights   the French Revolution

the Civil War   the Stone Age

Movements in Art, Music, Literature, and Philosophy

Capitalize the names of historical periods and artistic or aesthetic movements.

the Renaissance	Constructionist painters	Romantic poets
the Baroque	the Age of Enlightenment	Logical Positivism

Ships, Aircraft, Spacecraft, and Trains

Capitalize the names of individual vehicles.

Air Force One   the *Titanic*   *Voyager*

the *City of New Orleans* (train)

Derivatives of Proper Nouns

Capitalize words derived from proper nouns.

Newtonian physics   Marxist economics   Texans

Do not capitalize words derived from proper nouns that have taken generic and independent meanings.

french fries   herculean   quixotic

57 d   Titles

Capitalize the first word, the last word, and all other words except articles, conjunctions, and prepositions in the titles and subtitles of books, plays, essays, stories, poems, movies, television programs, pieces of music, and works of art.

Pride and Prejudice, Beauty and the Beast, La Traviata, Guernica, The Sopranos, "Chelsea Morning"

Words joined by a hyphen are usually both capitalized, except for articles, conjunctions, and prepositions.

Jack-in-the-Box   *The One-Minute Grammarian*

In academic papers, underline or italicize published titles (books, periodicals) and put quotation marks around the titles of chapters, articles, stories, and poems within published works. (See 53c and 61a.)

Proper Nouns versus Common Nouns

Capitalize proper nouns (the names of specific people, places, or things); do not capitalize common nouns (the names of general types of people, places, or things).

English, French	history, political science
Chemistry 2	chemistry
American Literature 23	American literature
Harvard University	a university
the College of Arts and Sciences	the arts and sciences
the School of Business	a school or college
Vice President Johnson	the vice president
Professor Wieting	my professor
the Supreme Court	a court of law
Haymarket Square	a town square
Representative Smith	a legislator
California	a state
October	a month
the Northwest	north, west
the Hebrew God	a god
Lake Champlain	a lake
Uncle John	an uncle

57 e   Capitalization and punctuation

Colons

Capitalization is optional after a colon that joins two independent clauses when the second clause contains the main point of the sentence.

The senators' resolve failed them: the health-care bill was dead for another decade.

Use capitals after a colon that introduces a numbered list of complete sentences.

His philosophy can be reduced to three basic rules: (1) Think for yourself. (2) Take care of your body. (3) Never hurt anyone.

Parentheses and Dashes

Capitalize the first word of a complete sentence set off by parentheses or dashes when it stands alone.

In 1972, Congress attacked sex discrimination in sports by passing Title IX. (The changes made in 1974 are called the Bayh amendments.)

Do not capitalize the first word of a complete sentence set off by parentheses or dashes when it falls within another sentence.

On many campuses Title IX has increased the number of competitive sports offered to women—even opponents agree—but its effect on men's sports is difficult to assess.

chapter 58 | *Hyphens*

Hyphens link words or parts of words to create new meanings. They can also separate words into parts to clarify meaning. In addition, hyphens have many conventional uses in numbers, fractions, and units of measure.

58 a   At the ends of lines

Use a hyphen to break words that are too long to fit at the end of a line. The following guidelines will help you determine how to hyphenate words.

Divide words only between pronounced syllables. Words of only one pronounced syllable—*eighth, through, dreamed, urged*—cannot be divided without suggesting an incorrect pronunciation.

Divide at prefixes or suffixes rather than dividing base words. Try to leave both parts of a word recognizable: not *an-tibody* but *anti-body,* not *ea-gerness* but *eager-ness.*

Don't leave just one letter at the end of a line or carry over only one or two letters to the next line.

A word with an internal double letter is usually divided between those letters (*syl-la-ble, wil-low*), but keep double letters together if they fall at the end of a base word; divide the word before a suffix (*access-ible, assess-ment*).

58 b   After some prefixes

Use a hyphen when a prefix precedes a capitalized word or a date. The prefix itself is usually not capitalized: *anti-Castro, pre-1994*.

Use a hyphen after a prefix attached to a term of two or more words: *post-World War II, anti-labor union*.

Use a hyphen in almost all cases after the prefixes *all-, ex-* (meaning "former"), *self-*, and *quasi-*.

all-inclusive   ex-convict   self-hypnosis   quasi-judicial

To prevent misreading, hyphens are often used when a prefix ends with the same letter that begins the base word: *anti-intellectual, co-ownership*.

Use a hyphen when two prefixes apply to the same base word. Add a space after the first hyphenated prefix.

We compared the *pre-* and *post-election* analyses.

58 c   In compound words

Many compound words (closed compounds) are written as one word: *workhorse, schoolteacher*. Other compounds are written as two separate words (open compounds): *hope chest, lunch break, curtain rod*. But some compounds are hyphenated: *great-grandson, stick-in-the-mud*.

Check the dictionary to see which compound words are written as one word and which are hyphenated. If you don't find a compound there, then it is written as two words.

Hyphenate compound nouns of three or more words: *mother-in-law, jack-of-all-trades*.

Hyphenate when two or more modifiers act as a single adjective before a noun: *late-night party, loose-leaf notebook*.

Do not hyphenate well-known compound terms: *post office box, high school student*.

Do not hyphenate words ending in *-ly: a highly paid worker*.

58 d   Numbers, fractions, and units of measure

Hyphenate two-word numbers from *twenty-one* to *ninety-nine*. Do not hyphenate before or after the words *hundred, thousand,* or *million*.

fifty-seven   twenty-two thousand

two hundred fifty-seven   six hundred twenty thousand

Hyphenate between the numerator and denominator of a spelled-out fraction unless one of them is already hyphenated.

one-half   two-thirds   twenty-one fiftieths

Hyphenate when *feet, inches, miles, pounds, yards* are used as modifiers.

The dump truck has a *nine-cubic-yard* bed.

Do not hyphenate when the unit of measure is used as a noun.

The dump truck holds *nine cubic yards* of manure.

Hyphenate ages of the form *year-old:*

my six-year-old nephew   my nephew, a six-year-old

chapter 59 *Numbers*

When you use numbers to describe data, follow the conventions of the discipline in which you are writing. In technical writing or any piece that relies heavily on numbers, figures are more common. In writing about literature, more numbers are spelled out. Here are some guidelines.

59 a   Figures or spelled-out numbers?

In writing about literature or any topic that uses few numbers:

- Spell out numbers of one hundred or less and numbers that can be expressed in one or two words: *thirty students, three-fourths of the forest;* but *517 students, 52,331 trees.*

- Use a combination of words and figures for round numbers over one million: *The U.S. population exceeds 250 million.*

- Spell out any number that begins a sentence: *Five students attended the concert.*

- Whenever you present numbers that readers must compare, treat them consistently: *Last year 87 cats and 114 dogs were adopted.*

- Spell out simple fractions: *Two-thirds of the members have paid their dues.*

In technical writing, use figures for numbers over nine, for fractions and with all units of measure.

The researchers identified 14 new compounds.

½ liter of water

3 pounds per square inch

---

59 b   Conventional uses of numbers

In all types of writing, convention requires the use of figures in certain situations.

Dates
11 April 1999   July 16, 1999   the year 1616

Addresses
2551 Polk St., Apt. 3
San Francisco, CA 94109

With Abbreviations and Symbols
3500 rpm   37°C
65 mph $62.23
74%   53¢

If you spell out numbers, also spell out *percent, dollars,* and *cents: seventy-four percent, fifty cents, five dollars.*

Time
12:15   23:30 hours

Numbers used with *o'clock, past, to, till,* and *until* are generally written out as words.

seven o'clock   twenty past one

Decimals
2.7 seconds   35.4 miles

Cross-references and Citations
Chapter 12   line 25   act 3, scene 2

Singular and Plural Forms of Numbers

A number—*dozens, hundreds, thousands*—used in a general sense rather than to indicate an exact count should be plural.

The news reported only a few protesters, but we saw *hundreds*.

You may need to add the word *of*.

Dozens of ducks arrived today, landing on the lake in *twos* and *threes*.

When *hundred, dozen,* or *million* is preceded by another number, use the singular, and do not use *of*.

There were approximately *two hundred* protesters.

At least *three dozen* geese flew over the lake today.

When unit of measure, of money, or of time is used before a noun, use the singular.

It was a *three-hour* movie.

chapter 60 *Abbreviations*

A bbreviations are used in tables, footnotes, endnotes, and bibliographies to help readers proceed through material quickly. The following abbreviations are acceptable in conventional and academic writing; scientific and technical writing may differ.

60 a Titles and degrees

Abbreviate titles of address when they precede a full name, except for *president* and *mayor,* which are never abbreviated.

Mr. Samuel Taylor   Dr. Ellen Hunter

St. Francis of Assisi   Prof. Ahmed Greenberg

Titles and degrees that follow a name, such as *Esq., MD, LLD, JD,* and *PhD, should be abbreviated.* Use either a title (such as *Dr.*) or a degree (such as *MD*), but not both.

Dr. Randall Marshall   Randall Marshall, MD

Abbreviate generational titles such as *Jr.* and *Sr.* In a sentence, they are set off by commas.

He talked to Thomas Burke, Jr., and to Karen Burke.

Do not abbreviate or capitalize titles that are not used with a proper name: *assistant professor of chemistry, doctor of internal medicine.*

Except for *Mr., Ms., Mrs.,* and *Dr.,* do not abbreviate titles that appear before a surname (last name) alone: *Professor Greenberg, Senator Obama, President Smith.*

60 b With numbers

Time

Use *a.m.* ("ante meridiem") or *p.m.* ("post meridiem") for specific times of day. You may also write A.M. or P.M., since capitalization is optional, but be consistent within one document.

3:45 p.m. (or P.M.)   12 noon

Year

Use BC ("before Christ") and AD ("anno Domini") for calendar years. Only AD precedes the year. To avoid religious reference, many writers substitute BCE ("before the Common Era") and CE ("Common Era").

425 BC (or 425 BCE)   AD 1215 (or 1215 CE)

60 c Degrees, numbers, and units of measure

Use *F* for degrees Fahrenheit and *C* for degrees Celsius (metric system measurement) when writing out temperatures. Use *no.* or *No.* for *number.* Use *mph* for *miles per hour, mpg* for *miles per gallon,* and *rpm* for *revolutions per minute.*

Whose address is No. 10 Downing Street?

The speed limit is 65 mph on the interstate.

In scientific and technical writing, abbreviate units of measure, usually without periods unless confusion is possible, as with *in.* for inches.

He added 200 mg of sodium cyanate to the beaker.

60 d   Symbols

Use symbols for degree (°), dollar ($), and percent (%) when they are used with figures. Spell out symbols when the figures are also spelled out. Be consistent.

It was 30°C and sunny 75% of the time.

It was thirty degrees and sunny.

60 e   Geographic names

Abbreviate geographic names when addressing mail. Use the U.S. Postal Service state abbreviations.

100 W. Glengarry Ave.
Birmingham, MI 48009

Do not abbreviate anything except the state name when presenting a full address in text. Do not abbreviate place names when you give a general address.

He lived at 11 West Sixth Street, Harrisburg, PA 17102.

She was born in Madison, Wisconsin.

60 f   Common Latin abbreviations

Use common Latin abbreviations in documentation and notes, but write out their English equivalents in your text.

ABBREVIATION	LATIN	EQUIVALENT
c. *or* ca.	*circa*	about
cf.	*confer*	compare
e.g.	*exempli gratia*	for example
et al.	*et alii*	and others
etc.	*et cetera*	and so forth
i.e.	*id est*	that is
NB	*nota bene*	note well

60 g   Acronyms and initials

An acronym is a word made up of initials and pronounced as a word—*NATO* for *North Atlantic Treaty Organization,* for example. Acronyms are written with no periods and no spaces between the letters.

Most initial abbreviations, such as *CD* for *compact disc* or *JFK* for *John F. Kennedy,* are written with neither periods nor spaces between the letters. Some abbreviations for countries do use periods but no spaces: *U.S., U.K.*

Make sure that acronyms and initial abbreviations are familiar to your readers. If you have any doubts, give the full term the first time, followed by the abbreviation or acronym in parentheses.

> Commerce is governed by a set of treaties called the General Agreement on Tariffs and Trade (GATT).

> The National Collegiate Athletic Association (NCAA) has posted new rules.

When you refer to the same organization a second time in your text, use the abbreviated version unless the initial reference is many pages earlier.

> Some have argued that the NCAA had no need for new rules.

Avoid Abbreviations in Formal Writing

In the text of a paper, spell out words you might abbreviate when writing informally. (Abbreviations are recommended for documentation references and notes in research papers; see Chapters 19–23.)

- Days of the week and months: *Tuesday,* not *Tues.; December,* not *Dec.*
- Text divisions: *page,* not *p.; Chapter,* not *Ch.* or *Chap.*
- Academic disciplines: *sociology,* not *soc; political science,* not *poly sci.*
- Academic institutions: *College of Arts and Sciences,* not *A&S*
- Academic titles: *professor,* not *prof.*
- Personal names (unless the person formally uses a shortened form): *Robert,* not *Bob; Susan,* not *Sue*
- Holidays: *Christmas,* not *Xmas*
- Units of measurement are abbreviated when used with figures in scientific and technical references: *30 ml, 2.5 kg.* In nontechnical text, spell out units of measurement: *six miles, three quarts.*
- Business names: *Company,* not *Co.; Corporation,* not *Corp.* Do use abbreviations that are part of a company's formal name: *Johnson Bros. Trucking.* And *Inc.* is acceptable as part of a business name: *Acme Products, Inc.*

To distinguish certain words in your text, use the slanted type called *italics*. In typewritten papers, or if your word processor produces italic type that is not easily distinguished from Roman (standard, nonslanted) type, <u>underlining</u> can be used as an alternative to italics. Check to see whether your instructor has a preference.

61 a For titles of major works

Use italics (or underlining) for the titles of longer published works.

- Books: *The Cat in the Hat, Moby Dick, Principles of Geology*
- Plays: *Hamlet, The Zoo Story*
- Operas and other long musical works: *La Boheme,* Beethoven's *Seventh Symphony*
- Films: *The Godfather, Star Wars*
- Recordings: *Tapestry*
- Newspapers: the *New York Times*
- Magazines: *The New Yorker, Time, Newsweek*
- Television and radio series: *ER, Friends, Prairie Home Companion*
- Long poems considered to be independent works: *Leaves of Grass, The Waste Land*
- Works of art: *The Last Supper, Nude Descending a Staircase, Venus de Milo*
- Web sites and publications: *Amazon.com, Encyclopaedia Britannica Online*
- Chapters, stories, poems, songs within longer published works use quotation marks.

  "Song of the Open Road" from *Leaves of Grass*

  "Homer Meets Godzilla," episode of *The Simpsons*

Do not use italics, underlining, or quotation marks for the titles of sacred works, parts of sacred works, ancient manuscripts, and public documents.

the Bible   the Bill of Rights   the Civil Rights Act

61 b   For individual trains, ships, and planes

Use italics (or underlining) for the official names of individual trains, ships, airplanes, and spacecraft.

City of New Orleans (train)   *Titanic* (ship)   *Spirit of St. Louis* (airplane)

61 c   For foreign words

Many words in English have been absorbed by the language and do not require italics. Recently borrowed foreign words do.

My favorite dish is lasagne, but try the *pasticcio di faglioni.*

Use italics for the Latin names of plants and animals.

Homo erectus is an ancestor of modern humans.

61 d   For words as words and for letters as symbols

Use italics for words used as words and for letters used as symbols in mathematics and other disciplines.

the term *liberal*   to substitute *y* for *u*

61 e   For emphasis

Use italics (or underlining) to indicate that a certain word or words should receive special attention or emphasis.

We all hear music in our heads, but how is music processed by the *brain?*

Be careful not to overuse italics for emphasis.

This glossary provides advice about word choices that are considered inappropriate for academic writing or that are considered incorrect. For example, *discreet* means "prudent" but *discrete* means "separate"—no one who knows that these are two different words would suggest that they are interchangeable. For further guidance, consult a more comprehensive reference such as *Choose the Right Word* by S. I. Hayakawa [New York: Collins, 1994] or *Merriam-Webster's Dictionary of English Usage* [Springfield, MA: Merriam-Webster, 1994].

Some of the usages described as incorrect or inappropriate in this glossary are common outside academic writing. For example, nonstandard usages (such as *anyways* instead of the standard *anyway*) reflect the speech patterns of particular communities but do not follow the conventions of the dominant American dialect. Colloquial usages (such as *flunk* meaning "to fail" or *awfully* meaning "very") are often heard in speech but are usually considered inappropriate for academic writing. Informal usages (such as using *can* and *may* interchangeably) may be acceptable in some papers but not in formal research or argument essays. Except as noted, this glossary recommends usage as found in formal academic writing.

a, an Use *a* before words that begin with a consonant sound (*a boy, a history book, a shining star*), even if the first letter of the word is a vowel (*a useful lesson*). Use *an* before words that begin with a vowel sound (*an antelope, an umbrella*).

accept, except *Accept* is a verb meaning "to receive" or "to approve" (*I accept your offer*). *Except* is a verb meaning "to leave out" or "to exclude" (*He excepted all vegetables from his list of favorite foods*) or a preposition meaning "excluding" (*He eats everything except vegetables*).

adapt, adopt *Adapt* means "to adjust" or "to accommodate"; it is usually followed by *to* (*It is sometimes hard to adapt to college life*). *Adopt* means "to take into a relationship" (*They considered adopting a child*) or "to take and use as one's own" (*I have adopted my roommate's habits*).

advice, advise *Advice* is a noun meaning "recommendation"; *advise* is a verb meaning "to give advice to" (*I advise you to take my advice*).

affect, effect *Affect* as a verb means "to influence" or "to produce an effect" (*That movie affected me deeply*). In psychology, *affect* as a noun means "appearance" or "outward display of emotion." *Effect* is a noun meaning "result," "consequence," or "outcome" (*That movie had a profound effect on me*); it is also sometimes used as a verb meaning "to bring about" (*Dr. Johnson effected important changes as president*).

ain't *Ain't* is a nonstandard (colloquial) contraction for *am not, is not, are not, have not,* or *has not.* Avoid except in reproducing dialogue.

all ready, already *All ready* means "fully prepared" (*They were all ready to leave*). *Already* means "previously" (*They had already left*).

all right, alright Spell as two words. The one-word spelling is widely considered incorrect.

all together, altogether *All together* means "all gathered in one place" (*The animals were all together in the ark*). *Altogether* means "thoroughly" or "entirely" (*The ark was altogether too full of animals*).

allude, elude *Allude* is a verb meaning "to refer (to something) indirectly"; it is followed by *to* (*Derek alluded to a rodent infestation*). *Elude* is a verb meaning "to escape" or "to avoid" (*The mice eluded Derek at every turn*).

allusion, illusion *Allusion* means "an indirect reference" or "the act of alluding to, or hinting at, something" (*The phrase "I have a dream" is often an allusion to Dr. Martin Luther King, Jr.*). *Illusion* is a noun meaning "misleading image" or "misapprehension" (*Mr. Hodges created an optical illusion with two lines*).

a lot Avoid in formal writing (*The students had many* [not *a lot of*] *opportunities*).

a.m., p.m. or A.M., P.M. Use only with numerals (6:30 p.m.). Do not use substitutes for *morning, afternoon, evening,* or *night* or with *o'clock*.

among, between Use *among* to signify three or more choices (*Competition among the oil companies is intense*). *Between* means only two choices (*He divided the cake between the twins*).

amount, number Use *amount* to refer to quantities that cannot be counted (*Fixing up the abandoned farmhouse took a great amount of work*). Use *number* for quantities that can be counted (*A large number of volunteers helped*).

an See *a, an*.

and/or *And/or* is used in technical and legal writing to connect two terms when either one or both apply (*Purchasers must select type and/or size*). When possible, avoid and/or by using the construction "A or B or both" (*Students may select chemistry or physics or both*).

anxious, eager *Anxious* means "worried" or "uneasy" (*Lynn is anxious about her mother's surgery*). Do not confuse with *eager,* which means "enthusiastic" or "impatient" (*I am eager* [not *anxious*] *to leave*).

anywhere Use *anywhere,* not *anyplace* (*You may sit anywhere you choose*).

as, as if, like In comparisons, use *like* only as a preposition followed by a noun (*Ken, like his brother, prefers to sleep late*). Do not use *like* as a conjunction to link two clauses. Use *as* or *as if* (*Ken sleeps late just as* [not *like*] *Carl does. Anne talks as if* [not *like*] *she has read every book by Ernest Hemingway*).

assure, ensure, insure *Assure* is a verb whose meaning is similar to "reassure" (*The lawyer assured her client that the case was solid*). *Ensure* and *insure* both mean "to make sure, certain, or safe," but *insure* generally refers to finance (*John hoped his college degree would ensure his future. He knew he would need to insure his house*).

at present, presently *At present* means "now, at this time." *Presently* means "soon."

awful, awfully   *Awful* is an adjective meaning "inspiring awe." In formal writing, do not use it to mean "disagreeable" or "objectionable." Similarly, the adverb *awfully* means "in an awe-inspiring way"; do not use it in the colloquial sense of "very."

bad, badly   *Bad* is an adjective, so it must modify a noun or follow a linking verb, such as *be, feel,* or *become* (*John felt bad about holding the picnic in bad weather*). *Badly* is an adverb, so it must modify a verb (*Pam played badly today*).

being as, being that   *Being as* and *being that* are nonstandard expressions for *because* or *since.* (*Because* [not *being as*] *her shoulder was injured, Anna withdrew from the tournament*).

beside, besides   *Beside* means "by the side of" or "next to" (*The book is beside the bed*). *Besides* means "other than" or "in addition to" (*No one besides Linda can solve this problem*).

better   The auxiliary verb phrase *had better* denotes obligation (*You had better hurry*). Do not use *better* alone.

between   See *among, between.*

biannual, biennial   Something *biannual* happens twice a year (*The biannual adjustments for daylight saving time occur in April and October*). Something *biennial* happens every two years (*The Whitney Museum opens its biennial exhibit of American art next month*).

bisect, dissect   *Bisect,* pronounced bi-sect with a long i, means to divide into two parts (*In geometry, we learned to bisect an angle*). *Dissect,* pronounced dis-sect with a short i, means to cut apart (*In biology, we had to dissect a frog*).

breath, breathe   *Breath* is a noun (*I had to stop to catch my breath*). *Breathe* is a verb (*It became difficult to breathe*).

bring, take   *Bring* describes movement from far to near; *take* describes movement away from a place (*Dr. Gavin asked us to bring our sketches to class; she said we could take them home afterward*).

busted   *Busted* is a nonstandard past tense for *burst* (*The state Senate chamber was flooded when a water line burst*). As a synonym for *arrested, busted* is also nonstandard.

cache, cachet   *Cache,* pronounced like "cash," is a French term meaning "a hidden supply or source." *Cachet,* which rhymes with "sashay," means "a hidden charm."

can, may, might   Informally, *can* and *may* are used interchangeably to indicate permission, but in formal writing, only *may* and its past tense *might* should be used this way (*May I borrow your dictionary?*). *May* also denotes possibility (*It may snow tomorrow. He said it might snow*). *Can* is used only to indicate ability (*I can see much better with glasses*).

capital, capitol   As an adjective, *capital* means "punishable by death" (*capital punishment*) or refers to uppercase letters (*A, B*). As a noun it means "accumulated wealth" (*We must invest our capital carefully*) or "a city serving as a seat of government" (*Albany is the capital of New York*). *Capitol* refers to the building in which lawmakers meet (*The civics class toured the state capitol last week*). Capitalize it when referring to a specific building: *The US House and the Senate meet in the Capitol.*

caveat *Caveat,* from the Latin phrase *caveat emptor,* or "buyer beware," means "warning" or "caution." Do not use it to mean "condition" (*He approved the purchase on the condition that* [not *with the caveat that*] *the house pass a structural inspection*).

censor, censure *Censor* means to remove material from a text or an image; *censure* means "to condemn strongly."

center, epicenter The *epicenter* is the spot on the Earth's surface directly above the site of an earthquake. Do not use *epicenter* when *center* will suffice.

center around, center on *Center around* is colloquial for *center on* (*The discussion centered on taxation*).

cite, site, sight *Cite* means "to quote for the purposes of example, authority, or proof" (*The brief cites several landmark cases*). *Site* as a noun means "place" or "scene" (*Signs of habitation were found at the site*). *Site* also can mean "to place on a site." *Sight* is a verb meaning "to see" or a noun meaning "vision."

climactic, climatic *Climactic* derives from *climax,* a moment of greatest intensity (*In the climactic scene of the play, the murderer's identity is revealed*). *Climatic* derives from *climate* (*Pollution might cause climatic changes*).

complement, compliment *Complement* as a verb means "to fill out or complete"; it is also a noun meaning "something that completes or fits with" (*The bouquet of spring flowers complemented the table setting*). *Compliment* means "to express praise or admiration" or "an expression of praise or admiration" (*Russ complimented Nancy on her choice of flowers*).

compose, comprise *Compose* means "to constitute or make up"; *comprise* means "to include or contain" (*Last year's club comprised fifteen members; only eight members compose this year's club*). Do not use *comprised of,* which makes no sense. Use *composed of* (*The club is composed of eight members*).

conscience, conscious *Conscience* refers to a sense of right and wrong (*His conscience would not allow him to lie*). *Conscious* means "alert, awake," "marked by thought or will," or "acting with critical awareness" (*He made a conscious decision to be punctual*).

continual, continuous *Continual* means "recurring" or "occurring repeatedly" (*Liz saw a doctor about her continual headaches*). *Continuous* means "uninterrupted in space, time, or sequence" (*Light refracted by raindrops forms the continuous band we call a rainbow*).

could have, must have, should have, would have Do not substitute *of* for *have.* Do not use these auxiliary verbs in both clauses of a complex sentence (*If I had* [not *could have*] *stayed longer, I would have earned more*).

council, counsel *Council* is a noun meaning "a group meeting for advice, discussion, or government" (*The council voted in favor of the plan*). As a noun, *counsel* means "advice" or "a plan of action or behavior" (*The bishop gave counsel to the young men considering the priesthood*). *Counsel* may also be used as a verb meaning "to advise" (*The priest counseled the young man*).

credible, incredible; credulous, incredulous *Credible* and *incredible* describe whether something is believable or trustworthy (*His descriptions of life at sea seem credible*). *Credulous* means "willing to believe" and carries the connotation of "too willing to believe" (*Such a charismatic leader depends on credulous followers*). *Incredulous* means "unwilling to believe" (*The claim of* *controlled, low-temperature fusion was challenged by incredulous physicists around the world).*

criteria, criterion *Criteria* is the plural of *criterion,* which means "a standard on which a judgment is based" (*Many criteria are used in selecting a president, but a candidate's hair color is not an appropriate criterion*).

data, datum *Data* is the plural of *datum,* which means "a fact" or "a result in research." Some writers now use *data* as both a singular and a plural noun; in formal usage it is still better to treat it as plural (*The data indicate that a low-fat diet may increase life expectancy*).

decent, descent, dissent *Decent* means "good, proper." *Descent* means "the act of going down, the opposite of climbing." *Dissent* means "disagreement, especially political disagreement."

defuse, diffuse *Defuse* means literally "to remove a fuse" (*They were able to defuse the controversy*). *Diffuse* means "to dilute" or "diluted, scattered" (*A diffuse sample revealed no particular pattern*).

detract, distract *Detract* means "to take away from" (*This discovery should not detract from Einstein's achievement*). *Distract* means "to divert attention from" (*We should not let the controversy distract us from our purpose*).

different from, different than *Different from* is preferred to *different than* (*Hal's taste in music is different from his wife's*). But *different than* may be used to avoid awkward constructions (*Hal's taste in music is different than* [instead of *different from what*] *it was five years ago*).

discreet, discrete *Discreet* means "prudent" or "modest" (*Most private donors were discreet about their contributions*). *Discrete* means "separate" or "distinct" (*Professor Roberts divided the course into four discrete units*).

disinterested, uninterested *Disinterested* means "unbiased" or "impartial" (*It will be difficult to find twelve disinterested jurors*). *Uninterested* means "indifferent" or "unconcerned" (*Most people were uninterested in the case until the police discovered surprising new evidence*).

doesn't, don't *Don't* is a contraction for *do not.* The contraction for *does not* is *doesn't* (*He doesn't* [not *don't*] *know what to do about it*).

effect See *affect, effect.*

elicit, illicit *Elicit* is a verb meaning "to draw forth" or "to bring out" (*The investigators could not elicit any new information*). *Illicit* is an adjective meaning "unlawful" or "not permitted" (*The investigators were looking for evidence of illicit drug sales*).

elude See *allude, elude.*

emigrate, immigrate *Emigrate* means "to leave one's country to live or reside elsewhere" (*His grandparents emigrated from Russia*). *Immigrate* means "to come into a new country to take up residence" (*His grandparents immigrated to the United States*).

eminent, imminent *Eminent* means "prominent" (*Her operation was performed by an eminent surgeon*). *Imminent* means "impending" (*The hurricane's arrival is imminent*).

ensure See *assure, ensure, insure.*

enthused, enthusiastic   Do not use *enthused,* the past tense of the verb *enthuse,* to mean *enthusiastic* (*Barb is enthusiastic* [not *enthused*] *about her music lessons*).

epicenter   See *center, epicenter.*

especially, specially   *Especially* is an adverb meaning "particularly" or "unusually" (*The weather was especially cold this winter*). *Specially* is an adverb meaning "for a special reason" or "in a unique way" (*The cake was specially prepared for Sandy's birthday*).

eventually, ultimately   Although these words are often used interchangeably, *eventually* means "at an unspecified later time" while *ultimately* means "finally" or "in the end" (*He knew that he would have to stop running eventually, but he hoped that he would ultimately win a marathon*). See also *penultimate.*

everybody, everyone, every one   *Everybody* and *everyone* refer to an unspecified person (*Everybody wins in this game*). *Every one* refers to each member of a group (*Every one of these toys must be picked up*).

except   See *accept, except.*

explicit, implicit   *Explicit* means "perfectly clear, direct, and unambiguous" (*Darrell gave me explicit directions to his house*). *Implicit* means "implied" or "revealed or expressed indirectly" (*His eagerness was implicit in his tone of voice*).

farther, further   Although these words are often used interchangeably, some writers prefer to use *farther* to refer to physical distances (*Boston is farther than I thought*) and *further* to refer to quantity, time, or degree (*We tried to progress further on our research project*).

fewer, less   Use *fewer* for items that can be counted and *less* for items that cannot be counted (*Because fewer people attended this year, we needed less food*).

finalize   Many writers avoid using *finalize* to mean "to make final." Use alternative wording (*We needed to complete* [not *finalize*] *our plans*).

first, second, third   Avoid *firstly, secondly, thirdly.*

former, latter   *Former* is used to refer to the first of two people, items, or ideas being discussed, *latter* to refer to the second (*Monet and Picasso were important painters; the former is associated with the Impressionist school, the latter with Cubism*).

further   See *farther, further.*

get   The verb *get* has many colloquial uses. In formal writing, avoid using *get* to mean "to provoke or annoy" (*He gets to me*), "to start" (*We should get going on this project*), or "to become" (*She got worried when he didn't call*). Do not use *have got to* in place of *must* (*I must* [not *have got to*] *finish by five o'clock*) or in place of *have* (*Do you have* [not *Have you got*] *a dollar for the toll?*).

goes, says   Avoid the colloquial use of *goes* for *says* (*When the coach says* [not *goes*] *"Now," everybody runs*).

good and   Avoid *good and* in place of *very* (*My shoes were very* [not *good and*] *wet after our walk*).

good, well   *Good* is an adjective; it should not be used in place of the adverb *well* in formal writing (*Mario is a good tennis player; he played well* [not *good*] *in the tournament*). In response to the question *How are you?* use *I am well* rather than *I am good*. (See 44c.)

half a, half of, a half a   For units of measure, use *a half* (*They had walked a half mile in pitch darkness*). For other quantities, use *half of, a half,* or *half of a* (*Half of the audience was not amused. Half an apple was plenty for Eve. A half ton of coal takes up a lot of room*). Avoid *a half a*.

hanged, hung   *Hanged* is the past tense and past participle of *hang* in the sense of "execute" (*Two prisoners were hanged at this spot*). *Hung* is the past tense and past participle of *hang* meaning "to suspend" or "to dangle" (*All her clothes hung neatly in the closet*).

hardly, scarcely   *Hardly* and *scarcely* are adverbs meaning "barely," "only just." Do not use double negatives, such as *can't scarcely* and *not hardly*. (*I can scarcely* [not *can't scarcely*] *keep my eyes open*).

has got, have got   See *get*.

have, of   Use *have* (not *of*) with *could, would, should,* and *might* (*We could have* [not *of*] *gone to the concert*).

he/she, s/he, his/her   When you require both female and male personal pronouns in formal writing, use *he or she* (or *she or he*) and *his or her* (or *her or his*) instead of a slash.

herself, himself, itself, myself, ourselves, themselves, yourself, yourselves   Use these pronouns only to reflect the action of a sentence back toward the subject (*He locked himself out of the apartment*) or to emphasize the subject (*I myself have no regrets*). Do not use these pronouns in place of personal pronouns such as *I, me, you, her,* or *him* (*He left an extra key with Bev and me* [not *myself*]). Do not use *hisself* for *himself*.

hopefully   *Hopefully* means "in a hopeful manner" (*The child looked hopefully out the window for her mother*). In formal writing, do not use *hopefully* to mean "I or we hope that" or "It is hoped that" (*I hope that* [not *hopefully*] *the class will prove interesting*).

hung   See *hanged, hung*.

if, whether   Use *if* to state a condition (*If it snows, I will wear my new boots*). Use *whether* (or *whether or not*) in a clause that expresses or implies an alternative (*In the morning, I will decide whether to wear my boots*).

illicit   See *elicit, illicit*.

illusion   See *allusion, illusion*.

immigrate   See *emigrate from, immigrate to*.

imminent   See *eminent, imminent*.

implicit   See *explicit, implicit*.

imply, infer   *Imply* means "to express indirectly" or "to suggest"; *infer* is a verb meaning "to conclude" or "to surmise" (*Helen implied that she had time to visit with us, but we inferred from all the work on her desk that she was really too busy*). Speakers *imply;* listeners *infer*.

in, into   Use *in* to indicate position (*The sun is low in the sky*). Use *into* to suggest motion or change of position (*The rats moved cautiously into the maze*).

The use of *into* to mean "involved in" or "interested in" is slang (*She is interested in* [not *into*] *astrology*).

incidents, incidence, instance   *Incidents* are occurrences or events; *incidence* refers to the frequency with which something occurs; an *instance* is an example (*The incidence of crime has decreased this year. For instance, our town had 30 percent fewer incidents involving armed robbery than last year*).

incredible, incredulous   See *credible, incredible*.

infer   See *imply, infer*.

ingenious, ingenuous   *Ingenious* means "resourceful" or "clever" (*Elaine came up with an ingenious plan*). *Ingenuous* means "innocent" or "simple" (*It was a surprisingly deceptive plan for such an ingenuous person*).

inside, outside   *Inside* and *outside* should not be followed by *of* (*The suspect is inside* [not *inside of*] *that building*).

insure   See *assure, ensure, insure*.

irregardless, regardless   The nonstandard *irregardless* is often mistakenly used for *regardless* (*We will have the party regardless* [not *irregardless*] *of the weather*).

is when, is where   Avoid these awkward expressions in formal writing to define terms (*Sexual harassment refers to* [not *is when someone makes*] *inappropriate sexual advances or suggestions*).

itself   See *herself, himself*.

kind of, sort of   In formal writing, avoid using the colloquial expressions *kind of* and *sort of* to mean "somewhat" or "rather" (*My paper is rather* [not *kind of*] *short; my research for it was somewhat* [not *sort of*] *rushed*).

later, latter   *Later* means "after some time"; *latter* refers to the last item in a previously mentioned series. (*Later in the evening, we were offered coffee or tea, and I chose the latter*). See also *former, latter*.

lay, lie   The verb *lay* means "to put or set down" and is followed by an object; its principal forms are *lay* or *laid*. The verb *lie* meaning "to recline" or "to rest in a horizontal position" has the principal forms *lie, lay, lain*. Do not confuse them (*I will lay out the blanket and lie down. He laid the book on the table as he lay on the bed*). (See 42c.)

lead, led   As a verb, *lead* (rhymes with seed) means "to go first" or "to direct"; as a noun, it means "front position" (*Hollis took the lead in organizing the files*). Its past tense and past participle are *led* (*The path led to the cave*). The metallic element *lead* is pronounced like *led*.

learn, teach   Students *learn*; teachers *teach*. (*Our parents taught* [not *learned*] *us right from wrong*).

leave, let   *Leave* means "to depart"; it should not be used in place of *let*, which means "to allow" (*When you are ready to leave, let* [not *leave*] *me give you a ride*). The expressions *leave alone* and *let alone*, however, may be used interchangeably (*I asked Ben to leave* [or *let*] *me alone*).

led   See *lead, led*.

less   See *fewer, less*.

let   See *leave, let*.

liable, likely   *Liable* means "inclined" or "tending" (*If you do not shovel the sidewalk, you are liable to fall on the ice*). *Liable* is also a legal term meaning "responsible for" or "obligated under the law" (*The tenant is liable for the damage*). *Likely* means "probable" (*a likely choice*). *Likely to* means "probably will" (*She is likely to refuse*).

lie   See *lay, lie.*

like   See *as, as if, like.*

likely   See *liable, likely.*

loose, lose   *Loose* means "not attached." *Lose* means "to misplace" or "to undergo defeat" (*Be careful not to lose that loose button on your jacket*).

lots, lots of   *Lots* and *lots of* are colloquial expressions meaning "many" or "much"; avoid them in formal writing (*The senator has widespread* [not *lots of*] *support; she is expected to win many* [not *lots of*] *votes*).

man, mankind   These terms were once used to refer to all human beings. Such usage is now considered sexist; use *people, humanity,* or *humankind* instead (*What has been the greatest invention in the history of humanity* [not *mankind*]?). (See 36c.)

may   See *can, might.*

may be, maybe   *May be* is a verb phrase (*Charles may be interested in a new job*); *maybe* is an adverb meaning "possibly" or "perhaps" (*Maybe I will speak to him about it*).

media, medium   *Media,* referring to various forms of communication—newspapers, magazines, television, radio—is the plural form of *medium;* it takes a plural verb (*They tried to get the message out in various media*).

might   See *can, may.*

mine, mines   *Mine* means "belonging to me." Avoid *mines,* a nonstandard form (*Did you find yours? I found mine* [not *mines*]).

moral, morale   *Moral* is an ethical principle or the lesson of a story or an experience (*The moral is to treat others as you wish to be treated*). *Morale* is the mood of a person or group (*The improvement in good weather lifted the crew's morale*).

most   Do not use *most* to mean "almost." (*Prizes were given to almost* [not *most*] *all the participants*).

must have   see *could have, must have, should have, would have.*

myself   See *herself, himself.*

nor, or   Use *nor* with *neither* (*Neither Paul nor Sara guessed the right answer*); use *or* with *either* (*Either Paul or Sara will have to drive me home*).

nowhere near   *Nowhere near* is an informal usage. Use *not nearly* instead (*This year's class is not nearly as unruly as last year's*).

number   See *amount, number.*

of   See *have, of.*

off of   Use *off* alone; *of* is not necessary (*The child fell off* [not *off of*] *the playground slide*).

OK, O.K., okay All three spellings are acceptable, but this colloquial term should be avoided in formal writing (*John's performance was all right* [or *adequate* or *tolerable; not okay*], *but it wasn't his best*).

on account of Avoid using *on account of* to mean "because of" (*The course was canceled because of* [not *on account of*] *lack of interest*).

or See *nor, or.*

outside, outside of See *inside, inside of; outside, outside of.*

passed, past *Passed* is the past tense of the verb *pass* (*She passed here several hours ago*). *Past* refers to a time before the present (*She has forgotten many details about her past life; the past is not important to her*).

penultimate *Penultimate* means "next to the last." The one before that is the *antepenultimate*. Do not use *penultimate* as a more intense version of *ultimate*.

people, persons A *person* is an individual human being. Use *people* for groups (*Only one person came, although we had hoped many people would attend*) except when emphasizing the individuality of the members of a group of people (*Three persons were injured in a one-car accident on Rohrer Road*).

per The Latin term *per* should be reserved for commercial or technical use (*miles per gallon, price per pound*). Avoid it elsewhere in formal writing (*Kyle is exercising three times each* [not *per*] *week*).

percent, percentage The term *percent* refers to a specific fraction of one hundred; it is always used with a number (*We raised nearly 80 percent of our budget in one night*). Do not use the symbol % in formal writing except in tables, formulas, or technical writing. The term *percentage* is not used with a specific number (*We raised a large percentage of our budget in one night*).

perspective, prospective *Perspective* is a noun meaning "a view"; it should not be confused with the adjective *prospective*, meaning "potential" or "likely" (*Mr. Harris's perspective on the new school changed when he met his son's prospective teacher*).

phenomena *Phenomena* is the plural of the noun *phenomenon*, meaning "an observed fact, occurrence, or circumstance" (*Last month's blizzard was an unusual phenomenon; there have been several such phenomena this year*).

plenty *Plenty* means "full" or "abundant"; in formal writing, do not use it to mean "very" or "quite" (*The sun was quite* [not *plenty*] *hot*).

plus *Plus* is a preposition meaning "increased by" or "with the addition of" (*With wool socks plus your heavy boots, your feet should be warm enough*). Do not use *plus* to link two independent clauses; use *besides* or *moreover* instead (*Brad is not prepared for the advanced class; moreover* [not *plus*], *he can't fit it in his schedule*).

p.m., a.m. or P.M., A.M. See *a.m., p.m. or A.M., P.M.*

precede, proceed *Precede* is a verb meaning "to go or come before"; *proceed* is a verb meaning "to move forward or go on" or "to continue" (*The attendants preceded the bride into the church; when the music started, they proceeded down the aisle*).

presently See *at present, presently.*

pretty   Avoid using *pretty* to mean "quite" or "somewhat" (*Dave is quite* [not *pretty*] *tired this morning*).

principal, principle   *Principal* means "first" or "most important"; it also means "chief executive" or "director" or "an amount of money" (*My principal reason for visiting Gettysburg was my interest in the Civil War; my high school principal suggested the trip*). *Principle* is a noun meaning "a rule of action or conduct" or "a basic law" (*I want to learn more about the principles underlying the U.S. Constitution*).

proceed   See *precede, proceed*.

quotation, quote   *Quotation* is a noun, and *quote* is a verb. Avoid using *quote* as a noun (*Sue quoted Jefferson in her speech, hoping the quotation* [not *quote*] *would impress her audience*).

raise, rise   As a noun, *raise* means "a pay increase." As a verb, *raise* means "to lift" or "to increase"; it takes a direct object (*Giving the workers a raise caused the owner to raise prices*). *Rise* means "to go up"; it does not take a direct object (*Prices rise during periods of inflation*).

rarely ever   Do not use *rarely ever* to mean "seldom." Use "hardly ever" or *rarely* alone (*We rarely* [not *rarely ever*] *travel during the winter*).

real, really   *Real* means "true" or "actual" (*The diamonds in that necklace are real*). *Really* is used informally to mean "very" or "quite." Do not use *real* as an adverb (*Tim was really* [not *real*] *interested in buying Lana's old car*).

reason is because   The phrase *the reason is because* is redundant; use *the reason is that* or *because* instead (*The reason I am late is that* [not *because*] *I got stuck in traffic. Yesterday I was late because* [not *The reason I was late yesterday was because*] *I overslept*).

reason why   *Reason why* is redundant; use *reason* alone (*The reason* [not *The reason why*] *we canceled the dance is that no one volunteered to chaperone*).

regardless   See *irregardless, regardless*.

respectably, respectfully, respectively   *Respectably* means "in a manner worthy of respect" (*Although we did not win, we performed respectably*). *Respectfully* means "in a manner characterized by respect" (*Even when you disagree, you should listen respectfully*). *Respectively* means "in the order given" (*The programs on the environment, woodcraft, and herpetology are at 10:00 A.M., noon, and 3:00 P.M., respectively*).

rise   See *raise, rise*.

says   See *goes, says*.

scarcely   See *hardly, scarcely*.

sensual, sensuous   *Sensual* means "arousing or exciting the senses or appetites"; it is often used in reference to sexual pleasure (*His scripts often featured titillating situations and sensual encounters*). *Sensuous* means "experienced through or affecting the senses," although it generally refers to esthetic enjoyment or pleasure (*Her sculpture was characterized by muted colors and sensuous curves*).

set, sit   *Set* is a transitive verb meaning "to put" or "to place"; it takes a direct object, and its principal forms are *set, set, set* (*Mary set her packages on the kitchen table*). *Sit* is an intransitive verb meaning "to be seated"; it does not take a direct object, and its principal forms are *sit, sat, sat* (*I sat in the only chair in the waiting room*). (See 42c.)

shall, will In the past, *shall* (instead of *will*) was used with the first-person subjects *I* and *we* to create the future tense. Now *will* is acceptable with all subjects (*We will invite several guests for dinner*). *Shall* is generally used in polite questions (*Shall we go inside now?*) or for requirements or obligations (*Jurors shall refrain from all contact with the press*).

should have See *could have, must have, should have, would have.*

sight See *cite, site, sight.*

sit See *set, sit.*

site See *cite, site, sight.*

so, so that The use of *so* to mean "very" can be vague (*Gayle was so depressed*). Use *so* with a *that* clause of explanation (*Gayle was so depressed that she could not get out of bed*). *So that* means "with the intention that" (*Gayle got out of bed early so that she would be in class on time*).

somebody, someone, something These pronouns take singular verbs (*Somebody calls every night at midnight and hangs up; I hope something is done about this problem before someone in my family becomes frightened*).

someplace, somewhere Do not use *someplace* in formal writing; use *somewhere* instead (*The answer must lie somewhere* [not *someplace*] *in the text*).

some time, sometime, sometimes *Some time* means "a length of time" (*We have not visited our grandparents in some time*). *Sometime* is an adverb meaning "at an indefinite time in the future" (*Let's get together sometime*); *sometimes* means "on occasion" or "now and then" (*Sometimes we get together*).

sort of See *kind of, sort of.*

stationary, stationery *Stationary* means "not moving" (*All stationary vehicles will be towed*). *Stationery* means "writing paper" (*Karen is out of stationery*).

supposed to, used to Do not use *suppose* or *use* in this construction (*Ben is supposed* [not *suppose*] *to take the garbage out; he used* [not *use*] *to remember regularly.*).

sure, surely In formal writing, do not use the adjective *sure* to mean "certainly" or "undoubtedly"; use the adverb *surely* or *certainly* or *undoubtedly* instead (*It is certainly* [or *surely;* not *sure*] *cold today*).

sure to, try to Avoid using *sure and* and *try and* for *sure to* and *try to* (*Be sure to* [not *and*] *come to the party; try to* [not *and*] *be on time*).

take See *bring, take.*

than, then *Than* is used in comparisons (*Dan is older than Eve*). *Then* indicates time (*First pick up the files, and then deliver them to the company office*).

that, which A clause introduced by *that* is always a restrictive clause; it should not be set off by commas (*The historical event that interested him most was the Civil War*). Many writers use *which* only to introduce nonrestrictive clauses, which are set off by commas (*His textbook, which was written by an expert on the war, provided useful information*); however, *which* may also be used to introduce restrictive clauses (*The book which offered the most impor-tant information was an old reference book in the library*).

thataway, thisaway Both these terms are colloquial. Use *that way* or *this way.*

that there, these here, them there, this here By themselves, *this, these, that,* and *them,* indicate position (*this* and *these* for things close by, *that* and *those* for things farther away), so *that there, this here,* and so forth are re-dundant.

their, there, they're *Their* is the possessive form of the pronoun *they* (*Did they leave their books here?*). *There* means "in that place" (*No, they left their books there*). *They're* is a contraction of *they are* (*They're looking all over for their books*).

theirselves, themselves *Theirselves* is nonstandard; use *themselves.*

then See *than, then.*

'til, till, until *Till* and *until* are both acceptable spellings; *'til,* however, is a contraction and should be avoided in formal writing (*We will work until we are finished; you should not plan to leave till then*).

to, too, two *To* often indicates movement or direction toward something (*Nancy is walking to the grocery store*). *Too* means "also" (*Sam is walking too*). *Two* is a number (*The two of them are walking together*).

toward, towards *Toward* is preferred, but both forms are acceptable.

try and See *sure to, try to.*

type In colloquial speech, *type* is sometimes used alone to mean "type of," but avoid this usage in formal writing (*What type of* [not *type*] *medicine did the doctor prescribe?*).

ultimately See *eventually, ultimately.*

uninterested See *disinterested, uninterested.*

unique *Unique* is an adjective meaning "the only" or "having no equal." Be-cause it refers to an absolute, unvarying state, it need not be intensified (by words such as *most* or *very*) (*Her pale blue eyes gave her a unique* [not *very unique*] *look*). The same is true of other adjectives that indicate an absolute state: *perfect, complete, round, straight* and so on. But modifiers that qualify are acceptable (*almost perfect, nearly straight*).

until See *'til, till, until.*

usage, use *Usage* means "an established and accepted practice or procedure" (*He consulted the glossary whenever he was unsure of the correct word choice or usage*). Do not substitute *usage* for *use* (*Park guidelines forbid the use* [not *usage*] *of gas grills*).

used to See *supposed to, used to.*

utilize The verb *utilize,* meaning "to put to use," borders on pretentiousness; *use* is generally better (*We were able to use* [not *utilize*] *the hotel kitchen to pre-pare our meals*).

wait for, wait on *Wait for* means "to await" or "to expect." *Wait on* means "to serve"; in formal writing they are not interchangeable (*You are too old to wait for* [not *on*] *your mother to wait on you*).

well   See *good, well.*

where   Do not use *where* in place of *that* (*I read that* [not *where*] *several of the company's plants will be closed in June*).

where . . . at, where . . . to   *Where* should be used alone, not in combination with *at* or *to* (*Where did you leave your coat?* [not *Where did you leave your coat at?*] *Where are you going?* [not *Where are you going to?*]).

whether   See *if, whether.*

which   See *that, which.*

which, who, that   Use *which* to refer to places, things, or events; use *who* to refer to people or to animals with given names; use *that* for places, things, events, or groups of people (*The parade, which was rescheduled for Saturday, was a great success; one man who* [not *which*] *attended said it was the best parade that he could remember*). *That* is also occasionally used to refer to a single person (*Beth is like the sister that I never had*). (See also *that, which,* and see "Choosing between *that* and *which,*" 44b.)

who   See *which, who, that.*

who, whom; whoever, whomever   Use *who* and *whoever* for subjects and subject complements; use *whom* and *whomever* for objects and object complements (*Who revealed the murderer's identity? You may invite whomever you wish*).

who's, whose   *Who's* is a contraction of *who is* (*Who's coming for dinner tonight?*). *Whose* is the possessive form of *who* (*Whose hat is that?*).

will   See *shall, will.*

-wise   The suffix *-wise* indicates position or direction in words such as *lengthwise* and *clockwise*. In formal writing, do not add it to words to mean "with regard to" (*My personal life is confused, but with regard to my job* [not *jobwise*], *things are fine*).

would have   See *could have, must have, should have, would have.*

your, you're   *Your* is the possessive of *you* (*Your table is ready*). *You're* is a contraction of *you are* (*You're leaving before the best part of the show*).

yourself, yourselves   See *herself, himself.*

ESL INDEX

INDEX

A

Abbreviations, 466–469
  acronyms and initials, 469
  common Latin, 468
  degrees, numbers, and units
    of measure, 467
  and formal writing, 469
  geographic names, 468
  numbers, 467
  symbols, 468
  titles and degrees, 466–467
Ability, designation of, 327
Abridged dictionary, 317
Abstract, 193
Abstract nouns, 401
Abstract words, 313
Academic Search Premier, 102
accept / except, 450
access / excess, 450
Acronyms, 469
Action, writing, 34
Active voice, 408
adapt / adopt, 450
Adding strategy, 87
Adjectives, 387–390, 409. *See
    also* Modifiers
  commonly confused, 388–390
  and comparatives, 390–391
  double negatives and, 391
  irregular, 391
  kinds of, 410
Adverbs, 387–390, 409. *See also*
    Modifiers
  commonly confused, 388–390
  and comparatives, 390–391
  double negatives and, 391
  irregular, 391
  kinds of, 410–411
affect / effect, 450
Age, designation of, 327

allot / a lot, 450
allude / elude, 450
allusion / illusion, 450
already / all ready, 450
altar / alter, 450
altogether / all together, 450
always / all ways, 450
American Chemical Society,
  147
*American Heritage Book
  of English Usage,* 317
*American Heritage College
  Dictionary,* 317
American Institute of Physics
  (AIP), 147
American Medical Association
  (AMA), 147
American Psychological
  Association (APA), 147
Analogy, 324
and, pronoun-antecedent
  agreement, 381
Antecedent, 374, 378
  pronoun references and, 377,
  403
Antonyms, 319
APA style documentation,
  191–223
  documenting books, 199–203
  documenting online sources,
  206–212
  documenting other sources,
  212
  documenting periodicals,
  203–206
  guidelines for formatting
  manuscripts, 192–194
  guidelines for in-text
  citations, 194–197
  guidelines for references
  page, 197–199

CREDITS

Text Credits

Pages 76–77: "We Real Cool" from *Blacks* by Gwendolyn Brooks. Copyright © 1987 by Gwendolyn Brooks. Reprinted by consent of Brooks Permissions.

Page 106: Copyright © 2006 by Yahoo! Inc. YAHOO! and the YAHOO! logo are trademarks of Yahoo! Inc. Reprinted by permission.

Page 107: Screenshot copyright © 2006 by Google, Inc. and is reproduced with permission.

Page 162: From *As I Lay Dying* by William Faulkner. "Copyright page" copyright 1930 and renewed 1958. "Title page" copyright 1930 and renewed 1958. Used by permission of Random House, Inc.

Page 168: Title page and first page from "The Challenge of Diversity" by Patrocinio Schweickart, *ADE Bulletin,* 88 (1987):21–26. Copyright © 1987 by Modern Language Association of America. Reprinted by permission of Modern Language Association of America.

Page 170: Table of contents and page 132, "Smashed" by Adam Kirsch, *The New Yorker,* 3/14/2005. Copyright © 2005 by Condé Nast Publications Inc. Reprinted by permission of the publisher.

Page 176: Courtesy of Dr. John B. Padgett.

Page 200: Title and copyright pages from *The Literary Book of Economics: Including Readings from Literature and Drama on Economic Concepts, Issues and Themes* edited with commentary by Michael Watts. Copyright © 2003 by ISI Books. Reprinted by permission of ISI Books.

Pages 204 and 232: Title page and first page of "Reading Texts, Literacy, and Textual Authority" by Henry A. Giroux, *Journal of Education,* Vol. 172, No. 1 (1990). Copyright © 1990 by Trustees of Boston University. Reprinted by permission of Henry A. Giroux.

Page 208: Courtesy of "Sea Grant Nonindigenous Species (SGNIS), a project of National Sea Grant". National Sea Grant is a division of NOAA, National Oceanic and Atmospheric Administration.

Page 230: Title and copyright pages from *Life and Thought in the Early Middle Ages* ed. by Robert S. Hoyt. Copyright © 1967 by University of Minnesota. Reprinted by permission of University of Minnesota Press.

Page 236: Reprinted by permission of *The Comics Journal,* Seattle, Washington. http://www.tcj.com.

Photo Credits

Page 1: Photos.com.

Pages 22 and 133: Courtesy of the Library of Congress.

Page 23: Dorothea Lange/Getty Images Inc.—Hulton Archive Photos.

Page 25: Courtesy of the Library of Congress.

Page 26: Courtesy of the Library of Congress.

Page 27: Thomas E. Franklin/Getty Images.

Page 31: Photos.com.

Pages 53, 55, 58, and 134: © Peyo—2006—licensed through Lafig Belgium—www.smurf.com.

Page 60: John Marshall Mantel/Corbis/Bettmann.

Page 68: Peter DeSantis/New England Mountain Bike Association.

Page 69: Bill Stevenson/The Stock Connection.

Page 91: Photos.com.

Page 96: Toby Fulwiler.

Page 123: Toby Fulwiler.

Page 139: Getty Images, Inc.

Page 143: Photos.com.

Page 145: US National Oceanic and Atmospheric Administration.

Page 146: L. Lefkowitz/Getty Images, Inc.—Taxi.

Page 148, top: Family of Vice Admiral H. Arnold Karo, C&GS/US National Oceanic and Atmospheric Administration.

Page 148, bottom: US National Oceanic and Atmospheric Administration/Commander Marcella Bradley.

Page 257: Cary Wolinsky/Aurora & Quanta Productions Inc.

Page 291: EyeWire Collection/Getty Images—Photodisc.

Page 333: Rachel Epstein/PhotoEdit Inc.

Page 415: Photos.com.

Page 447: EyeWire Collection/Getty Images—Photodisc.

Page 473: Photos.com.

Notes

Notes

Notes

Notes

Notes

Notes

Notes

Notes

Notes

Notes

WAC BOXES

WRITING ACROSS THE CURRICULUM